PSYCHOLOGICAL WARFARE AND PROPAGANDA
IRGUN DOCUMENTATION

PSYCHOLOGICAL WARFARE AND PROPAGANDA

IRGUN DOCUMENTATION

Edited by

Eli Tavin

and

Yonah Alexander

SR Scholarly Resources Inc.
Wilmington, Delaware

PUBLISHER'S NOTE

The documents in this book have been reprinted as they originally appeared in English. Only the most obvious typographical errors present in the documents have been corrected. The original spelling (and frequent misspelling) and punctuation have been retained throughout the work.

Scholarly Resources Inc.
104 Greenhill Avenue
Wilmington, Delaware 19805

Library of Congress Cataloging in Publication Data

Main entry under title:

Psychological warfare and propaganda.

Includes bibliography.
1. Irgun Tseva'i le'umi. 2. Palestine—
Politics and government—1929–1948—Sources.
3. Jews—Palestine—Politics and government—
Sources. I. Tavin, Eli. II. Alexander,
Yonah. III. Irgun tseva'i le'umi.
DS126.4.P72   956.94'04   81-52469
ISBN 0-8420-2188-4   AACR2
ISBN 0-8420-2189-2 (pbk.)

CONTENTS

Appendix

Historical Introduction

Eli Tavin and Yonah Alexander

I

One of the fundamental bases of Zionism[1] is the historical bond between the Jews and the "Land of their Fathers." Although the vast majority of Jews were scattered to every corner of the earth after the destruction of the Second Commonwealth, continuity of Jewish life in Palestine has been maintained. In addition, the millennial hope for national restoration survived and was expressed in the form of numerous attempts to resettle the "Promised Land," during the centuries of exile.[2]

This unique attachment of "a people without a country to a country without people"[3] has been reinforced in the Zionist ideology by the fact that the Jews have neither abandoned Palestine nor renounced their title to it. In modern times, an increasing number of *Olim* (immigrants) influenced by the rise of nationalism in Europe

---

[1]For the basic ideology of Zionism by the founder of the Zionist movement, see Theodor Herzl, *The Jewish State* (New York: Scopus Publishing Company, 1943); *Old New Land (Altneuland)*, trans. from German, with revised notes by Lotta Levensohn (New York: Herzl Press, 1960); *The Complete Diaries of Theodor Herzl*, edited by Raphael Patai, trans. by Harry Zohn (New York: Yoseloff, 1960), 5 vols.; and *The Diaries*, trans. and edited by Marvin Lowenthal (New York: Grosset and Dunlap, 1962). For works related to Zionism by other Zionist leaders, see Nahum Sokolow, *History of Zionism* (London: Longmans, Green and Co., 1919), Vol. 1; Arthur Ruppin, *The Jewish Fate and Future* (New York: Macmillan, 1940); Chaim Weizmann, *Trial and Error: The Autobiography of Chaim Weizmann* (New York: Harper and Brothers, 1949); David Ben Gurion, *The Rebirth and Destiny of Israel* (New York: Philosophical Library, Inc., 1954); Louis Lipsky, *A Gallery of Zionist Profiles* (New York: Farrar, Strauss, and Giroux, 1956); and Nahum Goldman, "Zionism: Ideal and Realism," *Confrontation: Viewpoints on Zionism* (Jerusalem: World Zionist Organization, 1970). For a brief analysis of Jewish or Israeli nationalism, see Israel Kolatt, "Theories on Israeli Nationalism," *Confrontation: Viewpoints on Zionism*.

[2]See, for instance, *The Historical Connection of the Jewish People with Palestine* (Jerusalem: The Jewish Agency for Palestine, 1936).

[3]Israel Zangwill, "The Return to Palestine," *New Liberal Review* 2 (December 1901): 627.

during the nineteenth century,[4] spurred by the brutal pogroms in czarist Russia[5] and the virulent antisemitism rampant in the west,[6] and inspired by the crystallization of a national consciousness advocated by *Chovevi Zion* (lovers of Zion), began to settle in Ottoman Palestine in the 1880s. These early *Halutzim* (Jewish pioneers) purchased and tilled the land, drained its marshes and swamps, reclaimed the uninhabited and barren desert, cultivated and irrigated the exhausted soil, established agricultural settlements, and built new towns.[7] To them and to the other settlers of the first and second *Aliyah* (immigration),[8] confrontation with the indigenous Arab population in Palestine was not a major concern, and they did not envision the necessity of having to resort to force in order to secure the right to a national entity in Zion, which they regarded as their only source of physical and spiritual safety and vitality.[9] Since they considered their ideology to be reasonable, uniquely human, and even messianic, they saw no inherent and objective reasons for conflict between Jews and Arabs.[10] Indeed, they believed that the aspirations and interests of both people were complementary and

---

[4]See Ben Halpern, "Zionism and Israel," in Benjamin Rivlin and Joseph S. Szyliowicz, eds., *The Contemporary Middle East: Tradition and Innovation* (New York: Random House, 1965), pp. 276–82, for a comparison between Zionism and other nationalisms and for an analysis of the reasons for the unique characteristics of Jewish nationalism.

[5]See Simon M. Dubnow, *History of the Jews in Russia and Poland*, 3 vols., (Philadelphia: Jewish Publications Society, 1916–20); and L. Greenberg, *The Jews in Russia* (New Haven: Yale University Press, 1951), vol. 2.

[6]See James Parks, *Antisemitism* (London: Vallentine Mitchell, 1963); and A. Roy Eckardt, *Elder and Younger Brothers* (New York: Charles Scribner's Sons, 1967).

[7]Among the earliest pioneers were students from eastern Europe belonging to an organization called BILU (initials of the Hebrew words "Beth Yaacov Luhu Venelha", "House of Jacob, come ye, and let us walk." [Isa. 2:5.]. See, for example, Leon Pinsker, *Auto-Emancipation: A Call to his People by a Russian Jew* (London: Rita Searl, 1947); David Ben Gurion, *Rebirth and Destiny of Israel*, 270–72; and Alex Bein, *The Return to the Soil* (Jerusalem: Youth and Hechalutz Department, World Zionist Organization, 1952).

[8]The Jewish population in Palestine in 1882 reached twenty-four thousand. During the first *Aliyah*, 1882–1903, some twenty-five thousand Jews immigrated to Palestine. In the second *Aliyah*, 1904–14, nearly forty thousand immigrants arrived.

[9]For background accounts on Arab-Jewish relations see, for example, Michael Assaf, *History of the Arabs in Palestine*, vol. 3, *The Arab Awakening and Flight— Nations and States Contend for Palestine, 1876–1948* (Tel-Aviv: Tarbut We-Hinukh, 1967); Shimon Shamir, *A Modern History of the Arabs in the Middle East* (Tel-Aviv: Reshofim, 1965); and Aaron Cohen, *Israel and the Arab World* (London: W. H. Allen, 1970).

[10]See "The Spiritual and Pioneering Mission of Israel: The Eternity of Israel," *Ayanot* (1964): 74. See also, statement by David Ben Gurion before Knesset, 2 January 1956, as quoted in *Israel Peace Offers* (Jerusalem: Ministry of Foreign Affairs, 1958), p. 56; and Martin Buber, "Zion and Youth," *Mission and Destiny*, (Hebrew) 2:219.

interconnected, and that the Arabs would benefit considerably from Jewish achievements.[11]

Dr. Theodor Herzl, the father of the Zionist movement, and his associates and successors,[12] who sought in Palestine a political and territorial solution to the Jewish problem,[13] concentrated therefore on the attainment of two objectives:[14] to convince the Jewish masses in the European Diaspora that such a redemption was both necessary and practical;[15] and to influence the custodians of the Holy Land and the important world powers to permit Jewish settlement there, and to secure some kind of autonomous status for those who would hearken to their call and come. Diplomatic interventions with the sultan of the Ottoman Empire, the kaiser of Germany, other European potentates of the time, and the statesmen of the British Empire were the principal political preoccupations of the early Jewish nationalist functionaries. The achievement of these stated goals, the Zionist leaders assumed, could be accomplished without

---

[11]See, for example, Cmd. 1700, p. 8; *Financial Aspects of Jewish Reconstruction in Palestine: How The Arabs Have Benefited through Jewish Immigration* (London: The Jewish Agency for Palestine, 1930); and *Zionism and the Arab World* (New York: The Jewish Agency for Palestine, 1946).

[12]See footnote 1 above. For diagnoses of Zionism's founders relative to the processes dominating Jewish life in the Diaspora see, for example, Martin Buber, "Aus einer Rede," *Die Welt* (29 March 1912), reprinted in *Juedische Bewegung* (Berlin: Juedische Verlag, 1916), p. 195; A. D. Gordon, "The Congress," *The Nation and Labor,* (1952): 198; Ber Borochov, "On Zionist Theory" in *Writings,* 1:2; Chaim Weizmann, "The Jewish People and Palestine," statement made before the Palestine Royal Commission in Jerusalem, on 25 November 1936; and David Ben Gurion, "From Class to People," *Ayanot* (1955); 23.

[13]Theodor Herzl stated that "The Jewish Question exists wherever Jews live in perceptible numbers. Where it does not exist, it is carried by Jews in the course of their migration." Herzl, *The Jewish State* (1896) 1:21–22. For a recent analysis see Jacob Neusser, "Zionism and the Jewish Problem," *Confrontation: Viewpoints on Zionism,* pp. 3–14.

[14]For the Zionist objectives as formulated in the first Zionist Congress, see *Protokill des I. Zionistenkongresses in Basel vom 29 bis 31 August 1897* (Prog., 1911), p. 131. See also *Constitution of the Zionist Organization* (Jerusalem: The World Zionist Organization, 1938); Israel Cohen, *The Zionist Movement* (New York: Zionist Organization of America, 1947); Gavriel Stern, "70th Anniversary of the First Zionist Congress," *Israel Horizons* 15 (November December 1967): 20–23; K. Israel, "The Zionist Movement and the Jerusalem Programme 1968," *Confrontation: Viewpoints on Zionism,* pp. 3–12; and Eliezer Schweid, "Israel as a Zionist State," *Confrontation: Viewpoints on Zionism.*

[15]Some Jews rejected the concept of unity of the Jewish people with Palestine as a beacon of national security. For anti-Zionist works see, for instance, Morris R. Cohen, *Zionism: Tribalism or Liberalism* (New York: American Council for Judaism, 1946); Alfred M. Lilienthal, *What Price Israel* (Chicago: Henry Regnery Company, 1953); Moshe Menuhin, *The Decadence of Judaism in Our Time* (New York: Exposition Press, 1965); Benjamin Matov, "Zionist and Anti Semite. 'Of Course!' " *Issues* (Spring, 1966): 21–26; and Jakob J. Petuchowski, *Zion Reconsidered* (New York: Twayne Publishers, 1967).

the slightest detriment to the Arab population in Palestine. Underlying this assumption was Dr. Herzl's pledge: "It goes without saying that we shall respectfully tolerate persons of other faiths and protect their property, their honor, and their freedom with the harshest means of coercion. This is another area in which we shall set the entire world a wonderful example."[16] Committed to this principle, the Zionist movement looked forward to Jews and Arabs living in peace within the envisaged Jewish state.

At the same time, Arab nationalism revived dreams of independence from the Ottoman Empire. As soon as the Arab press published reports on the emergence of Zionism as a national ideology, some concern for the fate of Palestine as part of the Arab world began to be articulated.[17] In Palestine itself, opposition to the semi-legalized Jewish immigration and settlement took the form of protests by some Arab notables to the Ottoman authorities, who at times acceded to Arab requests to impose various restrictions on Jews. These demands did not stem from nationalistic motivations, but rather were expressions of religious and ethnic assertiveness.

Since the Turkish administration did little to check small-scale attacks on Jewish settlements by Arab peasants and Bedouin, the Zionist pioneers had to rely initially on hired local Arab and Circassian guards[18] to defend their vulnerable villages. Only in 1907 did some of the settlers form a Jewish armed militia, the Bar Giora, named after a Jewish leader of the rebellion against Rome in the first century of this era. Two years later, it was succeeded by *Hashomer* (the watchman), which soon provided protection to Jewish settlements in the Galilee and Judea.

The Palestinian Arabs sought to merge Palestine into "Greater Syria" on the basis of common political, judicial, social, and economic foundations. It is not surprising, therefore, that no distinct Arab political-ideological parties developed in Palestine simultaneously with other Arab national movements elsewhere prior to World War I.

---

[16]Herzl, "Diary" (June 1895), in *Writings*, 2: 71.

[17]Anis Sayegh in her study *Palestine and Arab Nationalism* (Beirut: Palestine Liberation Organization Research Center, n.d.) reports that during this period the first articles attempting to expose the "Zionist plot" appeared in *Al-Manor* (Cairo) and *Al-Carmel* (Haifa). For a pro-Arab anthology of readings of the history of Zionism and Palestine from 1897 until the establishment of Israel see Walid Khalidi, *From Haven to Conquest* (Beirut: The Institute for Palestine Studies, 1971); see also Nevill Mandel, "Turks, Arabs and Jewish Immigration into Palestine," *St. Anthony's Papers, Number 17: Middle Eastern Affairs*, 4 (Oxford: Oxford University Press), p. 80, and Nagib Azoury, *Le Reveil de la nation Arabe* (Paris: 1905).

[18]Circassians are members of a Moslem ethnic group from the Causausus region who were transported to Palestine in the mid-nineteenth century by the Ottoman Turks.

II

When World War I broke out and Turkey entered the conflict on the side of the Central Powers, Arabs and Jews both appealed to the Allies for assistance in realizing their national aspirations in the Middle East. During the period between July 1915 and March 1916, letters were exchanged between Sherif Hussein of Mecca, on behalf of the Arabs, and Sir Henry McMahon, the British high commissioner in Egypt, on behalf of the British government. This correspondence culminated in the British promise of Arab independence in the Middle East in return for an Arab agreement to revolt against the Turks. Consequently, Bedouin tribesmen, supported by British funds, arms, and advisors such as the legendary Lawrence of Arabia, began to sabotage Turkish installations. Other Arab units, led by Sherif Hussein and his son Feisal, helped the Allies to hasten the disintegration of the Ottoman Empire.[19] About the same time, many Palestinian Jews, jointly with their brethren from England and the United States who enlisted in the Jewish legion organized by Joseph Trumpeldor and Zeev (Vladimir) Jabotinsky, fought alongside British forces in the Middle East in the hope that this effort would lead to Allied support of Zionism.[20] This expectation materialized on 2 November 1917, when Lord Arthur James Balfour, the British foreign secretary, in a letter sent to Baron Edmond Rothschild, a prominent Jewish leader, declared, "His Majesty's Government views with favor the establishment in Palestine of a National Home for the Jewish people and will use their best endeavors to facilitate achievement of this object."[21]

At the San Remo Conference of 25 April 1920, the victorious powers, acting as the Supreme Council of the League of Nations, decided to place Palestine in the British sphere of influence.[22] On

---

[19]For a general discussion of the period see Suleiman Mousa, *T. E. Lawrence: An Arab View* tr. by Albert Butros (New York: Oxford University Press, 1966).

[20]Some Palestinian Jews, at least initially, favored wartime cooperation with the Central Powers. See Alexander Aaronsohn, *With the Turks in Palestine* (New York: Houghton Mifflin, 1916), for a personal narrative of a well-known Palestinian Jew concerning the early part of World War I in Palestine. See also Yigal Allon, *Shield of David* (New York: Random House, 1970), pp. 32–34.

[21]For text see United Kingdom, 'Balfour Declaration," November 1917, quoted in Great Britain, *Palestine: Royal Commission Report.* Cmd. 5479 (London, 1937), p. 16. For resolutions, statements, and views by Jewish organizations relating to the Balfour Declaration, and for press comments see *Great Britain, Palestine and the Jews: Jewry's Celebration of Its National Charter* (New York: George H. Doran Company, 1918). See also Blanche Elizabeth Dugdale, *The Balfour Declaration: Origins and Background* (London: The Jewish Agency for Palestine, 1940); Leonard Stein, *The Balfour Declaration* (New York: Simon and Schuster, 1961); and Richard H. S. Crossman, "The Balfour Declaration, 1917–1967," *Midstream* 13 (December 1967): 21–28.

[22]This was done in accordance with the wartime secret Sykes-Picot treaty of 9 May 1916, whereby Britain and France agreed to divide the eastern Middle East

1 July of that year, a civil government was established in the country. The League of Nations approved the final draft of the Palestine mandate and incorporated the Balfour Declaration into the document on 24 July 1922. It charged the mandatory power with "placing the country under such political, administrative and economic conditions as will secure the establishment of the Jewish National Home."[23]

The promise given to the Jews in the Balfour Declaration, which was originally understood to cover all historic Palestine on both sides of the Jordan River, was successively circumscribed by the British. The British created the Emirate of Transjordan, transferring four-fifths of the territory of Palestine assigned to the mandate to Abdullah, the son of Hussein, in fulfillment of the wartime pledge to create an independent Arab state.

III

The conclusion of World War I began a new era of self-determination of nations, peace, and prosperity in the Middle East. The prospects for mutual recognition of the aspirations of both Arab nationalism and Zionism were forecast by the leaders of these two liberation movements. On 23 March 1918, Sherif Hussein, the exponent of pan-Arabism (the idea of uniting all Arabic-speaking peoples, Moslems and Christians alike, under one flag), wrote in the daily paper of Mecca, *Al-Quibla* "We saw the Jews . . . streaming to Palestine from Russia, Germany, Austria, Spain, America. . . . The cause of causes could not escape those who had the gift of deeper insight: They knew that the country was for its original sons, for all their differences, a sacred and beloved homeland."

Stronger support of the Arab nationalist movement for Zionism came on 3 January 1919, when Emir Feisal, son of Sherif Hussein,

---

between them. For an examination of the British and French role in the Middle East see Jukka Nevakivi, *Britain, France, and the Arab Middle East, 1914–1930* (London: Oxford University Press, 1969); John Morlowe, *Arab Nationalism and British Imperialism* (New York: Praeger, 1961); and Elizabeth Monroe, *Britain's Moment in the Middle East, 1914–1956* (Baltimore: Johns Hopkins, 1963). For an interpretation of Britain's Palestine promises, see Fayez Sayegh, "Two Secret British Documents," *Hiwar* 8 (January–February 1964) (Beirut):17–32, and *The Times* (London), 16 April 1964.

[23]See Great Britain, *Final Drafts of the Mandates for Mesopotamia and Palestine for the approval of the Council of the League of Nations* (London, 1921), Cmd. 1500, and Cmd. 1785, pp. 1–11, for official documents of the mandate. See also Albert M. Hyamson, *Palestine Under the Mandate 1920–1948* (London: 1950), for a Zionist view by a former mandatory official. For other works see Norman and Helen Bentwich, *Mandate Memories, 1918–1948* (New York: Shocken, 1965); and Edwin Samuel, *A Lifetime in Jerusalem: The Memoirs of the Second Viscount Samuel* (Jerusalem: Israel Universities Press, 1970).

acting on behalf of the Arab kingdom of Hedjaj, signed a formal agreement with Dr. Chaim Weizmann, president of the World Zionist Organization, which called for "all necessary measures . . . to encourage and stimulate immigration of Jews into Palestine on a large scale, and . . . to settle Jewish immigrants upon the soil. . . ." The preamble of the agreement stated,

> mindful of the racial kinship and ancient bonds existing be-
> tween the Arabs and the Jewish people, and realizing that the
> surest means of working out the consummation of their national
> aspirations is through the closest possible collaboration in the
> development of the Arab state and Palestine, and being desirous
> further of confirming the good understanding which exists be-
> tween them we have agreed upon the following. . . .[24]

Feisal's stand was reaffirmed in his subsequent correspondence with Felix Frankfurter, a prominent American Zionist, with the hope of obtaining the assistance of influential World Jewry in achieving the goals of the Arab movement for sovereign independence. On 3 March 1919, he wrote, "We Arabs, especially the educated among us, look with deepest sympathy on the Zionist movement. . . . We will wish the Jews a hearty welcome home. . . . We are working together for a reformed and revised Near East, and our two movements complement one another. The movement is national and not imperialistic. There is success without the other."[25]

These statements indicate that the Arabs looked upon the Zionists and their proposed state as a potential ally. Following this signal, the Palestinian Arabs were friendly at first to the idea of a Jewish National Home. Most of them showed a lack of political sophistication and expressed little interest in obtaining much more in the way of home rule or exclusive tenure than they had enjoyed under the Turkish regime. The Zionist leaders consistently assured the Arabs that their interests would be safeguarded. As Dr. Weizmann put it, "cooperation and friendly work with the Arab people must be the cornerstone of all our Zionist activities in the land of Israel."[26]

These early hopes were shattered by two events. First, the pan-Arab kingdom, in whose name Feisal spoke, never came into being.

---

[24]Quoted in Cmd. 5479, pp. 19–20, and The Jewish Agency for Palestine, *Documents Relating to the Palestine Problems* (1945), pp. 17–18.

[25]Quoted in Chaim Landau, ed. *Israel and the Arabs* (Jerusalem: Central Press, 1971), p. 48. See also letter by Sir Henry McMahon in *The Times*, 23 July 1937; Chaim Weizmann's speech to the Zionist Congress of 1931, quoted in Jewish Agency for Palestine, *Memorandum Submitted to the Palestine Royal Commission* (1936), pp. 87–89; and N. Mandel, "Attempts at an Arab-Zionist Entente, 1913–1914," *Middle Eastern Studies* 1 (April 1965): 238–67.

[26]Weizmann, *Speeches* (1937), 1:141.

Therefore those Arab leaders who were willing to recognize a Jewish state in Palestine could not implement the Feisal-Weizmann agreement. Second, and perhaps more important, the Palestinian Arabs turned all their efforts against the fulfillment of the Zionist vision. This occurred because an extremist minority faction of Palestinian Arabs assumed control over their own people and introduced a policy of terrorism to achieve specific political aims: (1) to reduce, if not eliminate, Jewish presence in Palestine and to frustrate Zionist designs to establish a distinct state there; (2) to reject any efforts of Jewish-Arab coexistence and cooperation; (3) to persuade or force the mandatory power to relinquish its policy as expressed in the Balfour Declaration; and, (4) to achieve national independence in Palestine under Arab control.

These goals were established at the All-Arab Palestine Conference, which met in Jerusalem in January 1919.[27] Palestinian Arabs, jointly with their supporters in the General Syrian Congress, declared the following June,

> We reject the claims of the Zionists for the establishment of a Jewish commonwealth in that part of southern Syria which is known as Palestine, and we are opposed to Jewish immigration into any part of the country. We do not acknowledge that they have a title, and we regard their claims as a grave menace to our national, political and economic life.[28]

Similar aims and demands were reiterated by the Third Palestine Arab Congress, meeting in Haifa in December 1920.[29]

Leading and inspiring these ultra-nationalists was Hajj (Muhammed) Amin al-Husseini, then president of the Supreme Moslem Council that had managed Moslem affairs in Palestine.[30] As the grand mufti of Jerusalem, he assembled a personal country-wide religious-political machine and also presided over the Arab Higher Committee, formerly the Supreme Arab Committee, charged with the coordination of the work of Arab nationalists. He and other members of the prominent Husseini family were the only Arab

---

[27]ESCO Foundation for Palestine, *Palestine: A Study of Jewish, Arab and British Policies* (New Haven: Yale University Press, 1947), 1:473.

[28]Quoted by George Antonius, *The Arab Awakening*, 3rd ed. (Beirut: Khayats, 1955), p. 441.

[29]For details see Issa Sifri, *Arab Palestine Between the Mandate and Zionism* (Jaffa: 1937); Robert John and Sami Hadawi, *The Palestine Diary 1914–1945*, vol. 1, (Beirut: The Palestine Research Center, 1970); Don Peretz et al., *A Palestine Entity* (Washington, DC: The Middle East Institute, 1970), pp. 1–21; and A. Kayal, ed., *Documents on Palestinian Resistance to the British Mandate and Zionism 1918–1939* (Beirut: The Institute for Palestine Studies, 1969).

[30]Maurice Pearlman, *Mufti of Jerusalem: The Story of Haj Amin al-Husseini* (London: Gollancz, 1947); Eliahu Elath, *Haj Mohammed Amin al-Husseini* (Tel-Aviv: Reshafim, 1968); and *Ha'aretz* (Tel-Aviv), 1, 2, and 6 March 1970.

personalities in British Palestine with whom the Zionist leaders did not meet to discuss a basis for mutual understanding, for the Husseini bitterly disavowed any proposals that did not entail the total abandonment of Zionist principles. Their constant incitements to violence against the Jewish community in Palestine resulted in the waves of Arab terrorism of the 1920s and 1930s.

IV

The first wave of Arab terrorism in Palestine began in 1920. Arab rioters attacked isolated Jewish settlements in Upper Galilee early in the year. Two villages, Metulla and Tel Hai, succumbed to the mob and had to be abandoned. The heroic death of Joseph Trumpeldor, the defender of Tel Hai, and his comrades became a symbol of dedication and sacrifice for future generations of Jews.

Palestinian Arab hostility against Jews spread to Jerusalem. Here, on 20 April, thousands of Arab pilgrims who had arrived for the Moslem festival of Nebi Musa were roused to join in an anti-British political demonstration. Soon the march turned into an anti-Jewish riot. Leaders and provocateurs shouted insults against their Jewish neighbors and incited the mob to attack their enemy. The Arab police, which was under British control, made no attempt to stop the violence and, in some cases, even joined their coreligionists in the rioting and plunder. These actions led Jabotinsky to organize Jewish self-defense units in Jerusalem (later known as the Haganah), which repelled the Arab attackers.

The communal violence claimed the lives of 5 Jews and injured 211 others. Four Arabs died in the incident. British troops arrived on the scene and detained several hundred Arabs for the night. Disturbances broke out again when the detainees were released the next morning. Order was restored several days later, but not before the government was forced to disarm the Arab police, proclaim martial law, and ask British troops to assume full control.[31]

The military governor of Jerusalem dismissed the Arab mayor of the city, Mussa Kazim al-Husseini, for inciting the anti-Jewish rioters. Soon afterwards, al-Husseini was elected as president of the Arab Executive Committee, the leading Palestinian Arab umbrella organization representing local political parties, which would not cooperate with the British authorities and refused to negotiate with the Jews.

The British took action against both communities. A member of the prominent Husseini family, Hajj (Muhammed) Amin, at that time the president of the Arab Club in Jerusalem (the organization that

---

[31]ESCO, *Palestine Study*, pp. 132–33.

supported an all-Syrian unity), was sentenced *in absentia* by a British military court to fifteen years' imprisonment for his direct responsibility for the 1920 disturbances. Bowing to Arab pressure, the British allowed him to return to Palestine from his Transjordanian refuge. In an effort to be evenhanded, Jabotinksy was sentenced by the British for fifteen years' imprisonment for his part in organizing the defense of the Jewish quarter of Jerusalem during the 1920 riots, but his sentence was commuted afterwards because of strong Jewish protests.

These developments tended to bolster the Yishuv's determination that it must rely on Jewish protection, in order to defend Jewish life, property, and honor. The *Haganah* (defense), the citizen-soldier militia organization established in the wake of the 1920 riots by veterans of the Jewish Legion, soon faced its first test.[32] On May Day of the following year, an Arab mob took advantage of a clash in the Jewish sector of Jaffa between a government-authorized Jewish labor organization's procession and a counter-parade by illegal Jewish communists, and unexpectedly attacked both groups. This was followed with the murder of thirteen Jews by a crowd in the Immigration House in Jaffa. On the outskirts of the city, Joseph Chaim Brenner, a leading Hebrew writer, was killed, along with the family whom he was visiting at the time. A series of reprisals by Haganah members followed in the Jaffa area. A number of people were killed, and many were wounded on both sides. Subsequently, violence spread to other regions in the country. Armed Arabs attacked and looted several settlements. The most serious attack occurred at Petach Tikvah, the oldest Jewish agricultural colony, which traditionally enjoyed good relations with its neighbors. The settlement was able to hold out against some two thousand attackers until it was saved by an Indian cavalry squadron that happened to be passing. Another Arab attack on Petach Tikvah was checked by a squadron of British planes, and then dispersed by an Indian military unit. Some fifty Arabs and four Jews died in this particular incident.[33]

The Haycraft Commission, sent to Palestine to investigate the causes of the 1920–21 disturbances, reported,

> that racial strife was begun by Arabs who were generally the aggressors; that the outbreak was unpremeditated and unexpected; that the general body of Jews was anti-Bolshevist; that the fundamental cause of the riots was a feeling amongst the Arabs of discontent with, and hostility to, the Jews, due to

---

[32]For details see, for instance, Munya Mardor, *Haganah* (New York: New American Library, 1966).

[33]ESCO, *Palestine Study*, pp. 269–70.

political and economic causes, and connected with Jewish immigration, and with their conception of Zionist policy as derived
from Jewish exponents.[34]

V

In reaction to the 1920–21 wave of terrorism and the Haycraft
report, the mandatory government in Jerusalem sought to appease
the Arab nationalists. When the Arabs refused to accept the establishment of a legislative council in Palestine, the mandatory administration formed, in January 1922, the Supreme Moslem Council
to administer the affairs of the Moslem community in the country.
Hajj Amin al-Husseini, who had been appointed the mufti of Jerusalem by the British high commissioner in Palestine, was elected
president. Although Al-Husseini had promised to exercise his great
spiritual and social influence to assure peace in Jerusalem, the
council soon became the mufti's powerful instrument to fight Arab
political opponents, Zionism, and the mandate's policy regarding
the establishment of a Jewish National Home in Palestine.

Several months later, Sir Herbert Samuel, the high commissioner, announced at a gathering of Arab leaders at Ramleh that
Jewish immigration would be restricted. This declaration was
formalized with the publication of the British White Paper of 3 June
1922, which proposed establishing a quota on such immigration to
be determined by the economic absorptive capacity of the country.[35]
However, the Arab nationalists were not completely satisfied with
the document because it did not put an end to the development of
the Jewish National Home in Palestine as promised in the Balfour
Declaration.

The White Paper led to changes in British policy. First, the
British banned the Haganah as an illegal organization. It went
underground and prepared itself to defend the Yishuv in the face of
continued Arab agitation reinforced by rising nationalism. Second,
in the absence of any representative institution in Palestine, resulting directly from Arab objections, the mandatory government
permitted the establishment in 1926 of the Va'ad Leumi (National
Council), to serve as "cabinet" for the Jewish community in the
country.

The years 1922–28 passed without any serious outburst of
violence. The Jewish immigration in the country almost doubled,
and, when an economic crisis developed in Palestine in 1926–27,
Arab nationalists expected that the Zionist effort to establish a

---

[34]Ibid., p. 271.
[35]Weizmann, *Trial and Error*, p. 342.

Jewish entity would collapse. However, the economic conditions improved, and the British strengthened the Palestinian Zionists by recognizing the Jewish Agency as a body to advise and cooperate with the mandatory government on matters concerning the National Home.[36] These developments, coupled with increased Arab agitation, disturbed the relative quiet in the country.

It began with the Wailing Wall (or Western Wall) dispute.[37] The mufti, who fostered the Islamic character of Jerusalem, injected a religious element into his struggle with Zionism when, in 1928, he challenged the right of Jews to pray at the wall in the Old City of Jerusalem, the most sacred site in Judaism. Jews, on the other hand, disputed the right of the Moslem Wagf, the Moslem religious foundation, to build on that part of *Haram al-Sharif* (the Temple Mount), with the Mosques of Al-Aksa and the Dome of the Rock, immediately overlooking the wall.

On 23 August 1929, Jews obtained permission for and carried out an orderly demonstration to reaffirm Jewish rights at the wall. The Arab leadership in the city then incited its followers to participate in a countermarch. Aroused by inflammatory speeches, the protesters burned petitions placed by Jewish worshippers in Wailing Wall crevices.

Rumors that Jews were planning to appropriate the Haram al-Sharif and to burn down the mosques situated there brought to the Old City thousands of Arabs ready to protect their sacred sites. The following day, on the Jewish Sabbath, groups of Arabs attacked Jews throughout Jerusalem, including the Mea Shearim quarter inhabited mainly by Orthodox Jews. The Arab police in the city were ineffective, and the British forces were delayed in providing assistance. As a result, the Jewish community suffered badly.

Violence spread to the outlying vicinities of the city, to the Jewish agricultural colonies of Hartuf and Motzah. In the latter community, an entire family was killed. Settlements in the southern district of the country, Hulda and Beer Tuvia, were also assaulted, but, in these colonies, the Haganah successfully resisted the Arab attack.

The most brutal attack that Sabbath day was aimed at the religious center of Hebron, which was populated mostly by older people supported by charitable contributions from abroad and by a group of young talmudic academy students. Almost the entire community was destroyed: more than sixty Jews were killed and over fifty wounded, included women and children; the synagogue was

---

[36]See *The Hope-Simpson Report* (Jerusalem: Government Press, 1929), pp. 53–54, and 78–79.

[37]See, for example, Jewish Agency for Palestine, *Memorandum on the Western Wall* (Jerusalem: Azriel Press, 1930); ESCO, *Palestine Study*, pp. 608–09; and Great Britain, *International Commission for the Wailing Wall Report, December, 1930* (London: His Majesty's Stationery Office, 1931).

profaned; the Jewish clinic, which had provided treatment for both Arabs and Jews, was ransacked; and other Jewish property was destroyed.

On 28 August 1929, another devastating pogrom-type operation took place at Safed, also an old center of Jewish piety. Here, too, the toll was high: forty-five Jews were killed or wounded, houses of worship and learning desecrated, and homes pillaged and burned.

In less than one week, a total of 133 Jews had died and 339 others had been injured in Jerusalem, Hebron, and Safed. In other cities, such as Gaza, Jenin, Nablus, and Tulkaram, the Arabs expelled the Jewish populations. Jews abandoned a total of eleven communities, in different parts of the country. The disturbances left 116 Arabs dead and another 232 wounded.[38]

The British government established, in the fall of 1929, a commission headed by Sir Walter Shaw to investigate the reasons for the disturbances. Its report blamed the Arabs for the outbreak of violence, but emphasized their fear of, and opposition to, the continuing development of the Jewish National Home. It recommended, therefore, that Zionist immigration to Palestine should be more tightly controlled.[39]

VI

The years 1930–36 witnessed a third wave of intermittent Arab-initiated disturbances and violence. These events unfolded in the wake of an increased Jewish immigration into Palestine, which resulted from Nazi repression and Polish anti-Semitism.

Al-Husseini, who had become the most important leader of the Palestinian Arabs after the 1929 riots, increased his pressure on the mandatory government to stop the flow of Jewish immigrants. The extremist faction of the Supreme Moslem Council supported his efforts. Mobilizing support from coreligionists outside Palestine, delegates from twenty-two countries met a Moslem congress in Jerusalem in December 1931 and warned against the dangers of Zionism. Similarly, the Arab Executive Committee, representing local nationalist parties, in its manifesto of March 1933 asserted that the Zionists had designs to take possesion of the country, with the active support of the British, and urged the Arabs to sacrifice themselves in the battle with their enemy.

This call struck a responsive chord, and the Arabs launched a campaign of violence against the mandatory government. The

---

[38]*A Survey for Palestine* (Jerusalem: Government Press, 1946), 1:24. See also Arye Hashavla, *This Month—Forty Years Ago, the Hebron Massacre* (Jerusalem: Prime Minister's Office, 1969).

[39]Great Britain, Cmd. 2530. For another proposal to limit Jewish immigration see *The Hope-Simpson Report.*

general strike of October protesting the accelerated Jewish immigration led to anti-British riots in Jaffa, Haifa, and Jerusalem. It resulted in the deaths of twenty-six Arabs and one policeman. The following year, an Arab terror group began to operate against the authorities, but the British forces killed and captured all of its members. Throughout this period there had also been a number of assassinations of Jews, attacks on Jewish farms, acts of vandalism against orchards and crops, and deliberate maiming of Jewish cattle.[40]

The dramatic events of 1929 and their aftermath had shocked the Yishuv. In fact, it rather expected that the national aspirations of the Arabs would be satisfied by the creation of Jordan and the establishment of other new Arab states and that they would not object to the establishment of a single Jewish state in the area. The Zionists maintained that the Arabs had neither a legal nor a moral title to Palestine. Any such claim, they asserted, was refuted by the fact that the Arab population of Palestine was of a mixed race and did not constitute a distinct "people," and by the failure of the Palestinian Arabs throughout history to fight for independence rather than surrender the land to successive conquerors. The Arab community did not accept this reasoning.

The Jewish leaders attempted to reach agreements with the more moderate Arab personalities. For example, David Ben Gurion and Moshe Sharett, representing the Yishuv, met with Musa Alami, a prominent Palestinian Arab spokesman, and agreed that there should be further discussion between the two communities, regarding the establishment of a Jewish entity, on both sides of the Jordan River, connected to an Arab federation in the neighboring countries. Ben Gurion and Musa Alami met again several times in the following year to continue their talks. Also, a small group of Jewish scholars, affiliated with the Hebrew University in Jerusalem and headed by Judah Magues, tried to promote among the Arabs the idea of a binational commonwealth in Palestine, in which both Arabs and Jews would enjoy equal rights. These contacts consistently failed as Arab apprehension in Palestine was converted into hostility by the more extreme Palestinian leadership orchestrated by the mufti and his followers.

VII

Encouraged by the failure of the mandatory authority to exercise its police power or moral suasion effectively and by the inability of the League of Nations to check the aggression of Italian facism and German Nazism, the militant Arab leadership decided to rise up in

---

[40]*A Survey for Palestine*, pp. 30–31.

open revolt against both the British administration and the Jewish community.

Two immediate events precipitated the prewar violence. First, the Arab Higher Committee, the all-embracing body representing the Arab parties in Palestine, was formed in April 1936, under the chairmanship of Hajj Amin al-Husseini. Despite some internal disagreements, this organization enabled the militant nationalists to command greater obedience from the population, and to direct the revolt without challenge from any other Arab leader. Second, the mufti realized that, with the growth of Jewish population in the country and the determination of the Yishuv to strongly resist Arab violence, terrorism rather than mob violence would become a more effective tactic. Therefore, he established Green Shirt paramilitary units to engage in terrorism.[41]

The violence began on 15 April, when a terrorist group held up ten cars on the Tel Aviv-Haifa highway, singled out three Jews, and shot them to death. Four days later, an Arab attack in Jaffa resulted in three Jewish fatalities. On 25 April, the Arab Higher Committee organized a general strike in the country until their demands for a fundamental change in British policy in Palestine were met fully. This strike was accompanied by violence. Jews were assaulted and stoned in various cities. In rural areas, Arab farmers attacked Jewish settlements and the British police. These activities were supplemented by guerrilla warfare carried out by organized Arab units from the hills.

Open support for Palestinian terrorism from the neighboring Arab countries came almost immediately. Their officials justified the violence on the grounds that the Arabs had lost faith in the value of British "pledges and assurances for the future." They also protested the mandatory government's use of force against the Palestinian Arabs. This political support was supplemented by training of local bands by outside guerrillas, such as Syria's Fazi al-Qawagji, who also joined the Palestinians in fighting. The local Arabs were reinforced by volunteers from Lebanon, Syria, and Transjordan. As a result of this escalation, sabotage and murder increased. Roads were mined, railways damaged, and the oil pipeline between Iraq and Haifa broken. The semiofficial Jewish Haganah responded with a policy of self-restraint (*Havlaga*), which led to sharp criticism in the Yishuv.

The London government established the Palestine Royal Commission headed by Lord Peel to investigate the violence. Its report, published in July 1937, declared the mandate unworkable and the British pledges to both parties mutually irreconcilable: "To put it in one sentence, we cannot—in Palestine as it now is—both concede

---

[41]See Leila S. Kadi, *Basic Political Documents of the Armed Palestinian Movement* (Beirut: Palestine Liberation Organization, December 1969).

the Arab claim to self-government and secure the establishment of the Jewish National Home."[42] The commission therefore recommended the partition of Palestine into a Jewish state and an Arab state that would be united with Transjordan as the best possible solution to the problem.

Although this proposal did not meet with full Jewish expectations, the Zionist Congress, sitting in August, decided to enter into negotiations with the British government for the creation of a distinct Jewish entity in Palestine as a decisive step in fulfilling Zionist aims. Only Jabotinsky came out against the Peel report; he insisted that the British return the mandate to the League of Nations.

Arab opinion was divided over the partition proposal. Transjordan's Emir Abdullah favored the partition proposal and hoped to incorporate the Arab portion of Palestine into his kingdom. Abdullah's supporters among the Palestinian Arabs, such as Rayheb al-Nashashifi, were inclined to accept this plan. However, the strong opposition of the extreme nationalists, led by the mufti of Jerusalem, and the coercion of moderate elements, coupled with the resumption of the insurrection with greater vigor, finally shelved the Peel proposal. When the British district commissioner in the Galilee was murdered, the mandatory authorities retaliated by outlawing the Arab Higher Committee on 1 October 1937 for its role in the violence. Five of the most important members of the committee were arrested and deported to the Seychelles Islands. The British authorities dismissed the mufti of Jerusalem from his position of president of the Supreme Moslem Council, which was disbanded. He fled to Lebanon, and then took up residence in Syria. From his exile, Hajj Amin continued to direct the violence in Palestine, and his followers resumed operations on a large scale.

Attacks against individual Jews and Jewish settlements increased. On 4 October 1938, Arabs attacked Jews in the town of Tiberias. Two large Arab units attacked the city for several hours before government troops drove them away. The violence left nineteen Jews dead and three wounded, including women and children. Violence was also directed at British police stations, as well as at Arab towns where local residents opposed the militant Arab nationalism. But, with the intensification of British military action, coupled with the support provided by the Haganah and the newly created Irgun's policy of counterterror against the Arabs, the revolt began to lose support by the spring of 1939.

Meanwhile, in another effort to resolve the Palestine problem, the British government invited the representatives of the Arab and Jewish communities and, for the first time, delegates of the Arab states to the St. James's Round Table Conference, held in London in February 1939. Because the Arabs refused to sit down with the Jews

---

[42]Cmd. 5479, pp. 110–11.

at the same table, the British had to meet separately with them and the Jewish delegation. The conference ended in a complete deadlock, and the mandatory government reverted to ruling Palestine by decree.

On 17 May, Malcolm MacDonald, the colonial secretary, published a White Paper enunciating a new policy whereby existing rights of Jews to immigration and land purchases were curtailed and the Balfour Declaration's goals were deferred. It also announced a plan for an independent Palestine, in which Jews would have a permanent minority status; the plan was to be implemented in ten years. The White Paper established that Jewish immigration would be limited to a total of 75,000 during the next five years and that additional Jewish immigration into Palestine would depend on Arab consent. Finally, the document determined that transfer of Arab-owned land to Jewish ownership would be regulated by an interim government.[43]

London's new policy, military realities, the severe economic damage suffered by the Arabs, and a joint appeal by pro-British leaders of the neighboring Arab countries finally convinced the Arab Higher Committee to end the revolt and urge quiet. The British agreed to permit the guerrillas to escape and made no attempt to disarm the bands. The general strike was called off, and the organized violence ceased, although sniping and other individual attacks still occurred. By the time World War II broke out in September 1939, the Arab revolt had been virtually suppressed. The final toll was 517 Jews, 3112 Arabs, and 135 Britons dead; 2500 Jews, 1775 Arabs, and 386 Britons injured.[44]

VIII

The Jewish losses from the Arab revolt would have been much greater had it not been for the defense efforts of the Yishuv, with support given by the British authorities. The Jewish Agency, representing the Yishuv, adopted a two-fold policy: *havlagah* (self-restraint) and *haganah* (self-defense). The Haganah, which was closely linked to the *Histadrut* (General Federation of Jewish Labor in Palestine), bore the main responsibility for the implementation of this policy.[45] It fortified Jewish villages with barbed-wire fences, redoubts, and searchlights; provided settlements and towns with fighting men; established dozens of stockades and watchtowers in

---

[43]For an excellent analysis of Arab, Jewish, and British policies from 1936 leading to the breakdown of the mandate, see Jacob C. Hurewitz, *The Struggle for Palestine* (New York: Greenwood Press, 1968).

[44]See *A Survey for Palestine*; and ESCO, *Palestine Study*.

[45]For details see Ephraim Dekel (Krasner), *Shai: Historical Exploits of Haganah Intelligence* (New York: Yoseloff, 1959); and Mardor, *Haganah*.

areas where no Jewish settlements had previously existed; made available armed escorts to protect vehicles and convoys; constructed new roads to enable greater safety of communications; and gradually organized operations against terrorist bands and their bases.

The mandatory government, in cooperation with the Jewish Agency, formed an auxiliary police known as *Ghafirs* or *Notrim* (Guards), which often served as a cover for the Haganah underground in communications, arms procurement, equipment transportation, and training. These units guarded railways, airfields, and government offices. Protecting villages against incursions by Arab bands was the responsibility of the Jewish Settlement Police, set up by the authorities, and of the Haganah's *Peluggot Sadeh* (field companies). Finally, special night squads, consisting of regular British forces and Haganah members, and commanded by Capt. Orde Wingate, undertook guerrilla operations against the Arab terrorists.

The Haganah continued to strengthen its underground forces, throughout the period of the Arab revolt. It purchased weapons inside and outside the country, developed its own arms industry, and trained its increasing membership. The cost of these and other security activities were met by *Kofer ha-Yishuv*, a voluntary tax which the Jewish community in Palestine imposed upon itself.

Simultaneously with such defense efforts, Jewish leaders, both official and unofficial, tried to improve relations with the Arab community in Palestine. These attempts were initiated by a few social, business, and labor groups. Several clubs to cultivate closer social relations were sponsored by the League for Arab-Jewish Relations. There were also sporadic instances of Arab-Jewish cooperation by the business leadership of both communities. The Arab chairman of the Nablus Chamber of Commerce participated in a Jewish nutrition conference in Tel-Aviv, and a number of joint meetings of Arab and Jewish orange growers were held. Histadrut, then an all-Jewish labor organization, launched a parallel Arab labor union, and the two groups cooperated in organizing joint strikes around the country and in initiating joint cooperatives. However, these efforts proved abortive because radical Arab nationalists discouraged and eventually, through intimidation and terror, stopped any contact with Jews. One newspaper correspondent concluded, "Extremist Arab followers of the Mufti . . . are rapidly achieving their aims by eliminating political opponents in Palestine who are inclined toward moderation."[46]

The Haganah's policy of self-restraint and defense had its critics, particularly among more militant members who owed allegiance to the Revisionists, the extreme nationalist wing of the

---

[46]*New York Times*, 15 October 1938. For Arab attitudes see, for instance, Great Britain, 3530, 5479, 5854, 6808, and 7044.

Zionist movement.[47] Revising an earlier split, they seceded from the Haganah in 1937 and formed the *Irgun Zevai Leumi* (National Military Organization) or, in its abbreviated form, Etzel (I.Z.L.), led by David Raziel.[48] It advocated not only a strong defense posture but also insisted on retaliation against Arabs. Thus, Etzel bombed Arab market places, cafes, and buses throughout the country, killing scores and wounding hundreds of people. The British response to this violence was severe. In 1938, the authorities hanged Shlomo Ben Josef, an Etzel member who was captured in an abortive attack on an Arab bus in Galilee. He was the first Jewish underground fighter to be executed by the British in Palestine. At that time, the Irgun started its first attacks against the British by bombing telephone installations, post offices, and the broadcasting buildings.[49]

Despite the activities of Etzel and constant Arab provocations, the Yishuv's policy of self-restraint prevailed for a time. A more militant attitude, particularly toward the British, developed within the Jewish community with the publication of the White Paper of May 1939. The Yishuv denounced this document as a violation of the Balfour Declaration and the British obligation under the League of Nations' mandate. Ben Gurion asserted at a meeting of the Haganah, "Until now, we have acted according to the spirit of the law. From now on some of our activities will be directed against the law and with the aim of making that law powerless."[50] When the British foreign secretary announced an immediate suspension of Jewish immigration to Palestine for six months, as of 1 October 1939, Ben Gurion declared, "The British closed legal entry to Palestine, so that Jews would force their way by the back door."[51]

To facilitate the organization and coordination of illegal immigration, also known as *Aliyah Bet* (Class B immigration)—organized initially by the Revisionists and the Irgun in Europe in the early 1930s—the Haganah set up a special underground body, the *Mosad* (institution).[52]

---

[47]The Revisionists established the World Union of Zionists Revisionists in 1925, and a youth movement, Betar (Brith Trumpeldor). In 1935 it seceded from the official Zionist Organization, only to rejoin it in 1946. Its leader was Zeev (Vladimir) Jabotinsky. See his presentation on *The Story of the Jewish Legion* (New York: Ackerman, 1945).

[48]The first split occurred in 1931 when these dissidents left the Haganah. However, most of them rejoined it in 1936. For details on Etzel by commanders who succeeded Raziel see Yaacov Meridor, *Long is the Road to Freedom* (New York: United Zionists Revisionists, 1961), and Menachem Begin, *The Revolt: Story of the Irgun* (New York: Henry Schuman, 1951).

[49]*Keesing's Contemporary Archives 1937–1940*, vol. 3, pp. 3177A, 3312A, 3513, 3642B.

[50]Quoted by Michael Bar-Zohar, *The Armed Prophet: A Biography of Ben Gurion* (London, 1967), p. 53.

[51]Ibid., p. 74.

[52]For details see Bracha Habas, *The Gate Breakers* (New York: Yoseloff and Herzl, 1963); and Jon and David Kimche, *The Secret Roads* (New York: Farrar, Straus, and Cudahy, 1955).

Other Jewish groups took more extreme positions. Etzel's response to the White Paper was more violent, and many of its activities were directed against the British authorities. When it called off its operations upon the outbreak of World War II, a more extreme splinter wing formed *Lohamei Herut Yisrael* (Fighters for the Freedom of Israel), also known as Lehi or the Stern Group, named after its first commander who was killed by the British in 1942.[53] Interestingly, Lehi initially sought to cooperate with Britain's enemies, the Axis Powers, in an effort to obtain from them a firm support for the creation of a Jewish state in Palestine.

IX

Although Arab terrorism ended at the outbreak of the war, the Jews of Palestine were alarmed by the growth of Transjordan's Arab Legion and Frontier Forces, which were officered and trained by the British and were stationed in camps west of the River Jordan.

The Yishuv turned its attention to the struggle against Nazism, despite this apprehension. Some 136,000 volunteers, almost the entire Jewish population between the ages of eighteen and fifty, registered for national service. Nearly 30,000 Palestinian Jews, including members of the Haganah and Etzel, joined military units within the framework of the British Army. They also formed the separate Jewish Brigade. They were equipped and trained by the British and fought alongside the Allies throughout the war. Some of them were recruited for special missions against the advancing Germans in the Middle East in 1941–42 and for guerrilla action in occupied Europe.

Palestinian Arabs made no similar contribution to the war effort. In fact, the mufti of Jerusalem established a direct contact with Hitler in Germany and encouraged the faithful in Iraq to join Rashid Ali's pro-Nazi coup against the British in April 1941. In a Berlin broadcast the mufti declared the following:

> *Salaam Aleikum,* children of Allah, Moslems of the World; this is your leader talking to you wherever you may be. This is Amin al-Husseini, calling on you in the name of Allah, besides whom there is no God and Muhammad is his messenger, to take up arms in this *Jihad* Holy War against the infidel British who want

---

[53]For an insight into the workings of Etzel and Lehi see Jerold Frank, *The Deed* (New York: Simon and Schuster, 1963). For a description by a former member of Lehi of some of the organization's activities see Avner (pseud.), *Memoirs of an Assassin* (New York: Yoseloff, 1959). See *The "Activities" of the Hagana, Irgun and Stern Bands* (New York: Palestine Liberation Organization, n.d.), and "Zionist Terrorism," United Nations, Doc. A/C.6/C.876, 22 November 1972, for Arab perspectives.

to subdue all children of Allah and kill all his soldiers, and against the cunning Jews who desire to rob you of your sanctuaries and rebuild their Temple on the ruins of our Mosque of Omar in al-Quds. Children of Allah, this is a Holy War for the glory and honor of Allah, the merciful and beneficent. If you die in this war, you will sit in Heaven on the right side of the Prophet. Children of Allah, I call on you to fight. Heil Hitler.[54]

Although the Iraqi revolt failed, the mufti continued his collaboration with Hitler in planning and executing the "final solution" of Europe's Jewry. For instance, at a rally in Berlin in November 1943, Al-Husseini declared, "The Germans know how to get rid of the Jews."

Many Arabs supported the Germans. In the streets of Palestinian cities, Arab crowds saluted Hitler. Many Moslems volunteered for German units operating in occupied territories in Russia and Yugoslavia, and for the mufti's legion carrying out sabotage activities in British Palestine. The mufti provided this assistance in return for Germany's assurances to liquidate the foundation of the Jewish National Home after victory.

The mandatory government persisted with its White Paper policy throughout the war against continuing Jewish opposition. When the British were about to deport seventeen hundred illegal immigrants aboard the ship *Patria* in November 1940, the Haganah sabotaged its departure. The boat sank and approximately two hundred and fifty Jews were drowned in Haifa Bay.[55] The authorities also continued the cordon-and-search tactic against the Jewish underground movements. In November 1939, forty-three Haganah members and thirty-eight Etzel members were arrested for carrying arms and participating in a military training course. In other instances, the British forces discovered hidden arms and ammunition in Jewish villages.[56]

Anglo-Jewish collaboration increased in the face of common danger. The British suspended these arms searches and arrests as the Italian and German threat to the Middle East became more acute. In return, the Haganah cooperated with the British in the invasion of Vichy-French Syria and Lebanon in 1941. Hundreds of the Haganah's Palmach, permanently mobilized commando units, were trained by British officers in guerrilla tactics in preparation for a resistance movement in case Palestine were to be occupied by enemy forces. Also, special Etzel units were trained in such fields as

---

[54]Quoted in American Professors for Peace in the Middle East *Newsletter*, (October 1969). See also Joseph B. Schechtman, *The Mufti and the Fuehrer* (London: Yoseloff, 1965), and Seth Arsenian, "Wartime Propaganda in the Middle East," *The Middle East Journal* 2 (October 1948): 417–29.

[55]Munya Mardor, *Strictly Illegal* (London: Robert Hale, 1964), p. 56 ff.

[56]*A Survey for Palestine*, 1:58, 61, and 63.

sabotage and espionage in Jerusalem, Tel-Aviv, and Haifa by Polish Army specialists connected with the Free French government.

As soon as the war tide turned in favor of the Allies, relations between the Yishuv and the mandatory government deteriorated again. The authorities resumed their arms searches, tried Haganah members, and blocked attempts of Jews to gain illegal entry into Palestine from Rumania. In February 1942, the *Struma*, carrying 169 Jewish refugees desiring to reach Palestine, sank in the Black Sea; some people believe that this was the result of deliberate British actions.[57]

An extraordinary conference of Zionist leaders from Palestine, the United States, and Europe was held at the Biltmore Hotel in New York, in response to British policy. On 11 May 1942, the conference adopted the Biltmore Program demanding the opening of Palestine to Jewish immigrants and the establishment of the country as an independent Jewish commonwealth. This plan met with strong opposition, particularly from Etzel and Lehi. Supporting a more radical solution, they insisted on a Jewish state within the historical boundaries of the ancient kingdom of Israel.

These more radical groups began active opposition to British rule in Palestine. Acts of individual terrorism by Lehi continued intermittently throughout the war. For instance in January 1942, there were a series of armed robberies and assassinations of senior British officers in the Tel-Aviv area. A month later, Abraham Stern himself was killed. Attempts by members of the group to assassinate the inspector-general of the police and one of his assistants on 24 April as a reprisal failed.[58] On 1 February 1944, the Irgun Command headed by Menachem Begin declared formally the beginning of the revolt against the British. The news about the Holocaust in Europe and the extermination of millions of Jews by the Germans, while the British refused to allow the survivors to enter Palestine, and the already obvious victory of the Allies, influenced the decision to start the revolt.

The Irgun demanded the establishment of a temporary Jewish government, which would organize a Jewish army, negotiate the evacuation of surviving Jews from Europe to Palestine, guarantee the exterritorial rights of Christians and Moslems to the holy places in Palestine, and ensure equal rights for the Arab population. It called on the Jewish population to refuse payment of taxes to the British, to strike both economic and educational institutions, and to engage in armed resistance against the mandatory administration until its aims were achieved.

The Irgun intensified its campaign against the British. Coordi-

---

[57]Thierry Nolin, *La Haganah: L'armée secrète d'Israel* (Paris: Ballard, 1971), pp. 159–63.

[58]*Keesing's Contemporary Archives 1941–1942*, vol. 4, p. 6798A.

nated attacks on British emigration and income tax offices in Jerusalem, Haifa, and Tel-Aviv were the first serious blows against the British, followed by attacks on the main police stations in the big cities and the Palestine Broadcasting Service in Romalla. Until May 1944, the Irgun avoided attacking army installations, but with the formal termination of the war those too were included as its targets. The revolt started by the Irgun became eventually the catalyst that spurred the Jewish underground to create the resistance movement. Lehi did not hesitate to carry its campaign against the British even outside Palestine. On 6 November 1944, two of its members assassinated Lord Moyne, British resident minister in Egypt, who was known for his anti-Zionist attitude. The assailants, Eliyahu Hakim and Eliyahu Betzuri, were arrested and, subsequently, tried and executed in Cairo on 22 March 1945.[59]

This wave of Jewish violence was strongly condemned by the Yishuv leadership.[60] It called upon the dissident groups to put an end to terrorism, hoping that, with the end of the war approaching, the British would take a more pro-Jewish position. Etzel and Lehi rejected this request and continued with their violence against the British in the belief that, if they were to destroy British prestige in Palestine, "the removal of their rule would follow automatically." As a result, the Haganah decided to collaborate with the British government by denouncing the Irgun activities, supplying names of suspected members, or kidnapping them and handing them over to the British police, after declaring an "open season" on the Irgun members in November 1944.

British policy continued to be basically pro-Arab. The mandatory government, on its part, resorted to repressive measures against all those suspected of belonging to Jewish terrorist groups. In October 1944, the authorities deported 251 suspects to a detention camp in Eritrea. Simultaneously, London encouraged the creation of the Arab League. The league was established formally on 22 March 1945 by Egypt, Iraq, Lebanon, Saudi Arabia, Syria, Transjordan, and Yemen. The Arab Higher Committee of Palestine was admitted as a permanent and voting member. The goal of the league became immediately apparent: the eventual unification of all Arab states, including an independent Arab Palestine.

---

[59]"The Assassination of Lord Moyne," *Jewish Agency's Digest of Press and Events* (11 November 1944), pp. 1–3. For a basic study see Frank, and his article "The Moyne Case: A Tragic History," *Commentary* 2 (December 1945): 64–71. See also Isaac Zaar, *Rescue and Liberation* (New York: Bloch, 1954), pp. 38–43; J. Bowyer Bell, *The Long War* (Englewood Cliffs, N.J.: Prentice-Hall, 1969), pp. 12–13, and "Assassination in International Politics: Lord Moyne, Count Bernadotte, and the Lehi," *International Studies Quarterly* pp. 59–82; and *Ha'aretz*, 26 March 1975.

[60]For details see *Palcor News Agency Cables*, 27 March, 13 April, 20 and 22 November 1944. Arab reactions are cited in *Jewish Agency's Digest of Press and Events* (10 April and 21 November 1944).

X

After World War II ended in Europe and the magnitude of the Holocaust became known, the Yishuv expected the British government to reopen Palestine to the Jewish survivors gathered in displaced persons camps established by the Allies. However, Pres. Harry S Truman's appeal to London to permit 100 thousand Jews to immigrate to Palestine was not heeded. The Labour Party, under Clement Attlee and Ernest Bevin, had promised their support for Jewish aspirations, before coming into office. Once in power, the Labour government stood firmly by the prewar White Paper, restricting Jewish immigration and, in effect, opposing the establishment of a Jewish state in Palestine.

These developments resulted in a unique display of the Yishuv's unity. The three underground organizations, the Haganah (headed by Moshe Sueh), the Etzel (commanded by Menachem Begin), and Lehi (led by Nathan Friedman-Yellin), decided to cooperate in a newly formed Jewish resistance movement.[61] Determined to engage in sabotage activities against the mandatory government in order to influence London to change its policy, each of the groups in the movement carried out specific operations separately but under a common authority. On 1 November the Haganah launched a major attack on the Palestine railway system at 153 different points, completely disrupting it. Several coastal patrol boats at Haifa and Jaffa were destroyed. Etzel caused heavy damage to the Lydda station, and the Haifa oil refineries were sabotaged by Lehi.[62] On the following day, Kol Israel, the underground broadcasting station of the resistance movement, called these activities "an expression of our strength and decision." It also declared: "We lament the British, Arab and Jewish victims who fell in the attack on the railways and ports of Palestine. They are all victims of the White Paper." Warnings to the British government of the consequences that would follow if it did not modify the Palestine policy were given by the Jewish resistance movement in subsequent months.[63] In a series of operations in February 1946, they directed attacks against police posts, coast guard stations, radar installations, and airfields. Describing these events, *Kol Israel* (Voice of Israel) in its 3 March broadcoast said,

---

[61]For activities prior to the merger of these groups see Valia Hirsch, "The Truth about the Terrorists," *Today* 1 (January 1945): 10–12, and Frank Gervasi, "Terror in Palestine," *Colliers* 116 (11 August 1945): 64–65.

[62]See George Kirk, *Survey of International Affairs: The Middle East, 1945–1950* (London: Royal Institute of International Affairs), p. 195; and *Hamaas* 2 (November 1945).

[63]See *Palcor News Agency Cables* (29 November 1945), and *Jewish Telegraphic Agency* (26 December 1945).

This last fortnight has seen a renewed intensity in the struggle of the Jewish people against the forces which aim to throttle them and their national aspirations for normal nationhood in their National Home.

The attack on the Radar Station on Mount Carmel by the Hagana was aimed at destroying one of the principal agents of the Government in its hunt for Jewish refugees. The sabotage of the airfields [by the Irgun and Lehi] was the sabotage of a weapon which has been degraded from its glorious fight against the evil forces of Nazism to the dishonorable task of fighting against the victims of Nazism.

Those three attacks are symptomatic of our struggle. In all cases the onslaught was made against the weapon used by the White Paper in its despicable battle to repudiate its undertaking to the Jewish people and the world, and not against the men who use this weapon. It is not our object to cause the loss of life of any Briton in this country; we have nothing against them because we realize that they are but instruments of a policy, and in many cases unwilling instruments.[64]

Railway stations and bridges were destroyed by Etzel and Lehi units on 4 April near Ashdod and Yavneh in the south and around Acre in the north. Communications with Lebanon, Syria, and Egypt were interrupted. On 23 April, the police station in Ramat Gan was attacked by an Irgun unit, two of its members were killed and four wounded. Among these was Dov Gruner, who was later sentenced to death and executed by the British.

When London rejected a recommendation for the speedy admission of 100 thousand Jewish refugees into Palestine, this time offered in the report of the Anglo-American Commission of 1 May 1946,[65] Kol Israel made the following broadcast,

> The Jewish Resistance Movement thinks it desirable to publish the warning it intends to lay before His Majesty's Government. Present British policy is executing a dangerous maneuver and is based on an erroneous assumption: Britain, in evacuating Syria, Lebanon and Egypt intends to concentrate her military bases in Palestine and is therefore concerned to strengthen her hold over the mandate; and is using her responsibility to the Jewish people merely as a means to that end. But this double game won't work. Britain cannot hold both ends of the rope; she cannot exploit the tragic Jewish question for her own benefit as mandatory power, while attempting to wriggle out of the

---

[64]*Eshnav* (Publication of the Jewish Resistance Movement), 116 (4 March 1946). For other activities by the movement see *Palcor News Agency Cables* (4 and 24 April 1946).

[65]This commission was formed by the British government in November 1945 for the purpose of involving the United States in the responsibility for a solution to the Palestine problem. See *A Survey for Palestine.*

various responsibilities which that mandate confers. From the Zionist point of view, the tepid conclusions of the Commission bear no relation to the political claims of the Jewish people, but even so, in the execution of these proposals, the British Government is displaying a vacillation at once disappointing and discreditable. We would therefore warn publicly His Majesty's Government that if it does not fulfill its responsibilities under the mandate—above all with regard to the question of immigration—the Jewish people will feel obliged to lay before the nations of the world the request that the British leave Palestine. The Jewish Resistance Movement will make every effort to hinder the transfer of British bases to Palestine and to prevent their establishment in the country.

Coordinated operations continued into the early summer of 1946. On the night of 10 June, the Irgun attacked railway lines between Jaffa and Lydda, Jerusalem and Lydda, and Haifa and Lydda, actually stopping all railway traffic for a time in the center of the country. Furthermore, in an attempt to disturb British communications, the Haganah blew up roads and bridges linking Palestine with neighboring countries.[66] Two days later, five British officers were kidnapped by an Etzel unit from a military club in Tel-Aviv.[67] On June 2, Kol Israel announced that three of the officers would be kept as hostages for two Etzel members who were under sentence. Under public pressure, the British high commissioner granted an amnesty to the two resistance members.[68]

In light of these events, the mandatory government decided to take firm steps against the Yishuv's leadership.[69] On 29 June, also known by the Jewish population as "Black Saturday," the authorities arrested many Jewish leaders and conducted searches for arms in dozens of settlements. In the following days, thousands of suspected Haganah, Etzel, and Lehi members were interned, and the British continued with their searches for weapons throughout the country.[70] Also, in a stiffening shift of its policy, London decided to intern all apprehended illegal immigrants in refugee camps in Cyprus rather than in Palestine, as had been done previously.[71]

---

[66]R. D. Wilson, *Cordon and Search: With 6th Airborne Division in Palestine* (Aldershot: Gale and Polden, 1949), p. 262.

[67]*Keesing's Contemporary Archives 1946–1948*, vol. 6, p. 7983.

[68]Itzhak Gurion, *Triumph on the Gallows* (New York: Brit Trumpeldor of America, 1950), pp. 80–81.

[69]*Palcor News Agency Cables* (30 April 1946).

[70]*New Palestine News Reporter* (12 July 1946), and *Palcor News Agency Cables* (30 July 1946).

[71]Emanuel Celler stated in the United States that "terrorism in Palestine is a symbol of despair resulting from British action and would be a tragedy if the British used it as a pretext to deny entrance of 100,000 Jews into Palestine." U.S., Congress, House, *Congressional Record*, 79th Cong., 1st sess., 24 July 1946:9944–45.

The unity of the Jewish resistance movement collapsed on 22 July 1946. In one of the most dramatic actions of that year, after a telephone warning, Etzel blew up one wing of the King David Hotel in Jerusalem that contained the British miitary headquarters in Palestine and all the offices of the government secretariat, except those of the high commissioner. The total casualties were ninety-one killed and forty-five injured, including soldiers and civilians—British, Arab, and Jewish. On the following day, the "Voice of Fighting Zion," Etzel's clandestine radio, declared that "the tragedy was not caused by Jewish soldiers, who carried out their duty courageously and with self-sacrifice, but by the British themselves, who disregarded a warning and refused to evacuate the building."[72] Despite the fact that the attack on the King David Hotel was planned and endorsed by the resistance-movement leaders, this action was strongly denounced by the Jewish Agency. It requested Etzel and Lehi to halt their activities against the British. But the so-called "dissident groups" continued with their violence. They ambushed and killed British policemen and soldiers, attacked government installations and army camps, blew up railways, and mined roads. Etzel even extended its sabotage beyond Palestine. On 1 October 1946, the British embassy in Rome, center of the British activities against the Jewish illegal emigration to Palestine, was badly damaged by bomb explosions.[73] British military clubs in Austria and Germany were attacked and military trains derailed.[74]

The British responded on two levels of policy. First, the mandatory government released the Jewish Agency and Haganah members who denounced the Irgun activities. Second, London proposed the Morrison-Grady plan of July 1946 (named after Herbert Morrison, lord president of the council, and Henry F. Grady, an American special envoy) that called for the division of Palestine into semiautonomous Jewish and Arab sectors, with a central British authority retaining supreme power for another four years. This was rejected by both Jews and Arabs.

The Jewish movements continued their activities against the mandatory government. On 27 December 1946 Etzel and Lehi units attacked British police centers in Jerusalem and Jaffa and a military camp in the outskirts of Tel-Aviv. About five thousand Jews were detained for questioning. The British fortified many administration buildings and police outposts and surrounded them with wire fences, and thus the so-called "Bevingrad quarters" were created in the main cities. In January and February 1947, many armed posts

---

[72]*Keesing's Contemporary Archives*, p. 8102–3. See also Begin, *The Revolt*, pp. 212–20.

[73]*Palcor News Agency Cables* (9 and 30 October and 7 November 1946), and *Keesing's Contemporary Archives*, p. 8222.

[74]*Palcor News Agency Cables* (12 November 1946), and Begin, *The Revolt*, p. 234.

and camps were attacked; arms and military equipment were appropriated by Irgun and Lehi units. The government was forced to declare a "military state" in March, which did not succeed in stopping the attacks of the two underground organizations.

XI

Faced with the failure of its policy of military restrictions, curfews, arrests, and deportations of suspected underground members, and coupled with the absence of any willingness on the part of the two Palestinian communities to accept various proposals for the future of the mandate, Britain asked on 2 April 1947 for a special session of the United Nations General Assembly to consider the question of "constituting and instructing a special committee to prepare for consideration of the questions of Palestine . . . "[75]

The Arab members of the United Nations objected to the terms of the British request because it implied recognition of Jewish claims, and the Arabs therefore demanded that the forthcoming meeting alternatively consider the questions of the termination of the mandate over Palestine and the declaration of Palestinian independence.[76]

The British item was placed on the agenda, when the special session of the United Nations General Assembly convened on 25 April 1947.[77] The assembly agreed to hear the cases of the Jewish Agency for Palestine, the Arab Higher Committee, and other interested nongovernmental parties.[78] The Jewish representatives complained of the British restrictions on immigration to Palestine. The Arab delegates, on the other hand, stated that the Balfour Declaration had been made without consent or knowledge of people most directly affected—the Arabs of Palestine.

The assembly set up a United Nations Special Committee on Palestine (UNSCOP)[79] to prepare the Palestine item for consideration by the forthcoming regular assembly. The Arab countries announced that they would boycott UNSCOP. After intensive investigation of the various aspects of the problem, UNSCOP issued its report to the General Assembly on 31 August 1947.[80] It unanimously resolved that

---

[75]United Nations, Doc. A/286.

[76]United Nations, Doc. A/287–291, 22 April 1947.

[77]For excellent presentation of the Palestine question as discussed by the special session of the General Assembly, see Jacob Robinson, *Palestine and the United Nations: Prelude to a Solution* (Washington, DC: Public Affairs Press, 1948).

[78]When the charter of the United Nations came into force on 24 October 1945, the Arab states of Egypt, Iraq, Lebanon, Saudi Arabia, and Syria were among the original members of the organization.

[79]Members of UNSCOP were Australia, Canada, Czechoslovakia, Guatemala, India, Iran, Netherlands, Peru, Sweden, Uruguay, and Yugoslavia.

[80]United Nations, Doc. A/364.

the mandate should be terminated. The majority recommended that Palestine should be divided into an Arab state, a Jewish state, and with an international status established for Jerusalem, all of which should be linked in an economic union. They further recommended that the Arab and Jewish states should become independent after a transitional period of two years, beginning 1 September 1947, during which time the United Kingdom would progressively transfer the administration of Palestine to the United Nations. Jerusalem was to be placed under an international trusteeship system with the United Nations as the administrating authority. Provisions for preservation of, and free access to, the holy places were to be contained in the constitutions of both the Arab and Jewish states. As an alternative to the partition of Palestine, a minority recommendation proposed a single independent federal state, comprising independent Arab and Jewish states, with Jerusalem as its capital.[81]

The Arab states and the Arab Higher Committee immediately rejected UNSCOP's recommendations. When Great Britain informed the regular session of the General Assembly on 29 September 1947 that it had decided to evacuate Palestine, the Arab Higher Committee proposed an alternative plan to the UNSCOP report with these recommendations: an Arab state should be established in the whole of Palestine; this state would respect rights and fundamental freedoms of all persons before the law; it would protect legitimate rights and interests of all minorities; and it would recognize freedom of worship and access to holy places, including Jerusalem.

This proposal for the future constitutional organization of Palestine was not accepted by the United Nations or the Jewish party. Rather, the General Assembly in its 29 November 1947 session adopted Resolution 181(II) on the "Plan of Partition with Economic Union of Palestine," as recommended by UNSCOP.[82] It established the United Nations Palestine Commission to implement the resolution and called for the Security Council to assist in implementation, as well as to take additional measures, if necessary, to maintain peace in the area.

Although this recommendation fell short of the Balfour Declaration, which according to the Jewish Agency referred to the whole of Palestine, most of the Yishuv readily accepted the partition plan. The major reservation registered by the agency stated that, since West Jerusalem is heavily populated by Jews, it should become the capital of the Jewish state and not be placed under an international administration, as proposed by the resolution.

The Arab delegates at the United Nations asserted that they would oppose the implementation of the partition plan. Several weeks later, on 14 December 1947, the Arab League, at the conclusion of its Cairo conference, released letters sent to the United

---

[81]The minority proposal was submitted by India, Iran, and Yugoslavia.
[82]The General Assembly vote was thirty-three to thirteen with ten abstentions.

Nations, United Kingdom, and the United States warning that the partitioning of Palestine would be considered an "hostile act towards 400 million Moslems." Britain, alone, capitulated to this pressure, declaring that it would not cooperate in the implementation of the United Nations resolution.

XII

As soon as news of the General Assembly's recommendation reached Palestine, a wave of Arab terrorism began. On 30 November, a bus was attacked by Arabs and five Jews were killed. The Arabs proclaimed a general strike and, on the next day, a mob of some two hundred youths broke into the Jewish commercial section of Jerusalem, smashed windows, looted shops, set goods on fire, and stabbed a number of people.[83] Riots also took place in Haifa and in the mixed quarter between Tel-Aviv and Jaffa. Convoys were attacked in different parts of the country. Dozens of Jews lost their lives in these incidents.[84] On 30 December, some two thousand Arab employees of the oil refineries in the Haifa-Acre area attacked their Jewish colleagues and killed forty-one of them.[85]

The situation in the country approached administrative chaos and political anarchy. The British were either unable or unwilling to prevent the intensification of Arab terrorism. Early in 1948, an Arab bomb planted in a postal delivery truck exploded in Haifa, causing nearly fifty casualties. Another twenty Jews were killed in an explosion of a British truck in Jerusalem. In the Hebron hills, a group of thirty-five men, composed almost entirely of Hebrew University students, were murdered and their bodies mutilated by their attackers.[86] Additional scores of Jews were attacked throughout the country.

Supplementing Palestinian Arab bands, led by local leaders such as Abd al-Qadir al-Husseini and supported financially by the neighboring states, the Arab League also began recruiting volunteers for an irregular Arab force for the purpose of participating in the Palestine struggle. Hajj Amin al-Husseini, the former mufti of Jerusalem, who had escaped arrest and settled in Egypt after the war, was particularly active as president of the Arab Higher Committee in this effort.

Early in 1948, the Arab Liberation Army, or Army of Deliverance (*Jeish al-Ingadh*), commanded by Fawzi al-Qawugji, sent some

---

[83]*The Palestine Post*, 3 December 1947.
[84]See, for example, *New York Times*, 11, 12, and 13 December 1947.
[85]*The Palestine Post*, 31 December 1947.
[86]Ibid., 20 January 1948.

five thousand men, mostly Iraqis, Syrians, and Lebanese, into Palestine.[87] Only after the force had been entrenched in the country did an increasing number of Palestinian Arabs join it. The army used small units to attack specific targets, usually Jewish settlements or convoys moving between settlements in northern and central Palestine. Other volunteers were sent to the southern part of the country by Egypt's Moslem Brotherhood, an ultraconservative religious and political organization.

Jewish response to the wave of Arab terrorism and its escalation into an organized armed insurrection was swift. While the Haganah focused on defensive actions, Etzel and Lehi, which continued to operate independently, also engaged in counterterrorism. On 11 December 1947, six Arabs were killed and thirty wounded when bombs were thrown at Arab buses in Haifa; there were also many casualties in an attack on an Arab village near the city. Two days later, eighteen Arabs died and sixty were injured in several attacks in Jerusalem, Jaffa, and the Lydda area. Houses blown up in an Arab village near Safed on 18 December left ten people dead.[88] Many Arab villagers were killed and wounded in the attack on Balad-el-Sheikh on 1 January 1948; this attack was apparently a reprisal for the murder of Jewish refinery workers.[89] On the same day, ten Arabs were killed in a Jaffa cafe explosion.[90] During that same month, there were heavy Arab casualties in Etzel and Lehi attacks on the Arab National Committee in Jaffa, an Arab-owned Semiramis in Jerusalem, and Arab crowds in various cities.[91]

As terrorism increased daily in the country, the United Nations Palestine Commission sent its First Special Report to the Security Council on 16 February 1948. It criticized "powerful Arab interests" in and out of Palestine for "a deliberate effort to alter the Partition Plan by force" and it criticized as well "certain elements of the Jewish community situation." The commission called on the Security Council to establish "an adequate non-Palestinian force which will assist law-abiding elements in both Arab and Jewish communities." Without such a force, the report warned, there will be "uncontrolled, widespread strife and bloodshed" at the termination of the mandate. Finally, it also quoted official British figures on casualties in Palestine during the period 30 November 1947–1 February 1948: 869 killed, including 427 Arabs, 381 Jews, 46 Britons, and 15 others.[92] The Security Council, aware of the seriousness of the situation,

---

[87]See Al-Qawugji's "Memoirs, 1948, Part I," *Journal of Palestine Studies* 1 (Summer 1972): 25–28; and the second part in *Journal of Palestine Studies* 2 (Autumn 1972): 3–33.

[88]*Keesing's Contemporary Archives*, p. 9237.

[89]Ibid.

[90]*New York Times*, 2 January 1948.

[91]*Keesing's Contemporary Archives*, p. 9238.

[92]United Nations, Doc. S/616.

conducted a long series of debates on the question of maintaining peace in Palestine.[93]

Both sides, during the period, continued their policies of violence and counterviolence. Moreover, there was the suspicion of British involvement on the side of the Arabs. On 1 February, the editorial offices of *The Palestine Post*, a Jewish-sponsored English-language newspaper in Jerusalem, were demolished by the explosion of a British armored car loaded with explosives and parked outside the building. Some twenty people were injured.[94] Similarly on 22 February, British armored cars parked near an apartment building on Ben Yehudah Street in the Jewish sector of Jerusalem exploded, destroying several houses and killing more than fifty residents.[95]

In light of these and other incidents, the general feeling within the Jewish community was that the authorities, on the whole, intervened on behalf of the Arabs. Etzel delivered a warning to the British stating that, since London was interested in kindling the fight between Arabs and Jews in order to remain in Palestine, it would direct its activities against the authorities inside and outside Palestine until "freedom is achieved."

London immediately denounced these actions and condemned the Jewish Agency for its failure to take steps to suppress "Jewish terrorism." In a statement addressed to the agency, the government concluded that the

> Haganah have from time to time foiled the terrorist groups, but there still remains no method of dealing effectively with these people except the use of the machinery provided by the law. The Government, confronted with the deliberate policy of the Jewish Agency to render their task as difficult as possible, desires to bring once more to the attention of the Jewish commuity the fact that the continuance of indiscriminate murder and condoned terrorism can lead only to forfeiture by the community of all right in the eyes of the world to be numbered among civilised people.[96]

The Arabs responded with more violence. Jerusalem was besieged by Arab irregulars and cut off from the coast. Jewish settlements in the Galilee were attacked by Arab volunteers. Clashes between Arabs and Jews near Tel-Aviv resulted in the deaths of seventeen Haganah members and fifteen Arabs. On 11 March, a device was smuggled into the courtyard of the Jewish Agency headquarters in Jerusalem, in a car belonging to the American consulate in the city, driven by an Arab driver. The explosion

---

[93]United Nations, Doc. S/PV.253, 24 February 1948.
[94]*The Palestine Post*, 2 February 1948.
[95]Ibid., 23 February 1948.
[96]*Keesing's Contemporary Archives*, p. 9238.

wrecked a section of one of the wings and caused thirteen deaths and other casualties.[97] Toward the end of the month, Arabs carried out repeated raids on highways, which blocked traffic and hindered the movement of people.

Lehi retaliated by heavily damaging the Haifa headquarters of an Arab military group under the direction of Iraqi and Syrian officers, destroying vehicles with explosives in the Arab sector, and killing 17 and injuring 100. Its units also mined a Haifa-Cairo train, causing a heavy toll in dead and wounded.[98]

The Arab boycott policy against the Jews of Palestine, which had been formally adopted by the Arab League Council on 12 February 1945, was further intensified in the spring. The government of Iraq stopped delivery of oil through the pipeline from Iraq to the refineries in Haifa. Encouraged by this display of support by neighboring countries, the local Arabs blockaded the Jewish quarter of the Old City of Jerusalem, cutting off the supplies of food, water, and medicine to the noncombatant residents of this sector.[99] A medical convoy, consisting of Jewish doctors, nurses, and teachers, was attacked on its way to the Hadassah Medical Hospital on Mount Scopus, killing thirty-six and wounding forty-five. Other units were ambushed elsewhere, among them the relief convoy of forty-six people, which was destroyed near Yechiam, a kibbutz in the Galilee.

In spite of these setbacks, the Haganah was able in April to establish control rapidly over the entire area allotted to the Jewish state in the United Nations partition plan. It opened the road to Jerusalem by occupying Arab areas along its route, dispersed the Qawuqji forces in the Jezrael Valley, and drove the Arab units from Safed, Tiberias, and Haifa.

Etzel and Lehi, meanwhile, continued to operate unilaterally, and sometimes jointly, against both the Arabs and British. On 6 April, a British military camp at Pardes Hanna, near Haifa, was attacked, resulting in the seizure by the Irgun members of thirty-five Bren guns, sixty-five tommy guns, seventy rifles, as well as light cannons, armored cars, and tens of thousands of bullets. A more dramatic incident took place on 9 April during a military operation of Etzel against the Arab village of Dir Yassin, near Jerusalem,[100] in

---

[97]See Netanel Lorch, *The Edge of the Sword: Israel's War of Independence, 1947–1949* (New York: Putnam, 1961), p. 63.

[98]*Keesing's Contemporary Archives*, p. 9239.

[99]The seige of old Jerusalem ended on 28 May 1948, when the Jewish quarter surrendered to the Arab Legion. See Harry Levine, *Jerusalem Embattled* (London: Gollancz, 1950); and John Bagot Glubb, *A Soldier with the Arabs* (London: Hadder and Stoughton, 1957), pp. 129–30.

[100]See "Dir Yassin," *West Asia Affairs* (Summer 1969): 27–30; *New York Times*, 10, 11, and 12 April 1948; Edgar O'Ballance, *The Arab-Israeli War, 1948* (New York: Praeger, 1957), p. 58; Arthur Koestler, "The Other Exodus," *The Spectator* (18 May 1961); Christopher Sykes, *Crossroads to Israel* (Cleveland: World, 1965), pp. 416–17; and Guy Ottewell, "Deir Yassin: A Forgotten Tragedy with Present-Day Meaning," *Perspective* (April 1969): 6.

conjunction with Haganah operations along the Castel road leading to Jerusalem. The Haganah commander of Jerusalem, Shaltiel, asked the local Irgun commander Raanan to clear Dir Yassin, a point en route to Jerusalem. The village itself was fortified and full of Iraqi soldiers. About one hundred Irgun members were selected to seize the village. They were equipped with a few rifles, pistols, and Sten guns; one light Bren gun; and some hand grenades. A small truck fitted with a loudspeaker accompanied them. A warning was repeatedly broadcast in Arabic to the civilian population to abandon the buildings, because an attack was imminent. Approximately one hundred villagers came out from their houses and were later transported to the Arab part of East Jerusalem. The Palestinians and Iraqis who remained in the houses hoisted white flags; but when the Irgun soldiers approached them, they opened fire. House-to-house fighting ensued. Some of the Arabs tried to escape in women's clothes and later they were found wearing Irgun military uniforms under the disguise. Many were killed when they resisted capture. The Irgun sustained forty-one casualties; the Irgun commander was among the four killed. The Arabs sustained close to two hundred casualties, including villagers who either believed the Arab soldiers would drive off the attacking Jews or were not allowed to leave the houses before the battle began.

At the United Nations, diplomatic activity continued. The Second Special Session of the General Assembly, which began on 16 April, rejected a United States plan for a temporary trusteeship for Palestine as a move to stop violence there. The Arabs favored the plan because it implied a single rather than a partitioned state; the Jews opposed it, holding that the trusteeship proposal was untenable and would negate the partition resolution. The Security Council, fully aware of "the increasing violence and disorder in Palestine," adopted a resolution on 1 April, which called upon the antagonistic Arab and Jewish armed groups "to cease acts of violence immediately."[101] Having failed to achieve this truce, the council called again on the parties on 17 April to cease all hostilities, to refrain from provocative political activity, and to safeguard the holy places.[102] On 23 April, the Security Council created a truce commission, composed of representatives of the United States, France, and Belgium, to assist in implementing the proposed cease-fire arrangements. During the same month, Haifa was conquered by the Haganah and Etzel units, and Jaffa was captured by Etzel.

As the United Nations was unable to stop the bloodshed, Golda Meyerson (Meir), in an attempt to avert what seemed to be a threatened invasion by the neighboring countries, met secretly on behalf of the Jewish Agency with King Abdullah of Transjordan on the

---

[101]United Nations, Doc. S/PV.277.
[102]United Nations, Doc. S/723.

night of 30 April. Although the Arab monarch was prepared to recognize some sort of autonomy for Palestine Jews, he could not resist both British and pan-Arab pressure advising him against concluding a separate agreement with the Jewish Agency. The dialogue failed, and the parties braced themselves for the inevitable confrontation.

The final two weeks of the prestate period were costly to the Yishuv. Transjordan's army, better known as the Arab Legion, commanded by British officers, entered the fighting in and around Jerusalem, killing and wounding hundreds of Jews and capturing scores as prisoners of war.[103]

On 14 May 1948, the mandate of Palestine ended, and the British completed the withdrawal of their forces. On that day, the Jewish Provisional State Council proclaimed the birth of *Medinat Yisrael* (the State of Israel). The Proclamation of Independence of Israel made a special plea: "In the midst of wanton aggression . . . We extend the hand of peace and good neighbourliness to all the neighboring States and their peoples and invite their cooperation and mutual assistance." It also called "upon the Arab inhabitants of the State of Israel to preserve the ways of peace and play their part in the development of the State on the basis of full and equal citizenship and due representation in all its bodies and institutions—provisional and permanent."

The Arabs responded to this appeal by sending the invading forces of Egypt, Iraq, Jordan, Lebanon, and Syria to guarantee the abrupt and conclusive demise of the Jewish state on the very first day of its existence. Azaam Pasha, the secretary general of the Arab League, outlined its purpose: "There will be a war of extermination and a momentous massacre which will be spoken of like the Mongolian Massacres and the Crusades."[104]

XIII

The independence of Israel changed the Jewish resistance movement from a group of underground organizations into components of the Israeli army. As such, their participation in the First Arab-Israeli War goes beyond the scope of this book. However, the perceptions and actions of the resistance movement, in general, and of the Irgun, in particular, continue to influence the attitudes and policies of Israelis and Arabs alike. While debate about this historical episode will continue as long as the Arab-Israeli conflict remains

---

[103]See Lorch, *Edge of the Sword*, p. 129, Edgar O'Ballance, *The Arab-Israeli War, 1948* (London: Faber and Faber, 1956), pp. 65–66; and Dov Knohl, *Siege in the Hills of Hebron: The Battle of the Etzion Bloc* (New York: Yoseloff, 1958).
[104]British Broadcasting Corporation news broadcast, 15 May 1948.

unresolved, the editors hope that the documents presented in this volume will shed light on the role of the resistance movement in the creation of the state of Israel.

The editors, who are solely responsible for the selection and organization of the material, wish to thank especially the Jabotinsky Institute of Tel-Aviv and its chief archivist, Pesach Gany, for providing assistance in locating relevant documents.

I
BACKGROUND

Irgun Zvai Leumi B'Eretz-Israel: Aims and Methods

THE AIMS OF THE IRGUN

The aims of the Irgun are the eternal aims of the People of Israel:—Return to Zion, National freedom and independence, Freedom and Happiness of the individual, Social justice.

Return to Zion

Ever since the people went into exile and till this very day, every Jew's heart has been imbued with the fervent striving to return to the Homeland from the blood-stained wanderings among the Gentiles, who are rising to exterminate us in the life-time of every generation. This striving has been taking varying forms until, in recent generations, under the two-fold influence of Jewish tradition and of national-political currents among the nations, it took the form of a *National* Movement. Then again, in our own life-time when it became evident that the means of action used by the Jewish National Movement would not achieve the purpose but, on the contrary, were liable *to perpetuate the dispersion*, there emerged the fighting—but truly fighting—Jewish *Liberation Movement*, bent on attaining the national aim in the same way done by all liberation movements known in history.

Return to Zion means:—Concentration of the People's masses in the Homeland; the concentration of *millions*; the concentration of the absolute majority of the People in its own country, which would put an end to the *unnatural* dispersion of the People of Israel.

1

National Freedom and Independence

Return to Zion cannot be the sole aim of the People. There were and are peoples who live on their own soil but are enslaved by foreign nations. Such is not the objective the Irgun is striving at.

Return to Zion must be accomplished by the achievement of national freedom and political independence. And national freedom can have one expression only:—a State, unfettered in its sovereignty by any outward bond and only restricted by a wise construction and by rules of international relationship—a State on the historical territory of the Nation.

The founders of the Irgun laid it down, from the very outset, that the achievement of political independence is not merely to *complete* the return to Zion, but, moreover, to serve as essential *preliminary* for this return which it ought to precede. Experience has proved how far-sighted they were and how they forestalled all the *other factors* in the nation in appraising the situation and estimating future developments. This is what they had said:—"The gathering of the diaspora into the Land of Israel cannot be effected on a million scale, unless it is *preceded* by the establishment of *Hebrew Rule* over Eretz-Israel; any 'Zionist' method, which might profess to execute this plan without preliminary establishment of Hebrew Rule, is a deceptive one." True, even under the present conditions, no other single effort should be abandoned, if it serves to bring to the Homeland, by one way or the other, the largest possible number of its home-coming sons; but, both from the historical and the practical viewpoint, return to Zion is impossible without *rule over Zion.* The direct and central aim of the Irgun must, therefore, be defined as follows:—the creation of Hebrew Rule in the Homeland, that rule which *alone* can attain and accomplish the process of repatriation and re-establishment in the country of our fore-fathers.

Freedom and Happiness of the Individual

The liberation of the country from foreign yoke, the establishment of Hebrew Rule, the revival of the independent Hebrew State with millions of Jewish citizens—this is the primary *condition* for rescueing the People from spiritual decline and physical extermination, and for securing its normal existence. This is why the *form of government* in the Hebrew State is *not* regarded by the Irgun as problem of decisive importance. A bad regime in a Hebrew State is preferable to the "Very best" regime under foreign domination. But, whereas it is the Irgun which is realising the People's aims and expressing its will; whereas the soldiers of the Irgun are the ones who are prepared at any moment to give the supreme sacrifice—the sacrifice of life—for the achievement of the aim,—it is their right, moveover—their *duty*—to strive that the Hebrew State, the fruit of their toil, the fruit of their fight, the fruit of their *blood*, should be a *free* state, which would secure for every individual full civil rights:— the Freedom of thought and speech, Security from persecution, freedom of enjoying the fruits of one's labour, safety of home and family and participation in the election of representative institutions (Local and Regional Councils, Houses of Legislature and Central Government), full equality before Law and Court, freedom of criticizing authority, the possibility to appoint fitting representatives instead of those who prove unsuitable,—in short:—the personal happiness of the individual in the framework of an organised, progressive and happy society. But there is no happiness in a state which is based on *tyrants' rule*, be it that of one man or of a sectional group, who by some or other way might have obtained the power. In such a state, the citizen either becomes a cringing coward, or a hunted beast. Such a state is destined to undergo periodical and heavy shocks, which may even lead to its ruin. Such is not the kind of state we are striving at. We want a state, wherein every single citizen will be proud and free, where the elected rulers will consider themselves not as "higher beings" but as *servants* of society and seekers of its benefit. We want a state, wherein high civilisation could flourish, where creative thought would develop in political, social and economic fields; a state which we would realise the prophet's saying:—"For out of Zion shall go forth the law, and the word of the Lord from Jerusalem."

Social Justice

What is the essence of social justice, what should be appearance of an accomplished society or of an ideal society? On this opinions differ.

There was a time when the idea of social justice was *identified* with the idea of absolute economic *equality*. This was so in the days when *absolute inequality* was prevailing in the countries of Europe. In those days the fate of a man and his station in life were not determined by his abilities, prowess, labour and so forth, but by his level of *origin*, or by his race, or by his religious belief and the like. The philosophers of that period—or those who were directly influenced by that period—were dreaming of a society where no distinction would be made between man and man. Thus according to the cliches devised by them every man should receive the same housing, the same ration of food, the same clothes, the same ration [of] pleasure, etc. On the basis of this ideal the kiboutzim and kvoutzot were established in Eretz Israel. But their experience, even if considered a success, still cannot be taken as a general rule. In the communal settlements there is a *limited* society, which lives a uniform way of (rural) life; while the society in a *state* counts *millions* of people, who are not bound together by personal relationship, who engage in different economic professions and differ in the main walk of life: rural, on one hand, and urban on the other.

This idea gained an interesting development in Russia. In the first years following the October Revolution, the experiment was made there to enforce unlimited economic equality; subsequently however, the Soviet State, introduced considerable distinction in the grades of salaries and living standards. Distinctions arising from the position and from the quality and productivity of individual work, and the slogan "*Absolute equality*" ('Curavnilovka' in Russian) became Contre revolutionary propaganda. The rulers of Soviet Russia today consider this slogan as *contrary* to the ideas of "*scientific socialism*" (which repudiates the thesis of "utopist socialism") and they are furiously persecuting the followers of that principle.

But whether we accept the opinion that absolute economic equality is possible and desirable and whether we take the view that such equality is unattainable or liable to produce *stagnation*—still the following two principles remain above any discussion from the viewpoint of social justice. The one principle is legal and political equality: *absolute* equality before the institutions of the State, absolute equality in achieving a station in life, or, in other words: the *equality of opportunity*, the chance of obtaining education, the opportunity of displaying personal ability, of rising the standard of living. This equality must prevail unrestrictedly and unconditionally. This is the meaning of *Social Democracy* which implies that every man should be honoured by all and by everybody and by himself as every individual will be given the full chance to develop his abilities and to secure his place in society.

The second principle is: *to abolish poverty*. An accomplished society is *bound in duty* to abolish poverty, in particular degrading poverty, that kind of poverty which does not enable the man to live as man should, a man of cultured necessities and of creative soul; for as the saying goes "not on bread alone shall men live."

Hence the conclusion that a progressive state *must* safeguard to all its citizens without exception those conditions of existence which are necessary in order to enable every one to freely develop according to his own abilities, initiative and energy. Sufficient food, clothing adequate living space, elementary school, medical care are the *minimum* requirements which organised society—namely the State—is obliged to secure for every man and woman. *To secure* does not mean to *give away* without the counter value of productive work, whether physical or mental, on part of the individual. For, should this be a grant without any return myriads and perhaps

hundreds of thousands of people would be found who would content themselves with the minimum required for subsistance and
would prefer to be idle rather than to make the effort to acquire
more for themselves and for future generations. Even today there
are such people and they are a minority of society—who are living an
idle life because they possess enough or too much. But this is a life of
parasites, and every man of self-respect ought to despise them. Life
demands progress; and progress is impossible without effort and
labour, both mental and manual.

The Ways of Achievement

In the life-time of the last two generations, two attempts were
made to restore Eretz Israel to the Hebrew People, with the view of
restoring the Hebrew people to Eretz Israel. One attempt was made
by way of so-called *"practical work,"* namely, by private or collective
land purchases, by erection of towns, colonies, communal settlements, etc. This endeavour, while fruitful in itself, came to a result
such as is invariably destined for similar ventures in the conditions
of a hostile foreign regime: to the creation of a magnificient enterprise indeed, but one which may be paralysed or destroyed at any
time,—the same as those magnificient enterprises, which the Jews
established all over the outside world, only to be wrecked by any
stray wind. It is clear today that under the actual political conditions all further growth has become impossible. There is no scope
for settlement except confinement in the borders of the ghetto, such
as the British oppressors had circumscribed by their "laws" even
before they cordoned it off by their barbed wire. The fate which is in
store for a ghetto in Eretz Israel is easy to anticipate, if one recalls
the history of Jewish ghettos in all other countries and at all times.

The second attempt was an effort to conduct the Jewish
struggle by means of moral-political argument, in the hope thus to
effect a fundamental change in Eretz Israel and enable, in a relatively short time, to settle the country and turn it into a Hebrew
State. It is evident now that this attempt has failed, too. The British
are ignoring moral considerations; they have firmly decided to
appropriate the country for themselves, under the pretext of doing
"justice" to the Arabs, and therefore any attempt at "persuasion" is in
advance doomed to remain sterile.

Hence the conclusion:—There is no other way to free our
Homeland and redeem our Nation except the way of the *Liberation
War*. A national Liberation War is a *just* war, which is conducted by
an oppressed people against a foreign Power that has enslaved it
and its country. And whereas the foreign Power is occupying the
conquered country by the sheer force of its arms—for otherwise it

would have been expelled overnight—it is unavoidable that the Liberation war should become *a war by arms*, a war by force of weapons, the weapons of freedom against those of enslavement. The Force, which the oppressed people sets up to wage war against the oppressor, is called the *Liberation Army. The "Irgun" is the Liberation Army of the Hebrew Nation.*

But the Liberation War—like any other war in modern times—is not conducted by military arms alone and is not limited to a *physical contest* between the forces of oppression and those of liberation. The Liberation War embraces many fields, and the Liberation Army employs *manifold* weapons. Such is the command of reality in an age where every war, between big and small nations alike, requires the use not only of troops, but also other means of attack or defence: political, economic, propagandist, etc. This is also *the great* chance of the Liberation War, because only seldom may the Liberation Army of an enslaved people overcome by *physical* force the occupation armies of the oppressory Power;—but with the aid of an ally, whether one who helps from the outset or one who steps in at the moment of the decisive clash, even the Liberation Army may beat the enemy and wrest from his hands the rule over the country. There are many examples in history to prove that an independent Liberation War, accomplished by *political action aimed at achieving an ally*, is resulting in victory for the Army of Liberation. *Thus* victory was gained by our Maccabees; thus the Italians defeated the Austrians in the 19th century; thus the Balkan peoples overcame the Turks in that same century; thus also, in the Second World War, did the European Underground Armies hasten the victory of their peoples and secure for them the fruits of victory.

The history of Liberation Movements shows that there are two more possibilities to gain victory. One of them occurs when, under certain political circumstances, internal or external (that is, by force of a given political constellation), the enemy finds himself compelled *to acquiesce* in the abandonment of his rule over the oppressed and fighting country, and therefor enters into negotiations with the national representative body of the fighting people with the view to establish a national regime; the other possibility arises when, under another political constellation, namely, in the event of war between the occupying Power and other Power or Powers—the enemy's *military might* desintegrates, thus rendering the opportunity for a well-poised Liberation Army to "strike," to dislodge the foreign rule, to set up a national regime and secure its existence against outward aggression, and to pave the way for sovereign institutions to be established by free elections of the people. The first example was provided by *Ireland* in the twenties of this century; the second possibility was exemplified by Poland, Czechoslovakia and the Baltic States at the end of the First World War.

All these possibilities may be summed up in one term: *the*

opportune hour. To exploit the opportune hour is the *primary* duty of the Liberation Army, and although such action also depends on subjective factors—namely, on the wisdom of decision of a courageous leadership, and on the readiness to sacrifice and preparedness for battle of the fighting forces—still, from the objective viewpoint it is *bound* to three preliminary conditions:

1) A continuous liberation war;
2) Incessant preparations for the decisive moment;
3) Political action, which should have two objectives:—
   a) to lift the problem, which is contested by the Liberation War, above local limits and to turn it into a world problem, into an international issue;
   b) to win over political factors—mainly sovereign Governments—as allies of the Army of Liberation.

By observing these three preliminary conditions, which are essential for the proper use of *the opportune hour* that carries freedom to every oppressed and *fighting* nation,—we arrive at the full clarification of the *essence* of the *Liberation War.* The Liberation Army is an Army of *Volunteers,* who impose their duties upon themselves, and not an army of compulsory recruits, whose duties are *forced upon them* by others; the *main* tasks of the Liberation Army are military ones; its duty is to strike at the enemy by modern weapons; its aim—to shatter and destroy the foreign rule and replace it by the rule of the Nation in its country; its aspiration—to become, on the Day of Redemption, the Army of Defence for the Homeland, to guard its frontiers, its independence, its integrity and development. Such an *Army,* fighting for the freedom of the Homeland and ready to defend it even at the price of life, is the one thing needed by the Hebrew people more than anything else. For without army there is no nation, no homeland, no *honour.* Without an army every people—even a great one—becomes what our own people has been: *a victim of massacres and pogroms during two thousand years.* Parties, institutions, *political movements*—all these the Hebrew People did possess in abundance; the one thing it did *not* have, one which it needs like air to breathe—is an *Army.* This was understood by the founders of the "Irgun," and therefore they did not establish a political-revolutionary group nor a defence organisation nor a new "movement"—but an *Army.* The *first* Hebrew Army, with its commanders and soldiers, its objectives and internal regime,—after two thousand years of Exile.

And still there exists a difference between our Army, which fights to free the Homeland, and a regular Army. The *main* difference is in the name itself. We are an *army,* but *not only* an army. We are an army of *Liberation.* And an Army of Liberation differs from a regular army not merely by way of recruitment (volunteering instead of compulsory draft), and not merely by its way of life (underground and necessary secrecy instead of open appearance) and not only by the kind of discipline (discipline by inner conscience as against discipline based on physical coercion); the Liberation Army differs from a regular army, first and foremost, in respect of the *political function* of the war. While a regular army in an established state—unless its regime is founded on *military dictatorship* which is as bad and ephemereal as any dictatorship—is leaving, can and *must* leave the political decision in the hands of its *Government*, the Liberation Army cannot and *ought not* waive the creative *political thought* and independent political action, which has the purpose of obtaining support, intensifying the war and accelerating victory. The *political* thought and action must *accompany* the military operations, must follow the Army of Liberation and pave before it the road to increased power and its use at the right moment. The Liberation Army educates revolutionary fighters; it raises soldiers; it also brings forth *statesmen*. For the Army of Liberation is both a *conquering force* and an *achieving movement*. Therefore, the Liberation Army cannot, and is not entitled to surrender the "political command" and the authority to conduct *the policy*, which is linked with the war for freedom, to any other body in the Hebrew people except to one—the *Hebrew Government*.

Background of the Struggle for the Liberation of Eretz Israel: Facts on the Relations between the Irgun Zvai Leumi and the Haganah

The conditions in which the Hebrew struggle for liberation is being fought in Eretz Israel are probably unexampled in the history of national or social revolutions. There are no mountains to serve as bases, to provide safe arsenals or to serve as hide-outs for the underground fighters. There is no difficult terrain which could be exploited against the foreign Occupation forces. The country is small, easily traversible and from some high points large proportions of its whole extent are visible. The underground struggle has therefore to be conducted in the midst of the population, soldiers have to be trained, men and material have to be moved, arsenals maintained and the intricate details of every operation planned virtually in the presence, almost under the very eyes of the enemy. Yet not only has the Hebrew brain found an answer to the gigantic problems created by these conditions: the Irgun Zvai Leumi has succeeded in mastering the conditions to such an extent that the whole British Occupation regime, and its 100,000 soldiers, cannot even find security in the ghettoes and camps, behind the barbed wire barricades it has been compelled to erect, or in the tanks and armoured cars without which their forces do not move a step in our country.

But the basic problems with which the struggle is faced are made infinitely more complicated by the fact that, unlike the two factors usual in a struggle against a powerful, ruthless Occupying force, there are in our country no less than four factors. There are the British Occupation forces, the Arabs, and the resistant liberation Movement; and then there is the Haganah. The "relations" between the Irgun and the British Occupation forces require no elaboration here. "War" is the only adequate description. The relations with the Arabs demonstrate the historic significance of the struggle and one of the great achievements of the Irgun. In 1939, the Arabs had just emerged from a successful "revolt," a "revolt" which, albeit with active aid from the British and the senseless, catastrophic "self-restraint" of all the Jews except the Irgun, had established them, at least in their own eyes, as the major physical factor in Eretz Israel, a power whose constant threat hung over the heads of the Jews, a power which enabled the British constantly to present the problem of this country as a never-ending dispute between Arab and Jew, liable to burst into armed warfare if only the British removed their "protecting" hand. The fight of the Irgun and the tremendous blows it has delivered at British power in Eretz Israel have removed that threat for ever, have exposed the utter nakedness of the British bluff. Notwithstanding persistent incitement by their British-instigated leaders, in spite of widespread propaganda, distribution of arms and promises of bribes by the British, the Arabs have refused to lift a finger to create even the semblance of an Arab-Jewish war. On the one hand they have been taught the healthy lesson of Jewish armed power *in action*; on the other hand it has exposed to many of them the hollowness of the British propaganda that the Jews bear hostile intentions towards them. The consequence has been not only the elimination of the Arabs as a physical factor of consequence but the real beginnings of understanding and sympathy. It is naturally impossible to give details here—but not once but many times have Irgun fighters returning from operations been given aid and blessing by Arabs; and these and other indications are convincing testimony that the struggle of the Irgun against British oppression has opened the way to Hebrew-Arab cooperation, perhaps even in the course of the struggle.

The one incalculable factor in the whole situation is, tragically, the Haganah. We have here an organization, reputed to count many thousand of members in all walks of life, with huge sums at its disposal and large quantities of arms of all kinds in its ramified armouries. Yet in the face of ever-increasing brutal aggression by the

British, inside our country, towards our brothers in exile, and towards our people as a whole; in the face of the ever-increasing clarity of the British purpose to crush us and to render impossible the attainment of our statehood, to frustrate the repatriation of our exiles and to doom us in Eretz Israel to a new ghetto and our exiles to disintegration—in the face of this most blatant, cruel and treacherous aggression—this organisation, with its reputedly massive and militarily impressive potential, has not only not fulfilled its mission as a national army to rise up and attack the enemy; it has vacillated, colourless and indecisive, from one policy to another. It has seldom been possible for the men in the street in Eretz Israel to know whether the Haganah meant to fight against the British destroyer of our people—or against the force which has taken up the fight for the liberation of our country and our people. For the most part the struggle against the British Occupation Forces in Eretz Israel has gone on as though this allegedly huge organisation did not exist.

The riddle of the Haganah can of course be explained—at least partially. In the first place it is not an ideologically homogeneous organisation. You do not have to believe in anything in particular in order to belong to the Haganah. One section in the Haganah strives for a Jewish State, but this section is subdivided into those to whom a Jewish State has meaning only if it is established in the whole of our country, west and east of the Jordan; others who have long forgotten that the lands east of the Jordan belong to us; and still others to whom a partitioned Western Palestine is not only sufficient but "a consummation devoutly to be wished." And there are yet others in the Haganah who are absolutely opposed to a Jewish State, regard the proclamation of our striving for it as dangerous. On the other hand there are some in the Haganah who are against "violence," and who believe the only possible military purpose to be served by the Haganah is defence against possible attacks by Arabs; and, because of the Irgun struggle there being now no serious Arab attacks, remain in the Haganah only to make propaganda against any action at all. There are others whose hearts are being eaten out in frustration at their enforced passivity in the face of the most dire threat to our people. But these are to be found mainly in the rank and file. They are not well represented in the leadership which of an older vintage and a political education both anachronistic and unduly influenced by the faintheartedness of the ghetto, nevertheless decides the policy of the Haganah. The Haganah has consequently no basic policy, no basic strategy, no basic approach to the searing problems with which we are faced, and its strength, or potential strength, has only too often been the strength of a body without a head, going through some automatic motions without clear purpose or vision.

These comments are not made in criticism. There are made in painful realisation that the facts must be faced; that these charac-

teristics of the Haganah have unfortunately determined its attitude—
or, more correctly, its varying attitudes—both to the national struggle
and to the force which is conducting the struggle: the Irgun Zvai
Leumi.

There would nevertheless be no need for the publication of
this account of the relations between the Haganah and the Irgun
were it not for the most violent campaign of vilification and distortion now being conducted by the leadership of the Haganah against
the Irgun. This campaign is the result of persistent pressure by the
Jewish Agency which (as is no secret) has tried to force on the
Haganah a campaign of armed violence against the Irgun. Such a
campaign—which would mean civil war—the Haganah has so far
refused to undertake. But the danger exists. And because of it;
because of the unbridled campaign of fabrication; and because that
campaign depends for any success it hopes to achieve on the
ignorance of the world at large of the historic facts of the past three
years, it becomes essential that the truth be now told.

Hitherto the Irgun has kept silent under extreme provocation—
and every poster-bedecked wall in Eretz Israel is proof of that
provocation—refraining from a complete exposure of the unchival-
rous, cowardly behaviour of its former comrades-in-arms—as long as
that behaviour did not threaten to go beyond the limit of words. Today the danger has appeared on the horizon that some irresponsible
elements in the Haganah may be incited to turn words into deeds;
and silence on the part of the Irgun becomes a liability to the cause
of internal peace.

Here, then, are the facts—facts which none will dare challenge.
For there are still, we believe, honest men in the Haganah.

The recent history of the Irgun struggle falls into five phases.
The first opens in February, 1944. It was then that the full horror of
the extermination of our brothers in Europe was revealed. It was
then that the full depth of perfidy of the British—realised by the
Irgun long before World War II—was exposed. It was then that the
heart of all of us was broken at the inexorable realisation that the
British had actively helped in the extermination of our people. It
became clear to the Irgun then that in the face of this most dangerous and treacherous enemy only one way to liberation was open: the
way of armed struggle.

Then the struggle started—though even then, because the war
against Hitler was still in progress, the Irgun avoided attacks against
installations required for the war against Nazi Germany, concen-
trating its attacks directly against British rule in the country.

What was the attitude of the Haganah? They explained to the
Irgun leaders that they were not yet certain that Britain had decided
against us. They still hoped. Dr. Weizmann, it seemed had per
suaded them that Mr. Churchill had promised that when the war
ended the Jews would be presented with the "plum in the pudding."

Should they, however, be forced to the conclusion the Irgun had reached—then, they assured, they would unloose a struggle against the British beside which the Irgun's was mere child's-play. But they opposed the struggle; and launched a vigorous propaganda campaign against the Irgun. Such, however, was the mood of their followers in the early stages that the Haganah began proclaiming that the reason they were opposing the struggle was that it interfered with *their* preparations for the real struggle. As Irgun attacks on the British continued—their propaganda against it grew in intensity.

Until finally in October, 1944, they presented the Irgun with an ultimatum—demanding that it stop the fight against the British. They, it seemed, had finally come to the conclusion that Jewish action should be confined to verbal politics, and they had hopes of a new, favourable Government coming to power in Britain. This however was not what they told the public. Their propaganda described the Irgun as "murderers," "Fascists" and "Hooligans."

The Irgun saw no reason for stopping the struggle. They saw before them the still closed gates of Eretz Israel—and the slaughter of our brothers in Europe was still going on. It was during that period that Britain openly rejected the opportunity of saving a large proportion of the Jews of Hungary, who could have left that country. The Irgun naturally rejected the ultimatum—though it contained the threat that otherwise it would be "liquidated" completely.

Then followed few months purgatory, during which the Haganah launched fratricidal strife on the Yishuv. They handed over to the British Gestapo lists of alleged members of the Irgun, including officers with whom they had had official contact. And the British flung them—in some cases after torture—into the concentration camp at Latrun, and deported several hundred Hebrew citizens to East Africa. The lists of those about to be deported were submitted by the Gestapo-C.I.D. to the Jewish Agency for confirmation; and it was then the Agency passively accepted the principle that it was permissible to exile Hebrews from their Homeland.

That two-faced pseudo-friend of our people, Mr. R. W. S. Crossman, M.P., has stated in the British House of Commons—on the strength of information from the Jewish Agency— that the Jewish Agency had handed over to the British authorities the names of 1,000 Jews. We do not place reliance on such a source. But we do know that several hundred Hebrew citizens are *still* (May, 1947) prisoners in Kenya as a result of denunciation by the so-called "National institutions."

In some cases there was actual physical identification by Jewish Agency or Haganah agents. A member of the High Command of the Irgun, who was personally known to the Haganah High Command, was travelling in a taxi from Tel-Aviv to Jerusalem when his taxi was chased and overtaken by a British C.I.D. car. With the British

Gestapo men was a Jew who pointed to the Irgun commander and said "That's the man." The Irgun officer was flown forthwith to imprisonment in Eritrea (whence he subsequently escaped and returned to active service).

Others were first kidnapped by the Haganah as a means of identifying them for the British. Still others were kidnapped and held by the Haganah itself and pressed for information. Some were beaten, some tortured. Men were chained to their beds for days on end, forced to perform even their natural functions on the spot.

Thousands of members of the Palmach (Haganah striking force) were drafted to the towns, where they did the work of shadowing and, where possible, kidnapping members of the Irgun. The British Gestapo being deeply interested in their work, they naturally did it openly for the British to see. The British did—and quietly gathered information at first hand on the identity of Palmach members. As the Haganah afterwards complained, the British used that information a year later when they arrested nearly 4,000 men as suspected members of Palmach.

Throughout that long period of terror and inhuman persecution, when the Haganah agents performed for the Nazi-British the same service as the Darnard Militia in Vichy France performed for the Nazis, all soldiers of the Irgun were under strict orders not to retaliate. In spite of all they saw their comrades suffering, the members of the Irgun rigidly obeyed those orders: there was no retaliation. The leaders of the Irgun were certain, despite everything going on around them, that the time would come when the Haganah would recognise the vital necessity of an armed struggle of liberation against the British. They were certain that this madness would pass: and decided to do nothing which might create a sea of blood and tears, which would erect an impassable barrier between Irgun and Haganah and make co-operation impossible for years to come. For the sake of that possible future fighting unity the Irgun suffered these fratricidal blows, instigated by blind leaders, without hitting back—and maintaining the struggle against the real enemy.

And the objects of the Haganah were not achieved. The Irgun was not liquidated. And the fight against the British went on. It was during that period that the Irgun made its first attacks against British oil installations and police fortresses.

There was a short period during which the Irgun carried out no operations—when the British Labour Party won the elections and formed their Government. Though far from sharing the optimism of the Jewish Agency and others, the Irgun leaders thought it fair to give the Labour Government a clear chance to show whether it meant to carry out the very definite promises it had made two months earlier.

By August it had become clear that Irgun suspicions of the Labour Government were only too well justified. Their treachery was so blatant that even the leaders of the Haganah saw it at once.

The Haganah war against the Irgun petered out; and the second phase of the struggle came to an end.

In September, 1945, the Haganah leaders made it known to the Irgun leaders that they had also decided to embark on armed resistance against the British. They asked them to interrupt operations until they were ready, when all should fight together.

The Irgun did not hesitate for a moment to stretch out the hand of co-operation and comradeship. The idea of a fighting Jewish unity, which they had cherished for so long, was more powerful than any other consideration. They had hoped for this moment, and suffered much for it. And though in their reply to the Haganah's request they reminded them that they could not lightly or quickly forget what the Haganah had done to them—they agreed to their request at once.

Several meetings took place between the two Commands to discuss strategy and organisation. The Haganah's first proposal was that the Irgun be liquidated and merged with the Haganah. This Irgun declined to do, not only because of the bitter memories of the recent past, but because they could obviously not be certain of the intensity of the Haganah's feeling for the struggle. At that moment, though they believed the Haganah's promise, they had in mind their years-long blood and suffering of their comrades. The Haganah struggle was still only a promise.

But they agreed to the Haganah's second proposal. In this they informed the Irgun that they would operate in the framework of an organisation to be called "Tenuat Hameri" (Resistance Movement) which should comprise both the existing Haganah and other forces they were able to muster. Under the banner of Tenuat Hameri would be carried out not only military operations but repatriation and civil disobedience. (Civil disobedience remained a dead letter in spite of many repetitions of the promise, and may be dismissed from this narrative at once). The Irgun was to carry out operations asked for, or approved by, the High Command of Tenuat Hameri. There was to be regular consultation, but in case of disagreement on plans the Tenuat Hameri leaders (that is, the leaders of the Haganah), were to have the last word. Operations for the capture of arms from the enemy were to be carried out independently, only notification having to be given to the other organizations. This agreement was tripartite, between Haganah, Irgun and F.F.I. (Stern Group).

It was explicitly understood that the agreement was for co-operation in *action*, and that should any party withdraw from the struggle, the agreement automatically came to an end. The Irgun for its part made it clear that the struggle would go on until the withdrawal of the British from Eretz Israel and the transfer of power to a Provisional Hebrew Government.

The period of actual joint operations began on 1st November,

1945. The railways were attacked simultaneously over 150 points throughout Eretz Israel, and a number of attacks were made on police stations. Then the Haganah attacked a number of British installations connected with the British campaign against Jewish repatriation. These included the police station and coastguard station at Givat Olga. There sixteen British soldiers were wounded, several subsequently dying. (Today the death of enemy soldiers in Irgun operations is screamed at as the "shedding of innocent blood. . .") They also carried out two attacks on radar installations, of which the second was partially successful.

It would be wrong to say that the Irgun and Haganah saw eye to eye completely. The Irgun had long been convinced that the British had determined to crush us, to prevent the attainment of our independence, to doom our brothers in Europe to extermination, moral or physical, and the Hebrews of Eretz Israel to permanent ghettodom, while Britain built up the country as one great military base and oil transit centre. If we did not surrender they were prepared and determined to use every means possible to enforce our submission. To this there could and can be only one attitude: a struggle by every means in our power to throw off the British yoke, to force their withdrawal from the country; to go the way of all small peoples fighting for liberation from oppression and the threat of extinction, and to frustrate their purpose. (Events have since shown how correct was the Irgun estimate, indeed how clearly it is possible to achieve victory for our people)[.] The Haganah, on the other hand, had been forced slowly, step by step, to an understanding that the employment of the "traditional" political means of propaganda and "enlightenment," appeals to honour, the sanctity of obligations, were useless: that the brute force of the British could be met only with force. Only, the Haganah leaders were not quite clear what precisely they wanted to achieve by their operations. Their notion, as far as the Irgun leaders could make it out in numerous discussions, was a perpetual compromise between a revolt against the British oppressors until they were forced to leave our country, and, on the other hand, a hankering, in spite of everything, after the good old days of "political negotiation." And it was their strange idea that if a few times the British were given blows and learnt that we were capable of smiting them as they had never been smitten before in their colonial history, then they would come begging—after the first half-dozen blows—for political negotiation. Consequently, there was always a tendency in the Haganah leadership to give a so-called warning blow and then go back and peep out to see whether the British were learning the lesson. This misreading of the psychology of warfare, this underestimation both of the enemy and of his determination to carry through his own purposes and retain control of our country, was something that time would cure if it were only the result of lack of understanding. Unfortunately it was a reflection of the spiritual approach of some of the Haganah leaders themselves who were often afraid of doing too much damage, who were anxious only to "pinprick" the British, afraid that really hard blows might make the British hit back. In other words they went into the struggle with the most dangerous of all states of mind: half-heartedness. It must be said again, however; this refers only to the leadership or what ultimately became the dominant part of the leadership, and it was not a constant attitude. But the general consequence was that the Irgun was compelled continually to press for more intensive and more frequently-timed operations.

Illustrative of the Haganah attitude and indeed of their attitude to comradely agreements, are the following incidents. At one stage the Haganah leadership agreed to an Irgun plan for attacks on C.I.D. buildings at Jerusalem and Jaffa, with the object of destroying the records on all the underground organisations, including the Haganah. They asked however, that the Irgun and F.F.I. carry these attacks out, but the communique on the operation should claim the responsibility for the Irgun and F.F.I.—and not, as provided for in the agreement—by the Tenuat Hameri. They explained that they themselves favoured these operations but that there were "certain" obstacles in getting official approval for them. The Irgun unhesitatingly agreed—they have never hesitated to accept the honourable responsibility for their actions. But the Irgun communique reporting to the operations was followed by a circular sent out by one of the Haganah commanders in Tel-Aviv denouncing the operations. The national HQ of the Haganah hastened to assure the Irgun Command that this had been done without their knowledge; and their explanation was accepted.

On another occasion the Haganah decided on a series of operations against the P.M.F. (Palestine Mobile Force). The points of attack were to be Sorona, Kfar Vitkin, Shfar'am and Jenin. The Irgun was to attack at Kafar Vitkin. The Irgun informed them that they proposed also to attack the British armoury in order to capture a store of arms. The plan was approved. But a day before the operation was due the Irgun was asked to cancel it. It was explained that there were strong local reasons for abandoning the attack. The next night Haganah forces attacked, inter alia, Kfar Vitkin. They did not attack the armoury nor capture any arms; but they did succeed in depriving the Irgun of the opportunity of acquiring a substantial quantity of arms from the enemy.

Shortly afterwards plans the Irgun submitted for major attacks on British aerodromes were approved by the Haganah leaders. The Irgun carried out the successful attacks at Kastina and Lydda (the F.F.I. attacking simultaneously at Patah Tiqwa). The results achieved were great, even from the purely military point of view—tens of fighter and heavy bombing planes were destroyed. It was followed by an appeal from the Haganah leaders that the Irgun again publish the communique accepting the responsibility. Which they did.

During this period the British Occupation forces made a number of attacks on Jewish agricultural settlements, searching for arms. Citizens from near and far rushed to the defense of national arms. Large numbers of Irgun soldiers moved to these places— where there were no Irgun arms. For to them *all* Jewish arms, as long as they are intended even potentially for use against our people's enemies, are sacred. Among the Irgun soldiers who came from a distance to the defence of Haganah arms at Shfayim was young Eliezer Kashani. In a clash with the enemy he was wounded, and captured and held by the British for some time. After his release he returned to the fighting front; and in April, 1947, he was murdered by the British hangmen at Acre together with Dov Gruner.

The last combined operation of the united struggle came in mid-June, 1946. It began with Irgun attacks on enemy railway transports, followed by Haganah attacks on the frontier bridges, and then by an F.F.I. attack on the railway workshops at Haifa. The Haganah lost fourteen men in those operations. As far as is known only two of the bodies of the fourteen were recovered. The other twelve, according to a Haganah statement, were killed by the British after capture and their bodies disposed of.

Thus ended the *third* phase of the Jewish struggle for liberation—the phase of *active* Haganah participation, the chapter of Jewish fighting unity, glorious in spite of some aspects of Haganah behaviour.

There fell into the hands of the Haganah details of a great offensive planned by the British: mass arrests of the youth, attacks on Jewish settlements, arrest of Jewish Agency leaders. Haganah published the details at once, in broadcasts and in bulletins. And it announced boldly to the British that no attacks would stop the Jewish struggle, that resistance would go on. "Even if they bomb us from the air we shall continue the fight" they proclaimed.

Then, two weeks later, came the 20th of June, 1946, when the British occupied the Jewish Agency, arrested some of its members, attacked Yagur, capturing a quantity of arms, and sent nearly 4000 young men from the Emek—suspected of membership of Palmach— to Rafiah.

The Haganah reaction, on its radio and in its proclamations, was bold and resolute. Day after day they broadcast to the people their determination to intensify the fight against the foreign Occupation. They promised the youth that the fight would now be pursued with great vigour, and called on them to be prepared. They boasted of their intention to smite the enemy whenever and wherever they found it most convenient.

Typical of their verbal reaction was their proclamation of
1 July, 1946. It ran as follows:

"Britain has declared war on the Jewish people.
"The Jewish people will reply with war.
"Jewish resistance will continue, Jewish resistance has only just
      begun. . .
"Down with the Nazi-British regime.
"Out with the unclean sons of Titus from the Holy Land. . .
"Long live the Jewish State."

And on the very day of that proclamation—forty-eight hours
after the British attack—the Haganah leaders sent a written instruction to the Irgun to carry out the operation against the British
Occupation Headquarters in Eretz Israel: the blowing up of the King
David Hotel. (The Irgun had submitted this plan to them earlier in
1946 but then they had rejected it). Technical difficulties prevented
the immediate execution of these instructions. Then, when the Irgun
was ready, Haganah asked for a postponement; and then for a further postponement. Finally the date was agreed on: the 22nd July.
      Meantime the Irgun operations expert met the technical expert
of the Haganah and submitted to him the details of the planned
operation. As in all previous cases, their expert approved the details.
Shortly after midday on 22 July, 1946, the operation against the King
David Hotel was carried out *exactly as planned*.
      It was intended to avoid civilian loss of life. For this reason
thirty minutes warning was given. For reasons best known to himself, Shaw, the Chief Secretary of the Occupation Administration
disregarded the warning: That is, he forbade any of the other
officials to leave the building, with the result that some of his
collaborators were killed while he himself slunk away until after the
explosion.
      The time chosen for the attack was an hour at which the cafe
situated in the same wing of the building as the British HQ (Cafe
Regence), through which the attackers had to pass in order to reach
the basement, was usually empty. From the lunch hour onward it
was always full of people. An attack at night was technically
impossible. The few hotel guests who were in that part of the
building were easily and rapidly got out, by the hotel manager. The
Arab workers in the kitchens were separately warned by the
attackers themselves. Indeed the Haganah expert had expressed the
opinion that a warning of 15 minutes was enough. But the Irgun
expert preferred to strengthen the effect of the warning by giving
sufficient time for the hotel to be cleared many times.
      Shaw thus sent nearly a hundred people to their deaths—
including Jews, including friends of our struggle.
      We are concerned, however, with the behaviour of the

Haganah. *A month after* the attack the Haganah issued a statement placing the responsibility for the casualties squarely on the shoulders of Shaw (who was recalled from his post). In this statement, the Haganah quoted the reply Shaw had given the Police Officer who conveyed the warning: "I'm here to give orders to the Jews not to take orders from them." But in the meantime the Irgun had been subjected to the most violent campaign of vilification by the Jewish Agency and its satellite Press, without any restraining hand from the Haganah and with their tacit encouragement—the Haganah at whose instructions the operation had been carried out and whose responsibility for it was omitted from the communique at the last moment. (Again, the Irgun had no hesitation in accepting responsibility for one of the greatest blows dealt at British colonial power in similar circumstances).

It having become apparent that the Haganah was trying to "cover" itself by whispering that while, indeed, they had approved the operation they had not approved its timing, the Irgun called for a "berur"—a thrashing-out of the matter, attended by both the experts involved. Here the Haganah expert claimed that he had been under the "impression" that the attack was to be carried out at 2 p.m. and not at 12.30. But when the Irgun expert pointed out that the Haganah expert had been told that the time chosen was when the cafe was empty, which could not possibly be 2 p.m.—it was agreed that this fact was established: that there had not been any misunderstanding about the details of the plan. But the discussion showed that the Haganah had already gone far not only towards denying any responsibility but even, under the pressure of the defeatists and anti-activists who had taken over the reins in the Jewish Agency, was condoning and encouraging the malicious attacks on the Irgun and the vigorous propaganda against the struggle, using the tragedy of the King David explosion as a basis. The Irgun leaders consequently demanded a thorough inquiry into the whole operation and expressed their readiness to have it conducted by a leader of the Achdut Avodah Movement—left wing of the Histadruth and a member of the Jewish Agency Executive or either of them sitting singly. This demand was rejected.

In spite of the malicious and dangerous propaganda campaign, in spite of the contemptible behaviour of the Haganah leaders, the Irgun has refrained to this day from revealing the whole story of that operation. They did not want to create even the shadow of an impression that they were in any way denying responsibility for the operation, one of the greatest blows dealt the brutal enemy; and, on the other hand, they did not want, by any word or action of theirs, to bring down on the heads of the Haganah or the Jewish Agency any repetition of what they had suffered on 29 June— suffering to which they were unaccustomed and which, as we have seen, was sufficient to break their spirit. Now, however, that the Haganah have gone so far on the path of denunciation, now that they have lent themselves to the new campaign of vilification demanded of them by the Jewish Agency and have, moreover, lent themselves to a cruel and vicious attack based on that very King David Hotel operation, now that it is clear that the honest ones among them who have done what they can to prevent this treachery to the memory of the united struggle, have not prevailed—it is essential for the sake not only of history but for the sake of the struggle itself, that the truth be publised as widely as possible. Moreover, the British destroyer of our people is at the moment so pleased with the services the Haganah is rendering him that publication holds no danger for the skins or safety of the Haganah. The Government which is murdering Hebrew prisoners, and murdering Hebrew repatriates without reprisal or even fear of reprisal by the husky members of the Haganah, would to-day not dream of attacking or weakening the Haganah.

To return to the summer of 1946: the Haganah went from strength to strength in its promise of action. In particular they emphasized that any attack on Jewish arms would be met by force, and any attack on Jewish repatriation would be met by force.

But time went on and there was no action. September, 1946 arrived and the meetings of the Jewish Agency in Paris. The Haganah approached the Irgun with a request for a temporary stoppage of operations. Though this was not in accordance with the agreement, nor with the Irgun's own reading of the situation, they took seriously the Haganah undertaking that the stoppage would be only temporary and that indeed their own stoppage was only temporary—and agreed. But the meeting in Paris decided on two things: first to ask the British for partition, in negation even of the officially proclaimed programme of the Zionist Organisation, and second, a cessation of the armed struggle, apparently as a quid pro quo for the release of the Agency leaders in Latrun. And immediately after that decision came a bold demand to the Irgun from the Haganah to stop the fight altogether.

The Irgun informed them that they would never agree to the carving up of our Homeland; and as to the authority of Tenuat Hameri the agreement was based on their explicit acceptance of the principle of *action*, of pursuing the struggle against the British. With Haganah abandonment of that principle, the agreement would be at an end—as explicitly provided for in the agreement. The Irgun continued the struggle and the Haganah sent a message to say that the agreement was dead. The fourth phase of the struggle was ended.

The struggle continued. Operations were interrupted for a few weeks, during the Zionist Congress in December—in order to remove any hint of pressure from the Irgun on its deliberations. It is instructive to note that of all the parties in Eretz Israel, only Aliyah Hadasha, came out in its election propaganda against the struggle and was rewarded with a paltry few thousand votes. Every other party, Napal, Revisionists, Achdut Avodah, Mizrachi, even Hashomer Hatzair, promised the people a struggle, the only reservation, in some cases, being a limitation of the struggle to a fight for repatriation which, the Yishuv was told, would be defended with arms.

The Congress resolutions themselves also called for a struggle.

But there has been no struggle by the Haganah except for the heroic efforts of the repatriates themselves who, armed only with their fists and with bottles, have stood up to the arms of the British Navy; while the Haganah leaders, who claim 70,000 followers, have been busy, from the security of their offices, writing brave declarations promising that the struggle will be "continued"; or composing attacks of a different kind: attacks on the only ones who are continuing the struggle.

Indeed it is their own withdrawal from the struggle which is presumably forcing them to concentrate on propaganda attacks on the Irgun. There is very great restiveness among the masses of the Haganah, whose patriotism and readiness for sacrifice are undeniable and who want to know why they are being chained in enforced inaction while the British proceed with their war against our people; while the British intensify their tremendous campaign against our brothers in Europe, not stopping short of murdering them if they find it expedient: while the British tighten their regime of bloody oppression against the Jews in Eretz Israel. They want to know what has happened to the uncompromising struggle in all circumstances which they were promised last summer. They want to know and they get no reply. The effect on them is easily imagined. Some of them have now joined the ranks of the Irgun. Many others, inside the Haganah, have kept asking those questions. The Haganah leaders have no reasonable reply; their only way out is to divert the attention of their youth, to try to inflame them against the Irgun, depending on their own authority and the group loyalty of their youth to succeed in doing so. Consequently no accusation is too farfetched for them, no distortion too blatant, no fabrication too immoral, no truth too sacred to them. We are the witnesses of an historic calumny and an historic betrayal of the struggle against oppression and tyranny, of the struggle for our people's liberation.

Incidents of the recent past will illustrate the nature of the campaign. The first is the story of the now world-famous "well" at Kiriat Haim, allegedly "destroyed" by the Irgun in rataliation for denunciations of Irgun members at Kiriat Motzkin. What precisely happed at Kiriat Haim? In one of a series of attacks on the British oil pipeline a misplaced charge damaged a water pipe instead. There was *no* well involved. Nobody's water supply was interrupted. And the Irgun did not even know that previous arrests in the area were the result of Jewish denunciation until after the pipe had been damaged when the local Haganah people, with guilty conscience, jumped to the conclusion that the Irgun *must* have done it deliberately because, after all, they had denounced alleged members of the Irgun to the British Gestapo. But the Haganah Intelligence Service soon satisfied itself that the pipe had been damaged in error. Nevertheless they have filled the world with the utterly mendacious story of a "well" "destroyed" as a "collective punishment." And the enemy propagandists thankful for the opportunity, have converted the well into "wells" and the "cutting of the water supplies of villages" into an Irgun policy.

A second incident. A certain Jewish police-corporal in Tel-Aviv, Berger by name, was clubbed to death in a Tel-Aviv street. The attack was carried out by a group of members of the Haganah. Not only did the Haganah not admit that they had done it (and presumably they had some reason for doing it) but, sensing that the murder had aroused some horror, they began a whispering campaign that the Irgun had done it. This charge, of course, never appeared in print. But it was used to kill two birds with one stone: avoid possibly awkward questions by Haganah members, and as part of the smear campaign against the Irgun.

The Haganah is afraid even to sign its name to the vicious propaganda material they publish. They now do it under pseudonym: they sign themselves "No 'emanei Havigbuy" which enables them to ward off protests by their own members at the mendacity and treachery revealed by these publications.

Hitherto there has been no armed attack by the Haganah on the Irgun. But considerable pressure is being brought to bear on them by leaders of the Jewish Agency to start an armed war. The Irgun leaders hope the Haganah will resist at least that to the end. For civil war, which is precisely what the enemy is waiting and hoping for, would be disastrous for all of us. There must be no mistake. This time the Irgun would retaliate; and would do so without slackening in the struggle against the real enemy. Nothing will deter them from that historic duty. But Irgun fighters will not again be subjected to the stab in the back without retaliation. We pray to God that that civil war will be avoided.

But already the propaganda campaign, carried on with such vigour by Jewish Agency leaders who have no other policy to offer, and by the Haganah who deserted the battlefield and betrayed all their promises, has had its tragic results. Dov Grunor and his comrades would never have been hanged if the British oppressors had not calculated that they could murder them with impunity, that there was sufficient disunity among the Jews to enable them to get away with it.

It is significant that even the case of Dov Grunor was made the occasion for vilification of the Irgun. The Jewish Agency Press publicly, and the Haganah in its whispering campaign, stated it as a fact that Grunor refused to sign an appeal to the Privy Council because he had been ordered not to do so—in other words, that Dov was prepared to sacrifice his principles but his superior officers would not let him. The truth is that Dov was given no orders at all on the subject. It is true that the Irgun does not recognise any British "court," or its right to "try" Jewish prisoners. But Irgun soldiers are free men; and Dov was a free man. He himself decided what to do. And in his refusal to sign he not only demonstrated all the more his greatness, but also his political sense. For, as the British have since revealed, they have never recognised the right of appeal from the Military "Court" "sentences."

It is tragic that this account must end on this unhappy note, tragic indeed that it has to be written at all. Tragic tenfold in that the vast majority of our people have realised that we shall attain liberation only by a struggle; that the yoke of the British will be thrown off only by a determined, unyielding fight, which will teach them that there will be no British base in our Homeland over the grave of our people's hopes. Tragic in that the wishes of the people, the fortitude and dignity and great determination of the people, are being falsified by a group of leaders who ignore the people's will and make ready to surrender their aspirations and their natural rights in the face of brute force. Tragic in that a large section of the youth is being frustrated and the struggle against the enemy drawn out, with consequent protracted suffering for the whole people, by paralysing large numbers of fighters, who are willing and waiting to fight. Tragic that in order to cover up their own confusion and defeatism those leaders are prepared to use every means to blacken and, if possible, to destroy those who every day risk their security and their lives for the liberation of their people and their Homeland.

It is tragic. Yet the Irgun has not given up hope that the day may come again when the fighting unity which for all too short a time reigned in our country will be re-established. If and when that day comes, the Irgun, in spite of everything, will join hands again; and as long as it is a *fighting* leadership accept its authority in the conduct of the struggle.

If it does not come the Irgun will continue the fight alone, confident not only of the justice and urgency of the struggle, not only of its expression of the will and the interests of the people, not only of the sympathy of all freedom-loving and decent people throughout the world, but confident also of ultimate victory.

And the people will help its fighters.

The Hebrew Struggle for National Liberation: A Selection of Documents on its Background and on Events Punctuating its Course

[INTRODUCTION]

The collection of documents that follows, is not a history of the Irgun Zvai Leumi or its struggle. The time for that has not yet come. It does however, present a comprehensive picture of the belief that animates the soldiers of the Irgun and the spiritual driving-force that has produced the greatness of a Dov Gruner and a Meir Feinstein; and of thousands of others who, young and loving life, are nevertheless prepared at any moment to give it up in the struggle for the freedom of their people.

The following pages include also a number of statements and declarations by the Irgun at various stages in the struggle, illustrating its background, and some of its incidents—pronouncements all flowing from the single mainspring of the Irgun's existence: the knowledge that national liberation and independence can be achieved only by an uncompromising, armed struggle against the tyrannous aggressor until he has removed himself from our country; that his determination to rob us of our country and to crush our people can be overcome by our even greater determination to be free, by our refusal either to be deceived by fine phrases or intimidated by brute force, and by the application of all our human resources to that task.

In the course of the struggle the British tyrant, having taken Irgun soldiers prisoner has, in accordance with the precedent set by the German Nazis, refused to recognise their rights as prisoners of war. In contravention even of the laws that he ostensibly recognises he has set up "courts" manned by Occupation Army officers, to try Hebrew citizens and to "sentence" them to long terms of imprisonment, or to death.

Irgun soldiers thus "tried" have naturally refused to recognise the authority of the Nazo-British courts, but continuing their struggle in the "court room" have made declarations elucidating the causes of the struggle, and the rights of Hebrew soldiers. Some of these declarations, in the tradition of the great martyrs of revolutionary history in all ages and among all peoples, are included in this publication.

The first of them is the statement made by Amnon Moscovitch, one of the "accused" in the "Trial of the Twenty"—twenty young men of Shuni village, "sentenced" in October, 1945 to long terms of imprisonment for the "possession of arms."

THE RIGHT AND DUTY TO RISE AGAINST OPPRESSION:
Declaration by Amnon Moscovitch
before a British Military "court"

You are going to condemn us to many years' imprisonment. You mean to deprive us of a civilized man's most precious possession: of liberty. This right of yours, which originates in physical force, imposes at least one human duty upon you. You are bound to learn and to know whom you are judging, whose hands you want to shackle, whom you are giving the cup of suffering, physical and moral.

Biographical details about me and my brothers, the other "accused," would tell you nothing. There are in Eretz Israel thousands and tens of thousands of Hebrew young men like us. Every one of them might be in our place here, for we are not, as you know, the first ones, and surely not the last ones, to be brought before you from the Acre citadel, in order to return, for a long time, to its dark cells. Therefore, if you wish to know the Hebrew accused, who awaits your sentence with absolute tranquility of mind, you have to look, not at his identity papers, but at his soul. You have to enquire, not into his age, social position or education, but into his convictions, creed and ideals.

We are sons of a certain family. In so far as it has been planted and has grown in Eretz Israel, it is a Hebrew family, but it is not only Hebrew. It is, properly speaking, a universal family. Its age is— eternity; the region inhabited by it is—the globe; the secret of its existence is—faith; its fate is—suffering; its happiness is—self-sacrifice; its enemy is—oppression; its banner is—liberty; and its name?—Its name is *resistance.* Yes, Gentlemen, we are sons of the great, Hebrew and all-human family of resistance. Our spiritual fathers left the village of Modiin, in order to stir up a revolt against a great empire, which sought to subjugate the land of the prophets both politically and spiritually. Our spiritual fathers went out of the crevices of rocks in the days of another empire, and, in their struggle against its conquering armies, erected eternal monuments: Massada and Jodefet. Our spiritual fathers repose for ever under the ruins of Beittar—those rebels of Bar-Kochba and disciples of Rabbi Akiba, who achieved an unsurpassable unity of Book and Sword. Such are our Hebrew fathers. But our spiritual brothers may be found, not only in this country, but in all the countries of the world, beyond seas and behind mountains, in the past and in the present. Their footsteps will lead you to the Greek Thermopylae, and your Runnymede, and the Serbian Kossove field, and the American Yorktown, and the French Bastille, and "The thousand" of Garibaldi, and the Yugoslav partisans, and the French maquis, and the fighters of modern Greece—in every country and in every age you will find those whom we proudly call our brothers in arms and brothers in faith.

There was a time—and how remote it appears to us now, in these days of filthy egoism—when that family used to behave as members of one family do: they helped one another. The Frenchman Lafayette, the Pole Pulaski, the Italian Garibaldi, volunteered to fight for America's freedom. The Englishman Byron—take heed, Honourable Judges—went to fight for Greece, and fell in the battle for her liberation. It was not only "Young Italy" that arose in Mazzini's days, but also "Young Europe," which united all the nations aspiring to liberty, whose oppressors were many, but whose enemy was one: oppression. But it is not the mutual help between fighters of various nations, that makes the peculiar characteristic of the human family of resistance. Something else has framed its unitary shape, in spite of all the chronological, geographical and ethnological differences. It is the S p i r i t. It is the unvanquished spirit of resistance to evil, it is the spirit of rebellion even against gigantic forces; it is the immortal spirit of revolt, it is the eternal aspiration to mount higher and higher, in spite of all the sacrifices, sufferings and persecutions. And I venture to say, Honourable Judges, that it is this spirit that propels the mills of human civilization, it is that which drives us forward, it is that which has given us fire and light, it is that which dispels the darkness, whenever anybody—a single dictator or a collective despotism—attempts to plunge us into it, or prevents our emerging from it.

I am not speaking of spiritual things only, although, in my opinion, they determine the ways of history. Everybody knows that without that spirit of resistance, which, in its manifold manifestations, is communicated by one generation to its successor, and by one nation to another, Hitler would have become the supreme ruler of Europe, and perhaps of the whole world. I am now referring to a very concrete event, which originated in the spirit of resistance, and without which we would not perhaps exist now, neither you, as British Judges, nor we, as Hebrew accused. I wish to remind you of that event.

About 170 years ago, there were still thirteen British colonies in North America. They were governed by a British Commissioner, and all their affairs were settled by British law. Their taxes were collected by a British tax-collector; their mutual relations, as well as the relations between the local population and the new settlers, were fixed by the British agent. How those British officials governed the American colonies, may be learned from an original and official document, dated 4th July, 1776. The following is an extract from it:

"He (the King of Britain) has refused his Assent to Laws, the most wholesome and necessary for the public good.
"He has endeavoured to prevent the population of these States; for that purpose obstructing the Laws for Naturalization of Foreigners; refusing to pass others to encourage their migration

hither, and raising the conditions of new Appropriations of
Land.

"He has made Judges dependent on his will alone.

"He has erected a multitude of New Offices, and sent hither
swarms of officers to harass our people, and eat out their
substance.

"He has combined with others to subject us to a jurisdiction
foreign to our constitution, and unacknowledged by our Laws;
giving his Assent to their acts of pretended legislation;

"For quartering large bodies of armed troops among us.

"For protecting them, by a mock Trial, from punishment
for any Murders which they should commit on the inhabitants of these States.

"For cutting off of trade with all parts of the world.

"For imposing taxes on us without our consent.

"For depriving us in many cases, of the benefits of Trial by
Jury.

"For transporting us beyond seas to be tried for pretended
offenses."

I have drawn your attention, Honourable Judges, to those
points, because one may learn from them that, just as the ways of
the struggle for liberty and justice are the same, so the method of
oppression is the same. The above words were written in Philadelphia, nearly 200 years ago. Nevertheless, one might dictate them
in Jerusalem, this very day, since all the charges, preferred against
you by Jefferson, might be repeated today by any Jewish representative. Moreover, that Hebrew representative could add a long list, an
endless list, of acts of fraud, and treachery, and oppression, and
murder. Most of all—murder. I am speaking not only of Abraham
Stern, Abraham Emper and Itzhak Zak, murdered in cold blood by
your high officer Morton, who did not even undergo a fictitious trial,
but, on the contrary, was promoted to a higher rank, and was
compelled only by the wrath of the Hebrew youth to flee the
country; I am speaking not only of those acts of murder, and of the
murder of Asher Tertner, a Hebrew youth, almost a child, in Haifa. I
am also speaking of that long list of murdered human beings, which
is unprecedented in the history of mankind—of the list of six million
Jews, murdered through the fault of your rulers.

But let us go back to the British colonies in America. After their
inhabitants and leaders had clearly seen that your rule was a rule of
despotism and oppression, they resolved to rise in arms against it, in
order to set up an independent government of their own. The
history and the outcome of that war are well known. One of its
turning-points was Yorktown, where your General Cornwallis surrendered to the rebel Washington. But let us suppose for a moment
that the course of events had been different. Let us suppose that
Cornwallis had succeeded in arresting Washington, and Jefferson,

and Lee, and Benjamin Fra[n]klin, and Taylor and Adams, and all the others who signed the Declaration of Independence and urged the nation to rise in rebellion against your rule. All those who dared to hold arms, use arms and fight against you, in defiance of your law, would have been brought before a Military Court (of course, a Military one!). It would have been a trial of twenty, of perhaps fifty, persons, and they would have been sentenced, no doubt, to five, ten, fifteen and twenty years' imprisonment. It would have been recorded in your history—if it had been recorded at all—that several American "criminals," who attempted to rise in rebellion against your beneficient rule, had received a proper punishment, and—what did Mr. Churchill say some months ago?—"Advance Britannia: Long live the cause of freedom!."

Think for a moment, Honourable Judges, of that eventuality. For its results would have been neither theoretical nor simple. If it had occurred, your Commissioner would have resided at New York to this day, and instead of the U.S.A., there would have existed, in the best case, a British Dominion, whose level of progress and number of inhabitants would not have exceeded, as may be learned from experience, those of Canada. And then? I believe that any Britisher, who thinks of that eventuality, must shiver and tremble. For in that case, Honourable Judges, you would have been doomed. It is possible that already Kaiser Wilhelm would have put an end to your world rule, to the results of your toil during generations, and there is no doubt that Adolf Hitler would have vanquished you, and would have transformed you, those who sing: "England must be free, or die"—into slaves or dead bodies. It would, of course, have been the fate of all the other nations too, and, as I have told you, you would not have been judges today, and we—the accused, *all of us* would have been today in a concentration camp or a grave. It is no secret that without the U.S.A., without her planes and armoured cars, her arms and equipment, her industry and soldiers, without all those things which are the outcome of America's rebellion and her victory over you— the entire free humanity would no more have existed. Now you see, Honourable Judges, that what is regarded as an evil by men like Cornwallis, is considered a blessing, not only by men like Washington, but also by the God of History, who sometimes saves the offspring of the Cornwallises through the agency of descendants of the Washingtons.

Do not be surprised, therefore, to see that we have learned from our brothers in spirit, not only to accuse the rule of oppression, but also to fight against it. Do not be surprised to see that we have also imbibed the moral teaching, contained in the simple words of that document of the 4th July, 1776, which says in its preamble:

> "We hold these truths to be self-evident, that all men are created equal, that they are endowed by their Creator with certain

inalienable Rights, that among these are Life, Liberty and the
pursuit of Happiness. That to secure these Rights, Governments
are instituted among Men, deriving their just powers from the
consent of the governed.

"That whenever any Form of Government becomes destructive
of these ends, it is the Right of the People to alter or to abolish it,
and to institute a new Government, laying its foundation on such
principles and organizing its powers in such form, as to them
shall seem most likely to effect their safety and Happiness.
Prudence indeed, will dictate that Governments long established should not be changed for light and transient causes, and
accordingly all experience hath shown, that mankind are more
disposed to suffer while evils are sufferable, than to right them
themselves by abolishing the forms to which they are accustomed. But when a long train of abuses and usurpations,
pursuing invariably the same Object evinces a design to reduce
them under absolute Despotism, it is their right, it is their duty to
throw off such Government and to provide new Guards for their
future security."

I have quoted the historic preamble, because it offers an
almost exact image of the conditions prevailing in Eretz Israel, as
well as for our revolutionary way. Your administration, deprives us
of all "the inalienable rights bestowed by the Creator upon all men."
It deprives us, it deprives our nation, of the right to live. Through its
fault, because of its "pretended legislation," which has closed the
gates of our homeland for our brethren, millions of Jews have been
slaughtered in the accursed Diaspora; through its fault, as a result of
the instigations of its agents and emissaries, nearly one thousand
Jews have been killed in four organised attacks in the Holy Land.
Through its fault, because of its Satanic will, tens of thousands of
Jews are still starving in concentration camps and refugee camps,
on the roads to Europe and on its shores. Your administration
deprives us of the right to freedom. Where is freedom, if we cannot
let our brothers enter our home, in spite of their cry "save us!"?
Where is freedom, if we cannot develop the natural resources of this
country, as our knowledge and abilities, which, as is well known,
are not inferior to yours, enable us to do—if we cannot develop the
natural resources of this country, so that it may give life to millions
of happy inhabitants, just as it gave life, even in ancient times, to six
or seven million citizens? Where is freedom, if you, British Officers,
are judging us, Hebrew soldiers? Where is freedom, if throngs of
your officials devour the fruits of the toil of the country's citizens,
and suck the marrow of their bones by heavy taxation? Where is freedom, if Jews have been pushed out, as in Tsarist Russia, to a "pale of
settlement," and are not allowed even to *b u y* lands in most areas of
Eretz Israel? Where is freedom if the Government is not our Government, if the laws binding our country are not our laws, if the
representatives who speak on behalf of our country, are not our

representatives? Where is freedom, if our homeland is governed by an administration which has violated all its obligations, and has brought all its promises into derision? No, Honourable Judges, under your rule there is no life for our nation, there is no freedom for us; you have deprived us of both, just as you have deprived us of our right to happiness. How can we aspire after private happiness, if we know that our brothers, fathers and mothers are being ruthlessly exterminated and murdered, only because you have not permitted them to come here? How can we think of happiness, if, day and night, there appear before us the appalling images, not only of the furnaces and the extermination camps, but also of refugee camps, where tens of thousands of our brothers live or agonize, hungry, scabbed, humiliated, beaten—and even they are not allowed by you to find shelter in their homeland?

And if so, if your rule has become a rule of tyranny in its most appalling sense, if it deprives a nation numbering millions of its right to life and freedom and happiness, then, as the American fighters said, it is our right, our d u t y, to fight for the overthrow of that rule and the establishment of another rule, a Hebrew rule, which will protect the security and the future of the exterminated nation. The right to oppose oppression is one of the natural rights of every civilized man; you will also find it in the second article of the "Declaration of Rights of Man and Citizen," of that Declaration which was born in the flames of the French Revolution, and which determines, to this very day, the ways of thought of civilized humanity. So far from committing a crime, anybody exercising that right fulfils his duty; and anybody who does not fulfil his duty, must despise himself for his egoism and cowardice; and anybody who persecutes those fulfilling their sacred duty, must be ashamed of his tyranny and baseness.

It cannot be argued against us that we started the struggle thoughtlessly. It cannot be said that we have not tried a l l the ways of explanation and moral influence. For twenty-five years, the Hebrew nation has been continually appealing to your conscience, to the British nation's conscience. You have contended that Eretz Israel is a barren country; we have proved that it may be converted into a flourishing garden. With that typical hypocrisy, expressly acknowledged by your most sober paper "The Economist," you have contended that we dispossess the Arabs—those same Arabs, whose brethren are deliberately left by you in the darkness of ignorance, in constant hunger and epidemics, in all those numerous States, whose governments are set up by you and your "advisers." We have proved to you that our colonization enriches the Arab population, which is thriving and prospering, in contrast to all the neighbouring countries. No pretext of yours, however artful and deceitful, has been left without a Hebrew reply and explanation. To all the unjust decrees, all the White Papers, all the restrictions of our rights, we have responded with a bitter cry and an appeal to your conscience, your fairness and your human feelings. But all has been in vain. Lack of resistance on our part has been interpreted by you as acquiescence; our requests have been interpreted as cowardice; our supplications—as weakness. One fraudulent act has led you to another; from one maltreatment you have passed to a second. And it all has ended in the declaration to the effect that we shall be, in our homeland, only one third of the population; and it has also ended in an act which we will never forget, even if we wish to forgive it after the free Hebrew State has been set up—in the act of closing the gates at a time when our parents and children were being slaughtered and exterminated.

All our appeals have been in vain. Not only have you paid no attention to them. You have even mocked at them. Evidence of it may be found even in a British source; you will find it in the words of Wedgwood, that great man, who was treated by your Lords as a Don Quixote and idle prattler, when he ventured to tell you, in his speech in 1942, that he would like to urge all the Jews in Eretz Israel to acts of violence, to acts of rebellion. For they sometimes are (so he said) acts of salvation—but your totalitarian censorship does not permit one single word of his to reach the public in Eretz Israel. In that speech, Wedgwood repeated what he had said while speaking to free America. Thus spoke the defender of the banner of justice in a dark world: "First of all arms; then land and then freedom," and he added:

> "Some think that all will be right at the end of the war; that 'Struma,' 'Patria' and all the killings were imposed on the British Government to prevent the Arabs from making trouble at this troublesome hour. Wishful thinking! The Arabs are the *excuse*, not the *reason*. Every change must be directed against the whole British Administration in Palestine. All of them have a vested interest to prove that the Balfour Declaration is not *realisable*, that they were right. There is nothing to hope from any British Government in Palestine. The bombs which blew up 'Struma' have dug too deep a cleavage between them. I tried to save for my countrymen the historic glory of building up Jerusalem, to do justice, to establish freedom. My words are of no avail. They won't do that. I can't help it. You must turn to America to take over the task. Don't ask anything more from Britain . . ."

If this is what an Englishman has said, one of the few who have not been dazzled by the cunning phraseology of your rulers; if this is the r e a l i t y in Eretz Israel, is it surprising that, after all the attempts to persuade you had failed, we have at last started our fight against you, and are urging all our brethren to rise in open rebellion against your treacherous rule? And what did you imagine? Have you really thought that one may endlessly maltreat a Zulu tribe? Have you not noticed that a new generation, healthy in body and firm in mind, has risen in this land, a generation endowed with a loving heart and thinking creative brains, as well as with h a n d s, skilled both in constructing and in fighting?

If in spite of your vaunted wisdom that is what you have thought, you have been totally blind, and you have not seen that a day will come, when this nation, which had regarded you as friends and benefactors, will rise in rebellion, and remove the mask from your face, and show the whole world: Here are those who break faith, here are those whose only aim is to subjugate others, here are those who are disloyal to their task, here are those who destroy International Law. And do not pretend that it is of no importance for you, since you have enough tanks and planes to protect your Empire and its routes. From your history you know that whenever a white oppressor comes across a white oppressed, the former must withdraw. You have learned it not only in North America. You have also learned it in South Africa, and in Ireland which is not distant from your Isles. The Germans, too, have learned it all over Europe. And you will learn it here too, in Eretz Israel. We are not over-estimating our strength. It is inconsiderable and small in comparison with yours. But there is a great principle in history: a big force aiming at despoliation and oppression is inconsiderable; a small force, aiming at freedom and justice, is powerful.

Of course, we have not started our struggle with a light heart. We know that the road is full of hardships, and our sacrifices will be numerous. We deplore these sacrifices. In the last generation, the Jewish people lost such a quantity of blood as no nation did. Therefore, every drop of Hebrew blood is today a thousand times more precious than ever. And, besides, I have already told you that we belong to the international and all-human family of resistance. One tragic feature marks the way of that family. It is compelled to use force, but the truth is that it d e s p i s e s physical force. It holds a rifle or a pistol, but the true desire is to work with a spade or a pen. Our family believes that man has been created, not in order to kill his neighbour, but in order to continue The Creator's work together with his neighbour. In the six days of creation The Creator laid the foundations of the Universe, but the rest—the discovery of fire and atomic energy—was left by him to man, created in his own image. A world of justice, a world of brotherhood, a world of peace, a world of mutual help and mutual understanding—this is the world, visioned by our spiritual fathers and brothers; and we, too, aim at establishing that world, and we want our nation to participate in it— because we have been brought up in the spirit of the Hebrew Law and the prophetic tradition and vision.

In spite of it—or perhaps for this very reason—all the seekers of freedom in the world, including ourselves, have always fought with arms in their hands. It is true that man has not been created in order to kill; but neither has he been created to be killed. It is true that man has not been created in order to subjugate; but neither has he been created to be subjugated. And if anybody rises to kill you, or to cause your murder, or to subjugate you—rise and fight him with the same weapons as he employs against you: iron against iron; force against force; brains against brains; blood for blood. This is the supreme commandment—the moral, human, and divine one.

This commandment is our principle of action; and the whole Hebrew youth will embrace this principle on the appointed day. That is why we are so calm when we enter the path of sufferings. For it is good to fight for Zion; and it is good to suffer for Zion. Everything is worth doing in order to save this nation. And we are not isolated, we are not abandoned. The free world, all decent men who took part in the war of liberation, will help us. They will not abandon an ancient nation regenerating its existence; a nation aspiring, not to subjugate, but to liberate itself; not to destroy, but to build; not to expand but to centralize; not to die, but to live—to live freely and honourably, like any other nation. The free world—and, perhaps, even the best sons of your nation—will stretch out their helping hand to us, and the result of our suffering will be victory, the victory of justice, the victory of truth.

And you, my brothers, prepare to spend your young years in the Bastille of Eretz Israel. Be proud that it is your lot to fulfil your sacred duty, and to follow the historic path, opened, for the first time, twenty-five years ago by the great teacher of our generation (Jabotinsky). Remember that although our sacrifice is great in itself, it is a mere nothing in comparison with the sacrifices brought by millions of our brothers for our people, its faith, its existence and its regeneration. Remember our oath. And remember also: any Bastille, no matter whether it was erected in Paris or stands on the shore of the Mediterranean, is doomed—to destruction.

The British Military "court" and the world were given an account of the reason for his joining the struggle by Isaac Ganzweich, former partisan fighter in Poland.

THE ROAD OF A HEBREW SOLDIER
(Declaration by Isaac Ganzweich)

The Statement I have to make is personal in content. I want to tell you some details of my recent past, not because these details are important in themselves, but because they illustrate the Jewish fate and the relations between Britain and my people. You, and your consciences, can draw the conclusions.

I have the honour to inform you, gentlemen, that I come from the valley of slaughter in Poland. I came to Eretz Israel only one-and-a-half years ago. You will not find any external marks on me to testify to my fight and the fight of my brothers. We appeared anonymously in the ghettoes; anonymously we went out to the woods; anonymously we attacked German convoys. Few in number, hungry and lonely we stood against the most powerful and most cruel military force that had ever arisen in Europe. Nobody recorded our deeds, nobody estimated our sacrifices. If it were not for this trial, if it were not for the spiritual need I feel to appear before a British court not as an individual, but as a representative, as a representative of the Jewish blood which was shed like water, as a representative of Jewish isolation the like of which the history of humanity has not known—if it were not for this I too would remain anonymous to the end of my days—like thousands of others who took part in the most difficult of battles—the battle of the decimated Jewish people against the destroying vandal.

Now that I have introduced myself in my invisible but honourable uniform, I want, I am entitled to demand that you concentrate your thoughts on this question: *how does it come that a Jewish fighter from Poland is on trial not before a German court, but before a British court?* I naturally emphasise the second part of the question. If the Germans still had military power and if I were captured by them, I would certainly get my portion of lead. But that is not the question. The question is—why am I standing before a British court? Why am I held in a British prison?

Only a year and half ago I and my brothers were your allies. True, unrecognized allies, unknown allies, but, nevertheless, allies in *fact*. We were on the same side of the barricade. You killed Germans, we killed Germans; you destroyed their means of communication, and we, too, sabotaged their railways. Of course, the quantitative difference between your deeds and ours was tremendous. But from a moral viewpoint, from the point of view of military honour, we were brothers-in-arms. We had one enemy, we fought against him with combined forces and according to the opportunities presented to each one of us. And now—what a difference! You are judges, and I am accused; you are judging, and I am facing charges.

This fact tells us a great deal. It tells us perhaps more than all the speeches, more than all the books that have been written, or that may be written on the Jewish tragedy and on your attitude to it.

I, gentlemen, was "there"; I went down to the deepest depths of purgatory. How colourless is Dante's artistic description compared to the reality created by the devil on earth! The true inferno was there in Poland, in the heart of Europe. It was there they burnt people alive, there that they turned synagogues into graveyards; there that they shattered children against rocks in the fields, that they turned human beings into hunted animals, into strange beings whom only some invisible force kept alive in spite of everything. And who were those people who were crushed, trampled on, strangled, burnt and slaughtered? They were—my father and my mother, my sister and my brother, my relatives, the friends of my childhood—all those I loved, all those who loved me.

Can you imagine our feelings? Can I, with my poor words, bring home to you that standing before you is a man who was dipped in blood up to here, up to the neck, who walked in an endless cemetery, who saw things that the eye of man has not seen since the world was created?

And I want to tell you the truth, you British. I want to tell you how we condemned ones, how we Jewish fighters felt. We hated the Germans, we hated them more than death. The idea of revenge became a programme, a sacred duty. And though we knew it was naive to believe that we should be able to avenge all they had done to us—it sufficed us to know that we, with our own hands, were doing something to them, that we were killing them, those mad dogs who tried to exterminate an ancient people and to enslave the whole world.

But it was not only the Germans that the inmates of the ghettoes cursed. They cursed you too. I tell you this openly because I know I speak in the name of millions of people who went down to the grave with a double curse: cursed be the murderers, their lips whispered, and cursed be that enlightened world which handed us over to them, which did nothing to save us, to save at least our children, our little ones.

That is what the slaughtered said. And the fighters added another accusation. Day and night they looked into the sky, waiting for help. They waited for arms. They waited for food. They had no doubt that you could send us the minimum requirements for carrying on the struggle, either in the flaming ghettoes or in the deep forests. But you did not do it. The heroes of the ghettoes had to be content with home-made arms, with a few revolvers and a handful of bombs against the Nazi-German machines of war and destruction. You forsook men whose readiness was unconditional but whose hands were empty. Yet if we had been properly armed we should not only have been able to smite our common enemy the more, but also—and especially—we would have been able to rescue hundreds of thousands of the condemned from slaughter.

And God willed that I should not die but live, that, after numberless wanderings, I should come to my Homeland. And what did I find? Oh, my judges, if you only knew what Eretz Israel looked like to us in the depths of the bunkers! If you only knew what we thought about her in the days of terror. Already at the beginning of the war a rumour spread in Poland that a Hebrew State and Hebrew army had been set up. That was the kind of thought that you call the son of the wish. The doomed Jews wanted a redeeming State, and therefore imagined that it already existed. But there were also logical reasons for sustaining this refreshing rumour. A war had broken out against Hitler. The whole Jewish people was against its enemy and the enemy of mankind. Therefore our people would certainly be recognized as an ally and Britain would immediately change her policy, and a Jewish army would be set up and a Hebrew Government, and so on and so forth. Dreams, not so? Fata Morgana? But that was what we all believed when the walls of the stinking ghettoes closed down on us, and from them we directed our prayers, in our faith and in our hope, eastward, to Zion!

Only after I came here did I learn the whole truth. Not only that there is no State, not only that we have no Army of our own—but that even the White Paper was not annulled and that just as the gates had been closed, so they remained closed. I shall confess: at first I did not believe what my eyes saw. I regarded the reality as a dream, just as there we had imagined the dream to be a reality. Was this the reward for our blood? Was this the compensation for our sacrifices? Was England too among the destroyers! But reality is reality. Eretz Israel is locked and barred. One may leave, but none may enter.

Then, my judges, I swore by the blood of my parents and my brothers and my sisters that I would not rest until the gates of our country are opened or are burst open. For I am but one of the few who succeeded in coming here, while tens of thousands remained there, in the great prison, in purgatory. I asked myself: why did I deserve to remain alive? How am I better than my brothers that I was not destroyed like them? And my conscience gave one reply: if the great God brought me here it is a sign that he wills me to be the messenger of all those who remained on the other side of the wall, that I should fight for them, for their redemption and their future. Otherwise there is no reason in my living; otherwise there is no content in my life.

If this mission, sacred not only to me, but also in the eyes of every honest man, Jew or Christian, is regarded by you as a crime, that proves that there is no end to the Jewish tragedy, just as there is no atonement for the crime of your rulers who have helped and are helping to destroy my people.

———————————

Another of the "accused" in the Trial of the Twenty was Jehuda Lemberger. In a detailed and documented indictment he placed the British in their rightful place—the dock.

THE RULERS OF BRITAIN FOR TRIAL
(Declaration of Jehuda Lemberger)

The Occupation Regime has given you authority to try us and to keep us in prison. But this is a purely formal authority, which flows from your seizure of power in this country by force. There is no connection between this authority and international law. By law, and in justice we should exchange our roles and our places. I am not, of course, referring to the judges personally. You are carrying out orders. I am referring to those who sent you, to those who sit not in this room but in Whitehall and who posture as our accusers and judges. It is they who should be in the dock. They are guilty of breaches of the law, of deceit, of breach of faith, of the use of force and of complicity in mass murder.

I have said we should change places. That is not precise. If these people, the rulers of Britain who sent you to judge us, were in the dock, it is not we or our brothers who would want to be their judges. The terrible crime they have committed is international in scope. Their court should therefore also be international. This demand is based not on brute force but on the power of conscience. Our demand derives from the same moral origin as gave a great Frenchman, Emil Zola, the human authority to accuse publicly the judges of Dreyfus, the Government which appointed them and the powerful State forces that backed them. In the name of that supreme authority *we demand the constitution of an international court to try the rulers of Britain for complicity in the murder of six million Jewish men, women and children.*

This is a just demand. Soon there will take place the international trial of the rulers of Nazi Germany, who are directly responsible for the world conflagration and for the mass extermination of our people. But in every legal text-book you will find the clause whereby not only the murderer himself is punished but also his accomplice and helper, whether the help is given directly or indirectly. And I shall prove that *the rulers of Britain actively helped the Nazis destroy the Jews of Europe.* I shall prove that although Britain fought against Germany—and there was a time when the British people awakened the respect of all free men, when they stood alone and unyielding against the wild and victory-intoxicated German forces—and though Britain was contemptuous of all the "collaborators" among the enslaved peoples of Europe, in this field, *in the field of the destruction of the Jews Britain was a confirmed "collaborator" and co-operated with the Nazi murderers throughout all the years of the war.* Consequently it is just that as soon as the case against the wild beasts, Goering, Hess and Ribbentrop, is ended a second trial should begin against their helpers—the responsible leaders of Britain.

This is, incidentally, not a new demand. It was put forward several months ago by Colonel Patterson. As you know, he is not a Jew. He is a Briton. In the previous War he commanded the Jewish Corps in Gallipoli and, in the course of his participation in that unsuccessful expedition, he learnt the qualities of the reborn Jew who goes out to fight, albeit on a foreign field, for his people and his country. Patterson's lieutenant was the one-armed Captain Joseph Trumpeldor; and it is well that you should know how that legendary Jewish hero agreed to lead Jewish youth and exiles from Eretz Israel to the wild Turkish peninsula and to shed his blood for the common cause. Yes, for the common cause, for Trumpeldor was given an explicit official promise that a British victory over the Turks would be the victory also of the Hebrew people, which would regain its land and its freedom. Trumpeldor has himself given an account of the negotiations, that led to this promise and I quote from his diary:

> "We did not want to be a transport unit and we did not want to go to any front they might choose. We said emphatically: we want to go into battle, in the front line and only on the Palestine battlefield. We would fight in and for Palestine. We would conquer, step by step, our country from which we had been exiled by force, we would liberate our Homeland. This idea was close to the hearts of all of us who had been deported from Palestine. This was our only request. And we made this clear to the General who was sent to Alexandria by the C-in-C. in Cairo, General Maxwell, to negotiate with us.

> 'We want to go into action, and in our Homeland.'

> But the General was a diplomat too and at the big and decisive meeting in the stuffy atmosphere of the barracks he said:

> 'The British people speaks to the Jewish people through me, in friendship. This friendship will certainly continue in the days to come in *Jewish Palestine.* Will you accept the proffered hand or reject it?' "

I have quoted this long extract in order to show you that only in consequence of the promise given to Trumpeldor in behalf of your Commander-in-Chief in the Middle East, did this man, who revived the tradition of heroism in the Jewish people, go out to fight outside of Eretz Israel—but *for* Eretz Israel. Trumpeldor took the hand proffered in friendship to the Jewish people in "Jewish Palestine." Trumpeldor fulfilled his obligation. The 'Zion Mule Corps' was formed and, as Patterson testified, did excellent service in exceptionally difficult conditions. But what happened to the British promise? Given in 1915, it was followed by innumerable further promises, the Balfour Declaration, Ministerial statements, "Times" leaders, the Mandate for Palestine, and so on and so forth. And the outcome? The Jewish people should do what the French did when they published, in a Yellow Book, a report of their relations with Germany and on the guilt for the Second World War. The collection of French documents begins with the "Paroles d'honneur" broken by Hitler and his lieutenants. We too should publish a Yellow Book, or a Black, and begin with all the words of honour you gave to the Jewish people and which you violated, sometimes by deceit, sometimes by brutality, always making them dead letters.

Even Patterson, the officer who commanded not only the Corps in Gallipoli but also the Legion which was raised by Ze'ev Jabotinsky and which took an active part in the conquest and—as we thought then—the liberation of Eretz Israel East and West of the Jordan, has admitted that British promises were trampled underfoot, that it was from Britain's attitude to the Jewish people, to Eretz Israel and to the League of Nations, which entrusted the country to your care, that Hitler, Mussolini and the Mikado learnt that promises could be broken and international law flouted; that this attitude was perhaps one of the causes that led to the world slaughter, and that, ultimately, the leaders of Britain aided in the destruction of the Jews by the legions of Hitler and Himmler.

That is the "J'Accuse!" of Patterson who, like Zola in his day, demands that your leaders be tried as war criminals. Zola demanded justice for one single man, while Patterson demands justice and a just trial because of the death of six million people, among them one-and-a-half million little children.

My demand is therefore not a new one. But it is a just one. The place of the authors of the White Paper, of those who shut the gates of Eretz Israel, who caused the sinking of the Struma, is not among decent people, not in Westminster or in Downing Street. Their place is here, in the dock.

I sometimes wonder and ask myself why they themselves do not ask for a trial. Is Britain so hard-hearted, is the demoralisation of our day so deep, is shamelessness so abundant that these people, who drove millions of people into the fire, and heard, but did not heed, the cries of the burned, do not feel any pangs of conscience, any guilt, any regret? For after all if we are concerned with guilt from the view-point of human feeling, theirs is the true guilt. It would be strange to say: the Nazis are guilty. What have they to do with human guilt? Are they human beings? If a wild beast attacks a peaceful village and kills men, women and children—will we say that the animal is "guilty"? Will we not ask rather: where were the people who had the good hunting rifles? What were they doing during the attack? Why did they not try to stop the beast? Why did they not try to save at least part of the village? We would all ask these questions. And if we were told that the armed men deliberately waited until the beast had made an end of the whole village, and only afterwards killed it, we should say, and you, judges, would agree, that it was their hands which had shed this blood.

Or if a ship is sinking in mid-ocean and sends S.O.S. signals, and a second ship, warship or mercantile, which can come to her aid, does not do so—what will you say? That the waters are "guilty" for having killed the unfortunate passengers? Or is the guilty one the captain of the second ship who could save, but did not? You are a seafaring people, gentlemen. The laws of the sea are well-known to you. Can you deny that such a captain would be treated by you as a dishonourable blackguard, as a criminal in the full sense of the word?

Or if a fire breaks out in a house full of women and children, and one man places himself opposite the burning house and watches quietly until the women and the children and the house are turned to ashes, and only then begins shouting "My heart bleeds for these unfortunates"—will you not see in such a man a despicable being, who would be blackballed from every club, and shunned by everybody. The concept "gentlemen" was created in England. Tell me, gentlemen, what would you think of such a man?

The parallels I have cited are no exaggeration. On the contrary—we are concerned with more than the elementary laws of humanity, which would in themselves be enough to place those who disobeyed them on trial. We are concerned here with an explicit, clear *obligation* that was imposed on you and that you accepted, and in spite of which you behaved like that man in the jungle who, gun in hand, cheerfully watched the tiger eat its prey, or like that sea-captain who unconcernedly smoked his pipe while the nearby sinking ship was tearing the ether with its S.O.S., or like Nero who sang songs of love in the light of the flames which consumed thousands of people. This country was destined, and could, rescue its exiled and exterminated sons. Its ruler is not just a neighbour who has heard something about a fire in the neighbourhood. His job is that of a fireman whose *duty* it is, in spite of danger, to hurry and save and save. And if the fireman does not do so, and moreover adds fuel to the flames, and obstructs others who are trying to save—there is only one word for him: criminal.

My charge, which is the charge of the whole Hebrew people, against the rulers of Britain, is based on facts, proofs, documents. I cannot bring them all before you today. It would require days, perhaps weeks, to submit to you the full, documented and reasoned charge-sheet. I shall therefore content myself with the principal facts and documents, which are sufficient to prove to anybody that the great crime was committed deliberately and with premeditation, and that those guilty are the rulers of Britain.

I shall begin with the pre-war period. Hitler already ruled in

Germany. The Nuremberg laws had already been promulgated. The Jews of Germany had already been murdered or deported. Austria was seized. Prague fell. About a million and a half Jews fell directly into the hands of Hitler and hovered between life and death. What fate awaited them you knew from the reports of international newspapermen. You did not trouble to hide your knowledge of the tragedy being enacted in the heart of Europe. Neville Chamberlain spoke of it in your Parliament. He said "From what happened in Vienna after it was seized by the Germans we know now, after the fall of Prague, what is likely to be the fate of the Jews of Czechoslovakia." You knew. You knew that a million and a half Jews were already in the burning house and that the flames were about to spread and embrace millions of others.

For in the years 1938–39, your rulers had no doubt that war with Hitler was unavoidable. They finally grasped the fact that, they having helped him arm, they having allowed him to turn the Versailles treaty into a scrap of paper, that after they had allowed him to crush the Jews in Germany and to throttle Czechoslovakia, the danger was approaching their own shores. That was why they hastened to sign a pact with Poland, and decided that this time they would fight. That war could no longer be prevented was the general view in London on the morrow of the fall of Prague and the Birmingham speech of Chamberlain.

And just as you knew then that war was approaching, so you knew the relation of forces between Germany and, say, Poland. You knew that in those European plains there would be no obstacle to the tanks of the Germans and that the Nazis would conquer their weaker neighbours. In other words you knew clearly that soon the majority of the Jews of Europe would be under the axe of destruction. I emphasise: under the axe of destruction, and not under the jackboot of the oppressor. The difference is important; the difference is decisive; and it was a difference well-known to the world. The peoples of Europe were enslaved by Germany, exploited by Germany, and naturally gave many victims in the struggle against Germany. But these people knew and believed that after the dark night the sun would shine again, and that after the evil arm was cut off they would be able to go out again into the light of life. Our people's situation was different. What threatened us was not temporary enslavement, but total physical destruction. It was no secret. It was known to every newspaper reader. Already in 1936 Hitler had ended a speech in Reichstag with these words: "The second world war means the complete destruction of the Jews of Europe "

I therefore sum up this point.

a) You knew in the years before the outbreak of war that war was coming soon.

b) You knew that when war did break out most of the countries of Europe would fall into Hitler's hands.

c) You knew that in those countries there lived millions of Jews who would be mercilessly destroyed by the wild invaders. You knew all this; and you were warned about it by Jewish leaders. And you even heard the cry of the Jewish masses themselves at thousands of public meetings: to Zion, to Zion! For the instinct of a living and persecuted people, the eternal Jewish instinct told them they were on the edge of the abyss. And what did you do in those decisive years? You locked the gates of Eretz Israel; you sent the well-known antisemite Winterton to Evian to say that there was no more room for Jews in their Homeland. When throughout the length and breadth of Europe the signs were up: "Death to the Jews!" you hung your sign over the gates of our country: "Entry to Jews forbidden!" And in May, 1939—remember the date: May, 1939—you published the White Paper and announced that Eretz Israel would not be a Jewish Homeland but "Palestine" with six hundred thousand Jewish inhabitants. And the rest? What was to be the fate of "the Jewish People" to whom, to all of whom, the promise had been given to help establish their "National Home"? Your answer was: "To the ovens! To destruction!"

Thus ended the first act of the gruesome tragedy; thus was committed the first part of the terrible crime.

Immediately afterwards the second act opened. War broke out. Poland was conquered. The Balkan countries fell. The bulk of the Jews of Europe were trapped. The sword of Damocles was no longer suspended over them; it came down on them. The mass murders began. Jewish blood was shed like water. At that time a number of Jews tried to escape and to reach their Homeland. They boarded rotten ships and ventured out into the mined ocean—for there on land certain death awaited them, while on the rotten deck there was a hope that they might yet reach their haven. Two of these boats reached Eretz Israel, but your mighty Navy captured the "enemy." Your warships detained the "Milos" and the "Pacific" and, covering them with their guns, brought them to Haifa. And then you published an official communique, a historic communique which will be inscribed in the chronicles of our people as the proclamation of Amalak of old was inscribed, which will be inscribed in your chronicles as a testimony of unforgiveable shame. Listen to the words of your Government in that document of 27 November, 1940:

> "Early this month two ships carrying 1,771 passengers were detained off the shores of Palestine and brought into Haifa harbour. These people must be regarded as illegal immigrants. His Majesty's Government is not lacking in sympathy for refugees from countries under German rule, but it is responsible for governing Palestine and must ensure that the laws of the country should not be publicly flouted. Moreover, it regards the

resumption of illegal immigration at this time as a development
likely to affect very adversely the situation in the country and to
become a grave menace to British interests in the Middle East.
The Government has consequently decided that the passengers
aboard the "Milos" and the "Pacific" will not be allowed to enter
Palestine but will be sent to a British Colony until the end of the
war, when it will be decided where to send them. But it is not
the Government's intention that they should remain in this
colony or that they should come to Palestine. The Government
will take similar steps in the case of any further groups who
succeed in reaching Palestine with the object of entering it
illegally."

That was what the communique said. And now permit me to
analyze it. The contents of the communique unquestionably reached
Europe too, that is to the Jews imprisoned there and to the Germans
ruling or about to rule there. To the Jews you said: "Do not try to
leave Europe. It will not help you. Even if you succeed in crossing
the ocean, you will not be permitted to enter the 'National Home.'
We shall send you to a prison far away (the deportees were treated
like prisoners in Mauritius) and at the end of the war we shall decide
what to do with you."

The news passed from mouth to mouth in the dark exile:
"There is no way out: the road to Eretz Israel is closed." That was
one push into the abyss. At the same time you gave another push.
The Germans also heard your humanitarian proclamation and, you
may depend on it, they understood its meaning perfectly. This is
what you said to the German murderers:

"The fate of the Jews does not interest us. Do what you please
with them. We shall not allow them to enter Palestine. They must
stay where they are. Our blockade of the ports of Europe is also a
blockade of the Jews of Europe. None of them will leave. Do your
work!"

Thirdly, you probably know that in logic and in law there is a
system of drawing conclusions a contrario. Think then, according to
this system, what conclusion was to be drawn from the statement
that the coming of the Jewish refugees, fleeing from the greatest
dangers threatening their lives, was likely to be a menace to the
British in the Middle East? Did not this mean that British interests
demanded that the Jews should remain in Europe, in the Hitlerian
slaughter-house? That is how you understood—and presented to the
world—"British interests"; and your rulers still have the impudence
to demand that these "interests"—the interests of the accomplices of
murderers—should be recognized as legitimate interests, as democratic interests, as interests against which it is forbidden to revolt.

It is no wonder that even the World Jewish Congress, which
does not consist of "extremist" Jews like us (and you regard every
Jew who wants to live as a dangerous extremist) that even that

Congress sent a telegram of thanks to the King of Sweden for helping save Jews in Europe—and not to the King of Britain. And, indeed, the King of Sweden deserved the thanks of our people. His Government did whatever it could to save. And our people is not ungrateful. Whoever does us the least kindness is remembered in our history with praise and thanks. And just as in the sending of that telegram to Stockholm the World Jewish Congress said "Thank you, little Sweden," so in not sending a telegram to London that Congress said "I accuse you, Great Britain. You had a mighty Navy; you built up a great Air Force; you dominated the seven seas; thousands of roads were open to you; above all, you ruled over the land of the Hebrew people. You could therefore have saved millions. And yet you did what you did and doomed them to destruction."

That was the second act of the tragedy. You blockaded the Jews in Nazi Europe.

Then began the third act. The first reports were vague. There was talk of "liquidation commissions," of mass deportations to "an unknown place." Until the truth was revealed in all its horror: in the heart of Europe, on Polish soil, death factories had been set up. Every day they were destroying tens of thousands of men and women and children. You knew all about it; but for months you concealed the facts. Afterwards you claimed that the reports were exaggerated, that it was inconceivable; and thus, behind the smoke-screen that *you* created, Himmler continued his work and extermi-nated the first two million of our brothers. At that time it was proposed that you should do at least one thing, that your planes should bomb the death camps, into whose building the Germans had invested much labour and technical experience. Your answer was: "We cannot do it, for our bombs might hit the unfortunate Jews in Treblinka and Auschwitz." Extraordinary humanitarianism, was it not? The death camps consequently remained intact, and reaped their harvest—the Jews of Poland, the pride of our people, were almost all exterminated.

But there were still Jews in Hungary. There were still Jews in Rumania. And these pleaded with you while there was yet time, before the satellite Governments had been replaced by the open rule of the Gestapo: "Take us out, bring us to our country." And they were not the only ones who asked. There are documents which prove that the Governments wanted to get these Jews out, and even sent emissaries to you to that purpose. Everything depended on you, on your giving them freedom of passage to Eretz Israel. You refused. "British interests" demanded that the Jews of Hungary and the Jews of Rumania, too, should fall into the hands of Himmler. And, indeed, you achieved that as well. A year after the extermination in Poland had been concluded, the bitter cup was passed to the remnant of the exile in Hungary and Rumania.

The story of Turkey is also well-known, and there too there are documents. The Turkish Government was prepared to give transit to any Jews who succeeded in reaching her shores, provided they had permission to enter Eretz Israel. Time out of number you were asked by Ankara: "Will you give these Jews entry permits to Palestine?" Again and again you answered "NO!" And Turkey closed her frontiers. Only in March, 1944 did you inform the Turkish Government that you would permit entry, but of course only within the limits of the White Paper, and on the basis of monthly quotas and with all the customary restrictions. Several hundreds were saved this way.

That is the story of Britain's collaboration in the murders by the Germans. That is the charge against your rulers, of a terrible crime, premeditated and carried out wilfully, as a result of which six million of the Hebrew people were strangled, slaughtered, burnt, suffocated and starved to death. Six million! Has your imagination grasped the figure?

And that is not the end. The fourth act of the tragedy begins immediately on the liberation of the conquered countries. Some Jews still remained. Remnants, shadows, wandering over the graveyards, without a yesterday, without a today and without a tomorrow. They want to leave the slaughter-house. They want life, they want freedom. They are hated by all the inhabitants of Europe. They cannot remain there, cannot breathe there; and their faces are turned Zionward, Zionward. But what do you do? You keep them in the Nazi concentration camps, you drive them by force into the countries of hatred. And Mr. Emerson, the bearer of British humanity, expresses the hope that the hard conditions of the Jews in the camps will force them to return to the countries from which they came— only that they should not come to Eretz Israel. As a consequence of this political decision, some tens of thousands of Jews more, whom Hitler did not manage to kill, have been lost.

And your rulers assume that at the end of the fourth act, the fifth act will begin: what you call "Jewish repatriation" to Poland, to Germany, to Belgium, to Rumania, and so on. "Repatriation" whose meaning is: eternalising Jewish dispersion and the continued slaughter of Jews. And then the curtain will fall. The Jews will continue to hover between life and death, and you will continue to rule in "Palestine."

But, gentlemen, the curtain is not going to fall. For the Hebrew youth has appeared on the stage. The youth which is blood of the blood and flesh of the flesh of the exterminated people; the youth which hears constantly that historic Jewish cry breaking from millions of throats: "Hear O Israel, the Lord our God, the Lord is One"; the youth which is contemptuous of death and is prepared to sacrifice everything in order to save those whom you did not succeed in killing; the youth which has straightened its back on the soil of the ancient Homeland and has armed itself not only with the arms of the Law, but also with the lore of arms.

This youth will not be silent. Eretz Israel, enslaved by you and closed to our brothers, will be an open, bleeding wound on your body. We shall fight by every means and in all ways.

The curtain has not come down and will not come down. The war of the Hebrew people is only just beginning.

David Kirpitchnikoff, another of the Twenty, gave the legal ground for rising against oppression.

HEBREW LAW AGAINST THE LAW OF OPPRESSION
(Declaration by David Kirpitchnikoff)

In this trial, as well as in the similar ones, the Court is trying to put obstacles in the way of making clear the whole of the circumstances of the problem, by contending that political matters are beyond its scope of jurisdiction, and by declaring that only the bare fact, contained in the indictment will be taken into consideration. This attitude is essentially wrong, and has no foundation either in law, or in legal practice, or in science. The function of a Court is not restricted to ascertaining facts. The machinery of the police will suffice for that. If a Court were to content itself with ascertaining the factual situation, the legal proceedings, as well as the personal evidence of the accused during the trial, would be superfluous. An inquisitional and secret investigation, without hearing the parties, and by giving heed only to the proofs of the prosecution, would be sufficient.

But if Justice nowadays requires public proceedings in the presence of the accused, it is because it does not take into consideration the bare facts, but the guilt; because it does not intend making an equation between the fact and the punishment, but examines the psychic conditions and the personality of the accused, his past and the motives which prompted him to the action attributed to him. The Court is bound not only to consider the question, if and how the offence has been perpetrated, but also to answer the question, who is the accused? Is he a bad man or a good one? A social man or an antisocial one? Are his motives base or noble? In short, the Court is bound not only to ascertain the true facts, but also to consider the problem of subjective guilt; and only after the latter problem has been elucidated can a just verdict be brought in.

In view of all these factors I shall endeavour to throw light on the whole problem before you; and I hope that you will have patience enough to listen to my words to the end.

Although we are required to account for our actions before a Court, and charged by the prosecution with many grave offences, we have no feeling at all of being transgressors. This fact may astonish you but it is nevertheless true. Our feeling of innocence is quite peculiar. Ordinarily, such a feeling is the result of being conscious that the crime attributed to the accused has not been perpetrated by him at all, and the accused, as a citizen recognizing the authority of his Government, agrees to the notions of legality and illegality expounded by the prosecution. In our case we are completely indifferent as to whether the action described in the indictment of the Attorney General has, or has not, in fact taken place. Moreover, our conceptions of legality and illegality of actions are not identical with those of the Prosecutor, but are directly opposed to them. It is of no importance whether the prosecution has actually proved that each one of us was carrying or holding arms—in compliance with the legal procedure, requiring that the task and the part of each accused in accomplishing the action be defined exactly and separated and distinguished from those of the other accused. It is our consciousness of law and justice that matters. Our conscience and our consciousness of law tell us that it is the right—and the duty—of every Jew in Eretz Israel to hold arms in order to defend himself and fight against the rule of oppression. Therefore we are indifferent to any factual considerations in this trial. For even if each one of us had been found in possession of arms, the factual situation would not, in our opinion, indicate a crime, but the fulfilment of an honourable duty. This opinion is not new to you. But the importance of this opinion comes more to the point than the reasons for it. You are Englishmen, who judge Jews in their country, in the Homeland of the Hebrews. You are also jurists, and have been taught at the University that a juridical rule is the result of opinions about right and wrong, prevailing in the society in question. A juridical rule is not a caprice or a ruler's will; it is not a regulation binding for ever; it is the expression of a society's conception of good and right. You, the English, are proud of the fact that many laws, which are theoretically obligatory in your country, do not actually obtain in English life, because the interest protected by them, or the procedure fixed by them, is not in harmony any longer with the English conception of justice and equity. You, the English, decided, when King Charles I was put to death by Cromwell, that whenever there is a collision between the views of the people and those of the ruler regarding good and evil, right and wrong, it is the popular sentiment of law and justice that is binding. Therefore, when you are to judge Jews in Eretz Israel, you must take account of the social consciousness of justice in this land of the Hebrew. If you choose another way, then let it be known to you that we deny your right to judge us; we repudiate your juridical imperatives, which we regard as means of oppression and iniquity.

The legal proceedings which have taken place hitherto, the explanations given by the accused in similar trials, revealed the conviction prevailing among the Jews:—they believe that in view of the conditions created by you, every Jew is allowed, and is even bound, to carry arms. And if it displeases you, if you can't suffer Jews to possess arms, blame yourselves, blame your Government which has brought about this situation. We have only drawn the right conclusions. There is no sentiment of guilt in our hearts, and you are looking for it in vain.

Now, after making a contradistinction between the Hebrew sentiment of justice and the British law in Eretz Israel, and after demonstrating that the gulf dividing them cannot be bridged, it is clear we still have to tackle another side of the problem. Science and history teach us that in a collision between two legal principles, the higher principle always gains the upper hand. So the question presents itself, which of these principles is the higher one? Is it the British law in Eretz Israel? Or is it the consciousness of justice of the Hebrew population? I wish to answer this question in a dispassionate manner.

With a feeling of pride we point out that we are Jews. We are sons of one of the most ancient nations in the world, and we have a tradition of national existence of 4000 years. Our forefathers built up a culture which has guided the whole of humanity, they laid the foundations of equity and justice, referred to by Mr. Churchill, in his letter to the Editor of the "Jewish Chronicle," as follows: "Once again, at the appointed time, he (the Jew) will see vindicated those principles of righteousness which it was the glory of his fathers to proclaim to the world." At that period the world had not yet heard of England, and the ancient inhabitants of the British Isles floundered in barbarism and ignorance. It is no shame that your nation is younger than ours, but it is a shame that a young nation should treat an ancient nation with cruelty only because the latter hesitated long before deciding to oppose force with force.

We gave you the Bible, which has fashioned your culture and language. Traces of our creative work are imprinted in Englishmen's daily life. Our cultural possessions have been acquired and adapted to English needs. And again it is no shame that somebody should have learned something from somebody else. It is a fine quality, to learn and outdo one's own teacher. But it is an everlasting shame, to treat the eternal nation as you do; to cheat, and deceive, and oppress it.

We lay stress on our national pride, not in order to boast, but in order to draw your attention to the fact that the notion of "natives" you are used to in your numerous colonies, the notion which determines your attitude towards the peoples ruled by you—is completely strange to us. Our cultural supremacy, our historical past, our achievements in civilisation and our religious Law, grant us the right to assert that the legal principles created by the Hebrew nation belong to a high category of juridical principles, in comparison with the juridical norms of your Administration. Even if your rule had been equitable and humane, we should have demanded that the supremacy of the Hebrew sentiment of justice be recognized. So much more now, when your Administration has become, as is universally known, a typical Occupation Administration using methods of oppression and despoliation, which need not be demonstrated, and which will be probably mentioned again at length in the course of this trial.

Accordingly, if an Englishman wants to judge Jews in Eretz Israel, he must take account of the sentiment of law of the Jews, and this sentiment tells us that every Jew is allowed to bear arms in this country, in order to defend both himself and his people, that is—in order to fight against your Administration, which encroaches on its primary rights. Therefore, even if arms had been found in our possession, which is not the case, even if we had been arrested while using them, there would have been no guilt with us.

Now let us briefly consider the problem of punishment. There is a controversy in science on the matter, but the prevalent opinion is that punishment must be of an educative and purifying value and that its aim is to improve the personality of the offender. We, therefore, ask: what is a punishment, even the severest one, likely to improve in us? Without submission, resulting from the consciousness of guilt, there can be no improvement. But, if we have no consciousness of guilt, if, on the contrary, we have a consciousness of injustice done by you, is there any room for submission? From which source will improvement come? The action we committed or could have committed is, in our and every Jew's opinion, good, desirable and sanctified. The conclusion is that, as far as improvement is concerned, to punish us would be aimless. Now allow me to analyse the other value of legal punishment. Although the science of law disapproves of punishment as a means of intimidation, the British Courts of Law in Eretz Israel have more than once adduced the intention to frighten, as a reason for the severe punishments imposed on the accused. Now the question is, whom do you want to frighten. The Hebrew fighting youth? Even you don't believe it possible. Every Hebrew young man, taking active part in the struggle of a military organization, has, before joining it, weighed all the pros and cons—to join the underground movement or not, to take the risk of punishments and sufferings or not. A man appears before a Court after joining an organization. A military organization is based on voluntary service, not on compulsory mobilization. Everyone knows beforehand of your punishments and courts, and everyone has made his mind up before appearing in the Court. A punishment cannot frighten him and will not attain its end.

Maybe you cherish the illusion that the punishment will

frighten others? It is your right. But, with all due deference, it is our right to tell you the truth; you are wrong in believing that the punishment will frighten anybody. A Hebrew young man in Eretz Israel has two alternatives: to live according to your wish, or to join a fighting organization. If he chooses the way sparing him physical pain, he condemns himself to terrible mental sufferings. The feelings of subjugation, oppression and humiliation is dominant in him. Every morning, the newspaper brings him terrible tidings of his brethren in Europe. And if he is a thinking man, he despises himself and curses his cowardice. There is no escape from the shameful feeling that he enjoys a quiet life, while his brethren and sisters are exterminated in Europe, and here, in the Homeland, strangers in police uniform, equipped with a stick and a pistol, assault citizens. In such a mental condition, he can't read a book or go to the cinema. In books, he finds descriptions of the heroic struggle of the underground against the German invader in Europe. Books teach him that war against oppression is good, and is the duty of every decent man. At the cinema, he is shown "For Whom The Bell Tolls," how a bridge is blown up, how acts of sabotage are organized, how patriots fight against the conqueror. At school, he is taught history. He sees and understands that all have done the same thing, without which the world would have been still sunk in darkness and barbarism. Little by little he comes to understand what eternal life is. The names of the judges of Socrates were forgotten long ago. Had they been remembered, they would have been symbols of scorn and derision. But Socrates is eternal, not only because of his teachings, but because he applied them in actual life, because he did not avail himself of the opportunity to run away, and of his own free will drank the poison. For Socrates was convinced that although the poison would put an end to his life, it would also eventually kill the regime of ignorance and barbarity. The same applies to Galileo and Giordano Bruno, who by their death conquered death.

Your rule is continually pouring oil on the flame of rebellion. Now infringement of our rights at the Jerusalem Municipality, now a sudden hunt in the streets of a city, now a commission of enquiry into land sales to Jews in prohibited areas, like in Tsarist Russia. Despoliation is steadily increasing and accumulating. Distress increases, and the desire to free oneself from mental pain grows stronger. The road to a fighting organization lies open. Among fighting men, one is suddenly relieved of mental distress, one gains an ideal and a faith. In spite of physical distress and incessant persecutions, life acquires a meaning, he knows what he is living for and what he is willing to die for. He becomes free and liberated. He doesn't envy the heroes of the past any longer, and he doesn't feel ashamed in the presence of their shadows. The doors of vigorous existence, with the glory of a just war, of self-sacrifice and the consciousness that his actions are good, are thrown open before a member of a military organization. And what is more important—he has a clear conscience. He is suddenly liberated from the embarrassing questions about his right to remain alive while all his relatives have been savagely exterminated. He stops envying his fellow citizens, who have the privilege of mourning their relatives at a funeral. He doesn't envy a son who takes part in his father's burial procession, who knows his grave, who recites the Doxology and lights a candle for the ascent of his soul on the anniversary of his death. Heroic deeds efface the images of Maidanek and Treblinka, where roads were built with the ashes of the victims; where bones of our brethren were used for manufacture of buttons, and hair of our sisters—for manufacture of mattresses and armchairs. On the other hand, the concrete figure of the British policeman, still watching over the closed gates, becomes clearer and clearer; and a thought buzzes in the brain: had we started our fight earlier, we might have abolished in time the obstacles meeting Jews on their way back home, and millions might have been saved.

Therefore, your punishment will frighten nobody. Mental distress induced by you is much more terrible and dreadful than the acutest physical pains.

To sum up, the way chosen by you is hopeless. Persecutions and despoliation will not attain their end, and punishments will not frighten. There is one way before you. It is the hard way of truth and justice. Your duty is to do justice. Restore us our robbed Homeland, redress the inhuman wrong done to the remnants of our nation, expiate your sin to the massacred victims, for it was your armed hand that hindered their rescue.

Menachem Binder, a soldier of the Irgun, captured with thirty of his comrades, during their withdrawal after an Irgun operation in Southern Eretz Israel, demanded, at the "trial" in June, 1946, their rights as prisoners of war. Characteristically, the British "prosecutor" contented himself with claiming that the "court" was not competent to decide the issue.

THE STATUS OF AN UNDERGROUND ARMY
(Declaration by Menachem Binder)

The arms enumerated in the indictment were not found in our hands. If they had been in our hands they would not today be in yours. Nor would we be sitting here, for that matter. For if our hands had really held those two Bren-guns and the tommy-guns and rifles then one of the following two things would have happened: either we should have broken through the columns of your soldiers although they outnumbered us 100 to 1, or all of us should have fallen in this unequal battle, killing many of your soldiers. There was no third possibility. But it is a fact which we stress not for our own sake but for that of truth and perhaps for the sake of history—that you found all those arms only after we had been captured, after most of us had been hit by your bullets and were bleeding from our wounds. And you found it very far away from the place where we were taken prisoner by you.

(By the way, I should like to point out that the prosecutor was not correct in referring in the indictment to *"bearing of arms,"* which he should, according to *his own* conception, have defined as *"possession of arms."* We do not think there is a great difference between these terms and we do not care which of them you use, nor do I want to interfere in the management and proceedings of this trial; and I make this remark for the sake of precision alone).

The fact that we have been captured under these conditions does not detract in the least from our honour as Jewish soldiers and fighters. At any rate, if you permit a somewhat incomplete comparison, it does resemble the fall of Tobruk or the surrender of your famous Singapore. Still I have to state emphatically that the conduct of the soldiers who captured us was far from being soldierly. I shall not mention that they misbehaved in words and with their fists against wounded men, which may be considered as an outburst of their feelings of hatred against us. Perhaps one cannot complain of such an outburst of instincts however shameful, though civilised people ought to be able to control themselves. I refer mainly to the intentional action of enlightened British soldiers which they carried out with German thoroughness.

They took from us almost everything of value: money, fountain pens, watches, purses, etc. They just "liberated" many trifles which we liked not for their financial but rather sentimental value. In general those objects were souvenirs or gifts which we had received from our relatives or friends. Is it fair to take such things from wounded people, bleeding and thirsty people who have been taken prisoners of war? Who taught His Majesty's forces to loot like this?

I think that the fact that we were taken prisoners however painful in itself, does not humiliate us, while the conditions under which this happened are a stain on the honour and uniform of the soldiers who captured us. Their behaviour was not soldierly, but reminded one of the behaviour of highwaymen.

However, this matter has another aspect, too. This was the first time that you captured a Jewish military unit, forming a part of the Jewish forces fighting against you and declaring openly that they would fight against you till the end: that is, until you hand over to the Jewish people the rule over its country and homeland, or until it is destroyed completely. Such a fighting unit you bring to trial in accordance with your usual, or, rather, unusual laws, as though these people were not soldiers, members of an independent underground army but ordinary breakers of the law. Is there any logic in such an attitude?

I state this problem intentionally as a problem of logic only. It is certainly possible to bring up the question of justice and human feeling that should compel a civilised man to take off his hat to people who could have lived quietly in their comfortable homes together with their beloved ones but who recognised their duty towards their brethren which demands that they endanger and even sacrifice their lives—which they do in pure idealism. One might expect from gentlemen who probably day in day out have the words "freedom" and "democracy" on their lips that they display an attitude of respect towards men fighting for freedom even if their fate made it necessary for them to fight against one another. But I shall not discuss *this* aspect of the matter. Experience has taught me that such an "old-fashioned" argument which was perhaps appropriate in the nineteenth century doesn't make any impression. It is therefore not worth while appealing to feelings that probably no longer exist in our times, the times of large-scale cruelty, the epoch of Hitler and Bevin. It is better to appeal to logic, cold reasoning, calculations of profit and loss, because if there is anything that can influence your rulers, I think that these are the *only considerations.*

Thus, Gentlemen, let us build our logical construction on one basic assumption. This basic assumption is that in this country there exists an independent, adequately armed Jewish force fighting against you, that is against your rule. The war waged by this armed force is a war of liberation, the war of an oppressed people against its oppressors, of a people whose homeland has been stolen against those who stole it. Therefore, this is a just war and this justice must be admitted by all those peoples who ever stood in battle for their freedom, against oppressors in their midst or foreign oppressors.

However, you do not want to recognise this force, and you call the members of the Jewish army "terrorists," while those who carry out its military plans you regard—or pretend to regard—as criminals. Gentlemen—this is not a novel attitude. The Nazis—the German Nazis as I must point out, because I regret that there are still many Nazis in the world who are not Germans—the German Nazis called "terrorists" the French Maquis and the partisan fighters of Tito and the fighters in Poland and the rebels in Slovakia and Greece, etc. This, then, is a very old term of abuse, used by all tyrants against the fighters for freedom, with the intention of casting a slur on the idealism of the fighters and their struggle.

However, as you know, Gentlemen, these names of abuse did not help the Nazis, who employed them against the fighters for freedom in the countries of occupied Europe. The oppressed people themselves regarded their fighting sons as fighters for their own cause and they supported their struggle wholeheartedly; while the other countries recognised the underground armies as semi-regular armies entitled to the same rights as soldiers in uniform. They even compelled the Germans to respect these rights of the various underground armies. If the Germans refused to do so they were threatened with retaliation. It is interesting to note that the Germans, who on the whole proudly trampled underfoot every international law, accepted this demand and recognised, officially or practically, the belligerent rights of the European underground.

On the basis of these precedents, and since from you one should be able to demand at least what was demanded from the German Nazis, the Irgun Zvai Leumi demanded two years ago the recognition of the fighting Jewish forces practically and theoretically as underground forces possessing the rights of belligerents. In our opinion this demand is in the interest of all concerned. It would even seem that it is to a great extent more in your interest than in our own. After all, Gentlemen, we are prepared for everything, for every sacrifice. We fight for our country and the lives of our children, while you in your war against us have let yourselves in for some very unpleasant business, which complicates your international relations, staining your honour in every respect; while, on the other hand, this small country, which is our all, is for you only a tiny part of the 40 million square kilometres at your disposal. One can, therefore, not compare our readiness for sacrifice in this war with your readiness for sacrifice. Our determination can be compared only to that of the Russians in their defence against the German invaders of their homeland, or to the determination you would have displayed had the German armies succeeded in landing on the shores of your Homeland. This is a particular kind of determination not to be weakened by any danger whatever.

If, therefore, you do continue with your ostrich policy and prefer not to face the fact that against you stands in this country an organised force, fully aware of its national and historic mission, a force backed not only by six hundred thousand Jewish citizens in the Jewish Homeland but by eleven million Jews all over the world, and, finally, or, as you say, "last but not least"—*by public opinion in all free countries:* (if you should like to examine this thesis you may study a few American, French or other newspapers;) if you continue in your blindness and bureaucratic obstinacy to regard the Jewish fighters and their organisations as ordinary law-breakers whom you can even hang like criminals, then, Gentlemen, I am afraid that the results of such an attitude are bound to become very grave indeed. By your very attitude towards our ever deepening struggle you are bound to liquidate all the laws commonly accepted in warfare, and which we are prepared to respect, provided, of course, that you too commit yourselves to act in accordance with them. But, Gentlemen, if these laws are indeed abandoned and if we realise that Jewish blood can be shed wilfully, there can be no doubt, as we told you two years ago, that British blood too will not be spared. Then the war between us will really develop according to lines that actually neither you nor we can know at present. I ask you to remember that in the course of our war there were numerous cases when our comrades disarmed your soldiers, your police constables, capturing dozens of your soldiers and police. It is true that after the men had surrendered they were not harmed but were released after our operations had been completed. Actually not even these facts can be considered as strictly equivalent because your soldiers were held by us for some hours only while we, once we fall in your hands, have to spend long years in your prisons and concentration camps. This inequality is due to the fact that under the particular conditions of our war we are not yet in a position to hold your soldiers in captivity for a longer time.

Perhaps these conditions will change and this inequality will be eliminated. In any case, it should be perfectly clear that the life of a prisoner should be "taboo": it should be safe, he should not be abused or tortured or refused the satisfaction of his needs as a civilised man. But what is going to happen if you discriminate against Jewish soldiers who fall into your hands? Do you think that the Jewish armed forces will pass over this in silence? It is obvious that they will arrive at their conclusions from your treatment and there can be no doubt that they will do so, because you should not forget in all your calculations, Gentlemen, that under the present circumstances there is one thing of paramount importance: the soldiers of Israel fight in the profound conviction that if they do not *succeed* in this war there will be neither life nor future for them, their children and their people. You should not take this too lightly. This is our situation. We are the generation of Maidanek and Treblinka. We have no illusions. We know very well what fate is in store for us—all of us—if we have no state of our own, capable of protecting us militarily as well as politically. Therefore we are ready for every necessity, for *every* necessity. For indeed the war that we are waging is a matter of life or death, a war for the survival of the Jewish people, and no dangers can hold us back, no sacrifices frighten us.

I have told you all this frankly and openly because this matter does not concern merely myself or my comrades here in this court-room. It concerns thousands and tens of thousands of people—English as well as Jews—who may be the victims of your blindness, of your treating as criminals the fighters of a nation struggling for its rights. I think that if you consider well what I have told you, you too will realise that it is incumbent upon you to recognise, theoretically and in practice the Jewish underground forces as possessing full combatant rights with all that this status implies.

The "objectivity" of these British "judges" having been illuminated by a characteristic Nazi remark by the President of the "court"—Irgun soldier Chaim Luster, one of the Thirty-One, made his reply in the "court."

GO HOME
(Statement by Chaim Luster)

In my statement I will confine myself to an interpellation. While I was in prison I heard that the clandestine radio of the I.Z.L. broadcast an announcement to the effect that you, Mr. President, said at a meeting with other officers: What a pity one has not done with the Jews in Palestine what one did with the Jews in Europe. I could then leave this damned country and return home to England.

You must not be surprised that these words reached the Jewish Underground movement. It is true that no guarantee can be given as to the precision of the words actually used but it would seem that their sense has been reported correctly. And you surely know that the Jewish Underground has many ears and many eyes, and sees and hears things that you never dreamed would reach those who fight against you.

As a matter of fact, Mr. President, your words stand in need of a detailed analysis and thorough discussion. After all, you are not an ordinary officer or an inferior official of your government. Your position is very high, it is perhaps one of the highest in this country, since in your hands lies the sceptre of justice—if one can speak of British justice—and the fate of human beings is sometimes subject to your decision. Acordingly I treat this opinion—and I am sure every Jewish citizen does the same—which you stated in front of your friends and acquaintances, very seriously indeed. I think it worth while considering these words.

Allow me to begin with the end: this country you chose to call a "damned country." You surely admit that this expression is no less amazing than it is insulting. Hitherto we were accustomed to the whole world calling our country the "Holy," since it is sacred to hundred of millions of people who see it, regardless of race or religion, as the source of divine wisdom, and the centre of monotheism. It was on these grounds that the Anglo-American Inquiry commission—or, rather, its English members—found it possible to announce that Christianity has a very great interest in the Land of Israel, and therefore they thought it necessary to leave you as rulers in it, you, the Christian English people. But if so, how can you explain that you as an Englishman and a Christian call the holy country a "damned country"?

Is it—and I arrive at this conclusion from the first part of your very suggestive statement—that the Holy Land became a "damned country" because the *Jews* live in it, or because the Jews want to possess it as did their ancestors? This opinion, too, is strange and surprising. For everyone knows that if this country did become a holy country in the eyes of mankind this happened precisely thanks to the Jews. Thousands of years ago they destroyed the idols of the heathens, they brought to this country the word of the Lord from Mt. Sinai. Nor should it be forgotten that the founders of the Christian religion too were the sons of our people and that the tree of Christianity whose branches now extend over all the countries of the world, was planted and grew up in our country.

But if you are nevertheless of the opinion that the Jews turned the Land of the Lord into a "damned country," I have to ask you another question. You have, of course, the right to hate us—you are not the only one in the world who hate us—but if you hate the Jews how does your conscience allow you to assume the function of a *Judge of the Jews?* I think that all legal books contain a passage stating explicitly that if a judge or any member of the jury has, for some reason or other, a hostile attitude to the accused, it is his *duty* to ask to be released from his function. I think you ought to have done so, Sir.

We think that all this jury is illegal, but still less can a judge be recognised who openly admits his personal hostility against the accused as members of a certain people.

However, in the continuation of your words there is a passage with which we agree wholeheartedly. It is splendid, isn't it, that we should agree with one another. Therefore, this fact should be recorded in the minutes of the proceedings and by public opinion. We certainly agree that you should return home to your family in England. We agree for two reasons. First of all, we highly appreciate your feeling called nostalgia, your longing for your home. This feeling, you should know, has been alive in our hearts for two thousand years. Oh, how we yearned for our home! All our prayers, all our dreams, were directed to the day on which the Lord would bring us back to our home. When the Lord brought back the Jews to Zion, our forefathers sang by the rivers of Babylon: "We were like *men in a dream.*" Yes, like men in a dream. For there is no greater happiness than to return home, home. Therefore there is no difference whether you return home from a palace or from a hut, from pleasant surroundings or from a "damned country," whether you return from a good people or, as happened to our nation, from people who want to murder you. The main thing is—to return home. And so all our desire today is to return home. But, of course, this does not apply to us alone. We are happy that we succeeded in reaching our home, but like us, there are millions of our brethren, who want to return home too. Can they be denied this right? Particularly since these are people who have not even got a temporary home, because the homes they built on the volcanoes of the Diaspora have been destroyed completely, burying in their ruins alive or dead all those who were near and dear to them. You should really understand, Sir, and Gentlemen, if you still can understand, that the whole issue, which has caused our trial too, is nothing but the return home of millions without a home. They do not return for the sole reason that you do not allow them to return, because you deny them this right, which as far as it concerned you, was so clear and natural and so *imperious*, that you are even ready to curse and desecrate sacred ideas when your superiors postpone for some time your voyage home. If there is in such a mentality a certain egoism—I regreat but I have no other name for it but *foul egoism*—this mentality has also certain implications. It would seem and this is something decided by you—that so long as your wish is fulfilled and you and your colleagues rule our country, you cannot return to your home and our people cannot return to its own home. And if so, Sir, you are perfectly free to return home! And not only you alone. Take along with you all your army and police, and all your officials, who too probably should like to go home. Return home and give us back this country which you have stolen from us. You know that we shall take it and that it will be ours as it once was. Your military commanders who appeared before the Inquiry commission left no room for doubt on this score. This country will be ours again, only we will rule it not in order to exploit it or in order to oppress others, or in order to make of it a military base against others; we will rule this country in order to carry out our great mission, given to us by Divine Providence, a mission for mankind as a whole.

We shall bring home millions of people who unless they have this home have no prospect of survival, no future. Thus, you see, in this case our hearts' desires coincide: if you return to your home, we too will return to ours and then there will surely be no reason to break the peace between our two peoples.

Do so! For heaven's sake—go home and give us back our home! And now, Sir and Gentlemen, permit me shortly to analyse the first part of your words. You expressed your regreat that one did not do to the Jews in Eretz Israel what was done to their brethren in Europe. Let us speak openly: you know, of course, Sir, what it was that was done to the Jews in Europe: they were put in thousands into gas chambers and were murdered in infernal agonies.

And you would like the same thing to happen in this country as well. Very interesting! Very instructive! And you surely realised that this time it would not be the Germans who massacred millions of men and women and children, but this time, in order to carry out this mass murder, it would be necessary to use the hands of your brethren, the English, who have the Bible on their lips and preach democracy and the brotherhood of man. And apparently you are prepared to assign this task to your brethren, to your people, and you surely hope they will fulfil it. Perhaps Mr. Chairman, you are right. Perhaps they will be no less ready to do so then the "civilised" Jerries. But this you and all of you should know: You shall not live to see this! No, No, No! You will never succeed in bringing the inhabitants of this country to extermination camps without resistance, without an enormous price that you will have to pay with your own *blood*. This was possible only there, in the damned countries of the diaspora, truly damned, on that soil of the Exile that robbed our brethren of the physical and spiritual will of resistance, which had led them to be completely defenceless, because of their naive belief in the image of man that you possess—only there it was possible and even there the Lion of Judah roared and went to fight at the last moment against the foul murderers and killed thousands of them. Here, however, this is not possible at all, here we stand in our country. Our country has given us the youthful vigour of the people of the Hasmoneans. Our country commanded us to take up arms again and to redeem it with our blood, as our forefathers once redeemed it with their blood, its ancient conquerors and liberators. Our country has revived in us the heroes of Massada and Jodefeth. It has given us strength, it calls us from the depths: "Arise and fight for me and for the People that has been led away from me into exile."

We have heard our country's voice, Gentlemen, for it is the voice of our mother, the voice of the motherland.

———————

There follow a number of statements of the Irgun, issued at different times since the summer of 1945. The first is the announcement made in July, 1945 with the coming to power in Britain of the Labour Government.

WE SHALL GIVE THE LABOUR GOVERNMENT
A CHANCE TO KEEP ITS WORD

In England a Government of the Labour Party has taken office. Before it came to power, this Party undertook to return the Land of Israel to the people of Israel as a free State, in which all those who long for Zion and its exiles would be concentrated.

This in itself gives no guarantee for the attainment of our national aim. The Hebrew people, tried in suffering, is also learned in experience. Men and parties in opposition, or in their struggle with their rivals, have, for twenty-five years, made us many promises and undertaken clear obligations; but, on coming to power, they have gone back on their words and continued with the policy which leads only to the robbery of our country and the destruction of our people. This experience, which has cost the Jewish people six million lives, teaches us that ONLY a war of liberation, independent and real, will set in motion political and international factors and bring redemption to our enslaved and decimated people.

This historic conclusion remains clear. The battle in which, as the advance-guard of the people, the fighting youth is engaged, is not being fought to obtain "friendly statements" or for the annulment of "decrees": the battle is being fought for the attainment of the FUNDAMENTAL aim: the establishment of Hebrew rule in the land of the Hebrews. And it will not cease except this aim be achieved. That is why, despite all the threats from outside and from within, we have not laid down our arms and, during the past few days, have entered a phase of widespread operations.

But in the presence of a Government ALL of whose members subscribed, as members of their party, to the programme for the mass return to Zion and the establishment of the Hebrew State, we consider it our duty, out of a sense of responsibility and of our free will, to give them an opportunity to prove whether they mean to go the way of all British Governments—the way of denial and betrayal— or whether it is their intention to fulfil without delay their public undertakings.

In view of the known situation of our people, *only a very short time—weeks and not months*—is required in order to find out whether their words are being translated into deeds, or whether to all the tragic illusions of the Jewish people there has been added another illusion, perhaps the last, whose shattering will demand from all of us:

WAR, WAR TO THE END, WAR TILL VICTORY.

On 29 June, 1946, the British counter-offensive was launched against the Hebrew people. It came at a time when all the three Hebrew armed organisations were co-operating in the struggle. The immediate reaction of the Irgun was a call and a plan for complete national concentration, for a National Government and a single National fighting Command, to which, as before, and since the Irgun was prepared to submit.

MOBILISE THE NATION!

The arrest of the heads of the Yishuv is a step in the campaign of liquidation, carried on systematically and brutally by the bloody

British regime against our people. This act of aggression was preceded by many acts of hostility, resulting in the destruction of one-third of the people, which have brought us to the edge of the abyss, and which have all had one purpose:

To put an end to the aspirations for Hebrew freedom; to rob us for ever of our only country; to turn us—as in the Diaspora—into dust and to blot us out from under God's Heaven.

The oppressive hand of the enemy—the teacher of Hitler and the executor of his plans—has been raised against the Jewish people. The existence of the nation is at stake.

In this situation there is no other way but to fight. In this situation vacillation is a misdeed, delay and retreat are crimes. In this situation the whole people—in Zion and in the far-flung Diaspora—must rise as one man and smite the cruel enslaver, by every means and in every way, until he is brought low.

In the face of the British aggression, which covers itself in a cloak of "law and order"—let there be set up the legal, independent State institutions of the Hebrew people—the only owner of this country:

a) Let the Hebrew Provisional Government be established—the legal Government of the country which will fight for the downfall of the British Occupation regime.

b) Let the Supreme National Council be established—the Parliament of the Jewish people and of Eretz Israel, which will make laws, impose obligations and give orders.

c) Let there be published the Declaration of Hebrew Independence and Freedom—the basis of the constitution of our country, whose principles shall be: Liberty, equality and social justice for all the citizens and inhabitants of the country.

d) Let there be set up Hebrew courts of justice and let the British courts be boycotted.

e) Let there be set up the Exchequer of the Hebrew people: all our payments must flow into this exchequer, and all payments of taxes to the exploiting invader must be forbidden.

f) Let there be set up the united Hebrew Liberation Army, which shall take an oath not to lay down its arms until our independent State is set up.

g) Let there be set up the Supreme Military Command, which will proclaim a general mobilisation of all who can bear arms in the people, which will set up an Emergency regime in our daily lives and will conduct the struggle.

h) Let the call go out to all the centres of the Diaspora to hasten to the aid of fighting and embattled Zion.

i) Let the call go out to the peoples of the world—to the United States, to the Soviet Union, to France and to all the free peoples—to give aid to the Hebrew fighters for freedom.

In this way—and only thus—shall we become a nation, fighting against the enslavers who have invaded our country; and stop being a "community" persecuted by its "law-enforcing" rulers. In this way the Jewish people will arise, and live and smash the chains of slavery.

An end, therefore to half-measures! Let the banner of revolt be raised! Let our camp be united, our hands firm, our aim clear, our faith resolute! For it is the cruel oppressor, the treacherous aggressor who places us before the alternative:

A war of liberation, or destruction: Freedom or Death.

The character of the leaders of His Majesty's occupation forces, and the spirit they have instilled into the soldiers under their command, was demonstrated by the anti-semitic order of the day circulated by the Nazi General Barker at the end of July, 1946, which, as it happened, did not remain secret.

It was published for the information of the public by the Irgun Zvai Leumi.

HIT THEM IN THE POCKET
Order by General Barker of 26 July, 1946

We publish for the information of the Hebrew public and the civilized world, the full text of the Order of the Day issued by the Nazo-British Commander-in-Chief in Eretz Israel.

"The Jewish community in Palestine cannot be absolved of the responsibility for the long series of outrages, which reached their climax in the blowing up of a large part of the Government Offices in the King David Hotel, causing heavy loss of life. Without active or passive help by the Jewish community for the terrorist groups who committed these crimes, they would have been discovered—and for this reason the Jews must bear part of the responsibility.

"I am determined that they should be punished and made aware of our feelings of contempt and disgust at their behaviour. We must not let ourselves be misled by hypocritical sympathy expressed by their leaders and representative bodies and by the protestations that they are not responsible and that they cannot curb the terrorists. I repeat that if the Jewish community really wanted to put an end to the crimes it could do so by co-operating with us. I have accordingly decided that as from the receipt of this letter all Jewish places of entertainment, cafes, restaurants, shops and private homes are out of bounds. No British soldier will have contact with any Jew, and duty contacts will be made as short as possible and will be limited to the duty concerned. I understand that these measures will create difficulties for the troops, but I am certain that if my reasons are explained to them, they will understand their duty and will punish the Jews in the manner this race dislikes most: by hitting them in the pocket, which will demonstrate our disgust for them."

———————

The following warning, which remained unheeded by the British regime of barbarism, who proceeded to carry out the flogging of a 16-year-old Hebrew soldier, was consequently implemented by the retaliatory flogging of a British officer and two N.C.O.'s. There have been no more British floggings.

WARNING

A Hebrew soldier, taken prisoner by the enemy, has been sentenced by an illegal British Military "Court" to the humiliating punishment of flogging.

We warn the Occupation Government not to carry out this punishment, which is contrary to the laws of soldiers' honour. If it is put into effect—every officer of the British Occupation army in Eretz Israel will be liable to be punished in the same way: 18 strokes.

IRGUN ZVAI LEUMI
b'Eretz Israel

January, 1947

———————

The striving of the Irgun for friendly and neighbourly relations with the Arab citizens of Eretz Israel has been made clear repeatedly both to them and to the world at large. In a special proclamation published in Arabic and Hebrew in 1945 it was given succinct expression. Despite the reign of terror of the British-instigated, self-appointed "leaders" of the Arab inhabitants of Eretz Israel, there have been many indications that the call of the Irgun has not remained without an echo in the hearts of the Arabs. The proclamation of the Irgun follows.

TO OUR ARAB NEIGHBOURS

The Hebrew youth, trained to fight, has launched the struggle for the liberation of its Homeland. The Irgun Zvai Leumi b'Eretz Israel, with its thousands of members, armed with modern weapons, is fighting against a treacherous Government which aims at putting an end to the eternal vision of the great Hebrew people.

This war of liberation, which is only just beginning, will grow in intensity and in scope.

This struggle is not directed against you. We do not regard you as enemies. We want to regard you as good neighbours. We have not come to destroy you or to deprive you of the soil on which you are living. There is enough room in Eretz Israel for you, for your children and your children's children, and for millions of Jews who have no other place to live but in this land. The Hebrew Government will accord you full equality of rights. The Hebrew and Arabic languages will be the languages of the country. There will be no discrimination between Arab and Jew in the appportionment of Government posts or public works. The Holy Places of the Moslem religion will be placed under the supervision of your representatives. The Hebrew Government will facilitate the education of your masses and there will be no illiteracy in the land of the Bible. There will be no more epidemics in your villages and towns. Wages will be raised to the European level. There will be great progress in your agriculture. You will build houses instead of tents. Electricity and water will reach every place where you live. The Hebrew State will be the common home for all of us, and there will be peace and neighbourly relations between it and the independent Arab States.

The treacherous Government does not want this. It tries to sow friction between us, to incite you against us, and us against you, in order to secure for itself the role of supreme arbiter, in order to leave you in the desolation of the desert and the gloom of illiteracy, and our brothers—to destruction in the lands of exile. But we do not listen, and do not intend to listen, to its cajolery. And we have proved this in *deeds*. In Ramallah, inhabited by Arabs, we seized the central broadcasting station, in spite of its proximity to the big police fortress; but we did not touch the inhabitants of the town. We delivered attacks in Jerusalem and Haifa, but we did not turn our arms against their Arab inhabitants. This has been our way in the past, and so it will be in the future.

But you too must beware of heeding the advice of the inciters. Do not try to raise a hand against the Jews or their property. For if, against your national and personal interests, you do raise a hand against us—we shall be compelled to cut it off without delay with the force of our arms. And both you and the whole world have learnt that the power of the new Hebrew youth is great.

It depends on you and your wisdom. If you wish it, and you do not listen to the inciters, peace and friendship will reign between our two peoples in this country for ever. Together we shall build this Holy Land; together we shall enjoy its resources and its fruits; together we shall develop its agriculture and industry; together we shall march with the free peoples of the earth to a life of justice and freedom, of dignity and happiness.

Our Arab neighbours,

We stretch out our hand to you in peace and fraternity. Do not reject it.

The following appeal was handed to the diplomatic represen-
tatives of the United States, the Soviet Union and France during the
participation of these three states, with Great Britain, in the Moscow
Conference in January, 1947.

AN APPEAL TO THE MOSCOW CONFERENCE

The representatives of the victorious Powers have gathered in Moscow, in order, as they put it, to establish lasting peace.

But peace is indivisible.

This rule was laid down, as it happened, in the very place where the present Conference is meeting, and reality has proved its truth.

Peace is indivisible. And freedom, too, is indivisible.

The Foreign Ministers of the United States, of the Soviet Union and of France should know that there is neither peace nor freedom in Eretz Israel. The peace is disturbed by the British Occupation Army, which has converted our country into a military base and a great camp of oppression. The illegal British Occupation regime robs us of freedom and even of the right to live. And in the light of the experience of our generation we must remind the representatives of the great Powers that war and enslavement in Eretz Israel threaten to endanger the peace of the world and the freedom of the peoples.

We, therefore, in the name of our people fighting for freedom against an aggressive and cruel oppressor, call to the Foreign Ministers of the United States, the Soviet Union and France, to take account of, and place on their agenda, the situation in Eretz Israel.

For the sake of peace and security, for the sake of the freedom of peoples and for the sake of international justice, Britain must be obliged:

a) To withdraw her Occupation forces from Western and Eastern Eretz Israel,

b) To abolish her illegal Occupation regime, operating directly in Western Eretz Israel and indirectly in Eastern Eretz Israel,

c) To transfer power in Eretz Israel to a democratic repre-sentation of the Hebrew people—to a Hebrew Provisional Government—which will carry out the repatriation of the sons of our people wishing to return to their Homeland, and will hold free elections for the Parliament and Government of our country which will represent all its citizens irrespective of nationality or religion.

Thus one of the most painful problems of humanity will be solved; thus peace and social progress will be assured in Eretz Israel and in the Middle East; thus an end will be put to the state of oppression and war reigning in this historic land and which threatens the peace of the world.

You, representatives of the United States, the Soviet Union and France, can do it. Do it for the sake of that lasting peace, to establish which your Conference is being held after a terrible bloody war that cost our people, bereft of independence, six million victims.

The following appeal was broadcast to the world on 21 August, 1946, in French, English, Russian and Italian.

DO NOT BE ACCOMPLICES TO THE CRIME—
GIVE AID TO JEWISH REPATRIATES

The Nazo-British enslaver has imposed a blockade on our country. It is the most cruel blockade in human history. It is not directed against raw materials or war material brought by sea to a belligerent; it is directed against human beings, against people who for years resisted Nazi-German tyranny, against people who were saved by a miracle from the destroyers, against people who have been left with nothing in their lives except a Homeland—the Homeland which alone can give back to them the reason for living, which must take the place in their lives of their dear ones, who were shot or strangled or buried alive.

The Nazo-British enslaver wants to make you accomplices in his crime and calls to you to help him decide the fate of the remnants of our destroyed people. DO NOT HELP HIM!

You too fought for years against a cruel oppressor, and you learnt that just as peace is indivisible, so is freedom indivisible. If one people is enslaved, other peoples follow. Therefore our war is your war and our victory—your victory. Therefore—help our brothers struggling to their only Homeland! Give them passage across your frontiers, give them shelter in their wanderings; show them the way to the ports; place transport at their disposal. For thus you are helping justice overcome evil, freedom defeat slavery, the victim to overcome the murderous aggressor. Thus you help not only our people, but also yourselves and your future!.

In their effort to break the spirit of the Hebrew people and to induce them to turn informer against the fighting underground, the British Occupiers, early in March, 1947, imposed "martial law," whose immediate purpose was to isolate Jewish centres from one another and from the outside world and to throttle Jewish economic life. But neither the Irgun nor the people was intimidated. The Irgun delivered a unprecedentedly heavy and widespread series of blows at British objectives; the people stood firm. After a fortnight martial law was ignominiously lifted. The Irgun issued the following communique:

WHY THEY LIFTED MARTIAL LAW

The tyrants have been forced to lift Martial Law because:

1) Britain is afraid of international complications. The Soviet Union and Poland could demand discussion by the United Nations Security Council of a state of martial law reigning in time of peace in a country which is formally under international supervision.

2) The blows suffered by the enemy at the hands of the Underground Army in spite of martial law rendered this means of suppression ridiculous.

3) Bitterness bordering on mutiny has become evident in the ranks of the Army of Occupation, whose patrols and camps were subjected to the incessant attacks of the Army of Liberation.

The enemy has suffered a stinging defeat.

The enemy has been compelled to retreat.

But we are singing no victory songs.

We are not fighting for the lifting of decrees. We are fighting for the liberation of our country, for the repatriation of our brothers, for the establishment of our State.

To this end we shall continue to fight until victory. And behind us we shall have the mass of the people, who proved throughout the period of trial that they are indeed worthy of Statehood.

From the depth of the underground we send our greeting to the poor of our people who, subjected to the severest of tribulations, courageously stood the test.

BE STRONG AND OF GOOD COURAGE, BROTHERS—VICTORY WILL COME.

---

*On the eve of the arrival of the United Nations Special Com-
mittee on Palestine on June, 1947, the Irgun issued a warning to
them against the inevitable British attempt to intimidate them and
to spy on them. The Committee subsequently learnt how well-
founded the warning was.*

THE ONLY DANGER TO MEMBERS OF THE UNO COMMITTEE
IS FROM BRITISH SPIES

The Inquiry Committee of the United Nations Organisation is
due to arrive in Eretz Israel in the coming days. From the experience
gained during the stay here of the Anglo-American Committee, it
may be said with certainty that the Nazo-British Occupation regime
will direct at the members of the international committee and at
their assistants a flood of horrific stories of plans for attempts on
their lives by the "terrorists." In order ostensibly to "protect" them,
the representatives of the eleven nations will be surrounded by
British agents who will not allow them to move a step without a
"bodyguard."

The purpose of these horror-stories and "security measures" is
clear to all. Bartley Crum, the member of the Anglo-American
Committee, even exposed it in his book. He knew that he and his
colleagues on the committee—whoever they might be—were in no
danger whatsoever; and that only the desire of the enslavers to
depict the Hebrew underground as a "group of gunmen," lacking
any political roots, and their desire to trail the footsteps of the
committee members—the desire, characteristic of all totalitarian
States, to spy on all visitors likely to keep their eyes open—were the
reason for surrounding the members of the committee with a tribe
of two-legged bloodhounds under the cloak of "protecting them
from attack."

There is no doubt that this miserable spectacle will be repeated
with the members of the international Committee. For this reason
we consider it necessary, even before their arrival, to make it known
that there is no danger to the Committee from Hebrew fighters. In
truth, we are convinced that the members of the Committee do not
require this statement in order to have a feeling of security. They
naturally know that plans for attacks on them, or their assistants, or
their offices, germinate only in the minds of *British provocateurs*,
and that the Hebrew underground, which fights the British enemy,
and only him, knows how to respect guests. But we make the
statement nevertheless because we want the members of the Committee to know in advance that the agents and policemen who will
surround them are not sent to ensure their safety—which nobody
threatens—but to spy on their movements, contacts, letters and so

on. The members of the Committee should beware of the spying eyes and dexterous fingers of the British "security officers."

As for the *general* conditions that will reign in the country during the work of the Committee, these will be dependent on whether the Committee, as the representative of the United Nations Organisation, will succeed in imposing the authority of the United Nations Organisation on the British Occupation regime in regard to the decision of the General Assembly. If the Committee succeeds in preventing the use of force by the enemy against Hebrew repatriates, Hebrew prisoners of war and in other ways, it will prevent *automatically* military attacks by the underground. But if in the very days of the presence here and the work of the Committee the enemy will continue to break the decision of the United Nations Organisation—it will be the duty of the underground to answer force with force.

The key is in the hands of the Committee itself.

The name of Dov Gruner has become history. It has become a symbol of heroism and endurance; a symbol of The Hebrew Struggle for National Liberation. The story of this quiet soldier, standing firm against the strength and intimidations of a mighty Empire, his heroic bearing in life, his dignified calmness in the shadow of the gallows, stirred the world. The cowardly manner in which his British murderers killed him was symbolic of the difference between the ugly purpose which animated them and the nobility of purpose of the Hebrew fighters.

When Dov Gruner was informed of his imminent execution he sent a note to the Commander of the Irgun Zvai Leumi in which he wrote, with characteristic simplicity: "If I had my life to live over again, I would do the same again."

We give here the words of Dov Gruner to the British Military "court" which "sentenced" him to death:

YOUR HAND WILL BE CUT OFF

I do not recognize your right to judge me. This Court has no lawful existence because it has been appointed by a regulation which itself is devoid of any legal basis.

You came to Eretz Israel by reason of an obligation which was entrusted to you by the nations of the world.

You were entrusted with the task of correcting the greatest injustice ever inflicted upon any nation, the injustice of the dispersion of the people of Israel, which made them the world's foremost victims of persecution and massacre. This obligation, and this obligation only, is the legal and moral basis for your presence in this country. You have committed a wicked breach of this obligation, brutally and with satanic treachery. You reduced your obligation to a mere scrap of paper, and then tore it to pieces. Though you did not declare it openly you acted exactly like the German Chancellor Bethman-Hollweg, who said: "What is an international agreement?— Nothing but a scrap of paper. Is it worth quarreling about?" Generally you have learned quite a lot from the Germans. Or perhaps, on the contrary, the Germans learned from you. In any case, in one respect their purpose and yours is identical: the extermination of my people.

For you know only too well that the rape of our country and the closing of its gates means a continuous mass attack on the lives of millions of men, women and children—my people. Notwithstanding this, or perhaps because of it, you are determined to transform this country into one of your military bases, one of the many—and to steal it from the people which has no other home in the world than this, given to it by God and by history. A history sanctified by the blood of generations, a land which has been made to flourish by the blood and sweat of its devoted sons.

After having cancelled and annulled the obligation which you solemnly undertook towards our people and our country you have no right whatsoever to be here. And if you are jurists, gentlemen, you will certainly remember the classic legal principle: If the cause ceases for which the law was enacted then the law itself ceases to exist. The cause for the international law under which you came to administer this country was other than the use to which you have corrupted this sacred trust. It was the revival of the Hebrew state in the country of our forefathers. Thus it is expressly stated, even in the text of the Mandate of the League of Nations. I say "even" because I know from reading the documents how the statesmen endeavoured— and they know how to find ambiguous definitions open to different and contradictory interpretations—to define in well-balanced words that Mandate, signed by fifty-two nations. In spite of their endeavours they failed to render ambiguous two provisions which without any shadow of doubt determine the nature of the obligations which you took upon yourselves.

One provision recognizes the historical connection between the Jewish people and Eretz Israel; and the other provision states that you undertake to reconstruct our National Home. What the historical connection between a nation and its country is, is something I need not explain. And what does "to re-construct" mean? It is only possible to reconstruct what has existed in the past and was destroyed. And what existed in the past in this country? Look into this book lying in front of you, the Bible, and you will learn.

But you mocked at, or attempted in your arrogance to mock at, the Lord's promise, as, in your vanity, you trampled upon the international treaty which you signed with our people and the nations of the world. Therefore nothing has remained of the legal basis of your rule, and it is now based on one principle only: brute force. The bayonet, and a reign of terror in the disguise of so-called "laws." These laws are drafted by the bearers of the bayonets, they promulgate them, they enforce them contrary to the fundamental right of man, contrary to the wishes of the local population and contrary to international laws.

That is why I cannot recognize your competence to try me. Because this, too, was ruled by the ancient Romans: No one can transfer to another more rights than he possesses himself. And if your whole rule is one of unlawful occupation, how can it confer upon you the power to try me, or any other citizen in this occupied country.

When a regime in any country is transformed into a rule of oppression, it ceases to be lawful; it is the right of its citizens— moreover *it is their duty*—to fight against this rule and to overthrow it. This is what the Hebrew youth is doing and this it will continue to do, until you evacuate this country and return it to its lawful owners—to the people of Israel. For this you must know: There is no force in the world that can break the link between the people of Israel and its one and only country. He who attempts this his hand will be cut off and the curse of God will fall upon him for ever and ever.

———————

Mordechai Alkoshi, one of the three Irgun soldiers captured in possession of whips designed to bring retribution on the British Army for their barbaric flogging of a 16-year-old Irgun member, was hanged together with his two immediate comrades—Eliezer Kashani and Dov Rosenbaum— and Dov Gruner. Before being brought to trial he and his comrades were subjected to tortures and humiliations of a kind made notorious by the German Nazis.
Here is his declaration to the "Court" that tried him.

HOW BRITAIN THREATS PRISONERS OF WAR
(Statement by Mordechai Alkoshi)

I want to say a few words about the behaviour of soldiers of enlightened Britain towards Hebrew prisoners of war. I want the whole world to know that at the same time as the denazification of Germany is being carried out (to whatever extent it *is* being carried out) there is in process the nazification of Britain and her armies. And here are the practical proofs:

After our capture on the road near Lydda one of our comrades was injured, not at all seriously, but he died after being transferred to the hand of the British Army.

As for us, we were brought, under a rain of blows, to one of your military camps, where we were immediately taken to an isolated room. British soldiers began tearing our clothes off us, not with their hands but with razor blades. Our clothes were torn; our flesh was torn too. We were beaten over the head and on the body with rifle-butts. We bled all over. But your soldiers were not satisfied. They took us out, naked as we were, and made us run round the camp, while other soldiers stood around and laughed. Our legs faltered, and we fell. They lifted us up, made us run again and beat us. Then they took us back to the room. They gave us no clothes. They gave each of us a sheet. But every few minutes one of the sadists would come into the room and pull the sheets off our naked, shivering and bleeding bodies. The next morning the tortures continued. They made us kiss the ground. They pulled out our hair and ordered us to sweep the floor with it. They poured dirty water over us three times and then again made us run naked round the camp. Then they began concerning themselves with our health. We were brought before a military doctor. After he had looked at us, he asked your fine boys: "Do you want to play with them a little longer?" Of course they did. And at the orders of the doctor, the comrade of the well-known doctors of Belsen, we were brought back to the camp, where the blows, the tortures and the humiliations were repeated.

These, British officers, are your features. This is the slumbering beast awakening inside the defenders of your Empire. This is how you treat prisoners. Do you wonder then that we are filled not only with disgust for you, but with the ever-deepening belief that you are destined to disappear off the stage as Adolf Hitler disappeared? An army that does what was done to us is not an army. It is a filthy gang, lacking all human feeling or human dignity, which threatens the foundations of human civilisation.

We have determined to purify the Holy Land of this Nazi filth; and no sacrifice will be too great for us to fulfil this historic duty, imposed on us not only by our freedom-loving people but by the whole of progressive humanity.

———————

Several hours before they were due to be hanged in May, 1947, by the British in Jerusalem Gaol, Meir Feinstein, a soldier of the Irgun, and Moshe Barzani (of the F.F.I.) blew themselves up in their cell. This is the declaration Meir Feinstein had made to his "judges."

[DECLARATION OF MEIR FEINSTEIN]

Officers of the Occupation Army,

A regime of gallows—that is the regime you want to establish in this country, which was destined to serve as a lighthouse for the whole of humanity. And in your stupid wickedness you assume that by this regime you will succeed in breaking the spirit of our people, the people to whom the whole land has become a gallows. You are mistaken. You will learn that what you have come up against is steel, steel tempered by the fire of love and of hatred—love of the Home-land and of freedom, hatred for the enslaver and invader. It is burning steel. You will not break it. You will burn your hands.

How blind you are, British tyrants! Have you not discovered yet who it is standing against you in this struggle, which has no prece-dent in human history? Do you think you will frighten *us* with death? We, who for years listened to the rattle of the wheels of those trucks that bore our brothers, our parents, the best of our people, to a slaughter which, too, has no precedent in human history? We, who asked and ask ourselves every day: How are we better than they, than millions of our brothers? In what lies our virtue? For we could have been among and with them in the days of fear and in the moments that came before death.

And to these recurring questions our conscience makes one reply: We remained alive not in order to live, in conditions of slavery and oppression, and wait for some new Treblinka. We remained alive in order to ensure life and freedom and honour for ourselves, for our people, for our children and for our children's children for ever. We remained alive in order that there should not be repeated what happened there and what has happened here and is likely to happen under your rule, the rule of treachery, the rule of blood.

Therefore, we shall not be frightened. We have learnt—and at what price in vain sacrifices!—that there is a life that is worse than death and there is a death that is greater than life. And if you have not yet understood this phenomenon of a people that has nothing to lose but the shackles of slavery and the "prospect" of a new Maidanek—it is a sign that you have been smitten with blindness, in order that you should leave the stage of history, from which the Almighty removes all those who rise up against the eternal people to destroy it. Assyria and Babylon, Greece and Rome, Spain and Germany came before you—and you will follow in their footsteps. It is an everlasting law.

That is what I wanted to tell you, British officers, you and those who sent you. As for me I have nothing to add beyond what my comrade has told you: I am a prisoner of war and demand the status of a prisoner of war.

Three soldiers of the Irgun Zvai Leumi are, at the moment of publication, in the death cell at Acre prison fortress, "sentenced" for participation in the attack on that fortress on June 4, 1947—an attack which, for the first time in history, broke open the walls of what the British have made the Bastille of Eretz Israel. Tens of Hebrew prisoners of war were liberated in the attack, described even by the enemy as a strategic masterpiece.

The three captives, Avshalom Haviv, Meir Nakar and Jacob Weiss knew the likely fate that would await them at the end of their "trial" by the British barbarians.

We give here the addresses made to the "Court" by the three. Avshalom Haviv dealt first with the treatment by British "soldiers" of their captives.

THE LESSON OF IRELAND
(Statement by Avshalom Haviv)

Officers of the Occupation Army,

After your brains and your heroism had proved incapable of preventing the breaking open of the walls of the Eretz Israel Bastille, blind chance helped you and gave you a mighty "victory" over some of the escaping prisoners, who were unarmed, and over the three of us after our ammunition had run out. And this gave you an opportunity to satisfy your sadism and compensate your inferiority complex. Your men behaved in the best Nazi tradition. They shot wounded men lying on the ground, they allowed no first aid for hours. They abused me particularly. They threatened me with death, they tied ropes around my neck, beat me with rifle-butts and kicked me in the most delicate parts of my body. When I fainted they brought me round with British urine mixed with sand and with my own blood. I am not telling you this in order to complain. I would not complain before you. God forbid. But the peoples of the world should know the horrible acts carried out by the British beasts of prey in this country.

I assume that you know the bloodstained history of your rule in Ireland. You will probably remember that there too you seized a small country and cultured people by force of arms and deceit, under the cloak of religion and under the cover of "law and order."

You will probably remember that there too you exploited the marrow of the bones of the working people and sowed discord among the various classes in order to maintain your rule. And when the sons of Ireland rose up against you, when the Irish underground started their fight against you, you tried to drown the rising against tyranny in rivers of blood. You set up gallows, you murdered in the streets, you exiled, you ran amok, and believed in your stupidity that by dint of persecution you would break the spirit of resistance of the free Irish, the spirit of resistance which is the gift of God to every man worthy of the name. You erred, Irish resistance grew in intensity. The blood of the fighters and of the tortured only solidified the people round the banner of revolt, until you were forced to retreat, leaving behind you ineradicable bloodstains and unforgettable memories. Free Ireland arose in spite of you.

Your supercilious rulers are really very ignorant. I refer not only to Bevin, who suddenly discovered that there are 4000 million people in the world. I refer also to those among you who know at least that there are only rather more than 2000 million people on earth at the moment. All of them are ignoramuses. All are blind. For they have not learnt the two foundations of life, and they will never know them. They are: the lessons of history and the spirit of man.

If you were wise, British tyrants, and learnt from history, the example of Ireland, or of America, would be enough for you to understand that you ought to hurry to leave this country of ours, enveloped in the flames of holy revolt which are not extinguished but, on the contrary, flare up the more with every drop of blood shed by you or in the fight against you. You would then pay heed to the words of warning uttered in the days of the Irish rising, in 1916, by Bernard Shaw, after your hangmen had murdered four Irish prisoners of war. Bernard Shaw is an Irishman, who became an English writer, steeped in your culture and living among you. And yet he had the courage to say these words to you:

> "My view is that the men who were shot in cold blood after their capture were prisoners of war, and that it was therefore entirely incorrect to slaughter them. An Irishman resorting to arms to achieve the independence of his country is doing only what Englishmen will do if it be their misfortune to be invaded and conquered by the Germans. The fact that he knows that his enemies will not respect his rights if they catch him, and that he must therefore fight with a rope round his neck, increases his risk, but in the same measure adds to his glory, in the eyes of his compatriots and of the admirers of patriotism throughout the world. The shot Irishmen will now take their place beside the Irish martyrs who came before them and beside the heroes of Poland and Serbia and Belgium, and nothing in Heaven or earth can prevent it. . . ."

These words were uttered by a wise man who is regarded as a cynic, thirty years ago and were vindicated to the hilt. And if your rulers were to study anew the results of wars for freedom, as we study them; if they were to consider the conclusions to be drawn from the words of Bernard Shaw and from the well-known developments that followed the murder of the Irish prisoners—they would long ago have foregone the attempt to crush, with the aid of gallows or the sword, the rising of a freedom-loving people. But, as I have said, they are blind and will not learn. And who knows? Perhaps this blindness has been given by the Almighty in order to bring upon you, in the course of time, retribution for all the blood and tears you have spilt in our country and outside it?

But not only the lesson of history have you, British tyrants, failed to learn. You also do not know the spirit of man. You believe that with a given number of armed soldiers and of tried intrigues it will be possible for you to maintain your rule over a country in revolt, whose inhabitants—all of them—regard you as invaders, sowing friction and exploiting. It is a fatal error. Neither the sword nor intrigues can stand up for long against the *spirit of man*, the spirit of *free* man. For this spirit can do wonders. It will continue to fight, to revolt and to inspire revolt, even if you deprive it of its transient body. But you, preachers of the idea of race, who regard yourselves as supreme rulers and other peoples as inferiors, you whose empty pride has robbed you of sanity, what have you to do with the spirit of free man who is ready to risk his life, and even to sacrifice it, for freedom?

It is no wonder, therefore, that you have failed to understand also the spirit of the new Hebrew generation. You wonder: "How come that these Jews, who we thought were cowards, who were the victims of slaughter for generations, have risen against our rule, fight our armies, mock at our orders and, when they stand in the shadow of death, hold death in contempt? How come that because of these Jews we are forced to shut ourselves in ghettoes, in which too we find no peace?"

You wonder, do you not? Yet the thing is simpler than you imagine. The spiritual character of our generation has been determined by two factors. By the soil of the Homeland and by the catastrophe in the Diaspora. It is the soil of the Homeland which has revitalized us and has given power to our muscles, courage to our hearts, belief in our future, which has restored to us in *practice* the tradition which our people carried in its heart for many generations: the tradition of heroism of the Maccabeans and of Bar-Kochba.

And the catastrophe in the Diaspora taught us that we are in a battle not only for our freedom but for our very existence. It taught us that perpetuation of slavery means extermination for all of us. It taught us that if we do not take our fate in our hands, we shall go down to the grave, that if we do not fight—we shall be destroyed.

And that is why fear has departed from the hearts of each one of us. Yes, British officers, there stand before you people not only here but throughout the country, who are no longer afraid. For what should we fear? Should death awaken fear in the hearts of sons of a people, millions of whose sons were killed in one nightmare night without reason and without purpose? When we remember our brothers who were destroyed—and we remember them always—our hearts are happy that we were enabled not to be [c]rushed like them, that we have been given the sacred privilege of *fighting* for our country, of living on the soil of our country, of writing a chapter—a heroic chapter—in our history, and of leaving a heritage, not of cowardice and slaughter, but of courage and of a war of liberation, for coming generations.

You, British tyrants, will never understand the spirit of free men, going towards death, as Dov Gruner and his comrades went— with a song bursting from their hearts, from their believing and loving hearts. And this too you will probably not understand: I, a young Hebrew, facing the threat of death, lift my heart to my God in Heaven, and give praise and thanks for the privilege that has been given me to suffer for my people and my country, and say with all my being:

"Blessed art thou, O Lord, King of the Universe, who hath kept us alive and maintained us and enabled us to attain this season!"

BRITISH BANKRUPTS AND BEGGARS
(Statement by Meir Nakar)

British Officers,

As we stand before you we ask ourselves: before *whom* are we standing? You call yourselves judges. We know that you are not judges but officers of an alien occupation army which has established itself by force in the country of another people and holds on to it for its own purposes, with the cruel clamp of oppression. But this is not the whole reply. For the question does not refer to you personally, but rather to those who sent you, to the tyrannical regime which has made you the judges of the free citizens of this country. Who is this regime?

This can be answered in the words uttered by the delegate of the Soviet Union in the General Assembly of the United Nations Organisation: British rule in Eretz Israel has gone bankrupt. And that is not the opinion only of Mr. Gromyko. All the world knows that you are bankrupts in Eretz Israel, just as in America you are beggars. A Government whose officials have to sit in ghettoes—is this a Government? A Government which spends about half the budget on police purposes and nevertheless remains helpless in face of the anger of the people in revolt—is this a Government?

One could bring many facts to prove that your rule here has bankrupted, and there is no power on earth that can save it from disintegration or withdrawal. But perhaps the following fact is most characteristic. The members of your Parliament argued a few months ago that there is only one way to crush the Hebrew revolt, and that is: to set up gallows in the Holy Land, to murder Hebrew prisoners. And you did it. You committed one of the basest crimes: You murdered prisoners of war! And what did you achieve? Did you succeed in frightening anybody? Did you weaken our people's urge for freedom? Did you succeed in crushing the national uprising? You know that you achieved nothing. The flame of revolt is spreading in this country and outside it. And you—you have brought only ever-lasting shame on yourselves by killing prisoners, which has been regarded everywhere and in every period as a crime against humanity.

In other words: even this crime did not help your rule, and your bankruptcy is *absolute*. And this being so, it is better for you to draw conclusions quickly. A regime which has failed in every sphere and in all its attempts at domination—must go.

And indeed, British bankrupts, the time has come for you to leave this country. It was ours and will remain ours. And we shall build it as a country of freedom, of peace and of progress—to eternal glory.

Your rulers feel insulted when people compare them to Nazis. When young Jews in New York paint the swastika on your flag your newspapers complain and your diplomats protest. Nevertheless you ought to think for a moment whether it is really possible to clean your flag of the swastika, which has been attached to it not by other hands but by your own.

For what does the swastika in our days represent? It represents the enslavement of peoples, the murder of masses, the cruelty of a wild beast, degeneration, corruption and many other things charac-teristic of the terrible moral deterioration of humanity. But above all—and this even you will admit—this unclean symbol represents the killing of Jews. Yes, the swastika will be remembered for genera-tions to come as the noose of strangulation placed by the mes-sengers of Satan round the necks of a whole people. It is a rule: the bearer of the swastika is a killer of Jews; the killer of Jews—bears a swastika, if not on his lapel then inside his heart. And now, British officers, ask yourselves, what task does Britain fulfil in this generation since the destruction of the killer of Jews in Berlin? Is it not a fact that she has taken from his hands the swastika and what goes with it? Is not Britain the only State in the world which as a State—as a State—kills Jews? Are not British soldiers today killing Jews in Jerusalem and in Famagusta, in Haifa and in the Sudan, in Eretz

Israel and in Europe? Is not Britain holding tens of thousands of Jews in concentration camps? Does not Britain threaten the lives of our people wherever they are to be found?

Britain—is killing Jews. That is the task you have taken on yourselves, that is the name you have given yourselves throughout the world. You will not be washed clean of it, just as Nazi Germany will never be washed clean. What use is it if you scratch the sign of the swastika off the Union Jack, off your flag? For it is not ordinary glue that attaches it to you but something which cannot be removed. It is attached to you with blood, with the blood of our brothers, which you have shed throughout the world, which you are continuing to shed here and outside our country.

Yes, Britain—a gigantic swastika today covers you, just as the hatred which it represents has filled your heart. You have accepted a mission: to finish what your teacher Hitler did not manage to finish. Therefore, like him, so will you too leave the stage of history and you will be inscribed in history with a name that will pursue you to eternity: killer of Jews. But you will not fulfil your plans. Just as the Nazo-German swastika was smashed, so will the Nazo-British swastika be smashed. God who helped David defeat Goliath will help the bearers of the Star of David defeat the bearers of the swastika, who defile the Holy Land.

Long live the people of Israel. Long live the Hebrew Homeland. Long live freedom.

AN APPEAL TO UNO
(Statement by Jacob Weiss)

Officers of the Occupation Army,

I cannot begin without exposing the barbaric maltreatment of wounded prisoners which I witnessed when I was captured. Ashbel, Amrani, Brenner, Benado, Daar, Moscovitch, Shmukler and others had scores of bullets shot at them at short range in spite of the fact they were unarmed—for they were not among the attackers but among the escaping prisoners. But your soldiers' efficiency is still low, and in spite of the many wounds inflicted, many of them did not die immediately and were brought bleeding to the courtyard of the police station. There they were thrown on the ground—not, God forbid, on a stretcher—and they lay thus for six hours while their blood flowed like water. Dozens of beasts in the image of human beings stood around with their hands in their pockets. Their only concern was to prevent us from bringing first aid. And in fact they succeeded in thus killing Ashbel, and Brenner, and Benado, and Amrani and Nissim Levi. It is obvious that these base murders will not succeed in frightening anybody. They will open the eyes of the people to see *whom* it is we are fighting. And if in the past you have enjoyed the advantages of a belligerent, in the future no doubt the law of retaliation will be applied; and though we shall not compete with you in the maltreatment of wounded men and in sadism, you will, for the rest be repaid in full.

And now as to what you call a "trial."

We do not recognise your right to try us, free citizens of the Hebrew Homeland, and we do not intend to take any part in these proceedings which you, in mockery and insult of the noble tradition of civilized humanity, call "justice."

Everything you are doing in this country is illegal. Your rule is illegal; your "courts" are illegal; your laws, which issue from the most totalitarian regime of all times, are illegal; and your very presence here, against which all revolt, is illegal. This country is ours, from time immemorial and for all future to come. What have you, British officers, to do with our country. Who has made you the rulers of an ancient, cultured and freedom-loving people? Who has appointed you judges over the people which gave the world the God of justice and righteousness when your people still inhabited the wild forests?

But your rule in this country is approaching its end. All the world knows it. And you know it too. You will not be able to stay here much longer. You have done all that cruel enslavers can do to grip the country in the shackles of slavery and to break the spirit of its citizens and rightful owners. You concentrated mighty military camps; you surrounded yourselves with scores of kilometres of barbed wire; you have spent millions on police and secret police; you have beaten, you have deported, you have threatened, you have introduced so-called laws the like of which did not exist even in Hitler Germany. And this also you have done: you murdered Hebrew prisoners, you led the best of the Hebrew youth to the gallows. And what has been the result? You have not only not broken the spirit of the Hebrew resistance but, on the contrary, before your very eyes, despite the gallows and perhaps because of the gallows, it is getting stronger and stronger, so that your Churchill is compelled to weep over his Empire, mocked and hated throughout the world because of the "squalid war" it is waging in the Holy Land.

In this situation, which all of the world regards as the bank-ruptcy of your rule, you were compelled to bring the problem of Eretz Israel before the United Nations Organisation. Of course your representatives did not go before the international institution with pure motives. It is not justice that they seek there, but authority to perpetuate your rule and a free hand for your cruelties. But the United Nations Organisation, in spite of the satellites of Britain sitting there, is not yet subject to the discipline of your rulers. Not all that you desired did you achieve there, or are able to achieve. And the first proof of this is the decision of the General Assembly to call both on *Governments* and on *peoples* to refrain from the use of force during the work of the International Committee on Palestine.

There is no ambiguity in this decision, seeing that your Government is the *only* Government using force in this country. It is obvious that it is she who was called upon by the General Assembly of UNO to stop threatening or using force until UNO reaches a decision. Your Government will be obliged to submit to this decision or to accept full responsibility for the breach of this decision. In this case I have no doubt that the countries who are not your satellites and who gave their names to this resolution will not permit you to make a mockery of the will of the international institution and of their signatures. UNO will demand that you carry out its decisions.

The peoples of the world know that to maintain military courts in a country not your own; to make alien officers judges of free citizens; and to threaten the murder of prisoners, is to threaten the use of force. Persistence in this course, which is intolerable in any circumstances, becomes, in the light of the decision of UNO, an international crime, and outrage against all the peoples who gave their support to this decision.

Consequently, from this place in which the decision of the peoples is being pridefully trampled upon, we call the United Nations Organisation, on its fact-finding Committee and to all the independent States who voted for the Norwegian resolution, that they intervene and that they do not permit the British enslavers, who break the laws of humanity, to place Hebrew citizens before a military court and to murder Hebrew prisoners. We hold your threats of murder in contempt, but we are certain that international intervention will come, now that this time, there have been placed in the scales, among other factors, the honour of humanity and the honour of many free States.

As for us—we know that there will be one result to this fight: our people will attain its freedom and its enslaver will depart from the stage of history. That is why we are composed. More than that: we are happy. For there can be no greater happiness than to give our life for a great ideal and to know, to know absolutely, that we are— directly—among those who are bringing about its fulfilment.

Listen, you British officers, and tell it to your rulers, who have been smitten with blindness and do not see the hand inscribing the great warning on the wall; tell them that there has risen to the people of Israel in this country a new generation, a generation that loves life, a generation that loves freedom *more* than life, a generation that will make the Nazo-British tyranny crumble, and will achieve freedom—even at the price of life.

The Jewish people lives. The Jewish State will surely arise.

II
THE PREWAR PERIOD (1936–39)

Heads Up!

Advance proof of editorial to appear in "World Jewry" New Year's issue, September, 1936.

We face the saddest of all the New Years since the defeat of Bar Kochba, by Julius Severus, who was brought from England by Hadrian, to conquer the Jewish forces. Hitler has smashed us in Germany, Mosley pesters us in England. The Nazis hold Austria and Roumania in the hollow of their unclean hand. Poland has provided us with a year of unceasing pain. The "balance sheet," which appears elsewhere in this issue, tells a terrible story. We have grown used to it. We have almost become callous to bad news, and expect no good.

Worse than all these things we have been stricken in the house of a presumed friend. England has outranged Hitler in the suffering she has caused us. A fool's paradise disappears, an illusion fades in the smoke of Arab guns. In a thousand forms, in a million words, high and low, wise and simple, we had faith in England, we believed in the British word. British honor lent pinions to our imaginations. Vanished! A sand castle undermined by a display of Arab terrorism. The thing was not, but it is hard to believe we were all fools, all blinded to the truth. We hug the illusion, for it is hard to break with it. It was ours—the first born of a new epoch in our blood drenched history is dead. Weep not. Heads up, dry eyes.

Yesterday is dead. Something has gone out of us that will not return. Great Britain has forfeited our confidence. Hitler wants to slay our bodies. England has determined to crush our hope, our outlook on life, to end those tomorrows that make existence possible. Smitten in every direction. Today gone. Tomorrow shall not be. Heads up, dry eyes.

No skulking, no lying, no subterfuge, no self-exculpation. We refuse to hide behind the misdeeds of the Palestine Administration.

That robot has performed according to orders. It is a mechanism whose wires are operated from London. We have no quarrel with the tool. Who tries to fool us in that respect is only fooling himself, and will suffer for his folly.

We have accepted sixteen years of misdirection, sixteen years of ever growing humiliations, in little things and in great things. "There is no righteous man on earth." We have all sinned, for in different degrees we have all believed in the mirage of a British alliance in the upbuilding of the Jewish National Home. Myth, legend, fantasy. We were the tool of an imperialism which has found a better or a more useful, or for its purpose, a more pliable tool. Let our children discuss why this was. Our task is to take a new position, to start a new struggle, to forge new weapons for a new fight.

We must become a purely political organization, uniting every possible Jew to a single purpose, for a single object, to shake off from Palestine the Mandatory Power which has rejected us in the hour of our greatest achievement, at the moment when millions of footsteps seek to hasten to Zion.

We must buy no land in Palestine. We must not enrich the Arabs so they can slay us at our expense. We must plant no new trees so that Arabs may win glory by their destruction. There is no security in Palestine. The Yishub is merely—the front line of a struggling force. We must strengthen it in man power, in numbers. We must refuse to be denied admission to Eretz Yisrael except at the point of a gun. Dry eyes and heads up. Against British steel Missi Jehudah "The stone hard as a Jew." It is an Arab term. We must make it true.

It is a political and a legal struggle against the greatest power in the world. David against Goliath. Judas Maccabeus against the Greek-Syrian hosts. We must make the Diaspora serve the Geulah. Struggle, not protest, in every land, in every form. We must organize resolutely to this end, and for no other purpose to avert doom and destruction.

It matters not whether the gates of Palestine be formally closed, or left partially ajar; whether the British yield two, or three, or all points demanded by the Arabs. It matters not whether at the last moment in these negotiations all the Arab demands are exchanged for an agreement to establish the Legislative Council. All these are petty details, tricks performed to mislead us, to quiet us, and We are ashamed to say they may be accepted, to justify a campaign and a collection.

We need money, much money for a wide and thorough political struggle, which will include the self-defense of the Jews in Palestine. Men and women cannot be too generous in helping in this holy struggle. But we must do nothing that enriches the Arabs, that helps Great Britain in creating a Crown Colony at our expense, with our investments, so that she may effectively bury the hope and the need of the Jewish people.

It is a hard and a trying doctrine. It will require great self-restraint. Some of the work of the last twenty years will go to smash. It is all crystal clear to us. But we have no option. We cannot say contradictory words at the same time and expect either the Jews, or the rest of the world, to understand us. Every penny available must go for this great struggle on every political and legal front, as every thought must be concentrated on the many phases and opportunities it presents. But not a cent for tribute.

The organization of the struggle, and the means and methods of it are matters for counsel and conference. We will go with all those who will go with us. The fight can be waged. Battles will be lost, but the war can be won. It is for every one of us, old and young, to dedicate himself anew to our people's cause. We went with England. She has broken faith. She has spurned us. She has forsaken us. Men will phrase it in a hundred ways. No more pleading, no more piteous telegrams, no more marching up Scopus to the High Commissioner. No more cap in hand to Whitehall. The roads separate. We must go forward without England, against England. The Royal Commission does not exist for us. Palestine is not British territory, and we must unmake British claims to rule our land.

We stand at another Masada. We repeat with Eleazar ben Jair: "Though he might live without either fear or danger can any man be so unnatural. . . . so mean and narrow spirited, as not to grieve that he has lived to see this day?" With him we stand erect, dry eyed. Courage, brothers. Endurance, men. Persistence, women. God keep you, children. Fate decrees. Heads up to the New Year. We pray for victory. "Here we stand, we have no other way."

To All Englishmen

A long time before the Balfour Declaration was given and twenty years thereafter, the Jewish People saw in Great Britain the symbol of Freedom, Firmness and Fidelity to the promise given to their persecuted and tortured race to build up their Homeland in the Land of their forefathers.

During the twenty years that passed, hundreds of thousands of Jews settled in Palestine, established hundreds of flourishing settlements, drained swamps and founded a faithful basis to British Rule in Palestine.

During the last three years of havoc and destruction, while in the predominantly Arab parts of the country, marauders left loose, murdered sisters of mercy, threw bombs upon children and slaughtered school children in Tiberias—the Jewish settlements and Jewish cities offered the only true shelter where British soldiers could rest, in a calm atmosphere from the atrocities of the Arab terror.

The Jews ventured to hope that at this most critical period in the History of their Nation, when brutal forces are driving hundreds of thousands of their brethren out of various Countries, when they are being robbed of their belongings, when their brethren are being locked up and tortured in concentration camps—they hoped that Great Britain in whom they had put their faith, would be their defender and last refuge.

This hope is now lost; terrible and menacing news are coming and it appears that the Jews of Palestine who are expecting hundreds of thousands of their brethren who are on the verge of destruction wherever they live, are being forced to surrender to their foes, to savages coming from the Desert who plunder and destroy everything which has been created with unceasing toil and unending solicitude.

ENGLISHMEN! Can you not understand that the Arabs who are daily firing and throwing bombs at you, who are rendering your children orphans, are not fighting only against the Jews?

Can you not understand that the Arabs are fighting the stranger and that after "solving" the problem of the Jews of Palestine by giving them the status of a minority, WOULD TURN AGAINST YOU, ENGLISHMEN and solve the English problem by means of bombs and bullets?

BRITISH SOLDIERS! Can you not understand the spirit that animates the Jewish National Youth in Palestine whose rifles have always been directed only against the Arabs, thus becoming your natural allies?

REMEMBER! that even after the execution of Ben-Yoseph at the news of which our Nation shuddered both in Palestine and abroad, no English blood has ever smeared Jewish hands.

YOU SHOULD UNDERSTAND that their duty is to fight to the end for their Homeland just as it is yours to fight for the Empire and for the future of your Nation.

Can you not understand that the Jews would be loyal to the British only as long as the British are loyal to the Jews and Zionism?

The National Military Organisation of Palestine

[A Letter]

September 12

Sir,

We were greatly surprised to hear that the British Administration in Jaffa yielded to the orders of the Arab gangsters and have evacuated that town. We would have considered it much fairer and more suitable, had the Servants of Great Britain crushed the nests of the Arab gangs instead of obeying their orders. But, since it so already happened, we are taking the liberty to make the following observations:—

The greater number of you has moved to the German Sarona to find refuge there and only those who could not find suitable accommodation in Sarona, have settled in hotels at Tel-aviv. May we remark that, if you find Sarona to be a safe shelter, it is not because it is inhabited by Germans, but only because it is surrounded by Jewish settlements and bordering with Tel-aviv.

The feelings of Germany towards Great Britain is well known to you from your experience during the great war as well as during the last years. Furthermore, you also know well that the fire-arms with which the Arab terrorists attack and murder are smuggled in from Germany (Except, of course, those arms stolen from Police Stations and Military Barracks. . .). And, must it be mentioned that the Arab gangs are trained and instructed by Hitler's delegates? The only conclusion is, therefore, that not the German inhabitants of Sarona will not safeguard you and your families from Arab bullets, but as we have already said above, the fact that Sarona is surrounded by Jewish settlements gives you security.

But, instead of, appreciating the fact that only in Jewish settlements you can find your safety, and instead of fostering the friendship with the Jews, the British Admisitration [sic] behaves in such a manner which is not at all likely to keep the so much needed friendship with the Jews.

The anti-Jewish policy of the Southern District's Authorities,
The arrests of the Jewish National Youth,
The searches for arms amongst Jews, instead of giving them the possibility to defend themselves against Arab murderers,
The brutal and disgraceful behaviour of the British Constables during the demonstrations of the Jewish Youth at the execution of Ben-Joseph,
All this EMBITTERS THE HEARTS OF THE JEWISH NATIONAL YOUTH.

Therefore, we address you with the following:—
REMEMBER, THAT IF YOU WANT TO KEEP AND FOSTER THE FRIENDSHIP WITH A NATION COMPRISING 18 MILLION PEOPLE, A NATION THAT HAS ALREADY SHOWN HIS FRIENDSHIP TO GREAT BRITAIN DURING THE LAST WORLD WAR (the Jewish Batallions which took part in delivering Palestine from Turkey, the Jewish Intelligence Service against Turkey and in favour of Great Britain) A NATION THAT CAN HELP YOU ALSO IN THE FORTHCOMING WAR:—

DO NOT ADD TO THE SUFFERINGS OF THE JEWISH NATION!
CHANGE YOUR INTOLERABLE ATTITUDE TOWARDS OUR NATION!
DO NOT TEMPT THE PATIENCE OF THE JEWISH NATIONAL YOUTH!
LEST OUR NATIONAL YOUTH MAY LET LOOSE HIS NERVES!

Friends

British Constables and Soldiers of H.M. Forces in Palestine!

The Jewish youth in Palestine as well as the whole Jewish people, were in the last years, subjected to a bitter disappointment, through the Government of Palestine. But in spite of that, the Jews want to believe yet in England, as they believed in England twenty one years ago *when they gave soldiers to Great-Britain.*

We are convinced, that the common interests of the British Empire and the Jewish people, in Palestine, will oblige England to change her policy toward the Jews, and to help them to reestablish their historic state, undivided, on both sides of the Jordan.

You have founded a mighty British Empire, and are very experienced colonisators.

You have introduced white rule and European culture and civilization to backward natives, in spite of their great resistance.

But we, Jews, don't want to colonise some strange country, we want our home back!

We, as a homeless people demand the reestablishment of our historic state in our fatherland!

The Arabs, inhabiting large tracks of land and own states (Iraq, Saudi-Arabia, Egypt, Yemen, Syria a.s.o.), attempt to rob the Jews of their little homeland. They attempt it by force already more than 26 months, against the British, as Mandatory, as well as against Jews.

British constables and soldiers!

You know too well that the Arabs are our common enemies. There never was a common front for Britain and the Arabs—never in the History—since the crusades until now. It is now merely getting rid of the Jews, what they desire; they want to expel British rule and influence from the Near East, whereby depriving the British Empire of its most important communications.

During the world-war they fought against the Turks not for the British Empire,—they fought for money and gold! (see Lawrence). *And now they are fighting against you, supported and lead by Italians and Germans!*

Remember that the Jewish regiments, the 38, 39, 40 and 41 Royal Fusiliers fought in Palestine under the Union-Jack and together with your brethren and fathers.

In spite of all what happened during the last two years, we still believe in the partnership between the British and the Jews.

British constables and soldiers!

You realize only too well what dangers await the Englishman in Nablus, Tulkarm, Jenin, and all other places intrabited [sic] by Arabs. You cannot have forgotten your comrades, who were killed by the same people, who have killed our comrades. You must realise and appreciate the safety you enjoy in Jewish settlements.

Do not fail to realize these facts!

Do not try to back those who desire to get rid of Great Britain in Palestine! Do not back those who desire to expel the British Empire of the Meditteranean!

Remember t h a t, when you are thinking about the difficulties of this country,

Remember t h a t, when you are on duty,

Remember t h a t, when you are sent to beat Jews,

Remember t h a t the same boys who demonstrate in the streets, whom you are made to fight with, are not your real enemies!

Look for the enemy where he is really to be found!

The Irgun Zevai Leumi in Eretz Israel (I.Z.L.)

Following the publication of MacDonald's White Paper on Palestine in May 1939, the following statement has been released by the command of the I.Z.L. for publication in the Press.

I.Z.L. Headquarters, Jerusalem, June 1939

The I.Z.L. was founded in the conviction that the solution of the Jewish problem through the creation of a Jewish Sovereign State within the historical boundaries of Palestine cannot be achieved without relying on a Jewish Military Force.

I. REASONS UNDERLYING THE ESTABLISHMENT OF THE I.Z.L.

1. The historical fact that the reclaiming of a homeland, independence and liberty of an oppressed nation never succeeds without the support of an adequate military force ready to stand up to threat and challenge.

2. The troubles in Palestine of 1920, 1921 and 1929 have proved conclusively that the Arabs use armed violence as a recurrent means to obstruct the establishment of the Jewish State, and

that the passive attitude of the Jews in face of this violence is only encouraging Arab terrorists to continue.

3. We cannot depend on the Mandatory Power to check Arab violence and keep Palestine in a state of peace, which is the preliminary condition for the development of a Jewish State. The British Administration in Palestine is outspokenly anti-Zionist and anti-Jewish. Arab violence was instigated, favored and allowed to continue by this same administration as a means to "justify" the whittling down of the ever-hated, by them, Balfour Declaration and Mandate, a process which culminated in MacDonald's White Paper of May, 1939.

4. Assuming even that we are free from British hostility in Palestine, it is essential in the present state of world affairs, that we prove to the world that our right to a Jewish State is not only an historical and human right but that we are ready and prepared to back it with military force, rather than relying on British bayonets.

5. In the event of war Palestine will be a most precious strategical point in the Near East, of the greatest concern to the Western European Democracies. It will be an all-important highway and air route to the Far East, an oil reservoir for the British and French navy and air fleet. Purely rational and sentimental claims of Jewry to Palestine will be even less respected by Great Britain in case of war than they were in times of peace. Only as an armed force of sufficient strength to assure the defense of Palestine shall we be able to attain a bargaining position which will induce Britian to agree to the creation of the Jewish State. In this conviction, the I.Z.L. is preparing to widen its cadres considerably, so that in case of war, over 100,000 trained, disciplined and partially equipped men be concentrated by it in Palestine.

II. STRUCTURE OF THE I.Z.L.

New recruits are enlisted by recommendation of veteran members. Before taking the oath of secrecy and allegiance a newcomer is under full surveillance and has to pass a special test. Everyone, irrespective of party, is accepted, provided he adheres to the governing principles of the Organization.

The principles governing the I.Z.L. are strict military discipline and hierarchy. The I.R.A. and similar national revolutionary organizations who fought for the liberty of their nations serve as an example. The organization is illegal in Palestine, hundreds of its members are in prison and suffering persecution in the hands of the British Administration. Some have become permanent invalids; several scores have died in action.

At the head of the I.Z.L. is the commander and the command. Under them is the general-staff composed of all the heads of departments. Officers, rank and file are organized in small secret units. Training is done secretly. Each member knows only his friends in the unit and his direct officer. He has no means of contact with other units. Each officer knows only his direct superior. All the strings are carefully concentrated in the command. The military order is the only means of unification. Nothing but the military order forms the direct contact between all members and the command. Under this system the command controls many thousands of people without fear of a major attack on behalf of the authorities in Palestine.

III. ACTIVITIES

1. *Military.* Fighting Arab terror by defense and retaliation measures. Since the publication of the White Paper in the beginning of May, 1939, the Organization is engaged in active resistance against Britain and the Arabs with the aim to defy the new Ukases. Already today, it is clear to Britain and the Arabs that no decision can be taken in Palestine without taking into account the reaction of the National Military Organization. Daily our military activities increase, and it is only the beginning of a warning that a Jewish Ghetto in Palestine will be established only over our dead bodies. In short, the I.Z.L. is the only body conducting the active resistance against the White Paper as reported in the world press. For us it is a battle for death or life.

2. *"Aliya Beth" (Extra-legal immigration).* It is a God-given right of the Jews to return to Palestine as free men to their fatherland. This right dates from times immemorial and was again asserted, in modern times, by the whole civilized world, in the Mandate for Palestine. Britain's action in closing the doors of Palestine for persecuted Jews is an act of black treason against a people with its back to the wall, as well as a cynical repudiation of a solemn international obligation. Here protests have no effect on the British. Only determined resistance will call them back to their senses. The I.Z.L. is responsible for organizing and conducting the mass extra-legal immigration to Palestine. Special squads have been set up in Palestine and Europe to look after the return to Zion of our brethren from concentration camps and prisons in Nazi-land, from hunger and misery in Eastern Europe. From April 1938 up till now we brought into Palestine over 15,000 people. Our principle in this work is: every Jew has a right to come to Palestine we will stick to it closely and, with all the devotion we possess, in defiance of the new British Nazi-Like laws untill we will transform that which Britain calls "illegal" immigration into our recognized legal right before the whole world.

3. *Enrollment, training and equipment.* The danger of war

being imminent, the I.Z.L. is training and enrolling in its ranks thousands of Jewish youth in various European countries. They are prepared as the army of occupation and defense of Palestine, if necessary in time of war, or as the reservoir of the I.Z.L. in Palestine at the present time. The I.Z.L. controls an aviation school and has a special squad of trained pilots. Equipment is undertaken only for Palestine. Especially in connection with the Aliya Beth we are now commanding hundreds of Jewish sailors, who, as already known, man the ships carrying our immigrants to Palestine under our supervision, and sail under the blue-white flag.

4. *Propaganda.* The secret broadcasting station "Liberated Zion" of the I.Z.L. in Palestine broadcasts twice daily in Hebrew and English. It is a most forceful weapon against the British Administration which suppresses free speech and press in the country. It informs the world of what is really going on in Palestine and calls upon the youth in Palestine and abroad to stand by us. We have two publications in Palestine: The "Sentinel" an English weekly bulletin distributed among the general Jewish public. Besides, frequent distribution of thousands of leaflets, posters, etc. All this is circulated secretly.

Outside Palestine we control one Jewish daily "The Action" appearing in Warsaw and three weeklies in Polish, French and English appearing in France, Belgium, Holland and Switzerland.

IV. POLITICAL AND MILITARY PROSPECTS

The tragic experiences of the last years have ultimately caused growing opposition and resentment to be felt among Palestine and World Jewry: opposition to the defeatists among us who have no belief in the strength of the Jewish nation and resentment toward the British Government that has openly broken its oath to the Jews and that proposes to create a Jewish Ghetto in the Jewish Homeland.

While we have every reason to expect that faced with a new and determined Jewry willing to battle and die for its survival, Britain will change its attitude and make possible a future understanding on the basis of a Jewish State friendly to Britain, we are quite prepared for the alternative: If England is not willing to help us, notwithstanding her solemn obligation to do so, the Jews will fight for their rights without England's help: for the Jews, after Britain's betrayal, are henceforward the masters of their own fate. An adequate solution of the Jewish problem is a profound concern of the non-Jewish world too, and England is in error to think that we will forever sacrifice our existence for the sake of H.M. Government's mistaken ideas about Palestine.

To the defeatists among us we say: Thanks for the lesson of "pacifism at any price." You have brought us to where we are now.

But tens of thousands of Jewish youth, young sturdy men with a desire to live like free men are being organized and well trained: they are being prepared for the decisive battle that will be fought in Palestine and which will decide the fate of our people and country. We have learned the lesson of Round Table conferences based on the idea of begging for justice and going unheeded, but tens of thousands, only the beginning, have not forgotten that theirs was a nation of warriors, and like the Macabees are ready to fight in order to reconquer the Land of Israel for Israel and their children. They are ready to fight as the English, French or Americans would have done in case their country were to be under enemy yoke, and as the Czechs are preparing to do now.

Of the world and the Jewish people at large, we ask to support us in our coming battles.

III
THE WAR PERIOD (1942–45)

To The British Soldier In Palestine!

We, members of the National Military Organisation in Erets Israel address you as soldiers address soldiers:

You have joined the armed forces, left your homes and families, exposed your lives to danger not as mercenaries, but as free and proud men determined to defend your country, against the enemy of yours, the monstrous enemy of all humanity—Hitlerite Germany.

The Hebrew Youth, however, was for 5 Years denied the opportunity. In spite of its most ardent desire, to fight our mortal foe, as it was robbed of the basic idea which inspires all nations participating in this glibal[1] war, the idea, that the goal of its fight and sacrifices is a free homeland.

The "political gamble" so cinically conducted by unsempulous politicians and so hipocritically camouflaged with fine phrases about "Justice" and "Freedom," resulted in our case in the following: that thousands of young Jews of Erets Israel who voluntarily joined the Army have been degraded to auxiliary services in the desert and elsewhere instead of taking part under their national banner, in the military operations on the many battlefields of the world; that the gates of our homeland, which must be a homeland for every Jew, have been shut and barred in face of the unprecedented massacres of our brethren in Nazi-Europe; that five millions of Jews—our parents, brothers, sisters and children—who, were it not for the bad faith of your politicians, should and could have been rescued, were exterminated in the European slaughter-houses.

This is the tragic situation we face and it imposed on us the necessity of starting a struggle for the liberation of our own country and for the rescue of our persecuted nation. It is not only our natural right, but above all our sacred duty to rise and fight, even with the cost of our life, in order to put an end to our people's sufferings, in order to give it, after so many ages of dispersion and persecutions, its home, so that it may live in peace, security and honour.

---

[1]Typographical errors in printed original. See Publisher's Note.

This struggle is not directed against you. We appreciate that you shed your blood on many fronts and in many countries; we know that many among you condemn the official hypocrisy and many are looking—as we are—for a better world in which every nation and every individual will be given an opportunity of free and undisturbed development.

Nor is this struggle historically directed against your country. No Jewish Government will pursue any other policy than that of friendship with the British Commonwealth and with other free nations. But friendship must be mutual.

Now, we are fighting against a regime based on bad faith, on repudiation of solemn pledges and international obligations, a regime of treachery and oppression. This little country belongs to us. It is our old historic motherland, dreamt of by tens of generations, sacred by the blood of heroes and fighters. It was promised to us. It is the only haven for millions of homeless Jews.

The declared aim, however, of your rulers is to prevent our people from repatriation and restoration: their policy is to keep by force the door of our country closed to the survivors of the Nazi massacres; their decision is to impose on us the status of a permanent minority, the well-known "existence" of a GHETTO.

It is this regime of oppression we are fighting against. And we are determined to continue our struggle, if necessary, to the last man in our ranks. And so is every free and proud Jew in Erets-Israel.

But it appears that the mercenaries and instruments of this regime, the police and C.I.D. men—those "heroes" of the Palestine Gestapo who succeeded in evading the dangers of the battlefield—are not strong enough and not courageous enough to overcome the revolt of free men. So they resort to you, soldiers on leave from the war fronts, in order to be assisted in their "noble" job. Recently, in Jerusalem, Tel-Aviv and Petach-Tikva, units of the Army took part in mass searches, chasing Young fighters, who shed their blood for a Justa Causa of no precedent in human history.

We are, indeed, proud of the fact the the Government of oppression has been compelled to bring in brigades and divisions, tanks and planes in order to try—in vain!—to destroy the spirit of freedom of the regenerated Hebrew Youth. But we are bound, on the other hand, to ask you:

Is it for that purpose, that you left your home and joined the Army? Does your duty consist in oppressing Jews in their homeland? Don't you realise the humiliation to which you are subjected by participating in such police-actions? Is THIS your task in this war, which is being called by Your politicians "war of liberation"?
THINK OF IT!

HAIRGUN HATZVAI HALEUMI
B'ERETS-ISRAEL
(National Military Organisation)

Notice

1.—On 27th September 1944, at night, attacks were carried out by our soldiers against the British Police Fortresses at Haifa, Kalkiliya, Katra and Beit Dajan. Heavy engagements took place, with casualties suffered by the Police and wounded on both sides. A considerable quantity of modern arms was seized.

2.—Our units are fighting, as we proved it in Jerusalem and Haifa, at Ramallah and Jaffa, at Katra and Kalkiliya, and elsewhere, according to all the laws of warfare, as they are recognised in this world of violence and oppression, which calls itself "civilized." In all these attacks the principle of face-to-face engagements has been followed. We have taken all precautions, in order not to hit the civil population, whether Jewish or alien; during the last attack our soldiers presented themselves bearing plain and distinct badges. Preparations are being made and plans scheduled for that very day, when we shall, as every Underground army did, come out, together with all the Jewish Yishuv, its movements and communities participating, for open conquest actions, and for decisive battles against the oppressors of our Homeland and the destroyers of our hope.

Therefore, and on the basis of the precedents, which have been created in the course of this World War, we will demand a de facto and de jure recognition of our rights, as an UNDERGROUND ARMY. For this recognition we will fight by all means in our possession.

HAIRGUN HATZVAI HELEUMI
B'ERETS-ISRAEL
(National Military Organisation)

[Untitled]

The deportation of Jews from their Homeland—
is an unbearable scorn, an inexcusable crime

All the Yishuv demands:
bring back the prisoners of Latrun to their Homeland

We will remember: no ship, no aircraft has been
found in order to SAVE Jews from extermination:
tens of planes have been made available in order
to DEPORT Jews from their Homeland

We will neither forgive,
nor forget the scorn of deportation

The Oppression Government dares to deport Jews
from their Homeland put an end to its crimes

Remember the scorn of deportation!
Remember the 251 prisoners of Zion and exiles of Israel

[Letter to a Friend from a Jewish Ex-serviceman]

Palestine, November, 1945

Dear Friend,

I have seen you in the street and felt like having a talk with you. I wondered whether you realised why you had been sent here. When soldiers are sent overseas, they naturally presume that it is to fight an enemy. It has occurred to me that someone may have tried to tell you that I am your enemy. You must not believe it.

I am a Jew, and I have come here from afar: I have come here to live and work in my own homeland. If, during your sojourn in Palestine, you can enjoy the pleasant shade of green young woods, I want you to know that it is people like myself who have planted them. If you find here the amenities of Western civilisation, remember that this is due to the efforts of myself and my fellow Jews, who have come here to redeem the soil of our ancient homeland from its desolation. Where have we come from, you may ask? All over the face of the globe have we wandered,—we, our fathers and our fathers' fathers. For many centuries have we wandered, ever since we were forcibly expelled from our homeland, the Land of Israel, known to you as Palestine. We have been hounded out of all the countries in the world, together with the cultural heritage of our people, who created the Holy Bible here in Palestine. We have been persecuted and tortured in every country under the sun. Our worst and most recent sufferings were undergone in Nazi occupied Europe.

Just stop and think for a moment. Six millions of my people have been murdered, burnt, gassed and subjected to the most frightful and protracted tortures till they died,—old and young, women and children. Helpless babes were mercilessly seized and beaten against walls or pavements until their skulls were smashed. No doubt you have heard something of this: you may even on your way here have seen with your own eyes some evidence of Nazi brutality.

The survivors of Nazi savagery have no other hope in life but to join us here. It is for them that we have been rebuilding our homeland. Their eyes are turned to us, and our arms are stretched out to them. Will you come between us?

Almost thirty years ago—in November 1917—the British Government publicly proclaimed its recognition of the justice of our claims and promised its fullest help in their realisation. The Balfour Declaration reads: "His Majesty's Government view with favour the establishment in Palestine of a National Home for the Jewish people, and will use their best endeavours to facilitate the achievement of this object."

All through these years we placed our faith in Britain and in the promises of its statesmen. We have worked and striven we have turned all our energies towards creating here a national home for our people. Many, like myself, enlisted in the forces and fought in the same cause as yourself. And now your Government is barring the entrance to their rightful home before the remnants of our people in Europe who have no other place to lay their heads.

The White Paper means the death sentence for our survivors in Europe. The White Paper transforms the promised "Jewish National Home" into a new Ghetto—a minority dependent on the charity of an Arab majority. This was certainly never the intention of your great statesmen when they declared that the Jews should return to Palestine as of right and not by sufferance!

We are not your enemies. We are only stretching forth our hand to give refuge to the starving survivors of our people, whatever the White Paper may say. And when we stretch forth our hand, you may receive the order to hack it off. Are you really going to hack off that hand stretched forth in succour?

A Jewish Ex-serviceman

IV
THE POSTWAR PERIOD (1946–47)

Fighting Judaea: The Battle Continues in the Court-Room (The Trial of 31)

Lord, how are they increased that trouble me! many are they that rise up against me. Many there be which say of my soul, there is no help for him in God. Se-läh. But thou, O Lord, art a shield for me; my glory and the lifter up of mine head. I cried unto the Lord with my voice, and he heard me out of his holy hill. Se-läh. I laid me down and slept. I awaked; for the Lord sustained me. I will not be afraid of ten thousands of people, that have set themselves against me round about. Arise, O Lord; save me, O my God: for thou hast smitten all mine enemies upon the cheek bone; thou hast broken the teeth of the ungodly. Salvation belongeth unto the Lord: thy blessing is upon thy people. Seläh.

INTRODUCTION:

With this dignified prayer, in which the grief of the persecuted mingles with faith and hope, opened the Jewish military unit, captured by the enemy after a night of fighting, its trial before a so-called British "military court" in Jerusalem.

Theirs was an unprecedented trial, but one that *created a precedent*. This time there did not appear before the British officers appointed to pass judgement on Jewish youths persons accused of carrying arms, or individual possessors of arms, or, "accused" men defending themselves in some manner or other. Before the court appeared a *Jewish military unit*, inspired by a *collective fighting spirit* even after they had become prisoners of war, even while they were standing in the shadow of the gallows. . . This spirit found its expression in many forms, one of which was their external appearance: military uniforms of a simple gray without badges of rank

101

or any other emblems except one—*the emblem of the Jewish people*, in whose name and for whose cause they had joined the fight, for whose cause they were imprisoned and on whose behalf they faced as *prosecutors and accusers* those who wanted to take their lives. Another expression of their spirit was revealed in the "stormy incident"—as other writers put it—when all the thirty accused men rose to their feet like one man protecting like a live wall the eldest among them from the brutal hands of the British police constables. The courtroom was filled with British soldiers and policemen, who did not hesitate, of course, to aim their guns at the dock of the prisoners in an unambig[u]ous threat. . . The youths, however, who had faced death often enough, sat down only when told to do so by their comrade in defence of whose honour they had risen.

However, over and above all these scenes, external as well as incidental, there was one scene in the proceedings which was so impressive that it did not only penetrate into the hearts of the disinterested observers—foreign correspondents and representatives of foreign broadcasting services, but even into the *brains* of the British "prosecutor" who of course, was far from disinterested. . . All the speeches and all the behaviour of these youths expressed their soldierly feeling, the feeling that there *is* a *Jewish army* in the Jewish homeland; that this army—like every other national army—fights for and defends its people; that this army is aware of its mission and aim; that this army knows *the rules of warfare* and to the same extent as it is ready to follow them it is ready *to force* the enemy not to violate them or, in the case they are violated—to apply the usual law of retaliation. Hence the self-explanatory statement that British officers, belonging to the occupation army, are not entitled to "judge" captured Jewish soldiers; hence the self-explanatory demand that the soldiers of the military unit should be considered as prisoners of war. It was this display of the feeling of Jewish sovereignty that compelled the prosecutor, for the first time in the history of trials in this country—to adduce arguments against the claims of the accused in order to prove that the British military court did possess the competence of jurisdiction over the 31 accused men. The prosecutor reminded them that the same military court had tried also Polish, Greek, British, Arab *soldiers*, etc. As for the demand to accord the Jewish soldiers the status of prisoners of war, the prosecutor did not refute it *as such* but argued that the court was not competent to make a decision to that effect.

The trial had attracted the attention of all the world. Millions of Americans followed the proceedings as reported over 218 radio stations; scores of millions read about them in their newspapers. For, indeed, this was an unusual trial even in our unusual days. Actually it was not even a trial at all, but a minor battle—a battle between the fighters for freedom and the representatives of oppression, between the clear understanding of a mission and the dull-wittedness, between readiness to bring the supreme sacrifice and the hatred of despots and murderers—a battle—or, more precisely, the continuation of a battle, which had been interrupted on an ill-starred day somewhere on the shore of our sea. From the development of this peculiar "battle" the other peoples came to know the character of the new Jewish generation brought up on the soil of the homeland, and they paid tribute, some in sincere sympathy and others while grinding their teeth, to the invincible spirit of the people of the Lord.

Blessed be the youths who had the good fortune to stand up for the glory of their people: happy the nation that can call its own such sons and soldiers.

I AM A HEBREW AND A SOLDIER!
By prisoner Menachem Shiff

Gentlemen,

When a man has to face a court, or an institution so called, which threatens to take his life, the gravity of the matter, if not the legal basis of the institution, demands that he present himself, saying who he is, where he comes from, what he wants and what views he has, why he left the ordinary paths of life and why he should have approached the orbit of the gallows; why he does not recognise the legal status of his judges to pass judgement on him; what it was that he believed in, regardless of whether he had to expect a long life or whether this was to be his last appearance in public; what motives he had that encouraged him to imperil his very life?

To the first question I have a simple and short answer: I am a Jew. I am a son of that ancient nation which thousands of years ago emerged from the obscurity of history, reaching this country, its Land of Promise, through seas and deserts and battles, establishing in it a flourishing state, making fruitful not only the fields of this country but also the idea of man and the universe. The Jewish state lay at the crossroads of international routes, a fact that explains its importance and its curse to this very day.

It was for this reason that from time to time conquerors and invaders intruded into this country, laying waste its towns and leading away into exile its kings and inhabitants. For many centuries this struggle continued between a small and yet great people and powerful empires that mounted and disappeared from the stage of history. Often it would appear to the other peoples that our state had fallen never to be resurrected. But nevertheless, it did rise to its feet again and again, resuming its war and preferring to die standing erect than to eke out a miserable life on its knees.

At the end of that epoch, after the fall of the last bastion of Bar-Kochba's rebels—or, rather earlier, when our Temple was destroyed, our people began to wander through all the countries of the world. These migrations are unexampled in the history of mankind. Traces of these migrations can be found in every country, but all these traces are those of blood shed in the name of religion or nationalism, in the name of economy or politics, in the name of the revolution or counter-revolution, in the name of racialism, or hatred or envy. This bloodshed, following our migrations like a shadow, has gone on for almost two thousand years. Now the Jewish people has decided to return home, its exiled sons come to it in their thousands from all over the world, while its sons in the homeland are waging, as in ancient times, the sacred war for their people, their country and their faith.

I gave you this short outline, Gentlemen, not in order to take up your time or to boast of belonging to a nation that preceded your people in the creation of sovereign institutions and a great civilisation. I did so because I want to explain to you the difference in our points of view as a result of which, in spite of the present situation, we do not regard you as judges and ourselves as accused, nor try to please you, nor worry about our personal future or life. This is, of course, something unusual and if there is any explanation for it, it is just that difference of which I have spoken. Our perspectives are not the same. It is true that you are sitting on the elevated chairs of the judges while we are sitting on the low bench of the accused, but I am nevertheless convinced that we see the matters involved in this collective trial, the relations between the people of Israel and England as well as the future of this country, from a level higher than that upon which you are seated. You see the relations between the physical forces of a great power, though no longer the greatest but still a great power, and those of a people having just now lost six million sons. Yours is a calculation of aeroplanes and ships and guns that you have got and we have not, and you compare this calculation with the number of rifles and machine guns and grenades possessed by the Jewish people. For you the result of such a comparison is clear enough: the Jews will be defeated, or exterminated, since, as Frederic the Great put it, "God is always with the stronger battalions." But I should like to tell you that you are mistaken, that your calculations are unfounded, while, as Churchill once said, there is a strong basis in the faith that lives in our hearts. Is this imagination? Is this mysticism? No, Gentlemen: it is neither imagination nor mysticism but a historical perspective that I have because I am a Jew and which you have not because you—are you.

We saw the Assyrian conqueror and his downfall; we saw victorious Babylon and its decline, the kingdom of the Seleucids and its ruin; we saw also how the Roman Empire went to pieces. All this we did see and—*we live.* Therefore we have not the slightest doubt that, whatever the outcome of the war between us may be, you will certainly *not* be the victors and all your victories over the people of Israel will be so many deadly blows to yourselves before history.

But when I say "I am a Jew" I have not yet said all. I should add at once that I am a *soldier*, a Hebrew Soldier. You are probably surprised to hear this as you have not yet heard of a Jewish army but only of Jews fighting in alien armies.

At best, you have heard of the Jewish Brigade within the British army which you have managed to disband because in your eyes it committed a terrible crime in helping too generously the remnants of our people, who in their effrontery wish to live in spite of the wish of your rulers who would have preferred that they had shared the fate of our six million dead.

Nevertheless, Gentlemen, there is a Jewish army, an independent Jewish army, serving the Jewish people alone, and I as well as my comrades here are proud of serving in this army, of fighting in its ranks and following its banner. It is true that this is not a regular army, it has no uniforms and does not recruit its soldiers on a compulsory basis. But for precisely this reason this army is so dear to us. We volunteered to serve in its ranks, we joined it of our own free will with the full knowledge of the dangers involved for those who belong to this army; no one forced us; no one enticed us. We went to enrol for service in its ranks because an inner voice told us: Rise and liberate your country!

Yes, Gentlemen,—our army has accepted the task of liberating this country from your rule or any other rule, and to return it to the Jewish people as its property for ever. Our army does not conceal this aim from you or any other factor in the world. On the contrary, we state our task quite openly. For we think that you have made yourselves the masters of our country by different means, by force and cunning, by making promises and by breaking them again, and it was particularly the aspirations, the claims and the *credulity* of our own people that you took advantage of in order to reach your aim. Our parents trusted you and gave you the mandate over Eretz Israel. They refused France and the U.S.A., they yielded their fundamental right of managing the affairs of their country themselves, they empowered you to act for them because they had put their trust in you. This is why they did not set up an army but built—built wonderful things. This is why they did not amass arms but collected money to invest in their constructive work, in the firm belief that under your protection and with your help, they were laying the foundations of the rebirth of the Jewish State.

And you deceived them. You simply deceived them. You invented all sorts of formulas, found all sorts of excuses and justifications, all of which amounted to just one thing: the people of Israel was to remain in the countries of the Diaspora, to which one more was to be added: the Land of Israel, under British or, British-Arab rule. Our parents were naive and the price they had to pay for their naivety is so horrible that no human mind can grasp it even. Suffice it to make one simple comparison: you, a people of 45 million have lost in the second world war three hundred thousand lives, while we, a people of 17 million, have lost twenty times as much as you have: six million lives, *six* million lives.

We have drawn our conclusions from the bitter experience of our parents. We realise that no power in the world will ever save us from destruction if we ourselves do not do so; nothing will liberate us from slavery if we do not free ourselves. On these basic assumptions was created and built up the Jewish army, the liberation army whose task it is to return to our people that without which it cannot live: its homeland and its independance.

You see therefore, that the Hebrew army is not a "private" army as your Prime Minister says, but it is an army created by the sovereign will of the People of Israel, which does not want the lands of foreigners nor the charity of foreigners nor the pogroms made by foreigners, but wants to obtain the right accorded to every nation, however small and weak: the right to a homeland, to self-determination, and an independent Government. Therefore, the Jewish army cannot be "illegal" as your rulers say. For the foundation upon which this army was built is the *law* that is recognised by all the peoples of the world, the law for which two world wars had to be fought. An illegal act is done by him who breaks this law; a legal and moral act is done by those who fight for its maintenance and realisation.

Therefore not we are the breakers of the law but your rulers, they who play havoc with the rights of man, of the citizen and human society. And if we fight against them, then we are doing our duty, our duty towards our own people and our duty towards free people everywhere.

And as a soldier of the free liberation army I have the honour of telling you on behalf of all my comrades that the officers of the army of the enemy have no right of jurisdiction over us and that according to the principles of international law we are prisoners of war, whose status is safeguarded by well-known international agreements.

And another thing let me tell you and my people: as happy as I was to fight for my people and my country so happy am I now to *suffer* for them. For suffering too, when it is borne for one's faith, is a kind of war. And history teaches us that from these sacrifices grows on the ruins of tyranny the tree of liberty.

This tree we planted with our blood: we are happy that we could do so.

INDICTMENT OF THE TORTURED JEWISH PEOPLE
AGAINST TREACHEROUS ENGLAND
By prisoner Baruch Shindler

Gentlemen,
You accuse us of carrying or possessing arms. I am not obliged to reply to this accusation because I do not recognise the right of your rulers to forbid Jews to carry or to use arms in their Homeland, just as I do not recognise the right of your judges to pass judgement on them for this matter. As regards my basic attitude it is perfectly clear and I do not intend to conceal it from you: every Jew in his homeland has the duty to carry arms, to train himself in their use and to employ arms in the sacred war for liberation of his Homeland. Moreover, our countrymen in the Diaspora, too, have the duty to undergo military training in order to prepare themselves for the war against those who deprive them of their country and expose them to extermination. I am sure that after all that the Jewish people, disarmed for two thousand years, has experienced, my brethren in the Diaspora know exactly as well as we here in the country of our forefathers what is incumbent upon them in these cruel times.

When, therefore, you make your calculations in your secret cabinet meetings as to the war potentials of the Jews on whom you have declared war you should not only take into account the 600,000 Jews in the Land of Israel with the extraordinary high percentage of youths among them who are fit for military service but all the eleven million Jews who survived the wave of destruction that came over our people all over the world. All of them will rise against you in due course because they feel that it is *their war*, and that without a reborne State they too—and certainly their children—can have neither existence nor future. II million, Gentlemen, who include hundreds of thousands who fought in the battles of the second world war, are in a position to raise strong armies. I am sure that they will do so if necessary. There are some precedents for this in our history. When Juda revolted in the days of Rome, she was immediately joined by all the essential centres of the Diaspora and the fire of the revolt against the oppressor flared up not in the Land of Israel only but in all the neighbouring countries as well. It is true that our brethren in the Diaspora possess also other means of fighting you in the field of economy. A boycott against British goods, organised by all the Jews in all the countries of the world—and it will be organised against you as it was organised against Nazi Germany, from whom you have inherited your attitude towards the Jewish people—such a boycott will weaken your economic position which is already unstable enough. But I am sure that apart from economic retaliations we shall be able to witness the unification of a dispersed people around the banner of liberty, around the banner of their war for liberation. Then not only thousands but tens and hundreds of thousands will rise against you everywhere, well trained and confident that they will fight indefatigably until you return to their people what you have stolen from them.

If, therefore, the front is to expand on such a vast scale, it would be a pity to waste time on such a trifle as the possession of a few automatic and non-automatic fire-arms. We had better direct our attention to the relations between our peoples, between the Jewish people and your people, as these relations which grew particularly strained during the recent decades, actually established their front and widen it more and more until, perhaps, they will leave their imprint on the history of the world.

In dealing with these relations it would be rather strange were I to confine myself to a stupid, arbitrary, bureaucratic indictment which contains one subject only: the carrying of arms without permission of those you think entitled to give such a permission. When we deal with these relations we must draw up and disclose before the whole world an indictment containing many paragraphs: the indictment of the Jewish people, being exterminated and deceived, against the treachery and tyranny of murderous England. Indeed—we, the soldiers and representatives of the Jewish people, accuse England of crimes for which it will have to answer before an international tribunal:

1. We *accuse England of the crime of the breach of confidence.* In 1917 England promised the Jewish people to exert all efforts to assist it in the achievement of the Jewish "Zionist aspirations." Though this pledge was in advance worded in an ambig[u]ous form, indicative of the premeditation of one who intends to evade its implementation, it was manifest to all what the meaning of the Jewish "Zionist aspirations" which formed the subject of the Balfour Declaration, really was. These aspirations had but one meaning, which was known to all your serious politicians: to Lloyd George and Balfour, to Churchill and Smuts, to Cecil and Amery: a Jewish or Hebrew State on both sides of the River Jordan. On the strength of this promise the Jewish people believed in you, helping you to defeat the Kaiser's Germany, and admitting you not as a conqueror annexing the Land of Israel but as the Mandatory over our country, entrusted with an international mission. This confidence you have violated and broken. Instead of endeavouring to help the people of Israel to realise its aspirations you did your *utmost* to interfere with the realisation of the aspirations of our people.

2. We *accuse England of the crime of the violation of international Law.* Although you drew up the text of the Mandate you endeavoured, as is the custom of your insidious policy to introduce definitions permitting of various interpretations, and to add "glosses" abolishing the principal obligations, etc., the Mandate of the League

of Nations nevertheless imposed upon you several definite duties which you have never fulfilled. You undertook to promote the repatriation of the Jews to their homeland. Instead of doing so, you have systematically limited it until it has ceased almost entirely. You undertook to promote the close settlement of the repatriated Jews. You undertook to make available for them Government land not required for public purposes. Instead you have frustrated every attempt at settlement in Transjordan—even when your satellite agreed to Jewish colonisation in Transjordan. You have enforced land laws based on racial discrimination, which were known before only in Czarist Russia and Nazi Germany. And above all, you undertook in the preamble of the Mandate to help in the *"reconstruction"* of the National Home of the people of Israel and to "reconstruct" can refer only to what existed before. In other words, you undertook to return the complete territory of the Land of Israel to its legitimate owner, the People of Israel, as its Homeland and independent State. Instead of doing so, you stole the country in order to keep it for yourselves, confining to a Ghetto, the part of our people that in spite of your intentions did succeed in reaching and settling in its Homeland, giving it a status that is no better—and in certain respects, even worse—than the status given to Jewish minorities in certain countries of the Diaspora.

3. *We accuse England of the crime of instigation to anti-Jewish massacres.* In order to obstruct us, in order to become the masters of this country under the mask of a supreme power enforcing peace in our country, you incited against us our Arab neighbours, with whom we actually have no conflict since we regard them as citizens with equal rights of our independent State, citizens who will enjoy rights, and social progress to an incomparably higher degree than under your regime of exploitation and instigation or under the rule of your satellites in Transjordan, Irak, or any other country. This unnatural and unjustified conflict is *your* work and was brought about by the foulest methods of agents-provocateurs. In this criminal work of instigation participated your governors, from Bolls and Storrs to Spears, as well as your military commanders, from the days of the military occupation of this country down to Mr. Glubb Pasha, who—as could not be expected otherwise—was given a high decoration for his instigation; in these activities participated also your ministers and journalistes, to say nothing of your petty agents—Government officials and mercenaries of your secret police who tour the villages and call upon the Arabs to "start." As a result of this instigation much blood has been shed in this country. Hundreds of Jews, men, women and children, were killed, many thousands were wounded, fields were set afire, settlements which had been built up under great sacrifices and with the toil of our pioneers were laid waste.

Your criminal propaganda of hatred actually continues to this very day. It would probably have led to renewed attacks against

Jewish Settlements, but in the meantime an armed Jewish force has risen in this country, whose efficiency could be seen by the Arabs throughout the years of our fight against you and your rule. Therefore our neighbours are not in a hurry to be taken in by your provocations and all attempts by your agents to spur them on to attacks against us have so far been in vain. But you will not easily renounce the spectacle of a Jewish-Arab war, that you would greatly enjoy since it would give again the possibility of appearing as the supreme judge who stands for justice and is "beaten" by both of the parties to the conflict.

Therefore you have brought to our country our agents, who during the war were Nazi agents, and made of them the leaders of the Arab population. When even these agents failed to involve the Arabs into attacks that would be sheer suicide for them, you brought to Syria the notorious agent and instigator who for two years served the death machine of the Nazis. You deny of course that you brought him to the frontiers of our country and for this purpose you staged the comedy of a search aboard the transport ship "Devonshire" in Port Said. But whom did you take in with these manoeuvres? A certain writer speaking of the Nazi gangsters said with regard to Goebels that though he was very cunning this fact did not help him so much since everybody had come to know him. I think that this is true also with regard to your wire-pullers. They are very cunning but all their cunning no longer helps them once the whole world has succeeded in exposing it. All the world knows who it was that needed the Jerusalem Mufti in the vicinity of the Land of Israel; all the world knows who helped him to "escape" from France. All your efforts of covering up this matter are of no avail to you: you brought him, you brought the Mufti in order to kindle up the fire of a war between Jews and Arabs, the fire of a war that was to help you to cook your soup. I do not know whether this man will succeed in achieving what his relative, Jamel Husseini, could not bring about. But if he does, if the Arab population is coaxed into attacks which are completely unjustified and whose results will be frightful, first of all for the Arabs themselves, then all the world will know that *you* caused the catastrophe, that *you* were interested in it, that you incited the Arabs and succeeded in doing so.

4. *We accuse England of the crime of being an accomplice to mass murder.* Ever since the day of Hitler's arrival to power you did all in order to prevent European Jewry from escaping the dangers of extermination prepared by the Nazis. It took Hitler six years to win Germany; the war against Nazi Germany took another six years. During those twelve years it would have been possible to save millions but you barred their way and compelled them to remain on the vulcano. Your aim was clear: you needed the disappearance of the greatest possible number of Jews in order to diminish if not

eliminate entirely the number of people claiming their Homeland, in order that you could, without difficulty, become the masters of our country for good, arguing that actually there are no Jews left who desire to return to the Land of Israel.

In those years the late President Roosevelt made an attempt to help the refugees of our people by bringing at least part of them to our country. This was the hopeless attempt of the Evian conference. The attempt failed only because you wanted it to fail. To the Evian conference you intentionally sent Lord Winterton, the notorious anti-Semite, his instructions were very clear: he was to inform the representatives of the nations participating in the conference that in the Land of Israel there was not room even for one Jew more.

Anyone who wishes to know in what troubled waters fish your hypocritical politicians, should recall with what sort of arguments you justified, throughout those years, your policy of closing the gates of our country. There was a time when you declared that the economic conditions of our country did not permit large-scale immigration. But after Jewish initiative had proved that it is the main source of the absorptive capacity of this country you arranged a pogrom and declared that security conditions—i.e., the "political conditions"—did not permit mass immigration. Then the war broke out. You immediately produced a new argument why the Jews could not be admitted into their country: among the Jews to be repatriated there might be—and this is what you really dared to say "German agents." This argument was abandoned when the total extermination of the German Jewry began. Then you argued that it was again impossible to bring Jews to their country because you could not spare transport for the rescue of the victims of the Nazi massacres because you needed all vehicles and ships in order to achieve victory over Germany.

When victory came and Hitler was defeated, when all your former argumentation was abolished by life itself you returned to your old arguments with regard to the political conditions, the resistance of the Arabs, the economic difficulties, etc. In these excuses and subterfuges which vary from time to time, every impartial observer can see all the hypocrisy and mendaciousness that you used throughout the years deciding the fate of our parents, our sisters and brothers. This is how you helped Hitler, directly as well as indirectly, in wiping out millions of Jews; this is how you lent a hand to the greatest and most dreadful crime of all history.

5. *We accuse England of the crime of murder of defenceless people.* Apart from participating in the murder of millions [of] Jews carried out by Hitler and his gangsters, you murdered and killed with your own hands Jewish citizens who strove to reach the shores of their Homeland, you murdered without trial Jewish citizens in their Homeland—the details of these crimes are sufficiently known. I

confine myself to quoting names which are inscribed in red letters with the blood of our martyrs: Struma, Patria, Mauritius, Haifa, Tel-Aviv, Sudan.

6. *We accuse England of the crime of permanent violation of the rights of Man and Citizen.* Our land you have turned into a prison. You have issued emergency laws placing every Jewish citizen in the shadow of the gallows. You are confining hundreds of citizens in concentration camps and prisons without ever bringing them to court. And if your courts acquit someone, the secret police appears without delay and places him under detention for many years, on the basis of special regulations. You have subjected our press to a totalitarian and provocative censorship. Your secret police, your constables and soldiers tyrannise and terrorise peaceful citizens. In defiance of all laws you have enforced a regime of oppression, terror and despotism.

7. *We accuse England of the crime of economic exploitation.* Instead of developing this country and raising the standard of life of its citizens you exploit the population of our country in the most impudent manner and hamper in this way its possibilities of development. You exact ruinous taxes from the Jewish citizens of this country. The immense bureaucratic machinery, mostly com-posed of youngsters from England who have no business here in our country sits like a leech on the body of the civilian population. You bring into our country British companies and grant them privileges enjoyed by no other company in our country. You prevent the productive exploitation of the natural wealth of our country—such as oil—in order to protect your profits derived from undertakings abroad.

8. *We accuse England of depriving a whole people the right to live.* The right to live is the first right of every human being. You deny this right to our people—our whole people—since without a Homeland it is not only unfree—and freedom too is one of the first things a man needs—but without a Homeland it cannot continue to live: exactly this—to live. Till this very day our brethren are being slaughtered in Europe; till this very day hundreds of thousands of Jews sit in concentration camps, while the wave of destruction has not only failed to show any indications of abating but, on the contrary, is on the rise all over the world. In your country too the Jews are exposed to the danger of destruction. Nor is this anything new. Already Lord Derby—as reported in the book of the ambassador, Henderson—spoke towards the end of the first war of a massacre (a night of St. Bartholomew?) against the Jews of Great Britain. And now? Does not Bevin head the Jew-baiters? Our indictment against you is not yet complete. I could have added much to the paragraphs I quoted. But I do not think that this is necessary. The paragraphs which I have ennumerated, though dealing with them only in a few words, suffice to expose you before the world as traitors and despots, liars

and instigators, international criminals inflicting catastrophes on other peoples and the world as a whole.

Therefore I stand here before you and tell you, in the shadow of the gallows—repent of your sins! Do penitence! Pray for mercy for yourselves, for your crimes have become insufferable.

THE REAL CAUSES OF THE TROUBLE
By prisoner Benjamin Kaplan

Gentlemen,

As we insist on the principle of the honour of soldiers, we think that it would be a mutual insult against our honour as soldiers if we recognised you as judges and ourselves as accused. Though we call you 'judges' we nevertheless do not forget for a moment that you are wearing the uniform of officers of a country fighting against the People of Israel. Furthermore, we do not forget that though you address us as 'accused' we are actually prisoners of war belonging to the Jewish people, which is at present at war with Great Britain.

Sincerity and frankness are considered the first virtues of a soldier. Thus, also we have been compelled to attend these proceedings in order to take part in the trial against us we can by no means agree to the function of accused forced upon us nor will we confine ourselves to the factual evidence relating to the case as demanded by the prosecution. The factual evidence of our case in itself neither explains nor discloses nor states anything at all. We therefore do not wish to discuss to what extent the prosecution succeeded in establishing the correctness of its basic assumptions, as demanded by legal proceedings. Experience has taught us that even the courtroom may become a battle-field for you on which England fights against the Jewish people. It is not always the legal principle of establishing justice that decides on this battlefield, but, quite on the contrary, in most cases justice bows her head to the requirements of an emergency situation. Therefore we consider it as our duty as soldiers to tell you frankly what we think of this trial and to show you what we regard as the principle matter in this case.

You will probably have no objections, Gentlemen, if we speak out aloud here what is usually not admitted openly and what people generally endeavour to hush up. The center of gravity in our case lies in the strategical and geographical situation of our country. It is this fact that induced England to carry on a campaign of conquest against our people.

The means of communication by air and land have again raised the importance of the ancient route crossing our country and leading to all parts of the globe. The interest you took in the fate of the people of Israel and the feeling of sympathy for its national aspirations you stated in the past, all derived from the wish to penetrate in the back of the Jewish people into this vital vein of your Empire. You needed some certificate, serving you as a pretext to justify your penetration to the country east of the Suez, just as, with the help of the gold of the Rothschilds and the Jewish brains of Disraeli you acquired the Suez canal against the will of many inhabitants of your islands. The persecuted Jewish people did not want to consider you always and everywhere as intriguers pursuing only selfish aims. It regarded you as decent partners. Under the influence of your fine declarations, in spite of the decline of your star during the Boer war, our people thought that it was the English fairness in business attributed to you that had motivated your declarations.

Gentlemen—we will not speak of the immense profit Great Britain gained in the past thanks to this state of the affairs. Your statesmen like Lloyd George, Balfour, Smuts, and others admitted openly that the pledges made to the Jewish people to help us in the reconstruction of our country were a compensation and a token of gratitude for all the help given to England by the Jews during the first World war. However, men like Lloyd George, Smuts and Wedge-wood obscured reality and resulted in the Jewish people going [sic] an incorrect impression of the real men responsible for British politics.

Who these men really are is admitted by Winston Churchill in his book on the leading men of his time. In the chapter on Asquith not only one must be liquidated [sic] how the latter decided after he had become Prime Minister to liquidate some of his political friends who were not convenient for his purposes. To Churchill's question why he was doing so, Asquith answered: "The most important quality of a Prime Minister is to be a butcherer." A characteristic answer, one should say. Let us examine it in the light of the situation in our country, in this part of the world.

In our opinion, Gentlemen, there is room enough for dozens of millions of people in the Near East, while there is room enough in our country for the repatriation of millions of Jews. These countries were the granary of the inhabitants in the times of the Romans. The expulsion of the Jews, the wars, the numerous conquests and the particular gift for destruction of the chance inhabitants of our country have turned into a desert a country that once flowed with milk and honey. Nowadays, thanks to the care of the Jews, the country is being reborn. Our country is ready to receive, to clothe and feed all those Jews knocking today at its gates. Our work of reconstruction may become a miracle of human creativeness, leading to peace and abundance. However, to make this miracle come true, it is necessary to have more qualities than those of a butcherer. Or, rather, one must not be a butcherer at all. When the executioner looked at our country, strange things began to happen in it. As officers you surely know the theory of the great strategical importance assigned to the mentality and mood of the inhabitants destined once to become an arena for the operations of war.

But even this theory permits different points of view: a human point of view—and that of a butcherer. The butchers were shocked to see what progress and civilisation the Jews were bringing with them to the Near East. They preferred ignorance and stagnation to reign in an under-populated territory euphemistically referred to as "the picturesque Orient." They preferred to support Arab rule and enabled scoundrels and good for nothings to do what mischief they wanted, without ever punishing them.

The Kurds, the Armenians and the Assyrians were destroyed— with the connivance of the British to such an extent, that there is no one left among them to rise and to ask: England—what about your pledges? But for the book written by the Jewish writer Franz Werfel, what would the world know about Musa-Daigh? 'Reuter' would have hushed up the true events in a maze of lies and the event would have been lost to the world of truth.

According to the point of view of the butcherer, the theory of strategy demands to win the "sympathy of the coloured people" in the territories on the way to India by means of the policy of "divide et impera" by delivering up all the peoples inhabiting those countries to the fangs of one of them.

For strategical reasons England decided not to enable the Jews to return to their homeland, which it tries to steal from them, in order to transform it into a British military base. This, Gentlemen, is the true reason why you are performing the function of 'judges' while the Jewish youth, the soldiers of our nation appear here as 'accused.'

The illusory belief in a "better England" than that of the 'executioner' has by now gone for ever. The victory and the sub sequent policy of the Labour Party, and the Foreign Secretary, Bevin, have done away with what may have remained of that illusion. Now the Jewish people as a whole sees beyond any doubt that the "New England" too is prepared to do, with the help of its ally and former accomplice of Hitler—the Mufti of Jerusalem—what the "old England" had accomplished with the help of those same Arabs in the case of the Kurds, the Armenians and the Assyrians after the first World War. England wants to exterminate the Jewish people. For this reason our people has decided to take up the arms. This war continues and will not come to a close as long as you bar the only way of rescuing our people.

A great man, a Jew, once said: "People think that the Jew is as weak as a match. But 17 million matches have power enough to set ablaze the whole world." Through your fault six million Jews were slaughtered. Eleven million Jews only survived. But today our inflamability is infinitely greater than it was at the time those words were spoken. Do not think that on the grave of our hope, on the grave of the Jewish people, you will be able to set up your military base.

The earth will burn under your feet and you shall not be able to predict wither the sparks of the conflagration will fly and what other conflagrations will incinerate your own houses. Your economy possesses many inflamable points. There will be no victory for you in this war. The cessation of military operations and the occupation of the country of the enemy, usually indicative of the end of a war, will not spell victory for you in this war. Our Homeland has been occupied by you. You have amassed in it armed forces and military equipment in perfectly ridiculous amounts. But nevertheless—this war continues. You have entrenched yourselves in fortresses and behind barbed wire and pill-boxes: but you are not the masters of this country, you cannot rule it—because we—the Jewish people do not want you to. The Jewish people with its eleven millions, scattered all over the world is in a position to extend help in human material and equipment to the Yishuv, the advance-guard numbering 600,000 of the Jewish people in its Homeland. Your entrenchment in our country will meet with much greater difficulties than those faced by the Roman Empire. This entrenchment will cost you much, both in losses of life and war materials. As traitors, as breakers of international commitments, as the oppressors of our people you shall not survive here.

Our people you will not liquidate as you succeeded in doing with the Kurds, the Armenians and the Assyrians. You incited and let loose against them the forces of destruction for you hoped to rid yourselves of your pledges which you never had the intention to make good. This was also your hope with regard to Hitler whom your Mufti served. You wanted that Hitler should massacre the Jews in Europe. You speculated that with the disappearance of our brethren the eternal pressure of the masses of the People of Israel against the closed gates of its Homeland would equally disappear. This is why you permitted the death machinery of the Nazis to operate undisturbed and mercilessly. But your plans have gone wrong. In spite of all your calculations the survivors of destruction try with increased force to reach their homeland.

The Jewish people sees in Great Britain the real guilty party in all these catastrophes and disasters, and so long as you stand as an obstacle between us and our salvation we shall fight you.

OD LO AVDA TIQWATEJNU
(OUR HOPE IS NOT YET LOST)
By prisoner Dvora Kalfus

Gentlemen,

After you sentenced the two Jewish youths, Ashbel and Simchon, to death, both of them rose, stood at attention and sang, inspired with an enthusiasm you will never understand, our Jewish national anthem, Hatiqvah. The B.B.C. reported this fact, among others, while it was giving in a few short sentences to the world at large a picture of proud unyielding Jewish fighters who receive a death sentence with a song on their lips. You cannot deny that this is an amazing scene and though I do not know what impression it made on you, I do know that in these dark days of *cowardly brutality*, their stand and conduct could fill the heart of every free man with a renewed faith in man, in individualism and the values of human morality.

However, your radio did not content itself with reporting the fact as such: faithful to your general line it found it necessary to add some comment of its own, giving the statement the following text: "The two sentenced men, sang in the courtroom the so-called Jewish national anthem." The B.B.C. did not say simply: "the Jewish national anthem" but the "so-called national anthem." I wish to explain now why I dwelled on the term employed intentionally by your radio, and what the connection is between this fact and this trial. I shall bring another fact, equally instructive, which is also connected, though not formally but in essence with our trial, or rather, with the circumstances that led to our trial. The fact in question was published in one of the official statements of your Government: A British destroyer stopped on the open sea, apparently in accordance with the universal law of the pirates, a ship carrying refugees, Jews on their way to repatriation, Jews, who in spite of you, were returning to their Homeland. When your naval officers went aboard the ship they saw a flag hoisted on the mast of the ship. That was our flag, the blue-white flag of the Jewish people. However, your officers reported and your official statement repeated and published that the flag was "an unknown flag."

In these two characteristic facts is actually contained all the meaning of the war between you and us; these facts also explain perhaps better than all our speeches the political background of our collective trial here. You English neither recognise our national anthem nor our flag. And since there is no nation without a flag and an anthem of its own, it follows from your attitude that you do not recognise the Jewish people either. In other words, in this respect you identify yourselves with Adolf Hitler. He too argued that the Jewish people is not a people but a conglomerate of inferior creatures. His conclusion was: to exterminate us. You, Gentlemen, accept Hitler's basic assumptions; during the war you even assisted him in carrying out his conclusions. Now you are ready to continue along these lines and to transform the eleven million Jews, who survived, and who, in your opinion have neither a national flag nor a national anthem, that is not the image of a nation, which in turn implies that they have not the image of a man—you are prepared to transform them into candidates for extermination camps, precisely as you assisted the Nazis in putting six millions of our brethren into those camps.

This is your plan: to carry out this plan, or, rather as a result of this plan, you have robbed us of our country and it is your wish that we should continue to wander amongst the peoples, without a Homeland of our own, without a flag or, without "an unknown flag," without a national anthem or, without a "so-called anthem," and in your villainy—and I should add, in your stupidity, you assume that we are going to acquiesce in all this and will prefer the existence of a respite granted to slaves sentenced to death, to a war that though it may cost the loss of human lives will lead to the concentration of our peoples in its land with its own flag, recognised by all nations as the flag of a free and independent people. Your scheme, has, of course, been frustrated completely and the main reason is that we have not yet lost our hope—yes, Gentlemen, we have not lost our hope—od lo avda tiqvatejnu!

If after centuries of persecution and massacres and humiliation and squalor we have lived to be and to see Jewish soldiers with arms in their hands for the liberation of their homeland—then we have not yet lost our hope.

When after 19 hundred years have passed since the quelling of Bar Kochba's revolt we have lived to see another revolt of the sons of Juda, distinguishing themselves by the heroism of Bar Kochba's rebels, then our hope is not yet lost.

If after the terrible slaughter of six million Jews we have not been weakened but, on the contrary, won, increased faith in the eternity of Israel and its soon rebirth in its homeland, then our hope is not yet lost.

Our hope is not yet lost. . . . Do your rulers with their obstinate hearts and their dumb minds realise what this song means to us and to millions of our brethren? Do they know by whom and where this song was song? Yes—the Jewish heart sang this song for two thousand years; the Jewish youths sang this song when they went into battle and returned from the fight. But apart from this, do you know who had these simple and great words on their lips? I will tell you: when the foul Nazi murderers pushed our teachers, our brethren and sisters into the death waggons, then our martyrs sang "Hatiqvah."

When those who were our nearest and dearest were lining up

in the cemetery facing the graves they themselves had dug—they sang "Hatiqvah."

When the best of our peoples, our sages and scholars, our elders and our tiny children marched in their thousands to the gas cells—they sang "Hatiqvah." To return to this land of our fore-fathers were their last words sent by the pale lips of millions of Jewish martyrs, and "towards the east" they raised their eyes, before they left this world for ever.

And such a song hallowed more than any other anthem in the world, with *blood* you call "the so-called anthem"? You shall know, Gentlemen, we, the sons of Israel, will fight against you, until the hope has come true of the millions who were slaughtered because of you, you together with your confederate Hitler, did not recognise their anthem, did not recognise their flag, because you had stolen their homeland. In this war of liberation our nation is being created anew and it will force you to recognise it and its right to a homeland and symbols, of independence which are accepted symbols in all civilised countries. And you, too will recognise the Jewish people: voluntarily or not, but recognise it you will, and then, only then there will be normal relations between Israel and other peoples. Then any naval officer who will look at a ship that sailed past his own, and perceive the flag will say: Oh yes, this is a Hebrew flag. On the mast I can see the flag of the Land of Israel. When on that day one of you will hear the "Hatiqvah" he will stand at attention and salute the anthem of a free people just as we, the soldiers of Israel, will salute the anthem of another nation. This day will come—and we give our hearts for this day.

HE WILL LIVE IN OUR HEARTS FOR EVER
By prisoner Chaim Ander

Gentlemen,

I should like to remind you that apart from us, 31 captured soldiers, in this courtroom you should, according to your laws, have brought to trial another Jewish youth. Then this trial would have been called in the history of our people not the trial of the 31 but the trial of the 32. However, this youth can no longer be reached by your hands: you cannot fetter his hands with handcuffs, you cannot put his body behind prison wall. This youth is on our lists as one of our ranks—but he is no longer alive.

One of the hundreds of bullets that your machine guns spit at us hit our young brother, Avner Ben Shem. Seriously wounded he collapsed. But it would have been possible for you to save his life. There can be no doubt that had he been given appropriate care—

appropriate for an injured man, appropriate for a prisoner enjoying recognised rights, he would be here today; among us, sharing our sufferings and our hopes. But this was not to be. No medical treatment worthy of the name was given to our injured friend. His condition deteriorated while he was in our hands, and he breathed out his pure soul. This is not the first time that youths, young Jewish fighters having fallen in your hands wounded or sick have perished in your prisons through the physical and spiritual agonies inflicted on them. This is what happened to Asher Tratner, a pupil of a Haifa secondary school, who was shot in the hip while pasting a pamphlet on a house wall, and whose wound, though relatively slight, led to his death. Why? Because instead of sending the wounded boy into a hospital you sent him to a filthy dark cell in Acre prison and chained him on his bed of agony. For many days and nights the boy was compelled to wipe off with his shirt the blood and matter trickling from his wound. The result was that blood poisoning set in, and it was only after his condition had become hopeless that he was transferred from Acre to Haifa—after all, he had been arrested in Haifa—and he was sent to a hospital where his leg was amputed.

But the operation came too late—and the youth—almost a child—the only son of his parents, died. You should compare this treatment which you accord to our people captured by you to the treatment given to the British officers captured and taken prisoners by us. I read in the news papers the report by your officers who were released after a few days. One of them had been wounded with a stick when he tried to resist his captors: He received good treatment, his wound was bandaged by a nurse, he was looked after by a doctor, and was even given the assurance that the circumstances under which he had been injured would be investigated and if it should be found that he had offered no reason for the use of physical force against him, the soldier responsible would be punished. Your officers were released healthy and unscathed, because they had been held by really civilised men, by soldiers who respect the laws relating to the treatment of prisoners taken by belligerents.

With you, however, people fall ill with dangerous stomach diseases; people confined by you suffer from tuberculosis; in your prisons the prisoner's body is weakened through the bad food you give him. And if your plans do not succeed completely and the treatment given to the prisoner does not lead to his death, he is frequently rendered an invalid for the rest of his life.

For these reasons, Gentlemen, we demand that an end be put to this sort of treatment. These conditions cannot be tolerated any longer, conditions under which our blood is shed by your fault—not only in the countries of the Diaspora, not only on the battle-field, but even in imprisonment, where the life and health of prisoners ought to be safe. Learn from those who fight against you! Treat those whom you capture as they treat those of you taken prisoners by them!

Our young brother Avner Ben Shem, is no longer your prisoner. He has been freed before you sentenced him. He has not been brought to trial by you; he faces today the judge of the world. But even though his body is not with us today, his soul is here in this courtroom, and with the spiritual ear that is given only to idealists who are prepared to sacrifice their lives for a good cause, we hear his voice speaking to us from heaven, from spheres as sacred and pure as the bright firmament: Do not be afraid, my brethren! Go your way of suffering proudly and hopefully for it is worth it. It is worth fighting for our Zion, it is worth suffering for it, and it [is] worth even to die for it.

May the memory of our brother, Avner Ben Shem, be blessed for ever!

––––––––––––––

THE VERDICT

The illegal court in contravention of the basic law of humanity, sentenced 30 of the Hebrew soldiers, including one girl, to 15 years penal servitude each, and one of them, Benjamin Kaplan to life imprisonment.

The sentence having been announced, all the fighters rose to their feet and sang the national anthem of hope and redemption.

This is the Resistance: Palestine's Fighting Army of Liberation

"When in the course of human events, it becomes necessary for one people to dissolve the political bands which have connected them with another, and to assume among the Powers of the earth the separate and equal station to which the Laws of Nature and of Nature's God entitle them, a decent respect to the opinions of mankind requires that they should declare the causes which impel them to the separation. . . .

"And for the support of this Declaration, with a firm reliance on the Protection of Divine Providence we mutually pledge to each other our lives, our fortunes, and our sacred honor."

—from the Declaration of Independence

A MESSAGE TO THE AMERICAN PEOPLE
FROM THE COMMANDER-IN-CHIEF OF THE IRGUN

In the name of our tormented people and for the sake of its freedom-loving sons, we have unfurled the banner of revolt.

We are in revolt in order to restore the land, sovereignty, liberty to the Hebrew nation.

We are in revolt in order to liberate Palestine from British rule; the despotic rule of oppression which arrogantly tramples international obligations underfoot; the rule which seeks to crush the fundamental rights of men and nations.

We are in revolt in order to bring political freedom, social justice, and cultural progress to the Hebrew Homeland.

We are in revolt in order to reunite our land, West and East of the Jordan, which was severed by the British tyrants with the aid of their puppet desert princes.

We are in revolt, and we swear that no sacrifice shall be too great, that we will not lay down our arms nor cease fighting until the whole of Palestine is a free and independent state.

For years we stood alone in the field. The war cut our land off from the whole world and from our dispersed people. From the continent of Europe we heard the death-cries of our parents and brothers and loved ones. We knew the identity of their murderers; we knew too who had prevented their escape to freedom. We knew that had it not been for British perfidy, the rule of a foreign oppressor in our land, had the gates to Palestine not been barred, the German murderers would not have trapped our people, and six million of our brothers would be alive today, free, proud, creative. We knew, and we have not forgotten.

We have not forgotten. And we did not yield to British intimidation. We did not mind standing alone, and we did not delude ourselves with vain hope. We began to fight. We made dozens of attacks. We made priceless sacrifices. Our soldiers fell in battle, and hundreds were wounded and taken prisoner. Harassed mercilessly. Tortured in cellars. Exiled. But we remained unbroken. When one soldier fell, another rose to take his place. Like our brothers, partisans fighting in the forests of Poland, we too acquired all that we needed by our own strength and our own skill. We raided enemy camps. We armed ourselves with his guns and with his ammunition. We took money too, and the money became steel. Thus did the few fight the many, the weak against the strong. And the entire world learned that a new generation had arisen in Israel; a generation drawing superhuman strength from the motherland, hallowed from ancient times with the blood of the brave and the holy; a generation that loves liberty and despises slavery; a generation that revolts against oppression, and fights for truth and justice.

The war against Germany and Japan is over. The nations of the world have celebrated the first anniversary of their triumph. We mourn six million. We mourn the land still occupied by a foreign power, still closed to our people who, with the last ounce of their strength, came close enough to see it but are shunted away by British bayonets. Shunted away to one of the concentration camps that ring the Mediterranean.

But precisely because of this the fight for Hebrew freedom and independence is gaining strength and power. Here in Palestine even the eyes of our cautious leaders have been opened to see that there is only one alternative: we either fight and are *redeemed*, or we humbly accept the status quo and are *destroyed*. Internal strife has evaporated. No longer do the appeasers point us out to our common enemy. No longer do the deluded collaborators condemn our great leaders to imprisonment and exile. Today, all Palestine is united against our British enemy.

Nor does Britain take its occupation lightly. It is not cheap. She has six fully mechanized divisions, an imposing array of fighting ships, and hundreds of bombers and fighter planes, all thrown into the battle against a tiny country and a numerically small resistance army. And she is rushing more troops and more planes and more ships.

And outside of Palestine the British oppressors are confronted by the united and determined spirit of our brothers in Europe—by the peculiar strength of a people tested as was no other people on earth; people who learned during the course of years filled with inhuman suffering that without a land of their own and without freedom there can be no life, and that freedom is acquired only through struggle. Hardened by persecution, tested by suffering, taught by war they stand on the blood-soaked continent of Europe determined to go home at any price, and to fight, and die if need be, to make that home free.

The British cannot prevail against us no matter what they do. More blood will be poured out. More hatred generated. But Palestine will be free. And we are the new people who will make it free.

Embattled Palestine needs help. It needs your help—in men, guns, and money. Help us and the tempo of our fight for freedom will be increased, its scope widened. Help us so that the fight for freedom and the dignity of man will not be in vain.

THIS IS THE RESISTANCE

Irgun Zvai Leumi (The National Hebrew Army) was born of sharp political cleavages in Palestine. It had its inception during the Arab riots of 1929, was formally organized in 1931 and today it spearheads the struggle for Palestinian independence.

Mobilizing an army to be devoted to a clear-cut struggle for the freedom of their country was a momentous step for men in Palestine. Out of the ranks of the Haganah and the militant youth of Palestine who had abandoned faith in Britain's promise to carry out the terms of the Mandate, sprang the Irgun.

These men watched as Palestine, promised as a homeland for the Hebrews of the world, diminished under Britain's trusteeship. They therefore made the decision to act before Palestine was lost to the Hebrews entirely.

Three-quarters of Palestine's land had already been arbitrarily taken away by the British Government and converted into the Arab "Kingdom" of Trans-Jordan. Within what remained of Palestine, Hebrew agriculture was cramped by land sale strictures, and Hebrews were barred from cultivating 95% of the land. Development of Hebrew industry and manufacturing was jealously watched by the British Government and curbed by crippling taxes and regulations. An alarming rise in Arab outrages and attacks was viewed complacently by most British officials, while evidence accumulated to prove that other officials were in fact instigating the Arabs to murder and pillage while at the same time "appeasing" them with continuous political concessions and grants. Surveying these factors, the men who created the Irgun declared that certain political decisions must be made to preserve Palestine. They recognized the fact that they would be facing not only the open enmity of the British Administration, but that they would also have to contend with collaboration forces within the Hebrew community. The rift between the Haganah and the Irgun deepened. And while the Irgun Zvai Leumi's chiefs asked for an open fight against the British, Jewish Agency leaders greeted each new disappointment with an appeal for further collaboration. While the watchword of the Irgun became "Attack," the slogan of the Haganah remained "Restraint."

STRIKING POWER

The Irgun Zvai Leumi is Palestine's second largest armed force. Superior to the Haganah in striking power and aggressiveness, the Irgun is a smooth running, efficient commando army; its 10,000 men are welded together in small, self-reliant commando units. It has its tactical staff, and its own political and propaganda branches. It regards itself as the army of the Hebrew nation, and acts in furtherance of policies which it believes will help that nation.

NOT TERRORISM

The Irgun is not a "terrorist" organization. It does not commit acts of violence or assassination having no tactical purpose. It does not believe in violence for the sake of violence. Its aims are political—the freeing of Palestine from foreign domination, the repatriation of all exiled Hebrews, and the establishment of a free and truly democratic government. When it fights, it fights for these political purposes, and in a legitimately political manner. It regrets every casualty it is forced to inflict, and it inflicts none that is not forced upon it. It proclaims its friendship for the British people, as for every other people on earth, but it opposes heroically and fiercely the treacherous and heartless policies of the British *sahibs* who rule Palestine without the slightest consideration for its Hebrew population or the dictates of humanity.

REPATRIATION

Though the Irgun was conceived in 1929, it did not have occasion to take the field until 1936. By that time it had become a unified, coordinated organization. Its objectives—repatriation, freedom, a democratic Palestine—were defined, and plans made to accomplish them. By 1937 it had placed key men in Eastern Europe, the Balkans, and Germany. Working underground and employing bribery and coercion wherever necessary, they succeeded in smuggling some 40,000 Jews out from under Hitler's nose and into Palestine by 1940. In 1940, however, when the European war was suddenly transformed from Sitzkrieg into Blitzkrieg, extra-quota repatriation had to be suspended. At this point a truce with Britain was declared, and the Irgun was temporarily absorbed into Montgomery's Eighth Army that chased the "Desert Rat" all the way across Africa and back to Italy. Its officers held the King's commission.

On V-E Day "illegal" immigration—repatriation—was resumed. Members of the Irgun now dot the capitals of Europe and infiltrate into the DP camps in Germany. In a highly coordinated system, DP's are provided with complete instructions as to how to travel, where to go, and what to do to escape detection, and are sent on their way. With the utmost secrecy and at great expense boats are purchased or chartered. When all the arrangements are completed and the passengers hidden from sight on board, the ship quietly departs.

Not all "illegal" repatriates land safely. British troops and police patrol the coast of Palestine very carefully, and do succeed in apprehending transports. This has been especially true during the past month since Great Britain has mobilized in and around Palestine a mechanized army of six full-strength divisions, a fleet of cruisers, destroyers, submarines, and auxiliary vessels, and a striking air force as large as that which took part in the Battle of Britain. The "illegal" repatriates thus apprehended are placed in internment camps in Palestine, Eritrea, the Sudan, and now Cyprus.

Preventing the deportation of Hebrews and freeing those interned in concentration camps becomes then one of the major functions of the Irgun. Surprise raids on the camps are staged, the sentries over-powered, and the barbed wire fences cut. The internees are then dispersed among the nearest Hebrew settlements.

FREEDOM

The battle for freedom which the Irgun has been fighting in Palestine is a constant factor; it will continue until freedom is won or every member of the Irgun destroyed. Their code is simple—Liberty or Death.

"Ours is a fight to resist extermination. Ours a war to return to the Hebrew people the Home taken from us through deceit and by force. Without a home we cannot exist either as a people or as individuals. Without a home we face extermination. Our way is dedicated to the resolve that we, the Hebrew people, shall not perish from the earth."

The Irgun Zvai Leumi is at war with the enemy. The enemy is not the Arab. It is the Mandatory Power, Great Britain.

—The Irgun Zvai Leumi
in Palestine

PROCLAMATION . . .

July, 1946
Hebrews:

The arrest of the leaders of the Hebrew community is but a stage in the course of the planned extermination of the Hebrew people. It is being conducted with systematic ruthlessness by the British Government which is now occupying our country. The destruction of six million of our fellow men is a crime to which the British Government is an accomplice; it barred their entrance into our country; it forced them to die in the gas chambers and crema-toria of Nazi Germany. The recent raid and arrests is another crime. Its purpose too is extermination.

There is no alternative. Either we die on our knees or we fight for freedom NOW. Hesitation is a sin, delay iniquity, retreat a crime. The entire Hebrew people, in Palestine and elsewhere, must rise as one man, must marshal every last ounce of strength, and must employ every means at their disposal to fight the ruthless British oppressor until he is defeated.

The British regime, cloaked in "law and order," must be

replaced by a democratic, independent government of Palestine. Therefore, be it resolved:

1. That a Provisional Hebrew Government be established to represent the Hebrew people and to carry on the fight to eject Britain entirely from our country.
2. That the Provisional Government establish a parliament, or supreme national council, which shall act as the legislative and executive branches of our government.
3. That the Hebrew declaration of freedom and independence be made public so that all nations may take cognizance of it.
4. The constitution of our republic shall be based on the American Declaration of Independence, and on the principles of liberty, equality, and social justice for all the citizens of Palestine regardless of descent, creed, or color.
5. That a Hebrew army of liberation be established—an army which will not lay down its arms until Hebrew freedom and independence be obtained. That a supreme army command be set up to lead the army and direct the fight for freedom.
6. That the British "courts" be liquidated, and that they be replaced by Palestinian courts democratically established.
7. That the payment of taxes to the occupying power be discontinued and prohibited, and that a Palestine treasury be established to collect taxes democratically levied. The funds thus received are to be disbursed only for the common good and welfare.
8. That a call for aid be sent out to all the friends of fighting and beleaguered Zion, and that all the nations of the world be asked to help us.

The time to fight is now. Only if we fight now will we attain freedom and independence. We will cease being a "community," a "ghetto," persecuted by the self-styled "keepers of law and order." Only by fighting can Israel rise and live again.

Let there be no halfway measures. The fight for freedom and independence is an all-out fight with no holds barred. Let us be united and bold. Let our arms be strong, our aim clear, our faith invincible.

The fight for freedom and independence can end only in liberation or destruction. The fight is for "liberty or death."

DEMOCRATIC PALESTINE

The Irgun is the fighting element of a renascent Hebrew nation. This nation seeks to build a progressive, enlightened society—an independent, democratic republic wherein full freedom and equal rights shall be accorded to all, whether Jew, Moslem, or Christian.

Upon this basis there is ample justice for the existence and functioning of a Provisional Government of Palestine. It is supported by every democratic precept and precedent. In the consideration of this moral justification and the urgent practical needs of the moment, the Irgun recently submitted a memorandum to 250 leading figures in Palestine, setting forth its political aims, and outlining a program of action for their attainment.

The memorandum proposed that "the outstanding personalities of the nation should convene and decide, as a primary revolutionary step, to establish: (1) a Provisional Government of Palestine; (2) a Supreme National Council.

The first measures of the temporary government would be:

1. To announce its establishment in a public declaration to the Hebrew nation, partly dispersed and partly in Palestine, and to the nations of the world in a statement signed by all the members of the provisional government.
2. To announce that, inasmuch as the Mandatory Government has become an occupying regime preying upon the fundamental rights of the Hebrew people, Palestine is to be considered an *occupied* country and that, therefore, the Hebrew people are constrained to fight for the liberation of their land. Men and women all over the world—Jews and non-Jews—are asked to aid.
3. To call upon the Hebrews in Palestine not to accept the laws of the British Government in Palestine nor to obey its ukases.
4. To stop all payment of taxes to the occupying power.
5. To assure international protection for the Holy Places.
6. To assure equal rights and social equality for all citizens.
7. To offer treaties of friendship to all the neighbors of Palestine.

"This is the basic program. We are not delving into details. What is important is that the time has come when the Hebrew nation can take the initiative into its own hands, and, through forceful revolutionary effort, cut the accursed noose that strangles it."

"VOICE OF FIGHTING ZION"

The "Voice of Fighting Zion" is the Irgun underground radio station. Established in 1937 to aid in "illegal" repatriation, it went off the air when the Irgun was forced to discontinue repatriation in 1940. Soon after V-E Day, however, it returned to the air serving the dual purpose of directing "illegal" transports and overcoming the iron curtain of British censorship by broadcasting accurate reports of developments in Palestine to the people in Palestine and to the outside world.

The "Voice of Fighting Zion" is so well hidden and carefully protected that it was able to return to the air within twenty-four hours after the British carried out their big July raids in which thousands of Hebrews were arrested and in which numerous caches of arms were found.

IRGUN UNDERGROUND PRESS

Members of the Irgun operate several underground presses which publish regularly a number of "illegal" newspapers and pamphlets.

Typical of the spirit animating soldiers of the Irgun is the following excerpt from the illegal newspaper, Kherut, "Freedom," which is a monthly publication:

> "Hundreds of brave resistance troops have thus far fallen in the fight to eject England from Palestine and to save their brothers in Europe—in the fight for freedom. Thousands have spent years in jail, many in the concentration camps of Eritrea, the Sudan, and Palestine. These brave soldiers suffered and gave their lives so that others might live; they rescued forty thousand of their brothers from the horrors of Hitler Europe, and brought them to Palestine."

IRGUN BATTLE COMMUNIQUES

"During the night of February 25, large scale operations were carried out by the Jewish Resistance in Palestine. The airdromes at Kfar Sirkin, Lydda, and Quastina were attacked and many aircraft destroyed."

"In the middle of February, soldiers of the Irgun Zvai Leumi held up a train near Hedera, in broad daylight, and captured LP 35,000 from the treasury of the Palestine Administration."

"In full daylight on March 5, soldiers of the Irgun Zvai Leumi attacked the military camp at Sarafand, where the Sixth Airborne Division and other units are stationed. The guards were over powered, and from under the noses of the British officers and troops, a lorry load of arms and ammunition was captured. An ammunition dump containing 15 tons of explosives was blown up."

"On July 22nd, at 12:05 PM, soldiers of the Irgun Zvai Leumi attacked the central British Administration, the secretariat of the occupying government, and headquarters of the occupying army. According to a plan that was thought out beforehand, the explosive was set to go off *only half an hour* after it was brought into the building. Immediately after the explosive was placed, telephone warnings were given to the main telephone exchange of the King David Hotel, and to press bureaus, telegraphic agencies, and the French Consulate which were in the vicinity of the hotel. In addition to these warnings, a warning bomb (not harmful) was placed in front of the square of the hotel in order to get the public away from the hotel area. The tragedy which occurred in the civilian offices of the occupying government was not caused by Hebrew soldiers who performed their duty with courage and who, as soldiers, carried out their orders with military exactitude and precision including the time required for evacuation or removal of civilian personnel from the military target. (Rules of Land Warfare not violated). The tragedy was caused by the British themselves who paid no attention to the warnings; they undertook to remove the explosives despite warning signs—in the three official languages—that the bombs would explode at the slightest touch. Furthermore, Sir John V. Shaw, Chief Secretary for Palestine, was informed by the manager of the hotel as soon as telephone warnings of the bombing were received. But Sir John V. Shaw ignored the warnings, and said: 'I am here to give orders to the Jews and not to receive orders from them.' Sir John then gave strict orders to his guards to permit no one to either enter or leave the building. But Sir John and a few senior officers left the building and saved themselves."

"There are more important things in life than life itself. Hebrew youth will never submit to a life of servitude. It will fight for freedom though the stake be life itself."

(From a broadcast of the "Voice of Fighting Zion")

"What the German Nazis did to our brothers in Europe the British Nazis shall not do to us. We shall fight them as fiercely as freedom loving peoples have always fought tyranny. We shall not be enslaved."

(From a broadcast of the "Voice of Fighting Zion")

HAGANAH—"DEFENSE AND RESTRAINT"

Haganah ("Defense") as organized in 1920 to protect Hebrew pioneers in outlying settlements against the sporadic raids of nomadic Arab bandits. Today, it claims more than 60,000 members. Haganah operates as a home guard in which most of the personnel are part-time soldiers available for emergencies. A nucleus of approximately 3,000 constitutes the Palmach, whose members are closely organized into shock troops. Well disciplined, they devote the major part of their time to military activities. The Haganah does not constitute an underground army in the strict sense of the term. It has been tolerated by the British Administration which shut one eye to its existence and gave it considerable leeway in the community.

Despite the 26 disastrous years of British occupation, the Haganah continued to consider itself in terms of the fledgling defense organization of 1920. Its concept of "self-defense" merely gave way to that of "self-restraint"—a concept imposed on the Haganah by the leaders of the Jewish Agency.

At the present time the Haganah leadership faces a dilemma. The temper of the population demands action. Yet they are committed to the cautious line set by the World Zionist Organization which favors parleying and negotiations with the British. As a result of the conflict between Haganah policy and the temper of the people, it has been following a dual course of action and restraint, of deed and disavowal. Occasional "incidents" are staged as demonstrations of militancy which are then disowned in a subsequent return to the old policy of "holding back." The Haganah was responsible for blowing the Jordan Bridges and scuttling the vessels which the British intended to use for transporting Hebrews to Cyprus.

Because of the British military authorities' recent grim decision to completely liquidate the Haganah, its leaders and membership are moving toward a policy of action and steadily abandoning the 26 year rule of restraint.

THE FIGHTERS FOR THE FREEDOM OF ISRAEL

The Fighters for the Freedom of Israel (Sternists or F.F.I.) is the third, and smallest of the Hebrew nation's armies. They are usually described as being "fanatics," "terrorists," or worse.

The Sternists were organized by a magnetic Polish-Jewish youth, Abraham Stern, who was one of the earliest leaders of the Irgun. Ultimately, personal anger at the betrayal of Palestine drove him to split (in 1940) with the leadership of the Irgun and to assume the command of the fighting movement which bears his name. Stern and a small group of Irgun soldiers bluntly refused to go along with the Irgun policy of aiding the British Army in World War II. They demanded that the British first evacuate Palestine. All of their political decisions are made exclusively on the basis of the situation in Palestine.

Among the striking characteristics of the Sternists are the

extreme youth of its members and the frank facing of all risk. The Sternists developed a skill in personal retaliation as the best weapon for their war, because they realize the vast disparity between the numbers at their disposal and those of the British Empire. Soldiers of the "Fighters for Freedom of Israel" killed Lord Moyne on orders from the leaders. Moyne was openly acknowledged as the man responsible for ordering the steamer, "Struma," headed for Palestine, back to sea where it sank with 760 refugees. In the eyes of the Sternists, Moyne was a guilty man, responsible for the death of thousands.

The F.F.I. have often been castigated for "terrorism" and "irresponsibility," usually by persons who have not taken the trouble to look into their background. Their group was born under circumstances of exceptional violence and repression; their goal is peace and freedom for their nation. While it is still possible to disagree with their methods, it should be difficult for a person of feeling and spirit to flatly condemn them after realizing the forces which motivate them. The intellectual level of the members of F.F.I. is extraordinarily high, it is reported by persons who have had contact with them.

Announcement

1. On the 23rd September, 1946, our soldiers attacked a train carrying fuel from the refineries situate at Haifa to Suez in Egypt, for the use of the occupation army of the British war machine.

The attack on the train began at 19.15 p.m., while the train was in motion, but cutting-off with explosives the wagon occupied by the train's escort from the remaining wagons of the train. The escort was driven-off by the attackers' fire without having time to put up any resistance. The train's civilian personnel (who happened to be Arabs) were removed from the train and were ordered to keep away from the danger area. The engine was completely destroyed. Trucks carrying fuel tanks were destroyed and severely damaged while others were set on fire.

Our soldiers returned to Base with their equipment intact.

2. We have nothing to do with what was described by the lies factory better known as the British Public Information Office, as "an attack on a railway bridge on the Jaffa-Lyda line." The attackers there were described as "dressed in uniform," and it is to be presumed, therefor, that they were a unit of the enemy's forces, who, for one reason or another, clashed with the sentries on the bridge.

[A Letter to Cpl. William Smith from a Well-Wisher]

1234567 Cpl. William Smith,
000 Coy., The Blankshire Regt.,
Palestine.

Dear Bill,—
    Are you the next?
    There are some terrorists being held for trial and liable to be sentenced to death.
    So someone will be kidnapped. And what happens to him after depends on who his parents may be. Are *you* the fall guy?
    The first hostages the terrorists collected were a bunch of Majors and Captains. There was some give and take. The hostages were taken back. The terrorists were given jail sentences.
    The time after, the Jews lifted an ex-Major and a Judge—who is an heir. *They* were sent back almost at once. Terrorist score: a four-months' stay of execution for their thugs.
    Last time the haul was not so hot. Officers were too well protected: they had to make do with sergeants. So the Government "refused to be intimidated" and hanged the terrorists. And the terrorists hanged Martin and Paice.
    You're only a Corporal, Billy. So it's time you started being the son of a Baronet.
    You're the mug, Billy-boy.

                                                            Well-Wisher

Geneva and Jerusalem

    What are the doings of the "national envoys" in Switzerland?— We have got *authoritative information* on this subject.
    They are pressing upon UNSCOP to make it recommend the plan of partition.
    They do not care about area: frontiers do not matter. What they want is partition—just partition.
    And those "national envoys" know—or should know—that:
1. *The partition plan is impracticable.*
2. A recommendation by UNSCOP on partition would require the *appointment of a new international committee* to fix an endless number of "details."
3. Meanwhile, the British rule of blood would remain on the scene.

4. Meanwhile, there will be no immigration.

5. The inmates of the camps will either starve or disperse.

Still they are besieging the members of UNSCOP: "Give us partition!"

But their pressure is so clumsy, and their replies to questions on *practicability* so idiotic—that several members of UNSCOP who at first were inclines towards partition have since gained the impression that all this partition affair is merely a means to obtain "Ministerial portfolios" for the members of the Jewish Agency.

Such are the doings of your "envoys." And such is their reward.

And their is a straight line leading from Geneva to Jerusalem.

There is a direct connection between what your "envoys" are doing in Geneva and what they promise to do in Jerusalem.

They have got to prove that they would be able to *rule* in the Jewish ghetto if such is recommended.

They know—and explain it to the Gentiles—that the "opposition" to the partition scheme is not serious. True, the "Hashomer Hatzair" are dispatching cables against partitioning the country; but they would go into the ghetto all the same, in order to keep "what they have." "Hatnua Le'Achdut Ha'avoda" have been indeed claiming in the past that, should the Jewish Agency devise or accept a plan of partition, "its authority would cease to be binding on the people"; but already it has become evident that all these radical statements were nothing but mere talk. The Agency has already devised a partition plan, but "Hatnua Le'Achdut Ha'Avoda" has contented itself with letters of protest. This party, too, would go into the ghetto—with a protest. Thus—the Agency envoys say—don't heed the opposition of various Zionist parties. "We shall settle this matter; the majority will be with us; the minority will acquiesce."

But there the Gentiles ask: and what about the Underground? Isn't it true that the Underground is opposed to any partition scheme, and that it usually translates its words into action?

The "envoys" are replying to this:—Yes, the Underground is indeed opposed to the partition plan—but (or just because of this) we shall liquidate it *already here and now.* We shall remove the last obstancle; Give us partition!

Now, Jewish compatriots, you will realize whence this surprising determination of the panicky institutions "to uproot terrorism *at any cost.*" Now you will understand why this Mapai—the most opportunist party of all times—has taken the lead in the crusade against the "dissidents"; now you will guess why Ben-Gurion—the most confused creature of our Jewish age—is demanding to expel "suspects" from their flats and jobs, i.e. practically to deliver them to the British C.I.D., and to kill, wipe out and destroy.

Now you will understand:—

For the sake of a *fata morgana*, for the sake of a childish illusion of a partition plan which will never realise but will merely prolong the sufferings of the people both in exile and in the home-land—for this they are prepared to cast upon all of us the disaster of fratricidal war.

They want to prove their ability to "rule" in the ghetto, and in their utter blindness they fail to see that their scheme is not only *criminal* but also *impracticable.*

They will not get the "puppet state."

And they will not liquidate us.

They will merely bring shame upon the people—and upon themselves. And in another couple of months, when it will mani-festly appear that we have not been liquidated but rather reinforced; and when it will be seen that partition has died even before it was born, or died at once after birth—then they will stand as an empty trough before Gentiles and Jews alike, and they will again seek confused phrases to cover their disgrace before the eyes of the world.

It is against these aberrations that we call upon the people: BEWARE!

Fighting Judea

January 1947   Tevet 5707

A REPLY TO AN AMERICAN FRIEND

Mr. Clark Baldwin, envoy of the President of the United States, has appealed to us publicly to postpone military action against the British oppressors until he renders his report to the President and Congress on our struggle for freedom and survival.

Mr. Clark Baldwin is a devoted friend of our nation. He asks for the reconstitution of Eretz-Israel, as a free and independent Jewish State. Therefore we are bound to reply to his appeal and this reply will be as simple and sincere as were the explanations given to Mr. Baldwin in the interview with our representative.

Mr. Baldwin, we whole-heartedly appreciate your friendship towards our tortured people and we believe in your sincere and noble intentions. We know that in your demand for the liberation of our country you are speaking on behalf of millions of free American men and women of all religions and races, who are convinced that the return of Zion and its liberation from the foreign yoke is an act of divine and social justice. We know that they all whole-heartedly support our struggle for freedom; that every one of them as a schoolboy learned how Washington compelled the British oppressors of his country to surrender to the American people those "Inalienable Rights" which they tried to deny to your forefathers.

Nevertheless we cannot, Mr. Baldwin, comply with your request. Because you are asking of us an impossibility: *to wait.*

We cannot wait. The hundreds of thousands of our brethren in the "liberated" concentration camps cannot wait. Those who freeze in the trains while trying to escape death cannot wait. Because of them *we* cannot wait. Furthermore we cannot wait because of the deeds and plans of our enemy, who strives systematically and cruelly for the liquidation of our last hope. He pushes us into a Ghetto. He bars the gates of our country before her bleeding sons. He dooms all of us to extermination.

You promise the help of the American Government for our just cause. But the American Government has had too many occasions to help a people in agony and to compel the British, dependent on its good will, to give back the home which they robbed from us. However your Government satisfied itself with lip-service, with declarations of sympathy and "recommendations" which accompanied millions of our brethren on their hopeless march to the gaschambers, and which reached the ears of the sons of Israel on their way to British concentration camps in Eritrea, Latrun, Acre and Cyprus.

We assume that some American statesmen, anxious to help, were simply deceived by the hypocritical British experts in treachery. We remember the experience of the Anglo-American Inquiry Committee. But on the other hand we have reason to believe that some other influential members of your Government are working hand in glove with our enemy in order to divert our nation from active resistance to the liquidation plot. We cannot forget the Gredey-Morisson plan. Now a new oil agreement has been reached between Britain and America and while it is premature to foresee its general international repercurssions, one thing is quite certain:

In every barrel of oil which your Standard and Socony Companies will get from the Anglo-Iranian Company, there will be at least one drop of Jewish blood.

Therefore, Mr. Baldwin, we regret that we are unable to comply with your appeal. We cannot rely on promises any more, not even when they are given by respected persons. What our tormented and fighting people needs is *real help.* And when this is not forth coming no other way is left to its sons than to help themselves, to rely on God, on their fighting spirit and their spirit of self-sacrifice.

In this struggle for freedom and justice we will certainly obtain the assistance of freedom-loving men and women in your great country and all over the world.

AFTER THE CONGRESS

Two negative decisions of a positive character were taken by the Zionist Congress. One is not to attend the London conference, and the second not to allow the man who symbolizes appeasement and complete capitulation to represent the official Zionist movement.

But that is all. The Congress which closed down without ending its deliberations did not indicate any new way to a people fighting for its survival. The Congress was unable to do so, because it was rendered helpless by political and personal friction.

The Congress decided not to attend the London conference, but left the door open for further negotiations. Negotiations about what? Everybody knows that the real plan of the Jewish Agency is the plan of partition, despite the theoretical reiteration of the Biltmore formula. And as this plan remains in force, the danger persists that the people will be deceived by a "compromise" between the partition plan of the Jewish Agency—a compromise which means liquidation and extermination.

In a few days we will see what the "radical" resolutions of Basle really mean. If they result in putting an end to the so-called armistice which the official armed forces were compelled to observe by a frightened leadership, they will be of great and perhaps decisive importance. But if the cursed "truce" continues and with it the besmirching campaign against the fighting forces, it will be a proof that the resolutions are no more than a theoretical and tactical camouflage of the policy of capitulation. Basle will be tested in Jerusalem. "Radical" resolutions can best be probed in one place: on the barricades.

One of the best camouflaged British agents—besides Mr. Richard Crossman—is Mr. Alston, known also as David Courtney. This agent plays the double role of a left-wing radical and of a devoted friend of the Jewish people, in order better to influence first the "progressive circle" with his anti-Russian propaganda and then to convince the Jews to aquiese in British bondage. These are well known tricks of British Intelligence men.

But some days ago Mr. Alston threw off his mask. He published an article in the "Haarez" in which provocation and blackmail are too evident for any doubt to remain as whom the able journalist is serving. Mr. Alston says that the fact that there were no attacks against the British occupants in Eretz-Israel during the sessions of the Zionist Congress, proves that the Jewish Agency is able either to stop or to renew the so-called terrorist campaign. This is the provocation. Mr. Alston says further that if military action is again undertaken, the occupation government will immediately institute wholesale reprisals against our people. This is blackmail—

We are not going to enter into polemics with a journalist who uses such methods to influence public opinion. But for the sake of the truth we state the following facts:

1. There was, and there will be, no truce in Eretz-Israel.

2. The Jewish People is in a state of war with Great Britain who occupies its country and endangers its very existence. It is a continuing state of war which will not cease until the British return the land of Israel to the people of Israel. Military attacks against the British occupants, their character, timing and location are planned and executed by the Underground Army, which alone is responsible for them. No Jewish official body, as is well known, is entitled to interfere with our decisions.

3. It is true that at the time of the sessions of the Zionist Congress in Basle we did not carry out military attacks in Eretz-Israel, but this decision was taken on our own initiative. We had appealed to the Congress in a special message, not to attend the London conference, to reject partition and to raise a united fighting front and we did not want to create a false impression that the Congress was under "pressure" of any kind.

4. The blackmail campaign of British agents and even the most cruel reprisals of the British occupants will not frighten our people and our youth who are determined to fight the oppressors until they withdraw from our native land.

HANUCCA 1946

Again we kindled the first candle of Hanucca, the feast of the renewal of heroism and of victory. In the light of this small candle we saw not only the glorious past, but also the present with its glories and calamities.

For some seventy or eighty generations our dispersed people was ruled—using the words of Disraeli—by tradition. And one of the most powerful traditions, which upheld the people's spirit was that of the Maccabean victory. But it was only a tradition, a remembrance of old days which only a God's miracle could bring again to an enslaved and persecuted nation.

Nowadays Hanucca has become more than a tradition. It has become a symbol of our own generation. Before our very eyes the spirit of the Hasmonaim has been rekindled and the banner of freedom raised by them thousands [of] years ago, is again in the hands of their descendants.

As Hanucca has become so near and real we see clearly the analogy between that remote time and our own days. At that time the Hebrews were—strange to say—a quantitive minority in their country. This is the case to day. Then the very existance of the nation was endangered by a mighty empire and by an inimical world. This is the case to-day. At that time appeasers and defeatists were the official leaders of the nation. This is the case to-day. At that time a minority of "unauthorized" but determined patriots—in other words, "terrorists"—raised the banner of revolt against the mighty oppressors.

It is indeed an almost complete historic analogy and as we look at the small candle burning again not only in our homes but also in our hearts, leading not only to prayers but also to battles—we know that the analogy will be carried out to the end. They, our forefathers, after long years of struggle, of victories and defeats, advances and setbacks—brought the lights of renaissance into the Holy-Temple, thus bringing freedom to the nation. They did it despite the physical superiority of a cruel foe and despite treacherous officialdom. The weak became strong and behind the fighting minority all the people united in war and in victorious peace. So will it be in our generation. After a period of struggling and suffering; of achievements and disappointments, of underground fighting and of open warfare, victory will be achieved by a united and fighting people. Fighting against a cruel foe and united despite—Weizmans.

BRITISH GESTAPO

We wish to bring to the attention of the world some details of the tortures to which the four youths arrested on the Lydda-Petah-Tikvah road on the December 29 were exposed during 4 days and nights, while in the hands of a wild soldiery, drunken with hatred. With regard to 5th man captured at the same time there is no doubt that he was deliberately murdered or tortured to death, as the wound he received in the car was very slight and he could with normal medical treatment have been saved.

The four a/m youths were brought into a military camp after having been beaten with rifle butts on their hands, faces, legs etc., with furious cruelty, so that an arm of one was broken, the nose bone of another broken and the face of a third prisoner covered with blood. But all this was not enough. The boys were put into a room, chained and their clothes hacked off with razor-blades—together with the skin. Then they were left naked all the night and were compelled to touch the floor with their lips. In the morning they were compelled to run wholly naked around the camp and when completely exhausted they were brought to a nearly police station. There a military doctor was sitting and after having examined the prisoners he asked the soldiers if they would like to continue "to play" with the boys. The answer was—of course. Then the Bergen Belsen doctor said that they would be all right. The prisoners were run back to the camp and the tortures went on. The soldiers poured excrements on their heads, cut their hair and ordered them to sweep the floor with it. "Heil Hitler" accompanied this Nazi spectacle. The pouring of excrement was repeated for 4 or 5 times.

It is to be noted that officers were present in the torture chamber. The men are now in Jerusalem central prison and are hardly recognisable.

EIGHTEEN LASHES
(A sentence of 18 strokes was carried out against a young soldier of the Irgun)

Eighteen lashes on the bare back of the youthful recalcitrant! Eighteen lashes to bring home to his inexperienced mind the austereness of British Justice, the force of its imperial might! A dozen lashes and yet another half dozen too to bruise his back, to crush rebellion from his heart: the crack of the whip, the victim's stifled moan to agonise his parents, to humble his race, to kill pride and spirit, to destroy the natural urge to shake the tyrant from his saddle.

One score of strokes minus two plied by puritans; the Empire's haughty counterblast against the right to want freedom, the right to speak for freedom, the right to fight for freedom, the right to strike at tyranny's shakles masquerading as a mandatory earnestly seeking a way out of a dilemma!

Let the sound of these lashes echo; let it reverberate; Hark, you who have survived the foul purposes of Hitler who in the light of contemporary events is slowly taking on the shape of a gentleman!

Listen to the fury of the British lash, you who are pining behind British barbed wire; you who are wondering in indignation behind British prison bars; you who weep for your sons and daughters, wives or husbands, your friends and dear ones; you who are in anguish, who chafe, who protest in every fibre of your being against the colonial concepts of human dignity, human law and human security. Listen and be tutored, you incorrigible ones! See the scouring flaying mission of the lash as it falls upon the stubborn back of unyielding youth! It has come to teach you the inviolable rights of Britons to maintain their Empire, to preserve their imperial routes to bask in the shimmering transluence of the most modern of Gods—Oil. The rights of a bureaucracy never in the wrong, to make arbitary decisions, arbitary "laws," arbitary and indiscriminate arrests; the rights of Britons to trample upon the sanctity of written promise, to trample upon the sanctity of the spoken promise, to violate the word spoken yesterday if it does not suit the purpose of today, the purpose of the drab, dreary fleeting hour! The sacred, the hallowed, the uncompromising right of Mistress England to shoot into the rooms—deliberately shoot—of a non-combattant population where women and children crouch against the walls or scramble under the furniture; the right, the noble right of self righteous England to hold women and children and all and sundry hostages against the rifle point.

Yes, let us drink fully the inspiring message of the eighteen strokes! England is now vindicated. Why should she be checked in her altruistic motives when all she asks is the mere sacrifice of a nation's right to freedom, air, the right to its track of territory under the sun and the right to fight for one's pride and one's place amongst the children of God!

THE FLOGGING INCIDENT

There is no doubt that in historical perspective, the flogging reprisals will be regarded merely as one of many episodes in the long history of the Jewish revolt. But in the records of nations, whether oppressors or rebels, incidents arise whose importance is incalculable. The incident of the flogging of British officers will rank among these. We are confident that the historian of the future will devote more space to the evaluation of the act than to its dry details.

Similar[l]y, the famous Boston Tea Party, in American revolutionary days, is remembered for its historic significance—a significance which had nothing to do with the losses caused to the British by the dumping of a shipload of tea, but which indicated the spirit and the steadfast resolution of a people in revolt.

In order to appraise the matter properly it should be viewed in its true historical perspective. Hebrew youth set out grimly in behalf of a fighting organization *which is particularly fond of keeping its word*—to retaliate against an insult to the personal, national and military honour of one of their comrades. This is the first time in two thousand years of Jewish history that such a reprisal has taken place. In British Imperial experience a thing like this has not happened for centuries.

For thousands of years our people has been the victim of the lash. In the diversity of our exiles the whip—figuratively and actually—has come down upon our bent, beaten and bleeding backs. Our ancestors became accustomed to it. One gets used to anything even humiliation debasement, beatings and scorn. Some were even able to stroke the rod that beat them or pay homage to the hand that wielded the lash. Some survivors of this school of thoughts, unfortunately are still with us even in the Land of Israel.

But—and here is the rub—a new generation was arisen in the meantime. They do not look upon questions of honour as the special province of gentiles of squires and drunken lords whom the "clever" Jew despised from the depth of his oppressed soul. To them honour is as natural as the air they breathe; as kinship with the native soil upon which they have been taught to tread, erect and proud. This new youth will no longer strive to devise ingenious excuses for its lack of healthy human reactions when the need arises. The era of humiliation and degradation has ended. Jews are not to be whipped any more—this is the moral which our people will draw from our reaction.

The lesson for the British is of a different nature. We were the flogged, the British the one to handle the whip which, for centuries has been coming down unopposed on the backs of subjected peoples.

The whip stands for the prestige of the ruling caste; it significes its might, its supremacy. Then something happens—in one of those "oriental" countries—to upset the well ordered apple cart. Somebody has been presumptious enough to knock the whip out of their hand. Once the flogger gets back a dose of his own medicine; the whip loses all its moral force as an "educative" factor, it becomes obsolete, and that cornerstone of Imperial authority, Prestige, breaks down completely.

The British have not been slow to grasp the situation. Their press is raising a furour over the "shocking insult" to the British army done by "ungrateful Jews." But it appears their comprehension stops short at that stage.

In the folly of their pride they still refuse to understand. Pride is something reasonable in themselves; but as for foreigners or natives it must be accounted sheer insolence for them to display a sense of wounded feelings and human dignity. Now that they have come to realise that the whip may be a double edged instrument, they may slowly begin to realise the metal of the human material they have to deal with in this country. And they might heed again the words of Disraeli—who is as much theirs as ours—: "When your ancestry were still contriving an existence amongst the wild swine of the eternal forests"—he once said to an non-Jewish listener—"of our ancestors it was said: a Prince of God thou art in our midst."

ACCOUNT OF ACTIONS
(Broadcasted on 5th January 1947)

We broadcast to-night an account of the attacks carried out by I.Z.L. soldiers against British military targets in the last few days. The operations started after a warning had been widely distributed, according to which inter alia, military vehicles moving on the roads of our country will be attacked:

1. On the night of January the 2nd the following attacks were carried out:

a. The Jerusalem concentrations of British troops were attacked with grenades and an armoured police car—with a flame-thrower.

b. In Tel-Aviv a concentration attack against British army H.Q. "Citrus House." A military armoured car park attacked and a police wireless vehicle blown up and destroyed.

c. In Haifa area an armoured car park attacked, a bren-carrier rushing to the scene of the attack destroyed and a big military armoured vehicle overthrown by a mine and heavily damaged.

d. In Hadera area army vehicle park attacked by explosives and two jeeps on the road blown up and destroyed.

e. In Tiberias armoured vehicle park attacked by flame-throwers.

2. On January the 3rd at 07.00 hrs. a military vehicle near Kfar Sirkin blown up and a jeep leading a military column destroyed near Raanana.

3. On January the 4th a military vehicle blown up on Jerusalem-Beth Lehem road and a jeep destroyed on Mt. Carmel.

Enemy casualties: one Captain killed, 20 other ranks injured, 5 policemen wounded.

Our casualties: 2 soldiers wounded.

The flame-thrower used in the recent attacks by us was constructed and made by our specialists. It will be used also in future attacks.

Following constant attacks against British military lines of communication, the Occupation Government was compelled to lift the road curfew imposed in part of the country as a collective punishment against the population after the flogging-retaliation against British officers. On the other hand military trafic was brought almost to stand still.

Fighting Judea No. 6

GENERAL BARKER'S LAST "DEED"

The baseness of the man and the degenoration of the criminal rule are fully symbolized in the murder order signed by the former GOC British occupation forces in our country General Barker. This Nazi-British General was to leave the country and his post before February the 15, while the so called "trial" of our four captured comrades took place on February the 10th. It is the normal procedure that at least some weeks pass until the file is sent to the GOC and he and his counsellors take their decision. In this last case a procedure was adopted without precedent. On *the morrow* after the "sentence" was passed the file was handed over to Barker and three days later his confirmation of the three death-sentences was given and published. All this has been done in order to enable Barker to still his blood-thirst and his lust for vengeance. On the very day of his leaving, the murderer in General's uniform left a "souvenir" to the country: an order to kill three Hebrew war-prisoners. The haste was unusual; the procedure was put aside—hurry, hurry, Barker must use his last chance to murder three sons of the hated race.

We are not in position to know whether this dastardly act was done by Barker himself or with the combined consent of the others, who wanted to kill, but did not wish, so to speak, to make things difficult for the new Commander of the occupying Army. In any case, the most shameful act in the country's modern history has been perpetrated and it proves how degenerated is this blood-stained rule.

Surely they all are glad now. Barker is glad that he "succeeded" in avengening his bitter defeats. The so called "socialist" Government is also glad; Churchil will be given proof that it is composed of "men."

The question however is to be asked how long will they be glad? We do not find it necessary to reiterate our warning in connection with the murder of prisoners. Killing defenceless prisoners of war is one of the basest crimes.

If the crime is commited, the Underground will do its duty. It will do it under any circumstances. And the responsibility for all that will occur in this country after the cold-blooded murder of our comrades will rest with the murderers.

TO DOV GRUNER

From the depth of the fighting Underground, from our heart of hearts we salute you, brother Dov.

How many are those who want thy life? Churchil, always ready to sacrifice millions of lives (other than British) for the sake of British "prestige"; the British Government—the so-called "socialist" Government, which seeks your blood in order to "repair its prestige"; and the whole of that Empire, which strives to destroy our people—with its ministers, commissioners and armies—have risen against you.

You, brother Dov, face all of them alone, from your lonely confinement in an isolated cell with but one neighbour—death. Nevertheless they are not able to vanquish you, all those blood-thirsty rulers. Because in their way they have met *you*, the man, who rose suddenly from the rivers of Jewish blood and proved that there is no force in the world which can break his spirit. Indeed, brother

Dov, if there is any meaning in the word "hero," *you* are the hero, from whom generations will learn the true nature of heroism.

Your fighting family did all in its power, in order to save you from the hangman's hands. This is its duty towards you; this is its duty towards other fighters. This is not a question of saving life. Everyone among us is ready at any moment to give his life for his faith, for his people. It is a matter of principle, of a sacred principle, which we will never give up, whatever the cost. *The life of a captured fighter, the life of a prisoner of war is inviolable.*

Brother Dov, the whole Jewish youth bows before your silent heroism and unsurpassed readiness for sacrifice.

AFTER LONDON
Words to the Jewish Agency

This is the fruit of your "diplomacy"; this is the result of your "truce."

Despite the raging British terror, despite the closed gates, despite the continuous deportation of our repatriates, despite the White Paper which continues in force, despite the evident liquidation plans—despite all—you suspended the struggle, initiated partition, went to London, and traded with the country's soil. For that you got—the Bevin-plan: no "independence," no Agency, no Aliya, no colonisation, no hundred thousand certificates—

a Ghetto!

A Ghetto in a British-Arab state, a ghetto, the fate of which will be sealed on the day of its establishing.

Now you claim that the "new" liquidation-plan is a disappointment and an injury to you. But the fault is yours!

You demonstrated more anxiety for your official "priviliges" than for the people's future—consequently you gave up the future and lost the priviliges. You promised the oppressor "tranquillity" and raised hope in his heart so full of hatred, that there will be no more resistance and that if it does not cease—you will stop it "by your own means." You fell into the trap of intended "negotiations" and turned a pawn in the enemy's hands. You brought upon yourselves a double shame:

In Jerusalem they dare to ask you to turn police-informers and in London they dare demand from you to "negotiate" seriously on the basis of federalisation, cantonisation—liquidation.

"This is not our last word"—say the satanically sly oppressors. Of course it isn't. They will put forward scores of new plans, but always they will have one purpose: to kill Jewish freedom and gain time, while we lose blood.

Will you again fall into the trap?

We call upon the masses of our nation and youth: put an end to the calamity! You now see that all our warnings came true and that the nation as a whole has been put on the brink of the abyss. Would you wait until we are physically fenced behind ghetto-walls? Will our fate be like that of the Warsaw-Ghetto?

Don't permit yourselves to be frightened by the bogey of "martial-law." Martial law will bring hardships and suffering, but it is now no longer a question of suffering; the question is to be or not to be, the question is of life or death—to our brethren in exile, to us, to our children—to the whole nation.

And the nation which choses life and not death, freedom and not serfdom, a liberated motherland and not a ghetto—calls upon all its sons:

Rally round the banner, of resistance, to the fighting front, to arms!

TAKE THEIR TROUSERS DOWN

Trousers, as everybody knows, are an essential and indispensable accoutrement of homo sapiens, masculine gender. There was a time when sundry gentry would yield to the night shirt in their bed-chambers, but today the Pyjama has come to the rescue and the current specimen of manhood goes betrousered by day and betrousered by night; in fact he is never to be caught untrousered—not even when napping. This brings us to recent events when no less a person than a Major, was stripped in certain grievous circumstances of this sacred and inseparable garb, as the prelude to a whacking or flogging in reply to a similar sentence carried out by his military superiors. The flogging side of the incident does not concern us here at all. What fascinates us is the letting-down-of-the-trousers aspect, which, the more we ponder over it, the more are convinced possesses implications deserving the ear of whatever there still is of civilised mankind.

We can imagine one of the gentlemen involved in this notorious ritual of firm and solemn detrousering, holding forth let us say, before some tribunal of Public Opinion listening tongue-tied to his Defence of Detrousering which would perhaps take on the following vestments:

"Gentlemen,

I am here today to set down my reasons in justification of the detrousering of civilised man. Why detrousering? Why this ignominy? this merciless unmanning this cruel stripping, this shameless divestiture?

"In explanation"—he would continue—"let me take you to primitive times. I want you to come back with me to the days when a spade was called a spade; black was known as black and white as white; when men—whatever their vices and shortcomings—had never yet ascended the heights of cultural attainments which have taught them to cover their thoughts, to distort their meanings, to cloud with ambiguity their commonest utterances, to speak with the voice of angels whilst doing the deeds of beasts.

"Consider for a moment"—and here the speaker's voice betrays just a wee suspicion of a break of emotion whilst the audience evince sympathetic tension—"Consider for a moment the barbaric tribesmen of old. They would kill one another, scalp one another, raid and harrass, make peace and war alternately and commit outrages untold, but what they did was never vernished [sic] with unspeakable cant or camouflaged with brazen pretexts.

"Your savage tribesman returning from an expedition would quietly enter his tent, get his wife to fetch him a beverage and to satisfy her curiosity would tell her very prosaically that he had clubbed so and so to death or ripped open somebody's bowels, or just scalped him, or merely hacked off his head or his leg, and taken away some of his property—had brought her a complete set of finger-nails as a memento. No excuses, no pretexts, no vernish. He didn't say he had gone off to civilize somebody, to maintain Law and Order, to keep the peace between two conflicting parties, to carry out his obligations under a Mandate, to protect a suffering minority or defend an indigent population against the wicked encroachments of plotting foreigners.

"He had none of the artifice that makes possible a description in the Press of an orgy of organized brutality as something that never took place or is merely exaggerated; none of the cold courage that orders people off a bus to show their identity cards and then lets off a shower of bullets against their unguarded heads and calls it a regrettable—*very regrettable*—accident! none of the exalted temerity that shoots at women and children, at anybody and everybody through open windows and then suavely "explains" that somebody was shooting at them on the roof-tops and of course they had to "defend" themselves.

"None of the arts and artifices of civilization; none of its wanton heartlessness, its base dishonour, its cowardly treachery, its mealymouthed sanctity of utterance.

"And now ponder, my dear friends, just ponder this: this savage, this downright consistent, outspoken, unspoilt creature of the elements—*he* never wore trousers; did anybody ever catch *him* with anything more than a loin cloth of the sparest proportions? Had he dared even so much as to toy with the idea of donning anything that bore the merest resemblance to trousers his life would no longer be worth living.

"Gentlemen, I declare byond all fear of contradiction that your thoroughgoing, real, genuine corruption, rot, humbug and deceit only took root when trousers became a fixed institution in human life.

"It may be safely asserted that a man's integrity and decency are distinctly related to the respective degree of indifference he displays towards his trousers. Your poet, your dreamer, your schoolmaster, your student in revolt against spreading tyranny, are distinguished by baggy knees, faded fabric, sagging and breadbare [sic].

"But your Diplomats, your Ministers of State, your Plenipotentiaries, your Bureacrats-in-chief your official spokesmen, your wealthy wire-pulling magnates, in short, those that make the world go round and give honest men heart-disease, they know how trousers should be worn and that no exellence is achieved without consummate perfection of the trousers.

"Watch the Minister of State as he delivers the speech of his career, upholding the rights of tyranny and oppression in defence of interest!

"Look below, look below, observe the trouser length, how haughty it stands, an unbroken line, a solid phalanx of unassailable respectability, a masterpiece of faultlessness; a spotless frontage; an irreproachable contour!

"I reiterate that Man's baseness is in proportion to the perfection of his trouser! Notice how he takes up the garment with tenderness, how he folds it, almost fondling it, placing it in its press with care, hanging it up like a painting by Rembrandt!

"They take care of their trousers these gentlemen, who are so careless of human lives and sign away the life of a whole people and the dearest hope of the mute mass without so much as a flicker of an eye-brow or a shake of their impregnable trouser line!

"Therefore I say and I believe you will all agree, 'Take down their trousers! Take them down I say: take their trousers down. . .! ' "

But they wouldn't let him finish. The idea caught on like wildfire. He had stirred something dormant in his listener's breasts. There was a dangerous glint in their eyes. "Take their trousers down!" they roared. They nearly brought the roof down. They almost rushed the speaker off his feet. They raised him on their shoulders and carried him out into the streets. The astonished crowds saw a wild-looking rabble of intelligent looking people carrying a wild-eyed person and shouting with a mad enthusiasm.

"Take their trousers down!" They wondered whose trousers they meant and nervously fingered their own. Little did they know that this fanatical demonstration was the vanguard, the portent, the warning of public conscience against the widening pools of blood and the deepening anguish wrought by Bureacrats, Leaders and Interests conspiring behind their elaborate facades of dissimulation and deceit!

LET THEM BE WARNED.

THE SOLDIERS OF THE UNDERGROUND TO THE SOLDIERS
OF THE OCCUPATION ARMY

It is not our intention to try to convince anyone of the justice of our cause, for we don't expect any good will from those who have deprived us of our country. But we know that a long and bitter struggles lies ahead, in the course of which it is unavoidable that many Jewish Soldiers and many British Soldiers should fall. And it is only fair that these people know at least why they may be killed.

Most of you have been in this country for quite a long time. You have learned what the word "terrorist" means, some of you may even have come into direct contact with them (and heartily desire not to repeat the experience). But what do you know about them? Why does a young man go underground?

To answer this question we can use the simplest example. Remember 1940. Then it seemed quite possible that your island country would be conquered and subjugated by Hitler hordes. If that were the case, what would you have done: Wouldn't you have gone underground and fought the foreign invader by all available means?

This is exactly our position. We have a country. It has been ours from time immemorial. But you have invaded our country. You deprive us of our home and of our freedom. So we must fight you. You are our mortal foe. Your rule here, which is illegal and immoral, is a parallel of a mass-assasination of a whole people, which wants to live and to live as free men.

We will fight you. It can't be helped. Nor does it help to speak about "Law and Order." Law and order means that each shall rule his own house and live on his own soil. That right is our cause—for which we are ready to fight to the last. Where is yours? Bevin's stupidity? Oil? Their Lordship's income?
IS THAT WORTH DYING FOR?

THE VOICE OF FIGHTING ZION
Broadcasted by the Irgun Zvai Leumi on 5th February 1947

To all free and freedom-loving Peoples:

The British occupation Government in our country has at last put aside its mask. It has put the same choice before our People, which Hitler put before other nations threatened with or subjugated by brutal force; either unconditional capitulation or merciless war.

We are not going to capitulate; and as we are sure that our freedom-loving people will not tolerate Quislings and Darlans in their midst, the possibility exists that in a week or so, a soldiery drunk with hatred, will run amok in our towns and villages— murdering, looting, burning. Even then we will not surrender. We know that the road to freedom and peace leads through tears, blood, pain and toil. But we shall fight the cruel foe until the last breath, until the last drops of our blood. And you, free peoples of the world, are bound in honour to assist our bleeding nation in its unparalelled struggle for freedom, for its future and perhaps for the future of the world. This is a struggle between liberty and serfdom, between justice and tyranny, between faith and treachery, between light and darkness. You cannot remain neutral in such a contest! Raise your voices against Nazi-British oppression! Help our fighters! Show the world—after all the years of undisturbed extermination of our people—that in spite of all, there does exist a conscience of a progressive mankind.

Occupied and fighting Zion calls upon all peoples: help us!

THE VOICE OF FIGHTING ZION
Broadcasted by the Irgun Zvai Leumi on 9th February 1947

From the talks in London and the shameful ultimatums in Jerusalem it is evident that we face one alternative only: either unconditional capitulation or a war for liberation.

It is no less evident that we will *not* capitulate. Capitulation means destruction, whereas the struggle offers hope for freedom and peace.

The question now faces the Zionist institutions: what are they going to do after rejecting the enemy's demand to turn police informers and spys. The negative reply to this demand is not of course a proof on their side of adherence to a sacred principle. We remember too well that two years ago they frankly cooperated with the British secret police in locating the so called "suspects." Today they are not able to do it and they know it—because they would be swept away by an outburst of mass indignation. In any case, it is a fact that no organised spying and informing will take place in this country in the near future.

But is this sufficient? Must not the Zionist institution ask themselves why it was possible that a hostile power—the Government of the White Paper—dared to come forth with such a humiliating demand? Should they not remember that similar demands were put forward by the German Nazis only to their Quislings and Vichyites?

The time has come for our nation, which fights for its freedom, to cease to be a "community," whose leaders are asked to "cooperate" with the enemy's secret police. Our nation must become a nation independent in its spirit in its fight and in its national institutions. This means the immediate creation of a national provisional Government, of an underground Parliament which would embrace all shapes of public opinion, of a united liberation army, a national treasury, and independent courts. Then normal relations will be created between us on the one side and the enemy on the other side and the foolish ultimatums will be a priori impossible.

As to the state of siege with which the British occupants are threatening our people—we have to make a simple and short statement. "Martial law" is probably an unavoidable stage in our struggle and we will pass through it as we did all trials in our long history of tears, blood and toil. But the enemy must know that if he is going to turn our country into a hell, we shall turn his life into a hell. Not only in this country. Our soldiers will strike at the enemy all over the world. Obviously we are nearing the decisive stage of the struggle between our freedom-loving people and British serfdom. And serfdom cannot and will not win the day.

Fighting Judea No. 7

THE FRUSTRATED ENEMY

What was the calculation of the British enslavers when they brought the question of Eretz Israel before the United Nations Organisation? Obviously they did not go to "Lake Success" with a light heart. They were not unaware that there are in the United Nations Organisation not only various types of British statellites but independent States, openly opposed to Britain's political purposes. They went there because they had no alternative. They even asked for a special session of the General Assembly, because we forced them to do it—by our blows just before Martial Law was imposed and during the period of martial law, which was lifted in consequence of the incessant blows of the Hebrew underground.

But when they came to UNO, the British came with a calculated plan:

First, there will be a discussion. The Arabs will make a noise and "Prove" that the dispute is between them and the Jews and not between the Jews and the British robbers of the country. Then a commission will be appointed. It will "investigate" the facts and will then submit a report, which cannot be unanimous. Canada and Yugoslavia will not subscribe to the same recommendations. Then the General Assembly will argue about the various reports. It will take decisions which are nothing more than *recommendations*. In order to carry them out—and this is the essential point—Britain will ask for authorisation "as a trustee" for UNO. Russia will oppose.

But the majority will decide against her—just as happened in the case of the composition of the Committee. There will be an "interim period" of some years. The British will continue to rule Palestine. This time "in the name of the civilized world."

And meantime—the British calculated—there will be peace. We shall breathe freely. We shall get out of our ghettoes. We shall fortify our bases. We shall continue to incite the Arabs and to arm them. We shall cook up many surprises in Palestine.

It is no wonder therefore that Mr. Cadogan supported "whole-heartedly" the appeal of the Indian chatterbox, Asaf Ali, for keeping of the peace in the coming months. And his support of the well-known proposal of the Norwegian delegate was undoubtedly un-hesitating. But here, through over-cleverness, he made a tactical blunder. He agreed to the text of the resolution, calling on *all Governments and all peoples* to refrain from the use of force during the work of the international Committee. His intentions were, of course, "good." He wanted to prove that there did in fact exist the possibility that many (Arab) Governments and (Arab) peoples would use force in order to impose a solution of the Eretz Israel question. But the cunning British diplomat fell into his own trap. The fact that the UNO appeal was directed also—or rather primarily—to Govern-ments has been interpreted throughout the world as meaning that it is the *British* Government which is called upon—together with the Hebrew underground—to refrain from the use of force during the coming period. This interpretation is correct, and there is no other. In Eretz Israel there are in fact two factors who are using force. One is the British Government, using the force of enslavement in order to seize our country and turn it into a military base; the second is the Hebrew underground, which uses the arms of freedom in order to put an end to British tyranny. The United Nations Organisation appealed to both of them. And only if the enemy responds to the appeal will the Hebrew underground be able to do so.

Our attitude, based on the natural feeling of ownership of the country and on true political understanding, has been explained to the whole world. And the world has understood it,—has understood that in the existing state of war in Eretz Israel, a truce is conceivable, even for a short period, only if it is *mutual*, that a *one-sided* truce is an impossibility.

We shall not be deceived by the treacherous enemy, with his intrigues and the sweet tones of his broadcasters. He will not be permitted to deport Hebrew repatriates with impunity. He will not be permitted to maintain a "pax Brittanica" in Eretz Israel. Hostile acts of all kinds which, in spite of the appeal of the United Nations Organisation, he may commit during the work of the Committee, we shall answer with hostile acts. Force will be answered with force.

That is the law of war. That is the imperative of Hebrew statesmanship. We shall fulfil them both.

WE ARE PREPARED

In repeated statements throughout the month of May, both during and after the Special Session of the General Assembly of UNO, the Irgun has made clear its complete willingness to observe a truce during the work of the Fact-Finding Committee, on the natural and axiomatic proviso that it is a truce—that is a mutual refraining from the use of force—and not just a surrender to the manoeuvres of the British Occupation authorities to pursue their oppression peacefully. The following pages contain the full text of the statements issued through our broadcasting station in May. They cover also the Acre operation; and include our warning, of June 1st, to the United Nations Committee to be careful of the "bodyguards" the British intend using as a means of spying on them.

UNO: THE ESSENCE
(Broadcast, 4 May, 1947)

We state again our basic attitude: the discussions in the United Nations and the decisions that may be taken after many months must not be accorded more importance than they inherently deserve in the light of the Charter of the United Nations and of the known precedents already established in other political questions.

This is a reasoned view of the situation. And whoever is capable of taking a reasoned view of what is happening and what is likely to happen at Lake Success will understand that the question, too, whether Jewish representatives will appear before the Assembly of the United Nations is not of decisive importance. The question is a formal one. It is possible to listen to arguments and then to take contrary decisions. It is also possible to take decisions and then not to carry them out—as British representatives have repeatedly made clear—and it is possible to take decisions which events themselves nullify.

Nothing has been changed by the fact that Jewish representatives have not appeared before the Assembly of UNO; and nothing would change if they *did* appear. Nevertheless we recognise the principled attitude of the representative of the Soviet Union on the question of the presentation of our national case. The Soviet representative demanded—according to radio reports not subject to British censorship—that the Assembly should hear the Jewish Agency and also the voice of the Jewish Resistance, the voice of those who are *fighting* the British regime of blood.

And though we do not know what will be the attitude of the Soviet representative to our aspirations themselves, his attitude and that of the Polish and Czech representatives on the subject of Jewish representation are to be welcomed.

But, as we have said before, what is important is not the formal question as to *how* the voice of our people, fighting for its freedom, is to be heard. What is important is *what* will be said in its name to the peoples. What is important is what will stand behind our demands. And here we must make it clear: the *true* voice of our people *will* be heard. It will be heard through actions; it will be heard through political documents. The world will assuredly learn that in Eretz Israel there is no war between Arabs and Jews—notwithstanding all the efforts of Britain's agents—open and disguised—thus to present the question. The world will learn that the war is between tyrannous Britain and our people, striving for freedom and returning to its country, which Britain aims at converting at the expense of our blood and our lives—into a British puppet country, with the aid of a number of vassal Arab families. The world will realise that the only way to assure peace in Eretz Israel is to remove the British Occupation Forces, to abolish the British Occupation regime and to hand over the government of our country to its legal owners: to a democratic representative body of the Hebrew people.

No One-Sided Truce

One more question raised at UNO demands a reply. Mr. Ali, the representative of India—we are not certain whether he represents the Government of Mr. Nehru or the British Viceroy—appealed for peace in Eretz Israel and that there should be no use of force until UNO takes a decision. Rumor has it also that, at Britain's initiative the UNO Assembly may take a decision in this spirit. We must therefore say at once: there will not be and there cannot be any *one-sided* laying aside of the use of force. Mr. Ali and everybody else should know that for twenty years Britain has been using her power—her power of deception and her physical forces—in order to rob us of our country and to break the links connecting it with our people. Her use of force has been murderous, it has cost us the lives of millions of our men, women and children, and this use of force continues. Our country has been turned into a Nazo-British concentration camp. For the third year now hundreds of thousands of our brothers languish in concentration camps throughout Europe only because Britain is employing her physical force to prevent their entering their Homeland. If Mr. Ali were really interested in justice— and he should remember that Britain is conducting incessant bloody war against our people—he should direct his appeal not to those who have taken up the arms of freedom against the arms of oppression, but to a different address: to the murderous aggressor: to Britain.

The same applies to all his colleagues at UNO. If they decide to order Britain to withdraw immediately her armed forces from Eretz

Israel—*all* her armed forces—and if they ensure that their decision will be carried out—then we for our part undertake not to attack the departing British forces. But the British forces and the British regime who trample our country underfoot and who by their very presence here conduct a permanent bloody attack on our people—we shall assuredly attack at every opportunity. "Truces" are the fruit only of the imagination of British newspaper correspondents who operate by the rule that the wish is father to the thought.

ACRE
(Broadcast, May 7, 1947)

In broad daylight, in Acre, populated entirely by Arabs, surrounded on all sides by mighty camps of the enemy army, our soldiers attacked the fortress defended by hundreds of police. They stormed the walls of the prison and liberated tens of veteran fighters who for years had been prisoners of the enemy, and brought them to safety.

"The greatest prison break in history" wrote a foreign observer. And, considering all the circumstances, this is probably no exaggeration.

This was not a "suicide action," as imagined by those people in their comfortable offices who, in their criminal blindness, are leading the whole people to perdition. It was an action of liberation, planned to the last detail. And though it appears on the surface as something bordering on the impossible, it was calculated—after a thorough weighing of the risks and the prospects—that the predetermined number of prisoners would be freed and that they and their liberators would return safely to base.

Maximum exploitation of the element of surprise, a powerful striking force, securing of their rear by seizing control of the town and its neighbourhood, and the selection of a *particular* line of withdrawal—all these were fundamental to the plan of operation. And only blind chance, which no plan can foresee, caused the casualties among the liberated and the liberators.

And our blood that was shed is being exploited by the defeatists and deserters in order to rub salt into bleeding wounds. Sadistically they ask "Was it worth it?" "See the price you paid."

Woe to you, brother-hating deserters! When the bridge at Azib was blown up and a whole unit of Palmach was destroyed we did not ask you "Was it worth it?" When the four were killed in the "terrorist operation" at the gate of Sarona, we accorded them the honour due to soldiers. We did not say: "See the price you paid for a failure." And when Bracha Fold fell and other fighters were wounded and captured in an action which brought no results and was distinguished for its general confusion—again we did not ask you: "Why and for what?" And when in the blowing up of the "Patria" you killed and sent to the bottom of the sea *two hundred and twenty* Jewish souls, we did not criticize you.

For when a people fights an essential war for its existence and its freedom—and there is no existence without freedom—only a treacherous defeatist who dooms his brother to slaughter will ask: "Is it worth it?" And only a coward, who passively awaits the slaughter, asks "Why and what for?" And only the blind will say "These are vain sacrifices."

War casualties are never vain sacrifices. Only the victims of slaughter, only the victims of surrender, only these are vain sacrifices. And sacrifices such as *these* we have made—*in millions, in millions*—throughout tens of generations, because we were afraid to die for life and freedom, because we went to the ghettoes, because we did not dare to revolt while there was yet time, because we had not the wisdom to hazard *an action for liberation.*

The Acre operation was a direct liberation, just as all our battle actions are, in their historic character, one great liberation operation. Not "suicide"; not a demonstration; and not the bursting out of prisoners who had got tired of sitting in gaol.

Achievement of the Struggle

Our comrades, the fighters of the underground, have shown that just as they know how to fight for their people they know how to suffer for it. They languish for *years* in prisons and concentration camps. They do not ask for mercy. They guard their dignity. They suffer proudly. But this they know too: though suffering is an inseparable part of the struggle, it is not an end in itself. The enemy is very cruel. *Our* suffering has not influenced him and will not influence him. On the contrary it brings joy to his Nazi heart. That is why the enemy does everything in order to make our people suffer more, in order that we should give up our country and be driven away from it, in order that we should go down to perdition and our name be blotted out from under God's Heaven. That is why we must fight against his rule of evil. The enslaver must be smitten by every means and wherever possible. His rule in our country must be undermined, his life made a purgatory, his base suspended over the abyss, his prestige a mockery in the eyes of mankind. And towards the attainment of these purposes the achievements of the Hebrew underground are neither few nor insignificant. These "world rulers" have been seized by fear and trembling. It is we who have driven them into ghettoes, in which, too, they find no peace. And our arm is still upraised. And all the world, east and west, says: Britain is no longer capable of ruling in Eretz Israel.

The war is the hope, the *only* hope. And it is the duty of every soldier who falls into enemy hands to seek ways of escaping in order to return to the front. And it is the duty of his comrades to help him. And this, too, the Hebrew soldier knows: there are no chains the urge for freedom will not break. And there is no prison wall which daring and an active brain will not smash. Underground soldiers have escaped from the camps in Sudan and in Eritrea, from Latrun and Jerusalem. And the fortress at Acre, which was regarded as unconquerable and impregnable, has not remained an exception.

Yes, our blood has been shed again in the hills of Galilee. But it is not the blood of slaughtered ones, but the blood of fighters and heroes, which raises new heroism, bringing freedom to the Homeland and a life of honour to our people.

Mourning our beloved brothers who went never to return and with their undying memory in our hearts—we shall go the way of war, the way of inhuman suffering, the only way to life, until the day comes when we shall go up to the fortress of Acre, whose walls we have pierced, and shall blot out from under our country's skies this British Bastille, the symbol of slavery, the fortress of tyranny.

That day, the day of liberation for all the prisoners of Zion and those who return to Zion, is not far distant. It will come because of those who stand in the front line for freedom, who fructify the soil of their country with their blood.

BRITISH BARBARISM AT ACRE
(Broadcast, May 11, 1947)

On the battlefield at Acre Hebrew soldiers stood up against powerful forces of the enemy—and overcame them. This is the chapter of *heroism* at Acre, the chapter of the overwhelming of the many by the few, the story of the victory of the spirit over the material. And thus will the Acre operation be recorded in the history of our people and of the country—as one of the great actions of the Jewish brain and the Jewish battle-spirit.

But together with this story there is another story—the story of the sheer barbarism of the enemy. The details of his behaviour became known to us only a few days ago. They were told to us *by eyewitnesses.* And it is our duty to make them known to our people and to the people of the world, in order that they should know to what depth of Nazi criminality the army of British Occupation have degenerated.

If any of our soldiers fall in battle we do not complain. True, we do not forget and never shall forget that every drop of blood shed in the Holy Land is on the heads of the enslavers who have robbed us of our country and have forced the best of the Hebrew youth to turn their ploughshares into swords. But a battle is a battle. Our soldiers are volunteers. They know why they have rallied to the standard and why they go out into battle. And they are prepared.

But what the soldiers of the enemy, drunk with hatred, did after the breakthrough at the prison, was not a battle action. It was the outburst of a barbaric tribe, lacking all semblance of human kind. For they abused the wounded. They murdered *captives.* They killed men bleeding on the ground, helpless and even unconscious. The wild Nazo-British beasts attacked our wounded captive soldiers with gunfire and with rifle-butts. They smashed their heads, broke their limbs and shattered their bodies.

Many, innumerable are the crimes the British enslaver has committed against our people. But the crimes committed by the barbaric murderers at Acre will be recorded as the most terrible of all.

Pay heed to what they did there. They abused the wounded, they tortured *to death* soldiers who had fallen captive in their hands.

This will never be forgotten or forgiven them.

THE ADDRESS IS: BRITAIN
(Broadcast, May 14, 1947)

The representative of Poland at the United Nations demanded from Britain the liberation of the political prisoners in Eretz-Israel, to do away with death sentences against Hebrew fighters and to open the gates of our country to the sons of our people knocking at them. The Polish representative denounced before the whole world the regime of oppression in our country, the intolerable foundation on which it rests and its most hateful manifestations, to which we drew the attention of the participants in the special session of the United Nations, in a memorandum sent last week to all the delegations except those of Britain and her satellites.

The Polish representative adopted a correct attitude. He did not follow the example of his colleague the Indian delegate, Mr. Ali, who for some reason, appealed to *us*, to the enslaved, who are doing their human duty—a duty recognized as such in the Declaration of the Rights of Man—and are rising, at the risk and sacrifice of their lives, against that unexampled regime of oppression which was denounced publicly at the United Nations. The Polish delegate addressed himself to the right quarter. He demanded from *Britain*, from the Power which has robbed us of our rights as human beings and as citizens, to stop employing force—the force of tyranny and enslavement—at least in its more brutal forms. And this call—or rather the address to which it was directed—should serve as an example to all the other Members of the United Nations, whether in the Assembly or in the Inquiry Committee, who may wish to issue a call against the use of force in Occupied Eretz-Israel. Remember, the address is: Britain, the address is: British tyranny which, with the aid of bayonets, is robbing a whole people of its *right to life*.

The Polish delegate has earned the gratitude of our people, of its fighters and of all lovers of freedom throughout the world for the attitude he adopted in the Political Committee of the United Nations Organisation. And this gratitude we express from here—from the war front, and the front of suffering in embattled Zion. But we do not deceive ourselves: the call of a member of the United Nations Organisation will also—like the call of other public figures fall on deaf ears. The British enslavers are not impressed by calls to their conscience, which they long ago sold, whether for oil or for strategic positions. They grip our country with the clamp of oppression and they intend to continue doing so. And they will not forego the use of force—the most brutal use, of the most illegal force, in the most enslaved land.

But British Tyranny is Unmoved

In the very midst of the United Nations discussions the Nazo-British tyrants added misdeed to misdeed. They exiled fifty Hebrew citizens from their country, from their Homeland; and they ordered the abuse of prisoners languishing in the prisons at Acre and Jerusalem. We know that these crimes are being committed as the vengeance of a disintegrating regime of oppression which, despite all its concentrations of troops, stood helpless in the face of the blow of the liberation army which burst open the most fortified prison and freed tens of Hebrew fighters—who have already returned to their tasks and are already helping to smite the enemy. These crimes—the exile of citizens from their country and barbaric abuse of prisoners—belong to the category of "crimes against humanity" for which the rulers of Nazi Germany were placed on trial. For these crimes there is no remission. And they cry out for just retribution.

In particular we warn the hirelings of British tyranny employed by the enslaver in his prisons and concentration camps. One of them, the superintendant of Acre prison, bursts drunkenly into the cells of the prisoners, beats them, kicks them, throws them into isolation cells and Indulges in other sadistic practices. His deputy and other gaolers both in Acre and Jerusalem do likewise. We do not know whether these outbursts are made at the orders of the great hangmen or on the initiative of the sadists on the spot. But that is not important, for just as the Gestapo men could not hide behind the "orders of superior officers" in order to save their skins, so will these hirelings not be able to evade punishment on the pretext that they were ordered to do what they are doing. We warn them, all of them, that we shall not tolerate the abuse of defenceless prisoners of war. Those who abuse our prisoners will be held *personally responsible* for their crimes.

You have been warned!

AFTER THE SOVIET DECLARATION
(Broadcast, May 18, 1947)

Consequent on our incessant warfare against the British domination of our country; consequent on the blows that have shaken the existence of the British military base; consequent on the unconquerable Hebrew resistance which has exposed to all the bankruptcy of the British Occupation regime—a change of great significance has occurred in the attitude of the Soviet Union to our people and to its aspirations for freedom. For the first time in thirty years the authorized representative of the Soviet Union has expressed support for the idea of a Jewish State. For the first time the spokesman of Soviet Russia has admitted the historical connection between our people and its country—that historical connection to which we drew the attention of the participants in the General Assembly of the United Nations Organisation when we recalled, in the document we submitted to them, the statement of Mr. Molotov at the Moscow Conference on the western frontiers of Poland and on the factor which was decisive—the historical factor—in their extension to the banks of the Oder. For the first time the representative of the Soviet Union spoke of the need—indeed, of the absolute need—for the Jews to leave the European continent of blood and for their reconcentration in the Hebrew Homeland.

This change will be welcomed by every Hebrew patriot. This attitude will evoke gratitude to the Soviet Union from all the dispersed of our people whose eyes are turned to Zion, and from the fighters of our people on the front for freedom.

True, the Soviet Union has not yet identified itself with the whole of our aspirations, than which there is none more just. But how can we complain about that if even among our people there are individuals and even groups who see a solution for our people in one of the two alternatives brought forward by Mr. Gromyko?

And this, too, must be remembered: the fate of a people fighting for its freedom is not dependent on this or that attitude of one Power or another. Its fate depends on itself. "Terms of reference" written in ink are not decisive in history for any length of time; what is decisive is the "terms of reference" written in the blood of fighters and of those who bring the fight to fruition. Thus it has been in all countries and in all times. So it will be in our country too. The renewal of our independence in our undivided country is the demand of reality and the imperative of history. That is why it will be attained. It will demand intensified efforts. It will demand further sacrifices. But it will be attained. There is no escape from history.

It is our struggle which has changed the situation from end to end. The aim is not yet achieved, the road is still long, the fight is still hard. But the tremendous achievements of our struggle are already evident. We shall intensify our efforts. We shall multiply our strength. We shall remain faithful to the eternal ideal of our people. We shall smite the enslaver, and victory will surely come.

THE ONLY CONDITIONS OF A TRUCE

The General Assembly of the United Nations which met to discuss the question of Eretz Israel adopted the following resolution:

"The General Assembly calls upon all Governments and peoples and particularly upon the inhabitants of Palestine to refrain, pending action by the General Assembly on the report of the Special Committee on Palestine, from threat or use of force or any other action which might create an atmosphere of prejudice to an early settlement of the question of Palestine."

This resolution has a double significance:

a) A demand from the British Government to refrain, during the work of the Committee on Palestine, from direct acts of hostility, by means of the "threat of use of force," against the Hebrew people;

b) A demand from the fighting Hebrew underground to refrain, during the same period, from military operations in Eretz Israel.

[1.] These two demands are parts of one whole and cannot be divorced from each other.

2. If the British Government, whose temporary rule in our country is approaching its end, will fulfil the demand of the United Nations Organisation, the Hebrew underground will also be prepared to fulfil this demand.

3. But should the British Government, whose very rule in our country is a manifestation of the use of brutal and illegal force, continue to drive away by force the members of our people returning to their Homeland, or continue to murder Hebrew prisoners of war, or continue to hold Hebrew citizens in illegal internment in Eretz Israel or outside its borders, or continue to maintain the military regime of oppression which threatens the fundamental rights of the man and the citizen—then *they* will be responsible for a breach of the decision of the United Nations Organisation and for the inevitable consequences of such a breach.

This attitude is common to the fighting underground organisations and has been adopted at the initiative of the Irgun Zvai Leumi.

The State Members of the United Nations Organisation should have regard to this attitude of the Hebrew underground which is a consequence both of the existing situation in our occupied country and of the decision of the General Assembly. The representatives of these States should immediately take the necessary steps to ensure that Britain should not defy the clear will of the General Assembly of the United Nations Organisation.

4. The Hebrew underground considers it its duty to emphasize that no body or group of countries is entitled to take decisions depriving our people of its unalterable right to establish its undivided country as a free and democratic Hebrew State. Our struggle has been directed to this aim and will continue until it is attained.

5. The deportation of the repatriates of the "Hatikvah" proves that it is not the enemy's intention to honour the decision of the United Nations Organisation. The consequence is clear: the use of force we shall answer with force. And the conclusion that will be drawn by the free world is also clear: the British regime of blood is responsible for ignoring of the call of the Assembly of the United Nations Organisation.

WHAT AN "INTELLIGENCE"!
(Broadcast, May 21, 1947)

For years now the British Intelligence has stood helpless before the Hebrew underground, whose blows always take them by surprise. The British Secret Service has at its disposal an unlimited number of spies and unlimited supplies of money. But neither has been of much use. The Hebrew underground is very deep. All the well-known "tricks" employed by British spies in various countries are not successful here. The walls of the underground are impregnable. Standing on guard are *faith and brains*—two terrible foes for the unclean methods of the British spy system.

It seems that in order to conceal this striking failure, which has been angrily discussed even in the British Parliament, the head of the British spy service has given orders for the spreading, with the aid of the B.B.C. and other propaganda instruments at his disposal, of sensational stories about our plans for the near future. The British have heard "from the horse's mouth" that today or tomorrow we are planning to blow up the house of the British "High Commissioner," or the house of the Commander of the Nazo-British armies, the headquarters of the military police and the "Public Information Office." Indeed, the British Intelligence has this time been smiled upon by success. They know not only "what" and "when"; they even know "why". They have read not only the plans of the Irgun Zvai Leumi, they have even read its *intentions*. Could there be a greater success for the Secret Service which has for so long been wandering round in this small country like a blind man?

But the World has Eyes

What, then, are our intentions according to these British spying geniuses? We want to blow up these buildings—they say—in order to bring about Martial Law, so that the Committee of the United Nations Organisation should see for itself that Eretz Israel lives under an oppressive military regime. We heard this profound exposition and we wondered: do the makers of British propaganda so deeply underrate the intelligence of listeners and readers? Or perhaps this is the measure of the intelligence of the spy-propagandists themselves—which could explain their failure as soon as they had to operate not in Bengal but in Eretz Israel? For every newspaper reader in the world knows that if we wanted "martial law" the choice was in our hands not to continue our attack when martial law was imposed in Tel-Aviv, Petah Tikva and Jerusalem. Had we been quiescent then the British would have said: "You see? We imposed martial law and the 'terror' stopped at once. This shows that this is the way to stop the terrorists, and that we must persist in it." But in despite of them what happened was quite different. We continued to smite the enemy in spite of "martial law," we continued to smite the enslaver both because it is necessary to smite him at every good opportunity and in order to prove that "martial law" too, which is nothing but a collective act of the well-known Nazi type, will not stop our struggle. And we proved it. And the enemy was compelled to retreat, and lifted martial law, and the British Press wept bitterly at its failure.

Secondly, is "martial law"—which the enslaver has chosen to give the more modest name of "controlled areas"—necessary in order to prove to the representatives of the United Nations Organisation that the country is living under a regime of military oppression? Cannot anybody with eyes in his head see—even without "martial law"—the gigantic military camps, the barbed wire barriers, the Nazo-British ghettoes, the Military "Courts" and all the other manifestations characteristic of a totalitarian regime, of a regime of military oppression, sitting only on its bayonets? Even the Anglo-American Committee exposed the transformation of Eretz Israel into an armed camp, and all the world knows that the like of the regime of military oppression that exists in this country, with its "laws" and its "institutions" did not exist even in Nazi Germany.

They are fools, therefore, these British spies who make a show of being magicians. They wanted to show that they know our intentions; what they have shown is that they are incapable even of lying successfully. As for our practical plans of attack, we have said before—and have proved that we did not speak in vain; the enemy, his spy service and the B.B.C. will learn of our plans—when they are carried out.

THE FIGHT AGAINST THE AMPHIBIOUS PIRATE GOES ON
(Broadcast, May 28, 1947)

As the deportation of repatriates from the shores of the Homeland has proved that the Nazo-British enslaver does not intend to honour the decision of the United Nations Organisation and refrain from the use of force during the work of the Palestine Committee, so did the attack—of limited scope—on railway installations, carried out yesterday by our soldiers, show that the Hebrew underground does not mean to give the enemy the advantage of a *one-sided* truce. The enemy, in his stupid vanity, pretends that it is not to him that the UNO appeal was addressed. The enemy, in his great stupidity, believes that the peoples of the world still regard what he does in the Holy Land as legal, and whatever is done against his tyranny as illegal. In fact, the truth is otherwise. The appeal of UNO was directed *in the first place* to the British Government, in that it is the *only* Government, among all the "Governments" to which the international body appealed, which is using force in Eretz Israel. Secondly, a revolution has occurred during the past few years in this country and in the attitude of the world to this country. There is not a Hebrew citizen—except for the few who would have been prepared to kiss Hitler's jackboot if only he had permitted them to "live" under him—who does not see in *the very presence* of British rule a manifestation of brutal and illegal force. All the more does he regard as illegal and criminal the acts of that illegal regime, directed against repatriates, against fighters, against the rights of man and citizen, trampled upon on all sides by the tyrants. In the same measure every Hebrew citizen regards the fight of the Hebrew underground as a legal and just fight, for every human being knows that "resistance to tyranny is obedience to God." And that applies to the whole world. Millions, tens of millions of people, irrespective of nationality or religion, see in the British regime in our country an Occupation regime, in his acts the acts of Nazi cruelty, and in his "laws" typical laws of tyranny, designed in advance to cover his brutal acts. The cloak of "law" with which the British tyrants cover themselves, has been taken off them long ago. Now it is clear to all the world that an amphibious pirate has, with the aid of the sword, seized a country not his own and with the aid of his fleet prevents its sons and owners from entering it. Whoever fights this pirate and his acts of robbery and murder performs the will of God and the command of humanity. He is legal and his acts are legal.

If the United Nations Organisation means to put an end to British gangesterism in our country—may its work be blessed. We are not unduly optimistic. But we were prepared to respond to the call of the international body and refrain from attacks during the next three months, on the self-understood condition that, the enemy would honour it as well. But the enemy has proudly disregarded it. Consequently—it is our *duty* to continue to smite him. It is inconceivable that there should be a *one-sided* refraining from the use of force. Only a *mutual* refraining is conceivable and possible.

Warning

We warn: the enemy is pursuing his corrupt way. He has placed before a "court" Hebrew prisoners of war and threatens to murder them. The United Nations Organisation must prevent the commission of this crime, which would have incalculable results.

Incidentally, the bomb placed in the Ramleh railway station was a time-bomb. The telephone warning of the explosion was given by one of our soldiers to the railway station at *Rehevoth* because at the time fixed for the attack the telephone at the Ramleh station was out of operation. Our soldier made it absolutely plain that the *Ramleh* station would be blown up thirty minutes later and that the local Arab inhabitants should be warned. Why did the British lie and say that a false warning was given to the Rehevoth station, and did not even mention Ramleh station? Was this a deliberate lie, or was it further proof of the chaos that reigns among them—chaos that expressed itself in the successful arrest of the four "attackers," dressed in British uniform, who left their lethal baskets at Ramleh and, with terrorist composure, continued their journey in the train to Lydda?

Chatterbox

The spokesman of the Jewish Agency has tried to justify Mr. Ben Gurion and to explain why the head of the Agency went on to the platform of the Assefat Hanivharim and, with a wave of his hand, sold the British the major part of Western Eretz Israel. Mr. Ben Gurion—said that spokesman—is an impulsive man and sometimes says things on his own initiative. This sort of thing—continued that spokesman—is not an unusual phenomenon in the world.

No, Mr. Spokesman of the Jewish Agency. The phenomenon is most unusual. Firstly, we have never heard that the spokesman of a Government—and the Jewish Agency likes to compare itself to a

Government—should say of the *head* of that Government that he is, with all due respect, a chatterbox. Second—what is more important—we have never heard of the "head of a Government" that his impulsiveness should be so great as to drive him into babbling about giving up two thirds of his Homeland.

If the Agency were an institution that had any self-respect it would, without delay, dismiss the man who, out of almost hysterical desire for his Lilliputian state, has broken the discipline of the Zionist Movement in the most brutal and damaging manner. But the Jewish Agency, being the Jewish Agency, will not do this. Will it at least do a good deed, at once national and humane, and give its chairman leave of absence so that he can cure his nerves of their surplus of "impulsiveness"?

Fighting Judea No. 8

(BROADCAST, 4 JUNE 1947)

We call to you, to every man and woman in Israel:

How long will you permit bewildered and groping "leaders" split and riven by disagreements, to *trade* publicly with the sacred principles of our people?

How long will you permit them to trample on the writ of the *people*?

How long will you allow it to be said *in your name* that Jerusalem, and Hebron and Shechem are "non-Hebrew territory"?

How long will you permit the proposal to the world *in your name* that there should be established a *Jewish ghetto* in the Homeland, in mocking mouthing of the terms "independence" and "national restoration"?

Have we not a Homeland whose frontiers were established by God and by history and by the blood shed in it and for it in every generation?

Who gave these blunderers the authority to surrender our eternal inheritance? Who has permitted them, to these deserters in Zion, to propose, whether publicly or behind closed doors, whether in secret conversations or in public speeches, the carving into pieces of our heritage?

See what is happening:

Like a chameleon changing the colour of its skin so do they change the "aims" in quick succession. Here you had (Western) Eretz Israel as a Jewish State *immediately*; here you had the immediate *proclamation* of Eretz Israel as a Jewish State; here—"continuation of the Mandate"—that is, continuation of the enslavement under the British jackboot; and here—a "State" in a part of (Western) Eretz Israel; and here a combination of "State" and "Mandate"; or a bi-national Government; or international trusteeship; and so on and so forth.

Has anything like this ever been heard of? Has there ever, in the history of all the peoples, been such opportunism as this miserable opportunism? Has our people "aims," or one sole aim, an aim which is unchangeable, the aim and the vision of all the generations: the liberation of the Homeland and the Return to Zion?

Now they are preparing again, these candidates for the offices of "president" and "minister," to come to the world and to propose to them the carving up of our Homeland, and again they will give assurances, as they once assured cunning British agents, that they will manage to maintain their leadership and to persuade the people that they must resign themselves to the plan of robbery. And again they will babble, publicly and privately, that they *know* that the establishment of Eretz Israel as a Hebrew State is impossible. And this treachery will be committed *in your name*, in the "name of the people," whom they have not asked and on whose aspirations they have turned their backs.

We call to you, to every man and woman in Israel:

Put an end to this shame!

Do not allow a handful of bewildered and panic-stricken "leaders" who have installed themselves in certain institutions to make trade with the sanctities of the people and with the territory of the Homeland. If they have no patience, if their hands shake and their knees falter—let them go home and not bring disaster and dis-grace on the people, which is fighting, is suffering and with sacri-fices, for its freedom and its future. And if in their vaingloriousness they continue to claim before the world that the people will back their "plans," let them be courageous enough to submit those plans to a referendum.

Let there be a complete, free and democratic referendum!

Let there be no more usurpation by "leaders" heedless of the people!

Let the world learn that our freedom-loving people is true to its heritage and is prepared to fight and suffer for the liberation of the Homeland—that there is no surrender of even one jot of the Homeland.

(BROADCAST, 8 JUNE 1947)

President Truman has appealed to the citizens of the United States not to encourage "illegal activities in Palestine." His appeal will be replied to—should be replied to—by the citizens of the United States. Yet we, citizens of Eretz Israel, fighting for the liberation of our Homeland, have also to react to it, seeing that we are one of the factors which indirectly brought about the appeal of the President.

President Truman should understand that we need no "encouragement" from anybody to fight, to continue our struggle. We derive that encouragement from the soil of our Homeland, whose every rock and every path recalls to us the heroism of our ancestors who, in defence of their Homeland, stood up against mighty Empires and overcame them. That encouragement—mingled with deep-seated anger—we derive from the rivers of blood which have poured from the body of our people *because* our Homeland was robbed from us by the British tyrants. We derive that encouragement from the concentration camps, in which there still languish tens of thousands of our brothers, whose eyes are turned to Zion. That encouragement we draw from the consciousness that our struggle is not only a struggle for freedom and independence, but a struggle for the very existence of our people. It is not the citizens of America, in whose memories are inscribed the days of Jefferson and Washington, who encourage us in the sacred revolt against bloody tyranny, but on the contrary; we who have risen, the few against the many, the weak against the strong—against enslavement, it is we who give encouragement to the citizens of America, and to the citizens of all free countries, to believe in the unconquerable spirit of freedom.

Only a few weeks ago, Mr. President, you repeated the inspiring oath of the father of all rebels: "I swear on the altar of the Lord that I shall devote my life to resisting every form of tyranny." And you know, Mr. President, not only from the reports of your representatives but also from your personal experience, that in our Homeland there has been set up a regime of tyranny more cruel than the regime of oppression against which your forefathers rebelled by force of arms and by "breaking the law"—the "law" of slavery which God commanded must be broken and removed from the world. You gained this experience during the past two years, when you addressed to the British Government, again and again, the demand to admit to Palestine immediately—you always said *"immediately"*— one hundred thousand of the inmates of the concentration camps. Your emissary Morrison reported to you that these people had only these alternatives: Palestine, demoralization and death. You told this to Mr. Attlee and Mr. Bevin. And what reply did they give you? They mocked at you and said that it was only in order to catch votes that you had put forward this demand—and they finally frustrated it by their Satanic tactics. You learnt—it was from your own experience that you learnt, Mr. President—that the British regime in our country is sending to perdition tens and hundreds of thousands of people without paying any heed even to your demands. You learnt that this regime is of a tyranny unprecedented in human history. Does not therefore the oath of Jefferson which you publicly swore oblige you to raise your voice against this bloody regime—instead of encouraging it, by one-sided appeals and by identification with its policy, to commit further acts of violence and murderous acts of oppression against our people?

We are, of course, proud of the moral support for our struggle of millions of Americans irrespective of creed or origin, just as we are proud of the sympathy of other free peoples for our struggle. But our struggle is not dependent on external factors. Whatever their attitude may be we shall continue to fight for the liberation of our country and the redemption of our people. We have determined never again to be the passive victim of international intrigues. We shall not go down to the abyss for the sake of oil which flows under the earth. We shall not bow our heads before the decisions of rulers who, for reasons of their own, decree slavery on us. Our physical strength may not be great. But we have already proved, in standing up to a garrison of 100,000 of the enemy, that there is within us another strength, with whose help we stand firm, deliver blows and do not fall. This strength is the readiness, in a degree possibly unexampled in history, to give our lives for freedom. And with this strength, which is accompanied by brains, we shall, with suffering and sacrifices, smash the British regime of blood in our country. This is our belief, and history—the history, too, of the Thirteen Colonies—teaches that this belief is not vain.

(BROADCAST, 11 JUNE 1947)

The prisoners taken in the Acre operation yesterday revealed a part of the Nazo-British barbarism reigning in our country. Before the whole world the shocking picture was unveiled of wild beasts armed with modern weapons, whose one purpose is to murder, to abuse and to rob. In truth, it is not in vain that the "Socialist" Lord Pakenham calls to the Germans to be proud of being Germans. For those who filled the ranks of the S.S. taught something to "His Majesty's Forces." *Those* looked through the windows of the gas-chambers and took pleasure in the spectacle of choking Jews writhing between life and death; and these, in their turn, made a sadistic spectacle of the death struggle, in inhuman suffering, of Hebrew soldiers and prisoners. Those and these abused the wounded and the dead; and both looted from prisoners and from those who had fallen.

It is added to the credit of our courageous brothers, who stand erect and with head high before their wound-be murderers, that they exposed once again the character of the occupiers of our country. Our people should know what awaits us if we do not smash this regime of blood which promises us gas chambers of first class British quality. And the civilized world should know that our war against the Nazo-British beast is a mission of the whole of humanity which does not want the Nazification of the world by the heirs of Hitler and Himmler.

And to our beloved brothers who fell victim to the wild sadists we may say only this:

WE SHALL PAY!

The British appeal to the United Nations Organization about the Hebrew repatriation confirms our warning that the British enslavers want to exploit the international institution in order to provide cover for their misdeeds and their seizure of a country not their own. With characteristic British hypocrisy the Conservative Mr. Cadogan writes, at the order of the Socialist Mr. Bevin, that prevention of repatriation will help in establishing peace in Eretz Israel. In other words: the enslavers picture to themselves only one kind of "peace": the "British peace" in a Jewish ghetto completely cut off from the people striving to return to its free Homeland.

But this is not what is most important. After all, there are today very few even among the blind Zionist leadership—who harbour any illusions about British intentions. What it is important to emphasize, as a lesson to be learned is that our professional "politicians" have again revealed that lack of understanding and lack of courage which have ever brought about their failures and will continue to make them fail.

The General Assembly of the United Nations Organisation adopted its well-known resolution calling on all governments and all peoples to refrain, during the international considerations of the question, from the use of force. The Jewish Agency should, of course, have called immediately on UNO to oblige the Government of Britain not to use force against the sons of our people who, in accordance with the fundamental law of humanity, are returning to their Homeland.

But the Jewish Agency did not do this. Nor they are still ruled by the ghetto spirit. *Internally* they make a pretence of being a "Government," but a true feeling of sovereignty is utterly alien to them. They still see themselves as candidates for "cooperation" with "the Government," that is, with the Government of Britain, that is, with the enemy of our people. They would not dare to say what any national representative body worthy of the name would say: the rule of these British is illegal and the call for peace by UNO was a call to all the parties; we consequently demand an end to British piracy off the shores of our country.

The Jewish Agency did not say this. That is why Britain found the convenient moment—especially after Mr. Truman's statement, which the fools in the Jewish Agency welcomed—to turn the tables and present the Hebrew repatriation as a breach of the law and a use of force during the deliberations of the International Committee.

Agency "diplomacy" comes back like a boomerang.

Our failure in the detention of the two Britons has nevertheless had its positive value. Against the background of this incident the character of those who claim to be the "representatives of the people" has been exposed. As usual, they were overtaken by panic—panic which drove them to loss of their sences and to hysteria. But this time their panic was accoumpanied by a certain "progress" compared to their behaviour in previous incidents. They demanded explicitly cooperation with the British enemies and murderers of our people. They called on the masses of the people to become detectives for Cunningham. Now all is clear to every one. And clarity is something very important in the struggle of the people for freedom.

See how great is their fear, how deep-rooted their ghetto spirit. They *knew* why these Britons were taken; they *know* what happened to young Rubovicz who was kidnapped by British Secret Police and whose traces have been lost. Yet they reacted to the "Galei Gil" incident with loud cries, demands, threats and with calls for treacherous collaboration—while in the Jerusalem incident they at first did not react at all and finally emitted the weak cry of the ghetto pleaders.

We have heard that they are very joyful today. Let them have their joy. They are blind and will not understand that nothing has destroyed their position in the eyes of the world and of the people more than their last call for collaboration.

Today the disgusted masses are saying: Vichy! Vichy!

We have heard that the enemy, too, is jumping for joy. He can have his joy too. We see that his feeling of inferiority in relation to the Underground has become so strong that he sees a victory in the finding of the two Britons, who were discovered because of an accidental error. He has not scored many victories over us in the past and they will be few in the future. Our failure does not decide anything. When we went out to war we knew that our path would not be strewn with roses. Defeats are an inseparable part of war. And they have their value, as we have said, for they teach many lessons. The enemy rejoices in vain. He will yet feel the joy of our strong right arm.

(BROADCAST, 15 JUNE 1947)

Tomorrow or the next day the United Nations Special Committee begins its work in the capital of our eternal country. We welcome the members of the committee to our occupied and fighting country; and we remind them not to permit the British spies and agents to spy on their movements and contacts under the mask of guarding their safety. Let the members of the Committee, not believe the horror stories of the British spy service about the dangers that allegedly threaten them. No danger threatens the members of the Committee, or their offices or their residences, from the Hebrew underground army. These horror stories are told them only in order to cover and justify their being surrounded by a horde of two-legged blood-hounds who will secretly read their correspondence, secretly listen to their conversations and will trail all their steps. That is why we warn the members of the international committee, whom we welcome as honoured guests—as the guests, too, of the Hebrew underground—without any illusions, but with all the respect that is their due.

You are listening to the Voice of Fighting Zion.

And so—they intend to stop the repatriation too. It is true there are excuses. One speaks of a shortage of fuel; another speaks of a shortage of food. But who is fool enough to believe these excuses. Everybody knows the reason for the stoppage of repatriation now—precisely now—and that American newspaper which has long identified itself with British policy spoke the truth when it said: "The Haganah has taken another step of appeasement by stopping immigration."

Another step of appeasement. Of course there have been previous steps of appeasement. There was the impudent call to treacherous collaboration, there was the attempt to convert the Haganah into a Darnand militia; and there has even been a payment by the enslaver. A small payment, but a very characteristic one; in glorification of the name of the benevolent King of Britain thirty members of the Haganah were pardoned on his official birthday. "Appeasement" for appeasement . . .

All this happened in the month of June, a year—only a year—since the three Hebrew armed organisations, bound by an agreement for a joint struggle, went out on offensive operations which had been planned jointly and agreed on together. These attacked railway transports, those—bridges, and the others—railway workshops. And before that: these attacked the Mobile Police, and the others airfields and aircraft of the enemy. And before that . . . but why should we recall forgotten things. For from a moral point of view it is not just a year that separates this June from that June, but a whole epoch, an epoch that began with the call: "Out with Nazi-British rule!" and ended with a call to spy on Hebrew fighters trying to save the lives of their comrades in enemy hands, with a call to frustrate in advance the plan designed to save them; an epoch that began with a great hope—perhaps the greatest in our generation—and ended in bitter disappointment; a period that began with a fighting unity and ended in civil strife.

It is clear now that surrender has no brakes. If you begin to surrender you cannot stop half-way. You end up at Vichy. They began, after the 29th of June, by giving up the active fight against the regime of blood as such, but promised to fight at least on certain sectors: in defence of Hebrew arms and in defence of repatriation— and did not keep their promise. They left their arms without defence, and when by chance one British Tommy-gun fell into their hands, they hastened to return it—in the apparent hope that for the one Tommy-gun the enemy would return to them the abundant arms he took at Yagour, at Ruhama and Dorot and Tel-Aviv. And they forsook the repatriants too, leaving them to be deported or killed. At first they still blew holes in a few deportation ships, but afterwards they forewent even this "retaliation". Thus came to an end the game that had cost precious sacrifices: neither a "limited" struggle, nor a struggle with intervals. Only the interval has remained, without even a "limited" struggle. All lies, all deceit. And now we have reached this point: repatriation is stopped, the British King's birth-day is celebrated by the Haganah on the liberation of its members by the grace of the enemy, and on every wall is displayed the call for collaboration with the Occupation Gestapo and army. In truth "Great is the pain and great the shame: Say you, O Man, which is the greater?"

But there is a no less important further aspect to the stoppage of repatriation—and to the public announcement of the stoppage, Repatriation has been stopped after the United Nations Organisa-tion adopted a decision calling on all the factors in the country not to use force during the international deliberations on the Eretz Israel question. It was clear to all men of goodwill that this decision obliges Britain not to employ her Navy her airplanes and her bayo-nets to deport repatriants returning to their Homeland. For repatriation is legal, and what is illegal is their deportation by force. And now these knights of surrender come and say, indirectly: in order that there should be peace in the country we shall temporarily forego the repatriation as well. In other words, they say: the return to the Homeland (the fundamental and unalterable right of our exiled brothers) is a manifestation of illegal force and must there-fore be given up in so-called accordance with the decision of the General Assembly of the United Nations Organisation.

Can greater moral and political damage to our cause be imagined than this "further act of appeasement"?

Communique

With regard to the statement about the King David Hotel matter made by the organisation of deserters which calls itself "Hebrew Resistance Movement" we state:

1. We did not say that Tenuat Hameri (Resistance Movement) had approved a plan "designed for mass murder." We said that

Tenuat Hameri *had approved our plan* for an attack on the Head-quarters of the British regime, a plan whose fundamental aspect was the *avoidance of casualties* in the attacked building.

This plan, which was approved by Tenuat Hameri and whose execution had been *demanded* of us by Tenuat Hameri after the 29th June—was carried out without any change. Half an hour was given for the evacuation of the building, and advance warning was given in three places.

2. Out of panic, characteristic of the leaders of Tenuat Hameri, they committed an act of cowardly retreat and denounced the "considerable fatal casualties caused by the dissidents," even though they *knew* that it was not we who had caused the "considerable casualties" but *the criminal Shaw*, who prevented the evacuation of the building.

3. Even now Tenuat Hameri, of blessed memory, has the brazenness to claim that the responsibility for the "horrible murder rests on IZL and only on IZL"—even though it was Tenuat Hameri who last year broadcast the statement—several weeks after the event—that the criminal Shaw had been warned to evacuate the building and that he had had enough time to do so.

4. After the 29th June and after the attack on the British Head-quarters Tenuat Hameri did not "draw all the conclusions." Then, too, they promised us to continue our joint struggle and even to intensify it. But after that there came the Paris meeting of the Zionist Executive and it was then that Tenuat Hameri "drew its conclusions." It laid down its arms, deserted the battlefield, broke all its promises, betrayed all its oaths. That is the "interval of inaction" which has continued to this day while repatriants are left to be murdered and driven away.

5. On the other hand it is true that we drew *our* conclusions from the shameless behaviour of Tenuat Hameri. We demanded an arbitration between us in the matter of the King David Hotel. *We repeat this demand.* And before the arbitration court, which, to-day too, we propose should consist of men *in the trust of Tenuat Hameri*, we shall produce the facts and the documents, which will prove who is right and who is the hypocritical evader of the truth.

6. Tenuat Hameri of today in its infinite stupidity boasts that it has frustrated planned operations against the enemy. It is true that it frustrated the attack on the Headquarters of the Occupation army in Tel-Aviv, but the number of attacks it has succeeded in frustrating or will succeed in frustrating are not many. Two other "plans" which Bevin's militia "frustrated" were the fruit of its own imagination, created only for the purpose of "frustrating" them. But the militia does not understand that it is these treacherous acts, which have disgusted the masses of the Haganah as well—especially after the blood-bath which the Nazo-British pirates prepared on the "Exodus Europe"—which made it permissible and essential to expose the

truth of the King David Hotel chapter. Made it permissible because today the danger no longer exists—as it did last year—that by revealing the truth we would bring troubles down on the heads of the Haganah. The Haganah, at its leaders' orders, is now serving the Nazo-British oppressor—through laying down its arms, through its promises to the oppressor that it will "liquidate the 'dissidents' " and prevent any serious resistance to him, and through its persistent preaching of civil war. The British oppressor is interested in all this, vitally interested. Consequently he will not hurt his lackeys. On the contrary he will show them the benevolence of his "pardon." The militia knows this very well. And it were better that it did not pretend otherwise. For nobody will believe it.

We had intended to publish our statement on the King David Hotel matter on 22nd July. At the last moment, following the events on the "Exodus Europe," we postponed publication and even considered cancelling it completely. We believed this might prove a turning point and Tenuat Hameri might resume the struggle. Many hoped so—also in the ranks of Haganah. But again a few threats by the negro-oppressor Gurney sufficed for the Haganah to publish its shameless statement—at the very time our repatriant brothers were being murdered—that it would "continue to frustrate the plans of the dissidents," that is to carry on civil war and to serve the enemy.

It was consequently *necessary* to expose that chapter. For too long have we allowed the hypocritical deserters, who have deceived the people and the youth with their warlike slogans, to pose as "fighters" and the bearers and preachers of morals.

Now—let the people know.

29 July, 1947.

V
THE UNITED NATIONS PERIOD (1947)

Memorandum to the United Nations

I

You are gathering to discuss publicly the problem of Palestine, one of the great historic problems of humanity. We would ask you, in this discussion, to bear the following facts in mind:

1. Eretz-Israel (Palestine), in its indivisible extent east and west of the Jordan River, is, according to all the accepted criteria: historical, moral, cultural and, as we shall show below, ethnic, the national territory of our people. It is its Homeland. In this country our forefathers set up their independent State and their original culture which, together with the culture of other ancient peoples, became part of the foundation of all human civilisation. They fructified its earth with the sweat of their brow and defended it with their blood. During tens of generations they heroically resisted invasions and rose courageously against enslavers. They were exiled from it—and returned to it. Throughout their long exile they never forgot it and never surrendered their claim to sovereignty over it. And they bequeathed the bond with their Homeland, and the urge to return to it and set it up again, to their children and their children's children until this very day.

In bringing up the historical connection between the people and the country, a connection whose effect is *natural* and ineradicable—as the experience both of our people and of other peoples has proved—we take the liberty to draw your attention not only to the preamble to the Mandate for Palestine of the League of Nations, but also to the statement made by the Foreign Minister of the Soviet Union at the recent meeting of Foreign Ministers in Moscow on the subject of the Western Frontiers of Poland. In this statement the Soviet Foreign Minister explained that in his Government's opinion the decisive consideration in favour of including the eastern territories of Germany in the Polish State was that these areas had been—in the words of Mr. Molotov—"the cradle of the Polish State and of Polish culture." In other words, the decisive factor is that of *history*.

We have quoted the statement by Mr. Molotov, which has been accepted in principle also by other Governments, not in order to provide proof of our right to our Homeland. We know that this requires no argumentation in view of the fact that the country is our *natural* Homeland and the Homeland of our brethren, just as America is the Homeland of the Americans, France the Homeland of the French, or Russia the Homeland of the Russians. We have quoted this significant statement in order to illustrate the accepted criterion in international relations. And criterion cannot vary; it is universal.

We must however emphasise at once that in bringing forth the enlightening Polish example of the return of territory to a people exiled from it for tens of generations we intend no hint of exclusion of the non-Hebrew population which has, in the course of time, taken root in our country. There is no section in our people which sees any reason or necessity for transferring any part of the non-Hebrew population from our country to some other country. We shall, without exception, regard the Arab population which has established itself in our country as citizens with equal rights in our free State. The only ones who, in their political "programme" demanded the transfer of the Arab population from Eretz-Israel to the neighbouring Arab States were the leaders of the British Labour Party who today constitute the British Government.

2. With the overwhelming of Judea by the Roman legions and with the crushing of the subsequent rebellions of its heroic sons, accompanied by campaigns of destruction and mass deportation, our people began its *abnormal* existence as a homeless nation, uprooted from the soil, disarmed of its weapons, and dispersed throughout the world. For nearly two thousand years this tragedy of our people has lasted. Throughout the whole of that long period our people was the only one that fulfilled unreservedly the principle of disarmament. But because it was the only people that staked its existence on conscience, on culture and on progress, our people became, in almost every generation, the victim not only of persecution, restrictions, humiliations and expulsions, but also of mass attacks and slaughters which reached their climax in the destruction of more than one-third of our people—in the systematic destruction of six million men, women and childred in the heart of Europe and before the eyes of the whole world.

An end must be made to this tragedy which, as we have

seen in Germany and in other countries, is exploited by the various enemies of humanity, by the disseminators of the poison of racial hatred, by reactionaries striving to attain power, by warmongers endeavouring to sow friction between people and people and to foster mutual hatred among them; an end must be put to this tragedy which is one of the factors permanently threatening the peace of the world. And an end can be made to it only by the normalisation of the lives of our people, that is by their concentration in their free and independent Homeland.

3. We constitute a clear majority of the population of Palestine east and west of the Jordan. This majority is composed of those of our people who have already returned to the Homeland (of whom at least one-third were able to enter the country only by breaking through the illegal barrier erected, openly or covertly by the British occupying authority) and of those of our people, numbering millions, who strive to return to it immediately but are unable to realise their right because the British occupation regime and the British occupation Army and Air Force, aided by the British Navy, have placed themselves in their path. We are faced by an example of an attack by brute force on the supreme and natural right, the right of return to one's Homeland. Might does not nullify a right. The ethnic Hebrew majority of the Palestine population is a clear majority. And this can be proved in a period of a few months or even weeks—with the removal of the illegal barrier set up by the British occupiers which separates the country from the sons of our people desiring with all their hearts to return to it.

4. Britain established her rule in our country by deceit and dissimulation. She promised—and undertook before the League of Nations—to help our people *reconstitute* its National Home, that is, to constitute anew what existed once and was destroyed—in other words, to help to establish our independent State. She made those promises and undertakings, however, not in order to fulfill them, but—exploiting and abusing an international trust—in order to maintain and perpetuate her own monopolistic rule in our country. To that end she shut the gates of our Homeland to our people; to that end she co-operated with Nazi Germany, indirectly and even directly, in the destruction of millions of our brothers in Europe; to that end she incited and raised up against us the Arab population, with whom we have no quarrel, and her agents organised—on four occasions in sixteen years—bloody attacks on our towns, our settlements and our villages.

5. Britain established her rule over our country by brute force when she saw that her intrigues, characteristic of the British colonial system, had begun to prove ineffectual in concealing her annexation of the country. When our people, like every other

oppressed and freedom-loving people, took up arms in order to fight against oppression and tyranny, Britain concentrated vast military forces of all kinds in our country and converted it into a British base for the whole of the Middle East.

6. In that part of our national territory known as Transjordan (that is the eastern side of the Jordan, just as the alternate name for western Palestine, in ancient historical records, is the western side of the Jordan) Britain has established her dominion by setting up as its ruler an alien prince, of the Hashemite family, who is her completely faithful vassal. This part of our country, once known as the granary of the east and called in Roman times *Palaestina Salutaris*, today lies waste for the most part, and its population numbers no more than three hundred thousand. What is today called the "Kingdom of Transjordan" is nothing more than a *British colony*, in which the British Occupation Forces organise their military manoeuvres.

7. The British occupation regime in our country is the most oppressive that has ever existed in any country. The citizen is subject to the mercy and the rod of every soldier or policeman, who may arrest him or kill him on the pretext of maintaining "law and order." Arrests and mass deportations; collective punishments; persecution of citizens are the phenomena which accompany this tyrannical regime which has converted our country into one great concentration camp.

8. The British occupation regime in our country is a reactionary regime of economic exploitation. Taxes which devour the marrow of the country's economy are imposed on the citizens, and most of the revenue is devoted not to the construction and development of the country but to police, secret police, army, prisons and concentration camps both in the country and outside.

9. There is a permanent struggle in Palestine. Our people, robbed of its country, deprived of its freedom and with its very existence endangered has embarked on a just war of liberation against the British enslaver, who is endeavouring—though unsuccessfully—to subjugate it by the most cruel means of oppression. This struggle will go on, and its scope will be extended as long as the British occupation regime and the British occupation forces remain in our country.

10. In contrast to the existing situation which, as experience has shown, endangers the peace of the world, our Homeland can be a country of freedom, of peace and of progress. Its citizens, irrespective of race or religion, can enjoy, under a democratic Hebrew regime, absolute equality of rights in all fields of life, political, social and economic. The wastes can be fructified, the swamps dried; the rivers can be converted into sources of vitalizing energy. The country can be—and with its liberation will be—a solid fortress of peace and fraternity.

II

Taking these facts into consideration, and in faithful fulfillment of the sacred principles of humanity in whose name and whose interest the United Nations Organisation aims to work, it is the duty of the representatives of the free and freedom-loving peoples to demand and decide:

a. To put an end to the British regime of occupation, in its direct form in Western Eretz-Israel and in its indirect form in Eastern Eretz-Israel;

b. To withdraw the British occupation army from our country;

c. To transfer the government of our country to the hands of a democratic representative body of our people—of a Provisional Hebrew Government;

d. To assist this Provisional Government in the immediate repatriation of the members of our people who wish to return to their Homeland.

e. To see to it that the Provisional Government, as soon as the repatriation has been completed, hold free elections, in which all citizens of the country shall have an equal right to participate, for the democratic institutions, legislative and executive, of the State.

III

We send this memorandum to you and to the representatives of all State-Members of the United Nations—excepting Britain and her satellites—and ask that the United Nations Organisation, to the extent that it is able to take practical steps to change the situation, should ensure that the solution of the problem of our people and our country—and there is no solution except the return of the country to our people and the return of the people to our country—should not be buried under a heap of protocols, or be obscured in the procedural maze of committees and sub-committees, or become a bargaining counter between opposing interests unrelated to the problem, or simply to be postponed by the unbinding text of a theoretical recommendation.

We ask you and all the members of the United Nations to see the problem under discussion for what it is: not a "dispute between two communities," but as a conflict between a people striving for freedom and an enslaving power which, with the aid of intrigues and brute force, has usurped control in that people's country and has thus in effect sentenced it to extermination; not as a subject for a diplomatic game, open or covert, and not as a subject for refugee philanthropy; but as the grave problem of a people, great though persecuted, enslaved and bleeding, which demands the natural, fundamental right of every people: the right to its own Homeland, to freedom and security and independence.

For indeed this people has determined to liberate its country and to raise it up again as a free State; and tens of thousands of its sons will prefer to die for their country and their freedom rather than to resign themselves to the shame of enslavement, to the humiliations of dispersion and persecution and to that "Jewish fate" which means extermination.

To this we subscribe from the front line of the war for the liberation of our country and the redemption of our people.

JERUSALEM, 1 Yiar 5707
                (21 April 1947)

HAIRGUN HAZVAI HALEUMI
B'ERETZ-ISRAEL
(National Military Organization of Palestine)

Memorandum to the United Nations Special Committee on Palestine

You are about to prepare a report on Eretz Israel for considera-tion by the General Assembly of the United Nations Organisation. Your report will doubtless include facts on the past and the present, as well as proposals for the solution of the question in the future.

In the name of thousands of Hebrew soldiers who are engaged in a fateful struggle for the liberation of their Homeland and the redemption of their people, we respectfully request you, when you sum up the results of your inquiry, to have in view the following facts and factors:

THE DECISIVE FACTORS

1. *The Historic Factor*

Palestine (Eretz Israel) in its indivisible extent East and West of the Jordan river is the national territory of our people. It is its Homeland. In this country our forefathers set up their independent state and their original culture which, together with the culture of other ancient peoples, became part of the foundation of all human civilization. They fructified its earth with the sweat of their brow and defended it with their blood. During tens of generations they

heroically resisted invasions and rose courageously against enslavers. They were exiled from it—and returned to it. Throughout
their long exile they never forgot it and never surrendered their
claim to sovereignty over it. And they bequeathed the bond with
their Homeland, and the urge to return to it and set it up again, to
their children and their children's children until this very day.

When you travel through this country you will see with your
own eyes the relics of the unforgettable past. In Jerusalem, the
eternal capital of David, you will see not only the barbed wire fences
symbolizing a cowardly regime of totalitarian oppression, giving the
City of Peace the appearance of an armed camp; you will also see,
both within the walls of the Old City and without, dumb but elo-
quent monuments proving that long before these British invaders
could call themselves a people, there already existed here the cradle
of our state and our culture, and a flourishing life of creation and
work and thought. And if you wish to make the difficult journey into
the desert of Judea you will see there a lofty and desolate rock. This
is Matsada [sic]. Here our heroes fought—to their last breath—against
alien invaders; and when they were faced with the choice between
slavery and death, they chose the death of free and unconquerable
men.

At another place, also not far from Jerusalem, you will see a
deserted railway station called "Bettir." This is Betar. Here there
fought and fell Bar-Kochba, one of the spiritual ancestors of the
rebels against slavery of all times and all peoples. And again not far
from our capital you will reach a little village. Its name in history is
Modiin. It was from here that the Maccabaeans went forth, here that
was launched the revolt which embraced in itself not only the
eternal spirit of freedom but also the exceptional phenomenon of
the victory of the few over the many, and the weak over the strong.

If you continue your travels through our small country you will,
on your way northward, reach Galilee. There you will find Gush-
Halav (Giskala), whence one of the leaders of the revolt against the
Roman Empire sprang; there you will come across Jodefet—another
monument to the spirit of freedom, the spirit of heroism and love of
the Homeland.

And when you proceed eastward do not stop at the Jordan.
This river which, with the aid of modern technical knowledge and
under a government interested in the development of the country
and not in eternalising its desolation, could be converted into a
mighty source of fructifying energy,—has never been the frontier of
our country. Cross the Jordan, therefore, and you will enter the
second portion of our Homeland. There, to a depth of hundreds of
miles—except for a narrow strip of cultivated land—you will find
fields covered with stones, burned and scorched, and here and
there a lonely impoverished village or the open tent of a nomad—
and many tanks of the British Occupation army. Remember then

that in the past these fields were covered with corn and with wheat, and *millions* of people—and not, as now, less than three hundred thousand—ate of their fruits. And there, in the fields of Gilead too, you will find places to remind you that our forefathers knew not only how to work and fructify this land but also how to fight for it and defend it with daring and heroism—as befits a people rooted in the soil of its Homeland.

We remind you of these facts not out of abstract "romanticism." We recall them because in our consciousness it is they that consti- tute the *decisive* factor in the bond between us and this country. These facts, though they are enveloped in the mists of history, are not dead. They are alive. It is they that demonstrate that it is a lie to say that ours is a people without a Homeland. Our people *has* a Homeland, only was exiled from it by force of arms; and it is by force of arms that new invaders and occupiers are preventing its return.

This consciousness of historic unity is not a unique phenome- non in our days. It is the consciousness and the feeling of every people. What the Field of Kossovo is to the Serb, Grunwald to the Pole, the White Mountain to the Czech, Verdun to the French, Valley Forge to the American, and Borodino—or in generations to come, Stalingrad—to the Russian—the Western Wall, Matsada, Modiin, Betar, Jodefet and the Fields of Gilead are to every one of us. These "imponderables" are one of the most *real* factors in human history. Their power is supreme and their influence ineradicable. To us here every stone and every rock speaks, and they all convey one message: this is our land, our country and our Homeland from the dim beginnings of time and for all future to come. It is not important whether things will go well with us here, or ill. It is immaterial whether any of us will be granted a long life here, or whether some of us are fated to die in the struggle for liberation and independence. This is our home. This is our country. Ubi patria, ibi bene.

You will find this out for yourselves when, in your travels in the country, you come into contact not only with the symbols of its past but with the realities of its modern life. You who have seen, whether closely or at a distance, masses of Jews degraded and persecuted, and even led—almost without resistance—to the slaughter, will see here a people risen to life again, with its language and its culture; a new generation, who have revived the soil of the Homeland, as the soil of the Homeland has revived them and restored to them the image of *free* men, free from fear, freed from the complexes resulting from two thousand years of persecution; a generation healthy in body and mind, whose sons know both how to plough and how to shoot, how to labour and how to fight. Here the wonder has come about, which is nevertheless only a natural consequence of the force of attraction and that driving force to which we have referred. An ancient people has come to life again, independent of mind, free in spirit, no better than other peoples, but no worse.

2. *The Double Connection*

But this nation is still in the process of its renascence. The seven hundred thousand Jews who have returned to their Homeland—in great part in defiance of the will of the British Occupiers—are only a small part of our people, in the east and the west, in the north and south, who want to return at once and without delay. Indeed, only a few years ago there were millions more Jews awaiting repatriation. They were exterminated. They were exterminated by the German Nazis and—as we shall show—through the guilt of the British Occupiers of their country. Nevertheless, there still remain millions of our brothers, who—after all their blood soaked wanderings—want to—and must—return home. And if they were not to return, if they were to be denied in the future—as the British Occupiers denied them during the years of war and extermination—the right and the possibility of repatriation, this would have a double result. They *there*—wherever they are—would be doomed to everlasting dispersion, to demoralisation, to persecution and, in the fullness of time, to that "Jewish fate" which from time to time overtakes our people: extermination. And we here would be doomed—let us not evade the truth—to life in a *ghetto*, irrespective of what it would be called: "autonomous zone," "community with equality of rights," "canton" or "state." The name is immaterial. What is material is the content—and the lesson of history. The fate of the Jewish ghettoes is only too well known.

Before us therefore is a dual connection: the bond between us and the soil of our Homeland, east and west of the Jordan: and the bond between us and our brothers who want—whose right it is—to return, like us, to their Homeland and to live a life of freedom, of labour and dignity. And just as it is impossible to sever the first link, so is the second link inseverable. We have not come here to save our lives; we were not born here in order to ensure life for *ourselves*. We have come here and live here and fight here, in order to save our *people*, in order to put an end once for all to the historic tragedy, from which it is not only we that suffer, but the whole of humanity—because that tragedy has ever been exploited by the various enemies of mankind, by power-thirsty reactionaries, by warmongers and poisoners of the international wells.

We hope that this explanation will enable you to understand the mind of a generation which is dominated by the consciousness—a consciousness stronger than death—that they are fighting not only for freedom and independence—without which life is not worth living—but for the very existence of their people. It may be that representatives of peoples who, while they have known wars, and risings, and blood and tears and sweat, have nevertheless *not* known an exile of two thousand years, have not known endless wanderings, have not known recurring slaughters, nor the planned

extermination of millions of men and women and children—it may
be that representatives of such peoples, proud, free, settled on their
soil, sure of their future, will find it difficult to feel what we feel. But
it remains a fact; there is not an iota of exaggeration in our words: in
fighting for the liberation of our Homeland, we are fighting for the
very existence of our people.

THE BRITISH DESIGN OF DOMINATION

Across the path to our freedom, security, and independence
Britain has placed herself—Britain who has succeeded for nearly
thirty years, with the aid of ambiguous declarations, intrigues and
well-tried Colonial tricks, in deceiving both our people—especially
the Zionist leadership—and the world as a whole, by hiding behind
her "mission" in Eretz Israel, a "mission" that began with the
promised "advancement of the Jewish National Home," developed
into the "protection of the defenceless Jewish minority from the
Arab majority," and threatens to end with the "protection of the
Arab inhabitants against the aggressive Jewish minority," or the
safeguarding of the peace of the country and the prevention of a
general civil war which allegedly will befall the country if the British
occupiers should leave it. The very fact that her "missions" have
changed several times in a comparatively short period demonstrates
that they are not the reason why she has tried by every possible
means—including the most brutal—to maintain her rule in our country. The real reason was and remains the British purpose of dominating the country and converting it into a military base for the whole
of the Middle East. The "missions" and the tactics changed with
circumstances; the true, hidden, purpose remained unaltered. And
the representatives of the peoples should know that Britain does not
want and is not prepared to transfer power in the country, either to a
Jewish independent Government or to anybody else. She wants—if
she can—to perpetuate her direct rule, or otherwise to perpetuate her
rule *indirectly* through a puppet, satellite Government, such as she
has established east of the Jordan, in Iraq and other places, or such as
Hitler established in Bohemia and Moravia, Slovakia, in parts of
Yugoslavia, etc. That is the purpose of every "solution" hitherto
proposed by the British, or that they will propose or support in the
future.

The British aim to dominate our country is part of a wider aim
of domination—domination of the whole of the Middle East. It is not
a new aim.

Ever since the days of Napoleon Britain has regarded the
Middle East as a key position in its Empire. Her relations with
Turkey in the nineteenth century, designed to keep Turkey alive but
weak and dependent are to-day well-known history.

After the Ottoman Empire had finally crumbled as a result of World War I, a new arrangement became necessary especially as information had already been received showing valuable oil resources of unknown but very encouraging extent in Iraq and elsewhere. Thus a plan was adopted by the British Colonial experts in Cairo and elsewhere of turning the whole of the Greater Middle East (Iran, Baku and the land of the Turkomen not excluded) into a new British Trade Empire, ruled by various native potentates, advised and financed by the British, free to develop splendour and luxury in their courts and to deal with their people in the old way; but held in complete subservience in all spheres connected with the requirements of colonial exploitation (cotton, oil, minerals and other raw materials) and of "imperial security."

Preliminary steps to achieve these ends were taken, marked by the new policy in Egypt (severance from Turkey and establishment of a Protectorate), taking the Hashemite family of Mecca into the British fold, establishing Ibn Saud as a check against the Hashemites, establishing British military administration in Palestine and Iraq, Sir Percy Cox's "treaty" with Persia imposing upon a weak Shah British advisers and turning Persia into a British protectorate, military missions in Baku and Ashabad, and turning the Greek Army against what was still left of Turkey.

Other steps were taken at that time to oust the French from the Middle East, or at least to weaken their positions. Feisal of Mecca was used for this end in Damascus, though haphazardly and unsuccessfully, and France revenged herself by assisting Kemal against the Greeks.

Eretz Israel "had to be" a strategic base. Britain consequently exerted every effort and, as we shall show, has committed the most unspeakable crimes in order to secure and retain control over our country. In recent years there has been added the possibility of economic exploitation of the country, and this has increased her predatory greed and her determination to hold on to it by every means in her power.

It is this determination, and only this determination, that has ever guided her steps in Eretz Israel: and her policy, in every phase and every aspect, has been framed in the light and at the dictates of this unchanging purpose.

Even before Britain was given the task of Mandatory over Palestine she had worked out the precise plan for securing and maintaining control over our country.

There is in existence a document, issued by the British Government—as a secret White Paper for the information of officials concerned—containing the report of the conference held in Cairo and Jerusalem in March and April, 1921, and attended, among others, by Mr. Winston Churchill, then British Secretary for the Colonies, and the notorious British agent T. E. Lawrence. It was at this conference that the broad, fundamental lines of long-term policy for the whole of the Middle East were laid down. It was then that the means and manoeuvres were decided upon which, through the instrument of the Mandate for Palestine, should place our country in British "tutelary" hands. There the long-range motives were defined which were to be achieved through emptying that Mandate of its content: first by the complete robbery of Eastern Eretz Israel and then by the gradual creation in Western Eretz Israel of conditions which, allowing the entry of a number of Jews sufficient only to provide Britain with the excuse of "protecting" them against "the Arabs," would justify her remaining here for good.

No inquiry into the situation in Eretz Israel is of much value without a knowledge of the contents of that document. We can only urge the Committee to call for its production by the British Government—which, for obvious reasons, has kept it secret for 26 years. Should the British not comply, we urge the practicability of calling for its production by the Jewish Agency for Palestine—which we understand once succeeded in securing a copy but, for reasons best known to themselves, have hesitated to expose it.

It was because of the British undertaking to the Jewish people to help in the *reconstitution* of its National Home, and because of the blindness or naivete of the Jewish official leaders, that considerable Jewish pressure was brought to bear on the State Members of the League of Nations to grant Britain the Mandate over our country; and because of it that the Mandate was, in fact, entrusted to her.

But in anticipation of being given the task of executing the Mandate, Britain did her utmost to render the text of the Mandate ambiguous and, by introducing as many loopholes as possible, to prevent the reconstitution of Hebrew Statehood. In the prevailing circumstances of international watchfulness and supervision she did not, however, succeed entirely. The Mandate *does* explicitly rest on the "historical connection between the Jewish people and Palestine"; and its object *is* explicitly set out as the "*reconstitution*" of the Jewish National Home. One can "reconstitute" only what once existed and was subsequently destroyed; and every child knows that what existed before in Palestine was the free and independent Jewish State. Jewish immigration, the Mandate said, *was* to be facilitated and close settlement on State Lands encouraged.

But these were only minor hindrances to the fulfilment of British designs. The basic policy for the rape of our country having been laid down in Cairo, and its control having been "legally" secured through the Mandate, there began the long series of crimes, possibly unexampled in the history of international rapacity, perpetrated by the British against our people. The full list would require a survey of international policies of the past thirty years, and an examination of the archives of many States. We present a brief, but adequate summary.

BRITISH CRIMES AGAINST THE JEWISH PEOPLE

I. *The Crime of Robbery of Territory*

The Cairo Conference had decided on the outright rape of Eastern Eretz Israel. One of the first documents submitted then was a letter by Sir John Shuckburgh, of the British Colonial Office, urging the prevention of Hebrew restoration beyond the Jordan. It will be remembered that there was a long-standing dispute between Britain and France over Eastern Eretz Israel. The British Government urged France to waive her claims in the territory—conceded to her by British in secret wartime agreements—on the ground that it was essential for the Jewish National Home and was required for the "forthcoming Zionist Government." In a powerful Press propaganda campaign France was told that Transjordan was essential for the strength and independence of the Jewish State.

On these grounds France waived her claim.

Having thus again successfully exploited the Jewish people, this time to drive out a serious competitor in the Middle East, Britain promptly proceeded to introduce into the text of the Mandate a loophole clause relating to Transjordan; installed her puppet Abdullah, who had come into the territory some months earlier, as "Emir"; and shut Eastern Eretz Israel to the Hebrew people. Through the following years the territory (three quarters of Eretz Israel in area) was gradually separated, in every respect except British control, from the Western part of the country, until finally in 1946 Britain proclaimed Transjordan's complete "independence," that is, as a puppet "State" completely under British domination.

It is relevant to add that the severance of Eastern Eretz Israel automatically cripples the development of Western Eretz Israel, from which it is inseparable from the point of view of healthy economics and for any plan of major development. This fact was no doubt not absent from the British calculation.

The eastern portion of our country is, moreover, richer, actually and potentially, than the western. Rainfall is more abundant and better distributed, its *known* cultivable area (that is without any serious research) is more than double. And its present density of population is less than 4 to the square kilometre even according to British figures.

The British "treaty" with "independent" Abdullah provides for the "acceptance" of British "experts and officials with technical qualifications," for Britain's "financing, arming and supervising 'his' forces," which are to be led by British officers in order "to ensure efficiency." And under an "Annex" to this "treaty" Britain is entitled to station its forces in Eastern Palestine in unlimited numbers with full freedom to build camps, aerodromes, stores, use roads and ports, to move trains, use her own signals, and enjoy exemption from duties, taxes and jurisdiction. In return Abdullah is given subsidies and grants-in-aid and a large quota of dollars for importing motor-cars, fountain-pens, lipsticks, silk stockings, tophats and other luxuries useless to nomads for sale at inflated price in Western Eretz Israel. The British have thus not in the least concealed their design in Eastern Palestine: naked annexation with Abdullah given the title King for purposes of local colour, in accordance with the dictum pronounced by Mr. Churchill at the Cairo Conference of April, 1921: "It does not matter what these chiefs call themselves as long as they do what we want of them when we want it."

Thus, converting the empty and fertile spaces of Eastern Eretz Israel into a strategic base, and maintaining its tiny population in utter stagnation Britain has robbed the Hebrew people of three quarters of its Homeland.

II. *The Crime of Fraud and Breach of International Law*

The story of the Mandate as such can be described only as an historic fraud by Britain on the Jewish people.

Having secured the administration of Eretz Israel, and severed three quarters of it, Britain ruthlessly and purposefully distorted, frustrated and violated every provision of the Mandate which would hasten the consummation of Hebrew independence. Ever since 1921 she has "regulated" and restricted Hebrew repatriation. At first she employed the excuse of "economic absorptive capacity" which gave her the arbitrary "right" to limit the entry of Jews into their Homeland so as not to permit the growth of their numbers beyond the figure she had set herself as being "safe" for her domination. Thus she evaded her undertaking to "facilitate Jewish immigration." From the very beginning she has prevented anything even approaching that large-scale close settlement on land provided for by her Mandate and alone commensurate with the requirements of a homecoming people.

Until, finally, when the number of Jews in Eretz Israel had topped the half-million and when any substantial increase in the number of Hebrew citizens would make clear to the world that her "Mandatory" task in this country was ended and that the country would have to be handed over to its rightful owners: and after she had created an appropriate political background, she introduced the White Paper of 1939. By this time, having organised the group of oligarchic Arab puppets whom she parades as the "Arab national representatives," she had dropped her plea of "economic absorptive capacity" for immigration (whose absurdity events had inevitably and, indeed, dramatically demonstrated) and bluntly proclaimed "Arab intransigeance" as the reason, and the "political criterion" as the guiding principle, for her new measures. These were designed to confine the Jews into a tiny area in their country and to crystallise their status as a "community," establishing Britain in Eretz Israel for good as a permanent "arbiter" between two comparably large "communities." This was the alternative to the outright robbery she committed east of the Jordan; and it was effected in the face of the explicit denunciation of the League of Nations authority.

III. *The Crime of Obstruction and Frustration and Economic Exploitation*

a) It was a natural requirement of the British design that the extent and strength of Hebrew reconstruction in Eretz Israel should be kept within the limits of "safety." There followed consequently the system of restriction, obstruction and frustration in every field of Jewish economic endeavour which, in view of the enterprising and dynamic character of the Hebrew human element and the spirit of national reconstruction behind it, nevertheless 'threatened' to create a solid, progressive and growing Hebrew economy in Eretz Israel.

"Government" development initiative has naturally been practically non-existent, except in the payment of salaries to the horde of British "officials" imposed on the country.

The system of frustration has been pursued in a mass of strangling regulations and processes. It is a characteristic fact, for example, that in the field of irrigation survey, research and development, vital to this climate and the previously neglected state of the country, the British Occupation Authorities did precisely nothing for over twenty years of their rule. In 1939/40, the total expenditure on the "Government Irrigation Service" was LP.2,375 of which LP.2,100 went on salaries. In 1946/47 the "approved estimates" amounted to LP.66,900. How much even of this sum (.02% of the total budget) was actually spent, and how, has not, however, been disclosed.

Such development as has been made (in this as in every other sphere) has been made by the Jewish people—in the face of British obstruction. And the occupation authorities make no secret of the fact that their primary preoccupation is with finding "legal" ways and means of frustrating and stopping Jewish development. It is openly revealed in the Occupation Government's "Survey of Palestine," 1946, that the limited degree of investigation and control of water resources has been pursued chiefly "in the hope of detecting some overdrawing" by Jews (and making this the excuse for frustration).

And the "prevention of overdrawing" has been the guiding principle of the application of British long-range policy in every sphere of life.

In agricultural development and research, there is practicably nothing to record beyond what has been established by Hebrew enterprise. Jewish industry has been held in an iron clamp, its development and expansion prevented in every way possible, and the only period in which it was permitted to develop comparatively freely was during the critical war-period when a near-by source of supply was required for the British forces facing Rommel in North Africa. It is heavily taxed, but starved of any assistance.

The Occupation authorities have avoided as far as possible any serious expenditure on constructive public works. Schools, hospitals and public buildings (except where built by Jews themselves) are hopelessly inadequate throughout the country. Government House in Jerusalem, the residence of the head of the Occupation regime, the Jerusalem Post Office and the Jaffa Post Office are—apart, of course, from the 100 and more police fortresses—the only modern Governmental buildings of note in the country.

The contrast between the spacious police stations and the lack of facilities for educational, health and constructive purposes generally is another exemplary illustration of the application of the British design.

Moreover, even private building, willy-nilly falling totally as a burden on the citizens of the country themselves—at a time of a severe housing shortage—is hamstrung largely by the Occupation authorities' own concentration on the building of roads, camps and installations for their military forces.

b) As, in spite of the British strait-jacket, Jewish economy developed, the possibility grew of extracting economic benefit from Eretz Israel for Britain. Eretz Israel has become a source of economic exploitation on old-fashioned Imperialist lines, which has now been woven into the basic British long-range plan.

The Jewish population of Eretz Israel, and Jewish industry in particular, are made to help swell the profits of the British oil companies. Though Palestine's position at the refining and shipping end of the Iraq oil pipeline should result in low fuel costs—fuel prices are abnormally high. Oil is "costed" here as though it were transported from the Gulf of Mexico.

The British oil companies are exempted in our country from the payment of any taxes, though they exploit our communications and port services; and though they make special payments to the satellite rulers in the neighbouring countries. Moreover, the rights to prospect for oil and mining rights in our country have been granted by the British rulers to British companies free of charge. And here too the "Government Statistician" has been frank:

"The nature of the oil companies" he has said "is such that they are best regarded as extra-territorial undertakings. . . . They produce local requirements of benzine, kerosene and fuel oil, but the prices are not based on local cost of production but on the price policy laid down by the London Headquarters of the oil companies."

The Occupation authorities' monetary policy is an integral part of the sabotage of Jewish development and the policy of colonial exploitation.

Palestine was granted a separate currency for no other purpose than to suggest deceptively to the "natives" the existence of one of the paraphernalia of "independence." It is used as a device for taking money out of Palestine and substituting for it a kind of "ghetto currency" (as the Jewish people under the German Nazis knew it), its circulation is limited, and exchangeable into the "real" currency only with difficulty: import of sterling into Palestine is prohibited.

Palestine currency is used by the "Palestine Currency Board" for buying sterling, which is then invested in British Treasury Bonds and British Empire Securities, of countries like Fiji, Jamaica and Zanzibar. Though Palestine is a country of capital scarcity and high interest rates, its currency is used to supply British colonies—or, rather, the colonial interests exploiting them—with loans at low interest rates. Every citizen of this country who owns money automatically and unknowingly lends it to Britain.

c) It need hardly be said that all the direct expenditure of the Occupation Government has always been borne by the population which has, of course, been starved of any substantial return.

The whole principle of the revenue system has been taken over from the Turkish regime. It is the ancient principle of primitive tax systems: "Where you see a head, hit it!"

Revenues are accordingly not collected in accordance with ability to pay. They are a prohibitive system directed against the economic development of the country, expecially against Jewish industry and trade. Customs duties are imposed on articles of mass consumption, on fuel and on building material (in a period of grievous housing shortage). Excise duty is collected on salt and cement equally with liquor and tobacco. Urban land is taxed (again, in a period of grievous housing shortage) for the sufficient reason that such taxes are easy to collect.

The manner of expenditure reveals at a glance the most blatant aspects of British financial policy. Regrouping and analysing the items in the "official" "Government Draft Estimates" for 1947/48 the following simple picture is revealed. In the four basic groups of expenditure (totalling LP.21,557,411)

35.4% is spent on police, prisons and a grant to the "Transjordan Frontier Force" (i.e. the Jewish people contributes to the maintenance inter alia of its own looted property);

40.2% is spent on emoluments of officials, including allowance and other administration costs;

8.1% is spent on subsidisation of the "Government Trading Account" (largely a fund for indirectly subsidising, or, rather, bribing the satellite Governments of the puppet "Arab League," by buying their products above world market prices) and

16.8%, is spent on social and public services.

A small additional item called "Estimated Extraordinary Expenditure," amounting to over LP.2,000,000, is intended, according to previous practice, for swelling the expenditure on "security," administration, and the building of roads for the Occupation Forces.

The police and prison forces of oppression alone have risen from circa 8,000 in 1944 to 19,446. This figure does not include the Transjordan Frontier Force which the British introduce into Western Eretz Israel from time to time to aid in oppressing the Hebrew population and in the faint hope of encouraging Arab-Hebrew discord.

(It is claimed by the British, with some justice, that this great increase in their police forces—as in their military forces—is due to our struggle. Yet it is a transparent fact that this increase has not helped to crush the Hebrew Liberation Movement; on the contrary in the same period its blows have grown stronger and more widespread. And the fact that the tremendous proportions of the police and Gestapo forces of the British have not succeeded in smashing or weakening the Hebrew struggle is a highly practical refutation of the suggestion of British propagandists that the Hebrew Liberation Movement consists of a handful of people, opposed by the population at large. The fact is that the Hebrew Liberation Movement has the backing of the Jewish people, both in Eretz Israel and throughout the world, with the exception of some bodies which, like similar bodies in other occupied countries, are prepared, for narrow interest of their own, to serve the enemy. The mass of the people is behind its fighters, and while it is obviously impossible for them openly to manifest their sympathy, very many of them give us their help, in a variety of ways seldom visible to the eye. And increase their forces as they may, the British Occupiers will never overcome the consequences of this vital fact: the continued ever-deepening struggle for Hebrew liberation until the British invaders have departed).

It is instructive also to record the British system of inflating budgets. First, estimates are drawn up which show a fictitious deficit. To meet this, additional burdens of taxation are imposed. Then at the end of the year, an "unexpected surplus" is found in the Treasury. This surplus provides an obvious reason for proposing still greater expenditure the following year. But then in the new estimates again a deficit or a very much reduced surplus is exposed. And then . . . and so *da capo al fine.* Thus the occupation regime extorts more and more money every year from the oppressed country. Thus, in the post-war years, 1945/46 began with an "estimated" *deficit* of LP.2,755,110 (and an estimated revenue of less than LP.18,000.000) and ended with an actual *surplus* of LP.2,186.358. By 1947/48 this surplus has not only been consumed but has been converted into an "estimated" deficit of LP.1,075.385; and expenditure which in 1945/46 amounted actually to LP.16,834.781 is now "estimated" for 1947/48 at *LP.24,635.066.*

d) It is relevant to add to this brief analysis that graft, bribery and corruption have become deeply embedded in the British Occupation system in our country, as the inevitable and foreseeable consequence of giving arbitrary powers to a large proportion of the thousands of officials pressed in parasitical profusion on the body of the country.

This is, of course, a traditional form of colonial exploitation, and even formal prosecution by the machine of "British Justice" is practically unknown. It is of interest to mention the case of a certain Mr. Walsh, the "Food Controller of the Palestine Government," who lost his life in the attack on Occupation Headquarters in the King David Hotel in July, 1946. A key found in his pocket led to the discovery of the sum of LP.285,000.—in cash held in a bank safe. This member of the Occupation "Cabinet," who had come to this country a poor man, was exceptional only in having been, posthumously, found out.

Another recent flagrant act of exploitation was the wartime introduction into Eretz Israel of a British firm from Burma, Steel Brothers, who were granted a monopoly for transport and for the trade in flour and all basic controlled commodities. Millions of pounds were thus transferred from the Eretz Israel economy into British hands.

e) It will be patent to the Committee that a proportion of the extortions from the Hebrew population is directed towards the Arabs inhabitants, but, of course, only sufficient to keep the Arab comparatively satisfied with his material lot and to give him the impression that the benefits he is deriving are the result of British benevolence. Moreover the bulk of the positive "benefits" are enjoyed by those Arabs who are in the direct service of the British Occupation authorities. The population at large benefits mainly from its exemption in practice from some of the extortions and restrictions of the Occupation authorities, such as income tax.

The most striking demonstration of the Occupation authorities' real attitude towards the Arab population is readily at hand: in the state of the Arab population in Eastern Eretz Israel, who have been subject *entirely* to British "benevolence." In the twenty-five years of the British occupation there is not a single sphere of life in which the slightest degree of progress has been made. To give but one typical instance of the stage of "progress" east of the Jordan: there is not a single newspaper in existence there.

f) It is claimed in Britain, to the accompaniment of bitter public protests, that the maintenance of the Occupation Forces in our country is a heavy drain on the British taxpayer. If this were only true the British taxpayer could be speedily relieved of this burden—

by the removal of the Occupation Forces from our country. The truth, however, is that the actual expenditure in Eretz Israel is met by issuing Palestine pounds. Against this the Palestine "sterling balance" in London is accordingly increased. The immediate effect is inevitably a devaluation of Palestine currency, price inflation and a lowering of the workers' standard of living. It is quite obvious that at least this part of the sterling balance will not be repaid. The inevitable consequence is that the Jewish people is paying for the establishment of a British base in its Homeland; and paying the expenses of its own oppression.

g) We must strongly emphasize that we have gone into some detail in listing some of the manifestations of British economic exploitation in Eretz Israel, not in order to "submit grievances." We have desired only to illustrate as clearly as possible the extent to which the motive of economic exploitation has became a part of the British design to enslave our country and our people, and by devious means to exact the maximum "tribute" to line the British imperial pocket. Even if Britain had installed an occupation administration in our country with orders to be "benevolent" and to treat the population as citizens, and not as milch-cows, this would not alter its character as a foreign occupation authority nor our obligation and determination to rid ourselves of it: for the country does not belong to Britain, but to the Hebrew people.

This comment holds good also for our exposure of details of the methods of subjugation employed *in all fields* by the British Occupiers. We have not brought them forward in order to suggest to the Committee that it should propose an "improvement" in British rule in our country, that is, an improvement in the conditions of our enslavement. In relation to the British we have only one demand, backed by our resolve to fight for its realization: the withdrawal of every vestige of British rule in our country. And we have dwelt on these details only in illustration of the evils inseparable from that British rule.

IV. *The Crime of Instigation to Murder of Jews in their Homeland*

In order to provide the excuse of "Arab opposition" for her policy of strangulation of the Hebrew national renaissance Britain instigated four attacks by Arabs on the Hebrews of Eretz Israel, and aided the mercenaries engaged in these attacks by effectively preventing the Hebrew population from speedily putting an end to them. Moreover Britain is guilty of persistent attempts to incite Arabs to further attacks on Hebrew life and property. Her recent efforts in this direction, though accompanied by promises of bribes, have failed—but the crime is not thereby mitigated.

V. *The Crime of Mass-Extermination of the Jewish People*

In pursuit of the object of ensuring that the control of Eretz Israel should remain in her hands and that consequently the Hebrew people should not re-attain its national independence, Britain has encouraged and participated in the greatest of all crimes in human history: the extermination of the Jewish people in Europe.

a) The extermination of our people under Hitler began long before the war. For six years before 1939 Hitler ruled in Germany and spread his doctrines of Jew-hatred all over Europe. In 1938 he seized Austria and, in March, 1939, Czechoslovakia; and the Jews of these countries were sentenced to death, slow or immediate. It was in those days that the work of free repatriation (which the Occupation authorities naturally called "illegal immigration") was begun by the then newly-born Irgun Zvai Leumi. But the number of Jews hovering between life and death under the Nazi heel was already before the war one and a half million. Only a handful could be rescued in this manner. The rest were left to be slaughtered—because Britain had determined to prevent their coming to their Homeland. They were left deliberately. When Prague fell, Mr. Chamberlain, the British Prime Minister permitted himself a crocodile tear in the House of Commons: "From what happened in Vienna after the entry of the German armies," he said, "we know what is in store now for the Jews of Czechoslovakia." They knew what was in store—and hastily double-barred the gates of Eretz Israel against any potential escape by the victims.

b) They knew, then, moreover, as all the world knew, what was the fate being prepared for the eight million Jews in the whole of Europe—for they knew then that war was coming, and that there was no force strong enough in Central and Eastern Europe, where the bulk of the Jewish masses lived, to stop the onslaught of Hitler's hordes. And it was no coincidence that two months after Prague fell, and the first shrill signal for the extermination of our people was given—the 1939 White Paper was issued, announcing the British Government's firm determination to shut Eretz Israel still more tightly; and thus to force the eight million Jews of Europe on to the knives and into the gas-chambers of Hitler.

c) The war broke out and almost overnight three-and-a-half million more Jews fell into the hands of Hitler; and three million more lived under the sword of Damocles. Desperately, many risked the perils of the mined ocean and the dangers of rotten ships to escape from the trap of death. Some did. But there, waiting for them, were the naval forces of the enemy, hypocritically still bearing the outward semblance of a friend: Britain. We recall in particular the case of two such boatloads of our people: on the "Milos" and "Pacific"—"captured" by the British Navy in the Mediterranean and brought to Haifa harbour—for their capture was accompanied by a significant, historic pronouncement by the British Government.

"These people must be regarded as illegal immigrants" said that statement on 27 November, 1940. "His Majesty's Government is not lacking in sympathy for refugees from countries under German rule, but it is responsible for governing Palestine and must ensure that the laws of the country should not be publicly flouted. Moreover it regards the resumption of illegal immigration at this time as a development likely to affect very adversely the situation in the country and to become a grave menace *to British interests in the Middle East* (our emphasis). The Government has consequently decided that the passengers aboard the "Milos" and "Pacific" will not be allowed to enter Palestine but will be sent to a British colony. . . until the end of the war, when it will be decided where to send them. But it is not the Government's intention that they should remain in this colony, or that they should come to Palestine. *The Government will apply similar measures to any further groups* (our emphasis) who succeed in reaching Palestine with the object of entering it illegally." (The British colony in question was Mauritius).

This proclamation was a warning to the Jews under Hitler not to leave the European death-trap. But it was also an open invitation to the German Nazis to "go ahead." It told them in case they had any doubt, that Britain too, was interested in sealing the fate of the Jews, that she would *never* let them enter Palestine, that her naval blockade was a blockade not only on Germany but also on the Jews. It told them that "British interests" demanded that the Jews of Europe remain in Europe.

Then the actual slaughter began. And when the first reports arrived of the murder of tens of thousands of men, women and children, and of the terrible comprehensiveness of the German plans for the extermination of our people it was the British Government which for many months effectively prevented the full truth being told the world. And when later it was proposed that bombers should attack the death factories at Treblinka and Auschwitz, etc. attacks which, properly directed, could have saved thousands of the candidates from the gas-chambers and the ovens, the British refused, on the typically hypocritical pretext that the poor Jewish inmates of the camps might be hit.

After the bulk of our people in Europe had been destroyed there still remained large Jewish centres in Europe where Hitler's control was then still only indirect. In Hungary and Roumania a million and a half Jews were imprisoned. The Governments of these countries were prepared and offered to allow the Jews out, and even made detailed proposals for effecting their transfer; moreover, Turkey was prepared to permit passage through her territory to all Jews with British permits for Palestine. But the British Government refused—

and the final million were handed over to destruction—because "British interests" required it.

d) Accompanying the great mass-slaughter was the British murder of the repatriates on the "Struma" and the "Patria": prevented by British brute force from entering their Homeland 220 repatriates on the "Patria" sank with their ship in Haifa harbour. And the repatriates on the "Struma," forced to return to Hitler Europe when Britain informed Turkey (in one of whose ports they had arrived in their flight) that they would not be allowed to enter Eretz Israel—sank with their vessel in the Black Sea.

e) Many of the repatriates deported to Mauritius died from disease, the unsuitable climate, and inadequate care.

Thus Britain ended the war with another great victory: six million Jews murdered, one-third destroyed of the strength of the people whose country she had robbed; and its consequent power to resist the final consummation of the robbery by so much reduced.

f) But her work of murder was not yet ended. After the war there miraculously remained in Central and Western Europe, a million and a half Jews, of whom about a quarter of a million remained in concentration camps. They are still there. For Britain maintains her determination that they shall remain there, to rot and die, crushing their personalities, driving them to suicide and encouraging the German Nazis to resume the actual killings as soon as convenient; and using all her diplomatic influence throughout Europe to prevent their escape to their Homeland.

VI. *The Crime of Deportation and Murder of Hebrew Repatriants*

Thousands of our people who have nevertheless tried to return to their Homeland have been captured and exiled to the British colony of Cyprus.

Britain has wounded and killed hundreds of these repatriants for daring to resist her pirate's breach of humanity's law of freedom of the seas; they have been tear-gassed shot or beaten to death.

VII. *Britain's Rule of Terror in Eretz Israel*

While Britain destroys our people still in exile, she has tried to crush the Hebrew people in the Homeland into permanent subjection and acceptance of whatever "status" her own design dictates as convenient.

And because the Hebrew in their Homeland have refused to allow themselves quietly to be subjugated, Britain has instituted a tyrannous totalitarian regime in Eretz Israel which has not its equal in human history.

This regime of terror has had a number of stages during the past ten years and has been intensified with the launching and widening of the Hebrew struggle for liberation.

The Emergency (Defence) Regulations, 1945, with their extensive and elaborating amendments are the outer frames of the British rule of terror.

The lives, freedom, well-being, property, and honour of every man and woman in this country have been delivered by this "Code of Oppression" to the whim of any British officer, constable or soldier.

The following is a short summary of some of the powers "conferred" on itself by the British occupation regime in our country:

Seizure of Property

The administration and the military have unlimited and unchecked powers of requisitioning any land and chattels, of selling such chattels, of prohibiting any work on any land, of removing and demolishing anything on any land; of prohibiting exercise of existing rights, and so on.

In addition to these powers of requisitioning, which have been used arbitrarily to seize Jewish dwellings all over the country, powers exist to order *forfeiture*. The Censor may order forfeiture of any printing press and instruments of printing, or prohibit their operation for an indefinite time. A military Commander may order forfeiture of any structure or land if he *suspects* that any firearms, or explosive or incendiary has been placed there even by a stranger or passerby; or if he is "satisfied" that *any* inhabitant of the town or area was involved in any of the innumerable "offences."

The High Commissioner may direct forfeiture of all property of any person of whom he is "satisfied" that he was involved in an offence. For this purpose the suspected offence may be, for example, wearing a military badge, or unauthorised dealing in Army food.

A vessel, aircraft, vehicle etc. may be arbitrarily declared forfeited if "suspected" of being used in contravention of the Immigration Ordinance (that is, for conveying Hebrew repatriants).

Abolition of Freedom of Speech, Writing and Association

No paper may be published without a licence, and it may be closed at any moment.

A rigid comprehensive censorship has abolished freedom of the press.

Freedom of speech has disappeared under the watch of a vast Gestapo. And far-reaching restriction are in force on the freedom of meeting and assocation.

Freedom of Movement

Freedom of movement may be restricted generally by the imposition of curfews or prohibiting movement on the roads. Individuals may be forbidden to move from one town to another, and ordered to remain indoors. Such orders have been imposed upon thousands of people, with effect for years.

Personal Freedom

Any person belonging to the same association or group as an "offender" is liable to punishment, including even the death sentence. A citizen can be arrested without charge, imprisoned without trial and held for years without opportunity to appeal even to a British "Court." Many thousands of Hebrew citizens have been thus imprisoned and many hundreds are at the present moment held in detention camps and gaols throughout the country.

Arbitrary Deportation of Citizens

Moreover, they can be deported at will outside the confines of his country and held there indefinitely. Thus hundreds of Hebrew citizens who know no other Homeland have languished for years in concentration camps in the Sudan, in Eritrea and in Kenya where, by collusion among the various British administrations, "laws" have been enacted "enabling" these alien administrations to incarcerate free Hebrew citizens for indefinite periods.

Murder of Prisoners

Such prisoners have been killed, in Eritrea, by the guards of their camp—adding to the list of British murders of our people.

Torture of Prisoners

Many of the prisoners taken by the Occupation regime have been tortured, with the avowed purpose of eliciting information on Hebrew resistance organisations.

Mass Repression of Citizens, Destruction and Murder

Faced with Hebrew armed resistance the British Occupation regime has let loose the full brutality of war measures against

combatants and non-combatants alike. Violent searches are carried
out at all times of the day and night. Curfews have been imposed
sometimes for days on end, bringing misery and illness, especially to
children, through the deprivation of elementary food necessities;
and children have been shot dead when seen allegedly "breaking
the curfew." Hebrew citizens have been killed throughout the
country, men and women and children—sometimes by British
armed formations, at others by individual soldiers or Gestapo agents.
Hebrew villages have been ravaged and looted.

Mass Intimidation

In March, 1947, so-called "Martial Law" was enforced on the
major centres of the Hebrew population, paralysing their economy
and cutting them off from each other and from the outside world—in
an attempt to break their spirit and to turn them into informers
against the underground resistance. The refusal of the Hebrew
population to submit even to this intimidation, and the large-scale
operations of the Irgun Zvai Leumi during the period of Martial Law,
compelled the Occupation authorities to lift it after a fortnight.

Military Courts

"Military Courts" have been imposed on the civilian population, consisting of the officers of a foreign occupation army, which,
even according to the Mandate, has no judiciary rights in Eretz
Israel. The authority conferred on these courts to sentence citizens to
death, or to life imprisonment, or to other long prison sentences, is
unlimited. The Commander-in-Chief of the Occupation Army is
the only "institution" supervising the "sentences" of officers appointed by himself.

Murder of Prisoners

These "courts" have pronounced "sentence" of death on
Hebrew prisoners of war who had explicitly declared that they were
soldiers of an enslaved people fighting for its freedom against a
cruel enemy and that they must consequently be regarded as
prisoners of war. In contravention of the fundamental laws of
civilized humanity, the British murdered six prisoners of war,
employing, moreover, methods of cowardly deceit and Nazi brutality
that aroused the protest of all civilised peoples.

Torture and Murder of Wounded

It has become a rule for the British forces to maltreat every Hebrew fighter they capture. The facts disclosed by Mordechai Alkoshi and Eliezer Kashani (murdered in Acre Gaol), on the barbaric tortures to which they were subjected in a British military camp, under the "supervision" of British officers, will be recalled.

If a man falling into the hands of these barbaric "defenders of the law" is wounded, he is denied all aid for hours on end. Many wounded fighters died slowly, surrounded by British soldiers, who for hours cheerfully watched their sufferings and their death agonies without giving them even a glass of water. These wounded men could have been saved, if they had been given medical First Aid. But "the soldiers of His Majesty" wanted them to die in agony— and murdered them. Many details about this terrible crime can be supplied by the three men, Absalom Haviv, Meir Nakar and Jacob Weiss, now in the death-cell at Acre Gaol.

The Effect on the Jewish Agency

Against the background of this regime of terror the Committee will readily understand why the spokesmen of the Jewish Agency are not free to submit the full list of Britain's crimes against our people, and to present its full aspirations. The Jewish Agency itself has been through some bitter experiences. Last year, after a period of united struggle against the British regime, which was conducted in agreement and understanding by the three Hebrew armed organisations: the Haganah, the Irgun Zvai Leumi and the Fighters of Israel, the forces of the Occupation regime stormed the Jewish Agency, seized its headquarters in Jerusalem and, with considerable brutality, arrested a number of its members. Explicit threats were then uttered that the Occupation regime would dissolve the Jewish Agency completely or that they would withdraw their recognition of it, if it did not "improve its ways," if the Haganah continued to carry out attacks, or if the Jewish Agency would not collaborate with the regime in fighting the underground Resistance,—as it had done in 1944 when it denounced to the British Gestapo hundreds of citizens "suspected" of belonging to the Irgun Zvai Leumi—or in any other way. Other threats were also made. Lord Winterton, a member of the British Parliament, suggested that the British army could turn Tel-Aviv into a heap of rubble—a threat repeated in a highly transparent hint contained in the report recently submitted by the head of the Occupation regime on the Irgun Zvai Leumi breaking open of the Acre fortress.

It is therefore not surprising that the Jewish Agency is frightened. It is afraid for its very existence as an institution. It is afraid for the safety of its members, who were freed from detention only after a Zionist institution had passed and published a resolution denouncing "terrorism." The Jewish Agency knows that after the departure of the United Nations Committee from Palestine, it will remain face to face with the British regime of terror; and fears its revenge. That is why it cannot tell the whole truth. Proof of this can already be found in the testimony of Mr. Shertok who, in answer to questions by your Yugoslav member, "could not remember" cases of racial discrimination other than those contained in the land regulations. Every child in this country could bring before you a long list of British attacks and acts of discrimination of a racial character.

It will be clear that in these circumstances the Jewish Agency is not a "free Agency." It is seeking a "compromise," which will enable it to live, somehow, with the British regime which—despite the enquiry on behalf of the United Nations Organisation—still behaves as though it is and will remain "master" in this country. That is why the Jewish Agency ordered those it is in a position to order to stop all resistance to the regime of oppression—in spite of the fact that the institution which elected it and to which it is responsible— the Zionist Congress—took an explicit decision, based on the will of the masses as expressed in the elections to this body, to offer active resistance to the "White Paper regime." That is why it went to the "London Conference," that is, to negotiate with the Occupation Government—again in clear contravention of the decision of that Congress and of the will of the electors. That is why it publicly proclaims surrender of Eastern Eretz Israel, and its members, publicly or privately, propose the carving up even of Western Eretz Israel, even though no institution has—or could have—the right to forego a part of our national territory, which is an historic unity.

The Jewish Agency is under the permanent threat of dissolution by the Occupation regime. That is why it does not say what the representatives of an enslaved but fighting people should and are in duty bound to say. This is a fact which we are compelled—with deep regret—to make clear. It may be possible to *understand* the special position of the members of the Jewish Agency, but it is not possible, in historic perspective, to condone their behaviour.

JEWISH-ARAB RELATIONS

In the light of the long-range British purpose their intense and predominant interest in the "organisation" of Arab-Jewish relations hardly requires any explaining. The proper manipulation of these relations and, what is more important, the form of their propaganda presentation to the world were the chief preoccupations of the British Occupation regime, for on a successful deception depended the British pretext for remaining in the country.

It was essential for this purpose to create an impression of undying hostility on the part of the Arabs to the reconstitution of the Hebrew Homeland. Only thus could they produce "justification" for their permanent war against Jewish national reconstitution. To this end, from the very first days of their presence in Eretz Israel, the British imposed on the Arab population a puppet leadership of feudal notables, neither elected nor approved by even a part of the population. Haj Amin el Husseini, after being encouraged to organise a massacre of Jewish unarmed men, women and children in 1920 (the first of the series of attacks), while British troops held the Jewish defenders at bay, was brought back from his hiding place, "pardoned" and forced upon the Moslems as their Mufti, in spite of his defeat in the election (the only Arab election on record). And he and his henchmen, under British instruction and with their direct aid, have ever since been presented to the world as the authentic Arab leadership. Any stirring of real democracy, any hint of opposition has been ruthlessly suppressed. The number of Arabs murdered in this country under British rule runs into thousands—all victims of the rule of terror of the British-directed Husseini family over the Arabs of Palestine. The price of opposition to the oligarchic "rule" of the Husseinis for the furtherance of British purposes has throughout all these years been death, or the threat of death. The result has naturally been that any leader who seemed likely to begin expressing the will of the people has been liquidated, or intimidated into silence, or intimidated into joining the Husseini clique. For example Mr. Henry Cattan—who recently appeared for the "Arab Higher Committee" in the United Nations Organisation was "converted" to Husseini orthodoxy at the point of a revolver.

It is this clique, maintained by the British in complete power over every Arab institution and form of life in Eretz Israel, who have fulfilled the purpose of the British and enabled them to deceive the world into believing that there was no possibility of the Arabs' agreeing to live together with the Jews returning to their Homeland; and made possible the fulfilment of Britain's purpose of presenting herself as a permanent "arbiter" between the two hostile communities. It has been essential for the British purpose to prevent the awakening of true democracy in the country. True democracy depends very largely on education; and the Arabs are predominantly illiterate,—a majority of the men and almost all their womenfolk. Those measures of the Occupation regime for education and for better health facilities for Arabs have been few, and have been forced on them by the necessity of making a *show* of "providing advancement" for the Arabs. It is significant that the only agricultural college opened for the Arabs is that provided by a Jewish bequest. And repeated proposals by Britain's own "commissions" for improvement of the lot of the Arab fellaheen (the bulk of the Arab population) have been ignored because this would weaken the hold of the Husseini clique.

As mentioned elsewhere, moreover, what little the Occupation authorities have done for advancing the lot of the Arab has been at Jewish expense—thus making it another means of attack on the Jewish economy.

We do not grudge the Arabs advancement. On the contrary, one of the early tasks of the future Hebrew Government will be the dissemination of education in all spheres and the democratisation of Arab life in general—but not in order only to provide headings in Annual reports. Indeed the fact that the Hebrew renaissance has already begun, and the Hebrew State will consummate, the liberation of its Arab citizens from the backwardness in which they still flounder, and in which "British interests" require that they should remain, has strengthened the British resolve to cruch[sic] Hebrew reconstruction.

The bulk of the Arabs still live in squalor and cultural backwardness—as will no doubt be observed by the Committee—and the bulk of them, at least of those who have been in contact with the Hebrew repatriants, realize that there is little hope of any improvement as long as the British rule the country. And the bulk of them do, and are prepared to, live at peace and in cooperation with the Hebrew population.

It is instructive that in spite of the permanent reign of terror by the Husseini clique one can still quote examples of the Arab desire for cooperation, which, too, throw light on the tripartite relations.

The continual murders of Arabs, notables and others, for selling land to the Jews tells its own story.

In November, 1945 the Occupation authorities appointed a committee to make recommendations for the easing of the housing situation. They recommended *unanimously* "the abolition of restrictions imposed by the White Paper on the acquisition of land by Jews in respect of land suitable for residential purposes." The Committee included Arab members.

In the Municipal Commission in Haifa Jews and Arabs have ever worked amicably together. And in that town there are none of the "intransigeant" Arab leaders: for the simple reason that the Occupation Administration is interested in not creating tension in the area holding both its naval base and the oil terminus and refineries.

In 1932, Abdullah "of Transjordan" himself offered to sell land in Eastern Eretz Israel to the Jewish Agency, for immediate settlement and development by Jews. The Occupation Authorities forbade it.

It is true that there are occasional quarrels and disputes, which may even result in blows. But they are in most cases less serious than similar quarrels and disputes between Arabs and Arabs; or such quarrels in other countries where the Governments have no interest in magnifying every local brawl into an international incident. The Arab, in spite of persistent incitement and promises of bribes by British agents—greatly intensified during recent years with the launching of the Hebrew struggle against British occupation—has not only refused to be misled into helping the British out by himself attacking us, but lives and works with his Hebrew neighbours in affability and friendliness. Moreover, we can testify from our own experience that, when occasion has arisen, the Arabs have given assistance to the Hebrew struggle for liberation. On a number of occasions Hebrew fighters returning through Arab villages or quarters from operations against British objectives, have been given aid, shelter and comfort by the inhabitants. To mention another instance: after a number of Arab-Jewish quarrels in British gaols which assumed serious proportions and which, according to the Arab prisoners themselves were the result of the British instigation of the Arabs, there has recently grown considerable comradeship and co-operation between Hebrew and Arab prisoners in the British gaols. At Acre the Arab prisoners have risked severe punishments from the British gaolers, manifesting solidarity with Hebrew prisoners' protests at maltreatment—though they know well that British favours can be bought cheaply by playing the game of hostility to Jews. Indeed, it is possibly in prisons, where the Arabs are, at least temporarily, freed from the intimidations of their British-imposed leaders that one finds the freest expressions of that desire for friendship and co-operation with Jews which, there can be no question, is common to the vast majority of the Arab inhabitants of Eretz Israel. But this desire will come it its full expression only with the departure of the British Occupation regime from our country, and with the opportunity that a Hebrew Provisional Government will then provide for a free democratic expression of the will of the Arab inhabitants, whom we regard as equal citizens with the Jews and with whom together we shall make Eretz Israel fruitful, prosperous and progressive.

MAJORITY AND MINORITY IN PALESTINE

The British Occupiers will argue before you that they cannot transfer power in Eretz Israel to a Hebrew Government because the Hebrew citizens in the country are a minority. When this argument is advanced by colonial exploiters who rule over tens of millions of people throughout the world as though this right had come to them from Heaven—it is only a further proof of their characteristic hypocrisy. We know, however, that this argument carries weight with men of goodwill, whose belief in the principles of democracy is sincere. We therefore feel it necessary to deal, inter alia, with the question of majority and minority in Eretz Israel.

It is the result of the use of *physical force* by Britain, preventing the Hebrew repatriation which, already before the war had assumed the proportions of a mass urge, that the de facto Hebrew population of Eretz Israel is at present smaller than the non-Hebrew. But it is not true that we Hebrew citizens of this country according to the law—not the British "law," but according to the *law*—constitute a minority of the inhabitants. The contrary is true. We are a clear de jure majority of the population of Eretz Israel, both east and west of the Jordan. Which we shall prove.

But before we prove this principal contention, we must touch on another question which, while it does not affect our rights, is not without importance and interest. We refer to the statistical figure[s] submitted to you by the Occupation authorities.

These figures are unworthy of the slightest confidence. They do not reflect the true situation; they have been manufactured in order to reflect a situation which the British Occupiers find it convenient to pretend exists. This is true of all aspects of life. Where it is a question of the extent of uncultivable land, the British experts will describe all uncultivated land as "uncultivable." This is, in fact, a mockery of reality. Most of the land fructified by Hebrew toil, was, twenty-five years ago, uncultivated and appeared to be uncultivable. And that is true of other lands now desolate. It is unquestionably possible to turn them into fruitful areas with the aid of modern technical methods and the toil of creative man. But the British Occupiers, who need these areas for their tank manoeuvres, will naturally say that attempts to irrigate land requiring irrigation and to dry areas that require drying will, of course, fail.

The distortion of figures is naturally brought into very wide play in the demographic statistics. Even in the Occupation authorities own Statistical Abstract (1944/45), you will find on pages 15-16, a carefully understated doubt as to the correctness of the figures compiled by the officials of the regime. And it is well that you should know that the figures for the total Arab population presented by the Occupation Food Controller vary from those of other Occupation Government statistics by more than *two hundred thousand* souls. With a stroke of the pen, over two hundred thousand were added to the Arab population in the country.

The "official" statistical estimates are based on a "census" held in November, 1931. How was this census conducted? Among the Arab population, where, thanks to the "cultural" work of the Government, illiteracy still amounts to more than 70 per cent, the enumerators were at work for months on end, which gave them time enough to adapt "their" figures to those previously "estimated" by the British Occupation Government—with generous additions to the figures of settled Arab population. This census, whose purpose was deliberate falsification, has served as the basis for all other and later statistical estimates. The picture presented by these estimates is consequently an utterly distorted one.

The statistical estimate nearest the truth is that in Western Eretz Israel there live today between 1,500,000 and 1,700,000 souls. Of these not less than 650,000 and not more than 750,000 are Jews, less than 200,000 Druzes and Christians of various nationalities and the rest Moslems, mainly of Arab nationality, part of whom—and no small part—are immigrant who came here from various countries during the last few decades. In summary, it may be said that there are in Western Eretz Israel approximately 700,000 Jews and some 900,000 others, the majority Arabs, all of them ruled by approximately twenty thousand British officials and police, who eat out the substance of the local population, together with 100,000 soldiers of an alien occupation army.

As for Eastern Eretz Israel, where there is, of course, not the semblance of a census, even the British have for the last twenty-five years been claiming only an estimated population of three hundred thousand, about half of it nomad (i.e. freely moving in and out between Eastern Eretz Israel and neighbouring countries).

As for the numerical relation between the Hebrew and non-Hebrew population there is of course, a great difference between the figures presented by British "statistics" and the true figures. The conclusion to be drawn from this difference is that the number of Jews who have to be brought into Eretz Israel in order to establish a de facto majority is considerably less than the British Occupiers would have the world believe—and this repatriation could be effected in a matter of months.

But this is a matter of mechanics. It does not affect the principle. In refuting the claim of British propaganda that we constitute only one-third of the population of Eretz Israel, we invoke the inalienable right of the sons of our people to return to their Homeland. We assert that their number is millions. And whether we are right or not can be proved very simply:

Under international authority our people in exile should be given the *option*, on the explicit undertaking that if they choose to go to Eretz Israel, they will be enabled to do so without interference and without delay: and that the physical illegal force, which the alien occupation regime employs in order to deny them this elementary right, will be removed. Physical force does not invalidate a right. The uprooting by Hitler of millions of Russians, or French, or Yugoslavs from their Homeland did not cancel the right of the uprooted to return to their countries and be citizens with full rights. That is true of our people and their Homeland. Not only those who still languish in the concentration camps are "displaced persons." Our brothers dispersed over various countries, are also exiled displaced persons, whose right it is to be recognised as citizens of Eretz Israel and to be

enabled and assisted to return to their country. They and the
Hebrew citizens already in Eretz Israel together constitute a clear de
jure majority of the population, even before the process of repatriation is accomplished.

The transfer of power in our country to a democratic Provisional Hebrew Government not only does not contravene the
principles of democracy, but, on the contrary, is the dictate of *true*
democracy, as it is the dictate of human justice.

"SOLUTIONS" AND THE ONLY SOLUTION

Taking our stand as we do on the historic right of our people to
sovereignty in the whole of our Homeland; seeing in the return of
the country to its legal owners an act of elementary justice—we
naturally do not feel obliged to go into the details of the various
"plans" brought before you, or before other institutions, for the
solution of the Eretz Israel problem. Even if these plans were
capable of execution, we should oppose them and fight them,
because all of them contain the element of robbery—in contravention
of historic right and the exigencies of life. But the truth is that all
these plans floating in the air are simply impossible of execution. To
propose such plans or to propose their detailed consideration—
something that would certainly require a new international commission—would mean simply to give Britain a further opportunity to
evade the primary solution required by our country; which is: the
withdrawal from the country of the British Occupiers. That is the
reason why we intend to dwell on the partition "plan" and the
"plan" for a bi-national state and to prove that neither of them solves
anything.

The Partition Plan

The main reason for the proposal of partition is that the Jews
and the Arabs allegedly cannot live together in one State. The second
reason is that it is not fair to let a Hebrew Government—even if it
includes Arab Ministers—govern the Arab inhabitants. Both reasons
are spurious. The first has no ground in reality. The second lacks any
foundation of justice if it is remembered that Eretz Israel is the *only*
Homeland of the Hebrew people, while the Arab inhabitants are one
fortieth part of the Arab people, who live in a number of countries
which could be independent if it were not for British "advisers" and
British bayonets. But assuming, for the sake of argument, that
neither of these arguments is spurious, that both are well-grounded,
what, from this point of view, does the partition plan give us?

Examine a map of Western Eretz Israel and note the lines

which have been drawn round the coastal area and a portion of Galilee in the plan of "autonomous zones," put forward by the British Government. The Minister who announced it "promised" that possibly, in the fullness of time, the autonomous Jewish zone would become an "independent State." It emerges that in this zone there live today 498,330 Jews and 430,480 Arabs. These figures are taken from the official statistics, and consequently require correction, but amendment of the figures does not change the principle nor the inescapable conclusion. Even if we assume that it might be possible to squeeze into this ghetto between 100,000 and 200,000 additional inhabitants there would still be living in it approximately 40 per cent Arabs. The question must therefore be asked: If it is true that Hebrews and Arabs will never be able to live together in the independent Hebrew State, in the whole of Eretz Israel, on what grounds is it assumed that they will be able to live together in the tiny Statelet? And if it is not fair to let a Hebrew Government, representing a majority of the inhabitants in the whole country, govern the Arab part of the population, why is it fair to let a Hebrew Government govern the Arab 40% of the population in the dwarf State?

A very similar picture—though with slight differences—presents itself if we increase the area of the small "Jewish State," as proposed, whether in secret or publicly, whether explicitly or in vague terms, by the Jewish Agency. It emerges that in this larger area—which includes Upper Galilee and the Negev—there is at present, as far as is known, an *Arab majority* (507,540 Arabs and 501,870 Jews). The very question asked by pseudo-democrats in relation to the whole of Eretz Israel—"how can you give a minority power over a majority?"—will be asked in this case as well. And if the answer is that the majority will be created in a short time by means of repatriation, the very same answer can, and must, be given in relation to the whole of Eretz Israel, as we have already shown. And if partition were carried out and the Jewish majority were already established, then again the two other questions remain in force: How are Arabs and Jews to live together in one, Hebrew State, and is it fair to give the Hebrew majority power to govern the Arab population?

There is no escape from this analysis. For there are only two alternatives: either the reasons for which various factors propose the carving up of our country are well-grounded, or they are not well-grounded. If they are, then they themselves—*in the light of reality*—rule out any partition plan. And if they are not well-grounded—and you accept the principle of a Hebrew State—then no ground is left for committing injustice or against converting the eternal Hebrew Homeland into a Hebrew State, free and democratic, based on absolutely equal rights for all its citizens.

Thus—either there will be peace between Hebrews and Arabs

in Eretz Israel, in which case it will reign—with the departure of the British—in the whole of Eretz Israel; or, if peace is inconceivable between the two peoples, it will be broken also in that part of the country—whichever it may be—which is allotted to the "Hebrew State" with its substantial proportion of Arab citizens.

We believe that there can and will be peace and fraternity between the two peoples but we know that they can be attained only with the withdrawal of the British from our country and its establishment as a Hebrew State, to which ends our struggle is directed.

The "Plan" of a Bi-National State

In order to avoid misunderstanding we suggest that an immediate distinction be made between a bi-national *State* and a bi-national *government*. It is clear that Eretz Israel will always be a bi-national *State*, in the sense that it will always contain sons of two peoples, whose origins are closely related but whose national characters differ. In elections to municipal institutions or to State institutions Hebrew citizens and Arab citizens will participate. It may be that there will be parties which, on the basis of joint economic demands, will include both Arabs and Jews, though this will be achieved only after some time. In the Parliament there will therefore be Hebrew Members and Arab Members, and it is probable that the Governments will include Hebrew Ministers and Arab Ministers.

The question is: what kind of Government will it be: Hebrew, or Arab? If it contains seven Arab Ministers and three Hebrew—as that British instrument, the Arab League, has proposed—it is clear that it will be an Arab Government, which is what the British Occupiers want and which will—in accordance with British wishes—do everything not only to prevent the entry of Hebrew repatriates into our country, but also, by various means to reduce the present Jewish population. It must not be forgotten that Amin El Husseini and Jamal Husseini have learnt the "lore" of the German and British Nazis.

On the other hand if the country is established on the basis of the recognition of the right of the Hebrew people to its Homeland, this Government will be a Hebrew Government, in which there will also be Arab Ministers; just as there will be Arabs, according to their ability, in the other democratic State institutions. But the *primary* duty of this Government will be to bring back to the country the exiles of our people who strive to return to it.

There exists, theoretically, a third possibility. This, according to those who created the bi-national "plan," is that the institutions of the State should be composed, for ever, of 50 per cent Jews and 50 per cent Arabs. This plan too is based on the assumption that *practical* co-operation between Hebrew and Arab citizens is impossible. That is why it is proposed that neither "side" should be able to secure, by a majority vote, a decision favouring its point of view in affairs of State. Consequently, the plan is nothing more than a Utopia. This Government will be no Government. It will be paralyzed ab initio. It will be impossible to reach decisions, and if they are reached they will not be carried out. And in order to maintain the Utopia, which will bring about complete anarchy, it will be necessary to pass reactionary legislation discriminating sometimes against Arabs, depriving them of the right to vote, sometimes against Jews, depriving *them* of the right to vote. It is clear that laws which, prospectively and on the basis of adherence to a specific ethnic group, deprive citizens, or those about to come, or those yet to be born, of the right to vote, are impossible in a democratic State. It is equally clear that such a State will never be independent— for in every question affecting the life and development of the country a *third* party will have to "arbitrate."

To summarize, it may be said that as logical analysis proves, the partition plan is an illusion and the bi-national plan a Utopia based on a lie.

The Solution

The Eretz Israel question, with which the fate and existence of our people is indissolubly linked; and with which is linked, directly and indirectly, the peace of the Middle East and perhaps also international peace can be solved in only one way, through the solution dictated both by history and by the exigencies of life itself.

This is the solution:

a) To abolish British Occupation rule in Eretz Israel, the alien, illegal direct rule in Western Eretz Israel, and indirect rule in Eastern Eretz Israel.

b) To transfer power in Eretz Israel to a democratic representative body of our people—to a Hebrew Provisional Government.

c) To provide for aid by an international body to enable this Government to carry out the task of repatriation in the shortest possible time.

d) To oblige this Government to hold, on the conclusion of the repatriation democratic general elections for the State institutions, to which it must hand over its prerogatives.

e) To help, by means of an international loan, the carrying out of development plans, making possible the settlement on the soil now standing desolate both of the repatriant Hebrew families and of the Arab fellaheen who suffer from chronic want under the double yoke of serfdom and exploitation.

This solution will bring to this alien-ravaged country—if not immediately, certainly with the passage of time—peace and fraternity of peoples, social and economic progress. This solution will put an end to the exploitation of the Holy Land for immoral aims of domination. This solution will assure for a persecuted and deci-mated people a life of security and creative work, and for humanity—liberation from the contagious and cankerous disease of a racial hatred the like of which has not been known since the beginning of time.

For this solution—and not for "solutions" that will solve nothing but will heap misery upon misery—it is worth while making efforts and even sacrifices. For great is the vision and great its blessing—for Jews, for Arabs, and for all the peoples of the earth.

Communique

In connection with the discovery of the tunnel underneath the building of the Headquarters of the British Occupation Army in Tel-Aviv, we state:

1. No prior warning was received from Adolf Bevin's militia that their spies had discovered the plan of attack.

2. There was never any inscription in the cellar; and the one that was shamelessly photographed only for purposes of exhibition was inscribed by the men of the militia only after they burst into our base in order to sabotage it.

3. Every one of our armouries and work-sites is protected day and night, and the leaders of the militia know it. We announced this explicitly.

4. The blood of Zeev Werber, who was left lying wounded by his "heroic" comrades, is on the heads of the quislings who sent him to serve the enemy even at the price of his life, instead of sending him to fight, as they once vociferously promised they would do, against the murderers of our people, the robbers of our Homeland and the deporters of our homecoming brothers in exile.

5. It was from this Nazo-British Headquarters which domi-nates the Hebrew city that the order was issued on "Wingate Night" to shoot to kill; it was from there that the instructions were given for the searches for arms and the mass arrests on the 29th of June; that decided on the strangulation of our economy and the starving of our children during Martial Law; from it that death-dealing bullets were fired at Hebrew citizens and children. This headquarters is a cancer in the body of the Hebrew city and the symbol of the enslavement of its citizens. In the planned attack on this centre of British terror, which was meticulously worked out, *not a single citizen* would have

been hurt; the date of the attack was not fixed and was made dependent on circumstances.

6. These voluntary slaves of the enemy, who desire the continued existence of the fortress of tyranny in the Hebrew city, should most certainly accept the invitation of the Military Intelligence Officer to "have a drink" with him. In any case, there is no doubt that the Occupation Government will raise its glass to its faithful lackeys.

But the people and the youth are filled with contempt for them and their despicable actions.

19.6.47

Report of Conference Between Representatives of the United Nations Special Committee on Palestine and the Commander and Two Other Representatives of the Irgun Zvai Leumi

The conference took place on *Tuesday 24 June 1947*, eight days after the arrival of the Committee in Palestine. The UNO Committee was represented by the Chairman, Mr. E. Sandstrom, Dr. Victor Hoo and Dr. Ralph Bunche.

This report, prepared in the first place by a UNO representative, has been passed by both parties.

The Commander inquired about Lisicky, whom he had expected to be along, and the Chairman explained that he had received word about Lisicky's inclusion in the group only that afternoon and it was too late for him to take any action upon it or even to inform Lisicky.

The Commander sat at the head of the table with his two colleagues on one side with their backs to the window, facing Mr. Sandstrom, who was flanked by Hoo and Bunche. Mr. Sandstrom began the discussion with the statement that the essential condition for the talk was that nothing should be released on this meeting during the period of the Committee's stay in Palestine. The Commander readily agreed to this.

The Commander then stated that first of all he wished to thank the committee for the action taken with regard to the sentences imposed on the three members of his organization "by the so-called Military Court." He and his organisation, he said, had no illusions as to the outcome, but they appreciated the action of the committee, the more so in view of the acceptance by the Committee of the interpretation of the U.N. Assembly's resolution, put forward in Irgun's letter, as obliging the British to refrain from the use or the threat of force.

Mr. Sandstrom then inquired as to the aims of the Irgun organization and the position which the Commander held in it, or rather, the authority with which he could speak for it.

The Commander stated that Irgun Zvai Leumi means "national military organization." It was organized some ten years ago. Its object is to bring about the liberation of the country from the foreign yoke, the attainment of freedom for the Jewish people and the restoration of Jewish rule in Eretz Israel. Before the war the Irgun had defended the Jewish people against the organized attacks of Arab groups which were instigated by the British rulers. It had also brought thousands of Jewish repatriates into the country as a major task of saving them from an unbearable future in Europe.

On the outbreak of the war against Hitler, the Irgun recognized the war as a war of all peoples against Nazism. The Irgun realized that Hitler meant his pronunciation concerning the destruction of Jews. For some years, therefore, the organization undertook no offensive measures in this country because of the danger facing Palestine from the Nazi aggression. The organization was kept intact, however. Some members entered various Allied Armies, others continued underground organization work.

In the last months of 1943 and the first months of 1944 it became obvious that all of the sacrifices of the Jewish people on the battlefields of the war would be in vain and that Jews in Palestine would be left under oppressive rule with no opportunity to bring back those who would wish to return to their Homeland.

Consequently, Irgun issued the declaration of November or December 1943 to the effect that there would be no more interruptions in its fighting for freedom. News had also come from Europe at the time, although it was unconfirmed, that the mass slaughter of Jews in Europe had begun in an unprecedented way. Irgun then began operations which concentrated on the local Government without harming the concentrations of troops in the country, since it was necessary not to endanger the fight against Hitler.

It was then proclaimed that Irgun's aim was Hebrew rule in Palestine and that Irgun would fight until that objective is achieved.

Following their proclamation the operations which Irgun carried out were sometimes large and sometimes limited in scope. This stage of its activity continued for nearly two years.

In the meantime the British Occupation regime continued to keep the doors shut against the Jews, even after they were fully aware of the process of slaughter of Jews which was going on in

Europe. The British continued to sabotage every effort in Europe to save the Jews. The Commander cited as one example, the fact that it would have been possible to save the Jews in Hungary before it was completely overrun by the Hitler legions. Turkey, he said, was prepared to give transit visas to Palestine but all efforts in this direction proved to be in vain, since the British refused such people admittance, even though this refusal meant certain death for them.

Thus Irgun continued its struggle. The British tried to overcome resistance with the aid of organized Jewish groups, including the Jewish Agency. Some Jewish bodies handed over to the authorities Jews suspected of aiding Irgun.

The British used the so called Emergency Regulations which had been promulgated in 1936 and 1937. In their effort to break the spirit of the Jewish people in Palestine, he said, they arrested people whom they claimed to suspect of Irgun affiliations, and put them in concentration camps. Some three hundred of them alleged the Commander, had been deported to a concentration camp in Eritrea. He emphasized that these were all alleged suspects, that no charges had been placed against them.

At this point the Commander referred to the letter from the Irgun organization which the Committee had received today requesting the Committee to call on three of the Irgun members now imprisoned at Acre as witnesses of the maltreatment of political prisoners by the British authorities.

He cited the example of the seventeen year old youth who in 1944 at Haifa had been shot in the leg for posting Irgun posters. Instead of being put in a hospital, the Commander alleged, this youth had been transferred to the Acre prison, had been given no medical treatment and for three days and three nights been chained to the cot in his cell, during which period his open wound became infected. The youth's leg later had to be amputated and he subsequently died. This, the Commander observed, was only one of many such cases of barbaric behaviour which he described as "an intolerable crime." A wounded man, he said whoever he is, has the right to medical treatment, and whoever withholds such treatment is a barbarian.

Continuing with his historical narrative, the Commander stated that when peace came and the elections were held in England and the new government of the Labour Party came into being, the Jewish Agency leaders and their supporters in Palestine had expected a change. He recalled that two months before the election a conference of the Labour Party in England had been held, at which Mr. Dalton, who is now Chancellor of the Exchequer, had said publicly that when Labour came into power it would do all in its power to bring about a happy and prosperous Jewish state in Palestine. Again, continued the Commander, one year earlier the Labour Party had said that the Jewish National Home has no meaning unless the Jews from the Diaspora were permitted to enter Palestine until they became a majority. The same resolution proposed the transfer of the Arab population from Palestine. This latter was an extreme position beyond any ever taken by any Jewish group.

But Britain, he charged, wishes to steal the country for itself and to give it neither to Jews nor Arabs, keeping it as a military base for herself.

At the time of the coming into power of Labour in Britain, Irgun did not share the illusions entertained in other quarters that the Labour Party would keep its promise and said as much in a public statement at the time. It was, however, prepared to wait, to interrupt operations and to give the new Government a chance to keep its promises and expose "British perfidy" to the Jews and the world at large. When Labour's intentions became clear Hagana (meaning defence) decided to raise the banner of armed resistance in Palestine. Hagana was the largest of the three organized groups. The other two being the F.F.I. (Fighters for Freedom of Israel), known as the "Stern Group" and Irgun. In October 1945 these three groups reached an agreement to join hands in armed resistance. This agreement remained effective for ten months and this was a period of large scale operations. For example, there were operations against the railways, on the first of November 1945, which effectively stopped them; there were other operations against air fields, bridges and the like.

In the Irgun tradition if a British official is regarded a criminal in his activities a court trial is held, with the defendant in absentis, in view of the circumstances of an underground organisation. A verdict is reached and the order is given to carry out the sentence.

In response to a question as to whether any action was ever taken against Jews, it was replied that Jewish informers on the British Secret Police have on occasion been condemned.

With regard to a question concerning the announcement by Irgun of the establishment of field courts to try British prisoners in consequence of the "British breach of the laws of warfare by killing Jewish captives" it was stated that such courts, though in existence, have not yet had any sentences carried out.

Reverting to the previous discussion on the relations among the three resistance groups, the Commander stated that all of the tasks of the three organizations which were combined during the period October 1945 to August 1946 were carried out under the name of the Jewish Resistance Movement.

After ten months of this operation Hagana decided not to continue the struggle. Irgun, on the other hand, decided to continue in the same way, and in fact was convinced of the necessity of intensifying the struggle, since in Palestine an oppressive rule had been instituted without precedent in history and hundreds of thousands of Jews were languishing without hope in the Diaspora.

The Commander emphasized that Irgun is an underground organization and must operate in the only way underground organizations can.

He stated that a document would be sent to the Committee by Irgun which would set forth clearly and in detail the objectives and demands of the organizatioń.

Asked what connection there is between Jewish Agency and Haganah, he said that question should be addressed to those bodies. "We are not spokesmen for either."

With regard to the organization of Irgun, the Commander explained that it was organized and governed by common consent of its members. To quote him "We are leaders of the organization and we will remain as leaders so long as we carry out our mandate."

Continuing his historical discussion, the Commander observed that the entire history of the Jewish armed organization began twenty-seven years ago with Hagana. In the early stages there were elections of officers by the nucleus of the Organization. Subsequently members of the organization accepted the original leadership. Irgun sprang from Hagana and followed the same method of leadership.

The Commander emphasized that no personal decisions are taken in Irgun. All decision, he said, are taken collectively and are, therefore, majority decisions. There is, he said, no dictatorship.

In summing up the aims of Irgun the Commander stated that these could be expressed very simply as follows:

1. Irgun considers that Eretz Israel (Land of Israel) is the homeland of the Jewish people.

2. Eretz Israel means both East and West of the Jordan, including Transjordan. "Transjordan," he said, "is an English translation that is incomplete." In the original Hebrew both sides of the Jordan were, in effect, called "Transjordan"—"Ever-Hayarden Ma'arava" (The Westward side of the Jordan) and "Ever-Hayarden Mizracha" (The Eastward side of the Jordan). The forefathers of the Jews, he said, conquered Palestine from the present Transjordan side and crossed into Palestine from east to west. Irgun, he said, considers the whole territory as Jewish territory and aims at the creation of a Hebrew republic under a democratic government.

3. Immediate repatriation of all Jews wishing to be repatriated to Palestine. The exact number of Jewish potential repatriates is unknown but would run into millions. The right of option should be given to all Jews who wish to return to Palestine. Their return is prevented only by British illegal rule and by British armed force, which should be removed. A Jewish government would undertake the repatriation of Jews with international help, perhaps under supervision.

4. We reject any statement made by the Labour Party as to the transfer of any Arabs from the country. There is enough room in Palestine for all, both Jews and Arabs.

5. Since Britain has decided to keep the country under her own control by force of arms there is no other way to accomplish our aims than to meet force with force.

In response to a question concerning Arab immigration from other countries, the Commander replied that the question of admitting Arab immigrants into the Jewish state when it is created would be a matter for the government of that state to decide, just as every state decides its immigration policy. The Irgun had no preconceived prejudice against anybody who might apply for a visa to the Hebrew State.

The first task of a Jewish government would be to bring back to the country all Jews wishing to be repatriated. He emphasized that every Jew had a natural right to return to Palestine, and that the Jews had a de jure majority in the country. In fact, he said, the Jews now are only a *de facto* minority in Palestine, because the British would not let in all of those from outside who wished to come in. Once that obstacle were removed, it would be only a matter of months before they were the majority *de facto* as well. In reply to a question concerning the technical and fiscal difficulties of transferring large numbers of Jews to Palestine, the Commander referred to the statement made by a United States Army general that he could evacuate Jews from the European camps in a matter of weeks. He referred to the mass Turkish-Greek exchange of populations in 1922, effected in a matter of months. What was possible then was emphatically possible now, what with the gigantic strides in modern technical knowledge.

The Commander explained that politically the Irgun proposal is not to establish immediately a permanent Jewish government in Palestine but only a provisional Hebrew government to which power would be transferred for the specific task of accomplishing the repatriation of all Jews who wish to be repatriated. After this is accomplished the provisional government will resign and then free elections will be held, participated in by both Jews and Arabs, and the permanent government would thus be established. In this Government there could be Arab Ministers, perhaps an Arab Vice-President. The provisional government would be democratic, because it would represent the rightful owners of the country but would not be based on elections. The Commander pointed out that this had happened in numerous states, such as France and twice in Czechoslovakia.

The question was asked as to how long the provisional status would last. The Commander replied that it would last until all of the rightful citizens of Palestine are in the country. But, he cautioned, it is necessary to understand that in the creation of the Jewish state and the repatriation of Jews to it one cannot take normal circumstances and criteria as the measure. The Jews in Europe, he said, have gone through such ordeals that they are prepared to live in tents in Palestine if necessary. They will suffer when they come here and it will take time, but it can be done quickly. He again referred to the one and one half million people who were exchanged between Greece and Turkey in 1922 in approximately nine months.

The question was asked whether if the British were out of the country and the Jewish state could be created the Irgun would dissolve. The Commander answered "yes." Asked what the Irgun would do in the case of partition, he pointed out that none of the Irgun members will accept any carving up of the territory which they consider to be the property of the Jewish state of Palestine but it was early to speak of what the methods of resisting the carving up would be.

The Commander was asked what the Irgun position would be if the Jewish state and Jewish immigration should not develop as quickly as he might think or hope for and the Arabs continued to have a numerical majority in the country and voted against immigration. He replied "How could such elections take place in Palestine?" Any such elections, he stated, would be illegal because they would exclude all those Jews outside who had a right to be in the country. Any Jew wishing to return to the country from which his forefathers were expelled has the right to do so.

The Commander observed that twenty-five years ago there were only one hundred thousand Jews in Palestine. The preamble to the mandate under the League of Nations refers to the historical relations between the Jewish people and Palestine. The Jewish claim was not based on the Mandate but on the natural right of the Jews to their country which was as self-evident as the right of a Swede or a Frenchman to his country. The Mandate only recognized that natural right. The Jewish state as he envisaged it could take care of all Jews wishing to come to it. He could not say how many of the American Jews or Jews in Sweden might wish to come.

With regard to the absorptive capacity of the country the Commander pointed out that in ancient times in Palestine there were between five and seven million people. Transjordan, he said, is absolutely empty, with only four people for each square kilometer. He emphasized strongly that Palestine belongs not only to the people now in the country but to the Jews abroad as well.

Asked how the Jews would solve the overcrowding problem that would arise after, say, 300 years even if they developed their state on both sides of the Jordan, his reply was "What will they do in 300 years in other countries, like China?"

It was pointed out to the Commander that the settlement of Jews in Palestine created Arab resentment and that this might lead to opposition by force, and he was asked what Irgun would do in such a contingency. He replied that Irgun does not believe in such a phenomenon as independent Arab opposition to Jewish repatriation. All Arab opposition, he said, is instigated by the British themselves. He quoted King Faisal's letter to Dr. Weizmann, in which King Faisal declared that Palestine should be a Jewish country. The British, he continued, instigated the Arabs to take a position of opposition to the Jewish state. Nevertheless, the Jewish population increased from one hundred thousand (ca.) to seven hundred thousand. Theoretically the Arabs oppose any increase in the Jewish population. He cited an article in the Egyptian press of the day before quoting Jamal Husseini to the effect that partition, too would mean war. But, questioned the Commander, are such threats serious and are they to be taken seriously. If so, and we are to have "war" anyhow, even unjust expediency is not served by denying Jewish rights. On the other hand, if these are empty threats and he believed that they are, then they are not to be taken seriously, also when uttered in relation to the satisfaction of Jewish claims in the whole of Eretz Israel.

Irgun, he said, will defend the Jewish people against anyone who will attack them, Arab or otherwise. But he did not believe that the Arabs would actually go to war. This, he said, is all British propaganda. If the British left the country, he continued, there would be peace. Should the Jews however be attacked, they could protect themselves. He was entirely sure of this.

Irgun, he said, does not think that Iraqii, Lebanese or Syrians would attack the Jewish State. They are not serious armies, except if they have foreign assistance. If they do attack, he had no doubt the Jews would win the day.

The Commander suggested that the Committee might ask Mr. Gurney, the chief secretary of the Palestine Government when the so-called Arab Higher Committee was elected by the Arab people.

The Commander was asked what proof he might produce for his allegation that Arab opposition had been instigated by the British. He replied that after the Balfour Declaration British generals made public speeches that there would be no Jewish state in Palestine, that there would be only limited immigration permitted, etc. Unofficially, he added, British officials, police officers, etc., go through Arab villages spreading rumors of threatened Jewish attacks, encouraging Arabs to oppose Jews, promising them arms, etc. He said the Haganah had in its archives detailed proofs of these allegations. He pointed out that despite Haj Amin El Husseini's instigation of the Arabs against the Jews in Jerusalem in 1920, he had been given a pardon and undemocratically given the post of Mufti.

The Commander was asked what his reaction would be to a proposal for partition. He replied that Irgun rejects partition and will fight against it. First of all, as a matter of principle. A country, he said, is a thing no one is entitled to trade. We cannot give up any part of our country, which has been defended for generations by Jews who hope to come back to it. Thus, he said, we reject partition first of all on the basis of principle, but partition is moreover unpractical. Allegations have been made in United Nations meetings that Jews and Arabs cannot live together, that their aims and aspirations are irreconcilable, and therefore partition is necessary; but actually if these allegations are true then partition is impossible since no line of demarcation can actually provide for the peoples of this country living apart from each other. We have no confidence in Government statistics, he said, which are fabricated for political purposes. For example, the British Government said that there were one million two hundred thousand Arabs in Palestine. But where are they to be found? A census was taken in 1931 and the bulk of the Arab population was illiterate. The Arab headmen in the villages receive a shilling for each birth they report.

The nucleus of large populations is always to be found in cities. Where, he asked, were the large Arab cities?

The only Arab cities worthy of the name are Jaffa, Nablus and parts of Haifa and Jerusalem. Irgun proposes a census of all of Palestine to be carried out under international control.

The Commander continued that if the larger plan of partition is taken (that is, along the lines of the Jewish Agency proposal) there would be an Arab majority, according to present government statistics. In order to establish the Jewish majority their repatriation would be needed, precisely as for the Jewish majority in the whole country.

He stated that Irgun is opposed to the transfer of population, either Arab or Jewish, which some people had suggested as a means of carrying out partition. It is not moral to take people from their homes against their will. There is no need, in fact, for any transfer of population from Palestine or within Palestine, since there is room for all here. There is no possibility, he said, of exchanging populations. Under a partition scheme the majority of the Jews now in Palestine would live in a ghetto state behind an artificial boundary. No exchange of population in Palestine could be made without the use of force.

The Commander was asked whether a solution might be acceptable to Irgun which would provide for a federal state in Palestine, with the different parts having self-government somewhat along the lines of the states in the United States or the cantons in Switzerland with an over-all central government.

He replied that the form of government in the future state of Palestine and the details of its constitution, etc., should be approved by the parliament of Palestine. It is first necessary to decide on the principle. What is Palestine from the point of history? Is it a Jewish state or not?

A federal state along the lines of the Morrison plan, he said, would mean the same thing as that on which the British are now trying to get the agreement of the United Nations in order to perpetrate her illegal occupation rule.

He stated that Irgun bases no claim on the League of Nations mandate but on the historical fact that Palestine has been Jewish territory for tens of generations. Already 3000 years ago there was a Jewish State here, from which ultimately the forefathers of present-day Jews were expelled by force by the Romans. The people of Lidice, whose town had been obliterated by the Germans, came back after the war to rebuild their homes and their lives. It was their natural right. So it was with the Jewish return to Palestine.

The Arabs never created an Arab government in Palestine. This was never an Arab country.

He said that the Irgun reply to any proposal is that if the Jewish people are allowed freely to return under their own rule and the principle of the unity of the whole country is recognized, then all the rest is mere detail.

The Jewish state should be the first condition as the repatriation of Jews is not possible except in a Jewish state.

Under a federal system the door might be closed to repatriation to some parts of the country and this would be against one of Irgun's basic principles.

A question was asked as to what the meaning of Palestine as a homeland for the Jews might be for the Irgun.

The Commander replied that the meaning was an independent country ruled by its rightful owners and that the Jews are the rightful owners.

He was asked what might happen to Arab land holdings in a Jewish state of Palestine. He replied that land now held by Arabs would be retained by them, but that in the new Palestine there would be need for agrarian reforms. As in ancient times latifundia exists in Palestine. There are vast lands held by Arab feudal landlords which are never worked, and large tracts held by the British. The government of the new Palestine would have to adjust this situation. Every Arab and every Jewish farmer would have to be assured of enough land for a prosperous self-supporting farm.

The Commander was asked whether Irgun would fight against a solution which might be acceptable to the majority of the Jewish people but which did not meet all of the aims and conditions set by the Irgun. He replied that no majority of this generation of the Jewish people has the right to give up the historic right of the Jewish people to their country, which belonged equally to all generations to come. He was convinced, he said, that the Jewish people as such would accept no solution contrary to Jewish tradition. If they should do so it was premature to say what Irgun would do. Irgun, he added, is educating its young men now on the question of principle. One does not give up his principle, he pointed out, for opportunistic reasons.

The Commander was asked if he would state the reasons for the opposition to the British by the methods used by the Irgun—was it to force the evacuation of their troops, to release Jewish prisoners, or for what other purposes. He replied that what Irgun might be able to attain would be a matter of careful action on the basis of proportionate forces. The British, he said, have more than we have, but they also know that we are not easily crushed. What we wish is complete evacuation of the British, the removal of British rule, the setting up of a provisional government and the creation of the Jewish state. The British, he said, had previously told the world that they were here to protect the Jews against the Arabs but General D'Arcy told the Anglo-American Committee that if the British left the country the Jews would control it in twenty-four hours—thus insinuating that the British had to remain in order to protect the Arabs from the Jews.

In response to a statement, the Commander asked the question "Is it true we have no support of the Jewish people? How could we resist if this is true, in the face of the great number of British police and troops here? We are convinced that we must fight or the Jewish people will be destroyed. We are not professional fighters, we don't take pleasure in shooting or being shot. Remember we have lost six million people and every Jewish life is the more precious to us. But we fight for a purpose, to avoid subjugation and utter destruction."

The Commander pointed out that the fight of his organization did bring troubles to the Jewish people—curfew, restrictions, retaliations, etc. But suffering, as every people that had fought knew, was inseparable from the struggle for independence. He added "We are not just a handful of fanatics. We exist and gain strength even though we bring troubles to the Jewish people."

There was no doubt that the overwhelming majority of the Jewish people were in favour of the struggle. When the Jews had an opportunity of demonstrating their support—which was not always possible—they did so. For example, he pointed out that when the Hagana fought the Jewish people had utilised the opportunity to applaud the struggle.

The Commander raising a legal point, contended that even under the mandate there is absolutely no right for a British Military Court in Palestine. The mandate, he said, differentiated between forces raised in Palestine, and British forces. The latter are regarded as foreign forces, and it follows that British military courts have no right here at all even on the basis of the Mandate. He emphasised that this point made no difference to the struggle, which would go on in any case, but should interest the Committee.

The Commander stated that the Irgun members consider themselves legal fighters, engaged in a legal fight and that they considered the British to be here illegally. He stated that Irgun has lost many of its men in killed and wounded and that it accepts this as an inevitable result of its operations. The British, he said, have executed four of their members, but Irgun did not cease its activities as a result of this, but rather it intensified them. "It inflicted heavy losses on the enemy and the price is not paid yet." After the executions, he observed, came Acre. Acre, he said, was no small feat. The fight will go on. The British suggestion that they might be prepared to forgo executing Irgun members if the Irgun stopped fighting is ridiculous blackmail. "Go to Acre, and ask the three boys sentenced to death whether they are prepared to buy their lives at the price of our struggle. They sent me letters, just as Dov Gruner sent, all saying: Whatever happens, fight on!" He added "We are all prepared to give our lives." No member of Irgun, he said, ever asks for mercy. The Commander was questioned as to the Irgun attitude toward the General Assembly's appeal for a truce during the period of the United Nations inquiry. He replied that in connection with this appeal Irgun had sent to the Committee a reasoned document and had stated publicly that it was prepared to cease operations during this period but only on condition that the British would cease their repressive actions also during this period. To illustrate this condition, he referred to the use of British air and naval forces to intercept ships at sea carrying Jews wishing to come to Palestine, the promulgation of death sentences, searches and the imposition of curfews. These, he said, are acts of repression which the British must cease if Irgun is to observe the truce. Any one-sided cessation of operations, he said, is impossible.

The Commander expressed the hope that the Committee would go to Europe and would see the men in concentration camps who have been there—first in Germany and now in the "Liberated camps"—for seven or eight years. He added that the camps in Europe were not the whole problem, only a part of it, but they reflected the problem in its most dire form.

The Commander expressed the fear that the General Assembly in September will not have time enough to deal with this problem and that a second committee would be appointed to come to Palestine again and that during all this time men, women and children would be languishing in concentrations camps in Europe.

He stated flatly that if the British execute Irgun men Irgun will execute British men—also by hanging. Irgun men, he said, are rightful fighters. Irgun, he said, is absolutely convinced that it fights not only for the independence of Palestine but for the right of free men.

In response to a question the Commander replied that the Anglo-American Committee had had no contact with Irgun. He

stated that Irgun had sent a memorandum to the American members of the Committee but had not sent it to the British members. He
added that some individual American members of the Anglo-
American Committee had tried to contact Irgun but that it was not
possible to do so at that time for security reasons.

The Commander explained that the Stern group had come out
of the Irgun. They too are fighters, he observed. The Stern group
came out as an independent group in 1940 as a result of the splitting
of Irgun for various reasons. It was widely believed, he said, that the
reason for the split was that Abraham Stern, then a member of the
Irgun command, had opposed the Irgun proclamation of an armistice during the war against Hitler. This was not true. Stern had
subscribed to that proclamation together with the rest of the Irgun
Command. The split had come a year later. The relations now
between the two groups are good. Irgun is larger but he would not
say Irgun is better.

In response to a question as to what the effect might be on
future Jewish youth of training them to disregard the law, the
Commander replied that the Irgun members are trained to oppose
what the British called law because it was the law of occupation and
oppression, but that in his view the adjustment to a Jewish state
would not be difficult for them. It might be a problem, but a minor
problem only, in a Jewish state, because there would be an
abundance of constructive work in which the youth would engage.

The Commander asked if there was any possibility of the
Committee taking a positive attitude toward the request of the Irgun
in the letter sent to the Committee that some of its members
imprisoned at Acre be called as witnesses before the Committee. Mr.
Sandstrom replied frankly "There is very little possibility. We have
done just about all we can do. We can ask why should these three
men be the best men to give evidence of terror in the camps."

The Commander replied that the answer to the latter question
would be that these men have been before the Military Court and
that they had themselves experienced maltreatment and witnessed
that of others. He added that he did not think this beyond the terms
of reference of the Committee and in fact he felt the Committee was
obliged to deal with it, since the Committee can investigate all the
problems of Palestine. It is a fact, he said, that the existing Occupation Government in Palestine is treating prisoners in a barbarous
way. Irgun could supply more witnesses than these three if the
Committee would have the time to hear them. Irgun, he added,
accuses the British of maltreating the prisoners.

Mr. Sandstrom observed that the point is that there must be
other witnesses who can testify similarly, to which the Commander
replied that the case of these three is special. They can tell of men
who were shot and wounded after the capture in the Acre prison
break, of wounded men who were shot dead while lying in agony on

the ground; of others who died because they were given no medical treatment or even water. The three referred to in the Irgun letter, he said, had been taken prisoner in that operation.

The Commander stated that he was not sure that the intervention of the Committee would give any results. Any such intervention in any case, would be couched in diplomatic terms as was the resolution adopted by the Committee. He added that in his view there was a precedent for granting this request which could be found in the Greek investigation by the UNO Security Council.

At the close of the meeting the Chairman mentioned the agreement which had been reached at its beginning that there would be no publicity concerning this meeting. The Commander replied "Irgun always keeps its word. Ask the British. They will tell you." He agreed, however, that at some later date when the Committee was gone from Palestine the Chairman could, if he saw fit, release the story of this meeting and the text of the notes taken at the meeting provided he would give a prior opportunity to review such notes before their release. This was agreed upon by the Chairman.

To All Other Ranks

Your generals, who serve the oil magnates and the blue-blooded aristocracy, are throwing away your lives.

They are doing it every day. They keep you in a foreign country which is rebelling against the enslavement and fighting for its freedom.

They lock themselves up in "fortresses" and behind barbed wire—but they send you to oppress—and to be killed.

But the best illustration of their complete disregard for your lives was given you this last week by the hanging of three Hebrew soldiers and the subsequent hanging of two of your Intelligence sergeants.

You will remember that when two others of our comrades were "sentenced" to death a year ago, we captured five British officers. Your generals quickly "commuted" the sentence on their Hebrew prisoners in order to save the lives of the officers.

One day before our comrade Dov Gruner was to be hanged last February we captured a British major and a British judge—of an "aristocratic" family. Your generals at once postponed the murder "indefinitely"—in order to save the members of their own class.

And now we captured, as it happened, two of your sergeants— and your generals did not hesitate for a moment to leave them to their fate, even though they knew that the Irgun always keeps its word. The Irgun demands the status of prisoners of war for its soldiers and is prepared to extend the same status to enemy soldiers falling into its hands. It has always done so. When thirty of your men were captured by us during an operation at the Exhibition Grounds in Tel-Aviv and were completely at our mercy not a hair on their heads was harmed.

But if Irgun soldiers are hanged, the soldiers of the enemy will be hanged too. Your Generals knew this. But in spite of it they murdered our three comrades—and sealed the fate of the two sergeants.

Why?

Because the two sergeants were not sons of the "aristocracy," or members of the ruling class, because they were just sergeants.

And so they throw away your lives—for their profits and their positions. So they send you to be killed—so that they should be able to live in luxury.

British soldiers!

How long will you continue to be blind tools of your rulers?

How long will you continue to shed your blood for their oil?

Demand your repatriation!

There, in your country, you can live in peace with your families.

There, in your Homeland, there is constructive work to be done.

Go home—and leave us in peace in our Home.

Do not give your lives to fill the pockets of your oil magnates, or to satisfy the stupid ambitions of the most stupid Cabinet Minister you have ever had.

IRGUN ZVAI LEUMI
b'Eretz Israel   August, 1947

To the Inciters, Shaking with Fear

When nine Hebrew fighters were led to the gallows by the British hangman—you did not denounce the despicable crime, you did not call to the world to rise against the criminals, *you did not express your condolences with the bereaved families.* Only when two British spies, sent to our country to crush us into dust, were hanged—only then did you open your mouths in abuse and imprecation against a *just verdict*, and hastened to "express sympathy."

Willing slaves that you are! Council of elders of the Ghetto—do not even you understand that by your hypocrisy and ghetto cowardice you are leading the people to the abyss of destruction. You have accustomed this people to everything: to the murder of its children, to the deportation of its sons, to the robbery of its Homeland, to the abuse of its holy of holies. Do you now want to accustom them to being *hanged in their homeland?*

We warned:

Ever since the day the British murderers "sentenced" the Hebrew prisoners of war, Ashbel and Simchon, to death—we warned repeatedly that if the enemy dared to violate the rules of war and hanged our captured comrades—we would set up gallows for their captors.

The murderous enemy, thirsting for blood, did not heed our warnings. He led *nine* Hebrew prisoners to the gallows.

Consequently we hanged his spies.

Not as a "reprisal"—for there is no adequate reprisal for the crimes of the unclean oppressor,

but as a *duty* to the Jewish people, as a duty to the people's volunteers.

If the "court" of the invading enemy dares to hang Hebrew soldiers fighting for the liberation of their Homeland—the court of the liberation army will certainly judge the soldiers of the invader and will order them to be hanged.

That is a law.

And we shall fulfil it whenever convenient.

And without mercy for the sentenced Britons, just as there was no mercy for the "sentenced" Jews. We shall not listen to the pleas of the British fathers, just as the unclean enslaver did not listen to the pleas of bereaved Hebrew fathers.

And you of the shivering knees, do not preach morals to us. Your morals are the morals of those who stretch out their necks to be slaughtered. We have rebelled against these "morals," which led us from slaughter to slaughter until we reached the gas chambers. We shall never again recognise them. War has one moral and there is no other: Hebrew captives will not be hanged in their Homeland—or their hangmen and their helpers will themselves be hanged.

Communique

September 30, 1947

At 5.45 on Monday, the first day of the Tabernacles Festival 5708 (September 29, 1947) our men attacked the headquarters of the British Gestapo for Northern Palestine.

Our men surmounted the fortifications, armoured patrols and

defence posts of the enemy, penetrated the heart of the Haifa Security Zone and destroyed it with a one-ton bomb.

The attack was rendered possible by a special technical device details of which will be published shortly. The attack was carried out at an early hour during the festival in order to avoid casualties among the civilian population. This military operation is known as *Hambuff* (Hamburg—Af-al-pi).

Today we have eradicated the shame of Hamburg, which would never have been forgiven to our generation if our reaction had been the ridiculous one of fasting and not that of cattle.

Today we have removed the disgrace of the expulsion of our returning brethren, the disgrace of the desecration of our nation's sanctities. Today we have requited the enemy for the bloodbaths on the repatriants' ships.

Nazi Britain has announced that it will be prepared to make plans for the evacuation of Palestine. This is bluff. Britain aims at imposing its own "solution" for the Palestine problem. That solution means servitude, dispersion and extermination for our nation. *Britain is trying to frighten the majority at the UNO in order to extort acceptance of her own plan: the establishment of a British Quisling government* to which the Jews of Palestine will be handed over. The remarks of Mr. Vishinsky, the Assistant Foreign Minister of the Soviet Union, in connection with Mr. Creech Jones' statement were not ironical. They reflect the real British intentions: Britain is bluffing. One week after "resolving" on the evacuation of Palestine the Nazo-British authorities put an ultimatum to the passengers of the "Exodus 1947," demanding that they should renounce their right to return to the Homeland or else perish of starvation. One week after that resolution the British have begun to bore for oil in the Negev. On the day following the statement of the British Colonial Secretary the British pirates staged a fresh blood-bath on a maapilim ship and expelled the passengers by force from the shores of their homeland. The regime of repression continues. The hostile acts towards our nation have not ceased for even a single day.

Britain is bluffing. For twenty-five years it has bluffed our nation and the entire world by its intrigues and declarations, the outcome of which has been the destruction of six million Jews. Britain will no longer succeed with its deceit. We, men of the Irgun Zvai Leumi will continue to fight against Nazo-British occupation forces. Fortifications will not protect them. We shall fight for the liberation of our country until the British actually take to their ships and return to their own home, and our exiled brethren return from the four corners of the earth in the ships of deliverance to their liberated and *undivided* Homeland.

One thing leads to another.

Communique

27 October, 1947

1. The "Haganah" spokesman has claimed, before foreign correspondents, that our communique on the events in the southern settlements was untrue. Nobody will believe him.

Every correspondent, every Jew and every non-Jew knows that from the very first day we began our struggle, we have not published an untrue statement. On the other hand, every newspaperman, every Jew and every non-Jew, knows that the spokesman of the traitorous militia is a cowardly liar:

a. Several weeks ago Haganah men killed an Arab family in an orange grove near Kfar-Sirkin. In the internal Haganah bulletin it was explicitly stated that this was "retaliatory action" for the murder of two Hebrew settlers of Kfar-Sirkin. But the Haganah spokesman— and his brother propagandist of falsehoods, the Jewish Agency spokesman—brazenly told the correspondents that "no organized Jewish body" had executed that attack in which an old woman was killed and a small child seriously injured.

b. Haganah men attacked two enemy officers on the Lydda Highway. The Haganah spokesman denied responsibility.

c. Haganah men killed the Hebrew policeman Berger in the streets of Tel-Aviv. The Haganah spokesman denied this.

d. The Haganah spokesman promised the correspondents that there would be immediate retaliation for each and every deportation of repatriates by the oppressor. The Haganah spokesman did not keep his word.

e. The Haganah Command gave its consent to the attack on the headquarters of the Nazo-British regime in the "King David." The Haganah spokesman denied this.

These are but a few facts, out of many, which prove that nobody can take the announcements of the militia seriously or put any trust in them.

We have investigated what occurred in Rishom-le-Zion and the following facts have been confirmed beyond the shadow of a doubt:

Our comrades pasted up our posters. A group of Haganah rioters led by the local ruffian Shafran, came over to them and told them, with the customary audacity of the pupils of Ben Gurion, *to take the posters down with their own hands.* Our comrades, of course, refused. Shafran then took out a revolver and threatened to use it. At the same moment the man in charge of our group drew his revolver and warned that fire would be answered with fire. An argument ensued. Our men reproved the incited rioters for using Hebrew arms for internal terror instead of against the enemy. In the meantime an enemy car with soldiers passed by. The Haganah "heroes" hurriedly hid their arms and ran away. Our comrades continued their posting. This angered the rioters and they immediately opened fire on our members. Two of our men were wounded. Then—only then—did the man in charge of our group open fire.

Further: The Haganah command are responsible for the use of firearms in all clashes with posters of our notices, for it is *they who gave the implicit order to fire at them.* At Rehovet our men were *fired on twice* before the incident at Rishon-le-Zion.

2. On Saturday night the rioters ran amok in Rehovot and Rishon-le-Zion. They broke the limbs of young men—most of whom have not the slightest connection with us—and did not even spare old men, women and children.

3. Our comrades consequently went out to punish the chief ruffian and informer on the spot, the *young Kossovi.* The "hero" slipped out of the house. There was no intention to hurt his father, but the latter attacked one of our men with a heavy club. We regret the fact that the father was hurt. The rioters, however, have not yet expressed their regret at the fact that they attacked an *eighty-year old woman* as well as many other women and children.

4. We shall pay the rioters back for the broken arms and legs of our comrades.

5. The Haganah spokesman assured newspaperman that the Haganah is starting an offensive to *liquidate* us. The implication is a *physical liquidation.*

We have taken note of this announcement of the traitorous militia.

They will *not* liquidate us, even as Darnan's militia did not liquidate the Maquis in France.

And, should an attempt be made in earnest to liquidate us, let the traitors remember this:

We shall give went[*sic*] to all the anger which has accumulated inside us from the first day they began to hand over to the British Intelligence the best of our men, so that they might be tortured with the tortures of hell and that they might have their limbs broken.

We, the men of the Irgun Zvai Leumi, are ready every minute to give our lives for our belief. And in this uniform struggle which Ben Gurion, in his madness, wants to force upon our people, only one kind of liquidation is possible:

Mutual liquidation
We have warned!

Declaration to the British Military "Court"—by Gad Sulami

Representatives of the disintegrating British Occupation Regime,
Officers of the retreating British Occupation Army!

During the past year, there have appeared before you, tens of
Hebrew young men, soldiers of the Hebrew Army of Liberation.
They refused to recognise your authority. They saw in you the
servants of an illegal regime which was doomed to final liquidation,
and they warned you—even in the shadow of the gallows—that the
day was not far-off when you would be forced to leave this country.

You probably scoffed at their prophecy in your unclean hearts.
You no doubt thought then: Is it possible that *we* might have to leave
this country—a land of Gold and oil? Where is the power that can
force us out?

The prophecy of our tortured brethren is about to become a
fact. All your efforts to break the spirit of resistance of our nation
have not availed you. You sent our heroes to the scaffold; you
murdered women and children. You declared Martial Law in order
to starve the masses. You concentrated in this country many divisions of your Army. And you brought in thousands of policemen—
from the ranks of Mosly and of the type of Farran—the very same
Farran who tortured his victim—a youth like myself—until he died
and that—with the aid of your rulers and "judges"—criminal
cowards like himself—erased the clues of his crime and "acquitted"
him with the aid of a miserable institution, which insults the very
conception of law and order by calling itself a "court."

All the cruel and terrible acts you committed in our country,
such as the torture of prisoners and the murder of wounded dying
prisoners—as was the case at the approaches to Acre—did not help
you. You did not frighten the Hebrew youth. The Hebrew nation did
not retreat.

On the contrary. The hatred of the barbaric enemy, the cruel
enslaver, increased, and the desire grew to throw off his grip even at
the cost of the most precious possession, even at the cost of life itself.
My comrades, the soldiers of the Irgun Zvai Leumi, warned you
against these inevitable consequences of your rule of bloodshed.
You paid no heed to their warning. You thought you were dealing
with what, in your arrogance, so typical of Colonial exploiters, you
term "natives"; you thought you were dealing with Jews from the
diaspora, whom it is permissible to torture, as did Hitler: without
punishment. You were wrong. A new generation has arisen here in
Israel. A generation without fear. A generation in whose heart there
is the consciousness that there are things in life more important
than life itself; a generation which has decided to be free or die; a
generation which has grown up on its home soil; whose courage has

sprung forth to life from the blood of the heroes of Israel of days gone by and out of the ashes of millions of tortured and massacred, whom *you*, British enslavers, killed together with your teacher, Hitler.

It is therefore not surprising that you did not succeed in breaking our spirit and subjugating our souls, despite all the rude strength at your disposal. Our struggle against you continued and increased. And you were forced to retreat. Your rulers announced that they had no alternative but to evacuate Eretz Israel. True, it is an open secret that even behind this announcement there lurks a plot and you will yet make many manoeuvres in an effort to maintain your hold on our country and exploit it. But you will not be able to maintain your bankrupt rule much longer. Your regime is inherently no longer real. Everybody recognises that it is in the process of dissolution and eagerly awaits the day when your soldiers and policemen will no longer be seen on our streets and highways, in our towns and villages. That day is not far off. Thus, I a Hebrew soldier in your captivity, have but three things to say to you:

First—I do not recognise your right to try me,

Second—True, I was taken prisoner in an Arab vicinity, but it was not to an Arab stable that I was leading my camel.

Third—and this is most important—Why do you still maintain your courts—military and otherwise? You have announced your withdrawal. Go therefore back to your own country! Good-bye and may we *not* meet again!

October 29, 1947.

[A Warning]

Though your Government has announced its intention of evacuating our country, it is making plans for a bloody struggle between Jews and Arabs, out of which it means to gain renewed control of the country.

The British representative at the United Nations has made it clear that the Government plans to withdraw the civil administration but to keep the Army, *in military occupation* of the country. The Army is not only to organize its departure. It is going to *rule* the areas in which it remains while the evacuation is going on.

The evacuation is to be carried out in such a way as to encourage and aid the Arabs to attack the Jews who, on account of the continued British occupation of *their* key areas, will be tied hand and foot in their efforts at defending themselves or counter-attacking.

Officially, the British troops will be "looking on." They will not lift a finger—except to crush any military activity by the Jews still "subject" to British Occupation.

The long-cherished dream of the British Foreign Office is thus to be achieved: an Arab-Jewish war in which (it is planned) the Arabs are to have the upper hand. And the Jews are thus to be crushed—or driven to beg for British aid. British aid will then be offered, on condition—that the country remains effectively under British control.

That is the master-plan. In accordance with this plan, Arab attacks have already begun even before the evacuation begins and they are being carried out with the cooperation of the British forces. British forces are thus providing cover for the Arab attacks, preventing the Jews from putting their defensive measures into operation, killing Jewish defenders and disarming them. Already the British forces have made it possible for their Arab hirelings to paralyse communication between Tel-Aviv and Jerusalem and forced the evacuation by Jews of part of the Tel-Aviv-Jaffa border area. A substantial proportion of Jewish casualties have been inflicted by British arms—including a woman and her child crossing a street.

These events of the past few days have only made clearer your Government's intentions and plans. And we want to warn you that we shall act to counter and frustrate them. If Arab dupes and mercenaries, misled or paid by British wire-pullers, and encouraged to believe in an easy victory, continue to attack us, we shall not only defend ourselves against them. We shall attack the real enemy, who sends and helps them. If there is more bloodshed in our country it is not, as Mr. Bevin plans, going to be only Arab and Jewish blood that is shed. It will be British as well.

We want you to know this because it is your sons and brothers, sent to risk their lives for your Government's squalid policy, who will pay the price of that policy. We want you to know this because we are not interested in killing them. We want to be left in peace in our country and have no objection to their remaining in peace—in yours.

But as long as they are here and we know the purpose of their presence is to ensure the shedding of Jewish blood we shall attack them.

Moreover, as your Government's war against our people and its efforts to crush us are world-wide (remember the sea blockade against our repatriates, remember the "Exodus 1947")—our counter-attacks will not be limited to Erets Israel.

We have determined to liberate our country and re-establish our independence, and we mean to finish the job.

It is for you to decide whether your sons and brothers are to risk their lives in order to carry out a senseless policy of hate and oppression.

If the British Occupation Administration withdraws from our country and if the British troops in our country, while they are organizing their evacuation, concern themselves *only* with evacuation they will not be attacked by us.

But any attempt by whatever means to perpetrate British rule in whatever form and in whatever part of our country will result in a new offensive by the Irgun.

We feel it is right to give you this warning because we know that your Government is not telling even its own people the truth. We prefer you to succeed in changing your Government's plans by your own means. If you do not—we shall have to do it.

Demand of your Government therefore that it carry out its evacuation from our country speedily, in orderly fashion, and without further interference of any kind in our affairs or our relations with our Arab neighbours. So that your soldiers may return Home in peace.

IRGUN ZVAI LEUMI
b'Eretz Israel

[An Appeal]

TEL AVIV
DECEMBER 26, 1947

WE, THE UNDERSIGNED,[1] RESIDENTS OF HATIKVAH AND EZRA QUARTERS, APPEAL HEREWITH TO THE COMMAND OF THE IRGUN ZVAI LEUMI IN TEL AVIV TO COME TO OUR AID IN THE DEFENCE OF OUR NEIGHBORHOODS, AND TO CRUSH OUR ENEMIES AROUND THE ABOVE QUARTERS.

---

[1]Scores of handwritten signatures were attached to this petition.

VI
THE LAST DAYS OF THE MANDATE (1948)

Communique

16 February 1948

The British enslaver is plotting to retain and perpetuate his rule in Jerusalem. The British enslaver who, in his overt and covert actions, is converting the UNO decision on Eretz Israel into a scrap of paper, has suddenly revealed readiness to "cooperate" with the UNO Trusteeship Council in the implementation of the constitution of Jerusalem, which is part of the UNO Assembly decision. The cunning enslaver knows that the setting up of an international force of 5000 volunteers for Jerusalem will meet with considerable, perhaps insurmountable, difficulties and will in any case require a long time, much longer than the three months left before the ending of the "Mandate" as announced by Britain. Bevin therefore assumes—and is endeavouring to achieve—that the Trusteeship Council, which is entirely under the influence of the "Western bloc" should appeal to Britain to "maintain law and order" in the Holy City even after the ending of the Mandate and until an international police force is set up, that is, for an indefinite period. Jerusalem would be like Trieste: an "international" city in theory and in practice a city occupied by the British. The British Press has confirmed that this is indeed the British "plan" for Jerusalem, which is part of the master-plan designed to turn the wheels backward and perpetuate British rule, direct or indirect, in Eretz Israel.

In relation to this we state:

Under British rule, in whatever form, "civilian," "municipal" or military, whether under "international" auspices or not, there will be no peace in the Holy City, the eternal capital of Eretz Israel. Under British rule, whatever form such rule may take, Jerusalem will be a *permanent front of battle* between the Hebrew Underground army and the enslaver.

Communique

April 11, 1948

The comedy goes on. Britain has already been requested at the Security Council to stay on in Eretz Israel after 15 May. And Cadogan, Britain's representative, did not this time stand up and declare: Britain will not, under any circumstances, consent to carrying this unbearable load. On the contrary: Cadogan promised to transmit this request to his Government for consideration and decision.

The comedy goes on. Very possibly Nazi-Britain will, in a few weeks' time, crown herself, with the aid of her Washingtonian partners, the representative of Civilisation and the executor of the United Nations' will in Eretz Israel. But the comedy will not avail her. It will end in great tragedy, particularly for those who act it out for the whole world to see and at the expense of a fighting and bleeding nation. Nazi-Britain will not rule in our country. Not by herself nor in partnership with other enslavers. Any attempt to extend or renew a regime of occupation in our country, under one guise or another will bring on such an offensive against the oppressors as has not yet been seen during all the years of our fight for the liberation of our country.

And this warning is being issued to Britain and Company not by Mrs. Golda Meyerson, but by the Irgun Zvai Leumi in Eretz Israel.

Speech of the Commander-in-Chief of the Irgun Zvai Leumi

Citizens of the Hebrew homeland, soldiers of Israel, Hebrew youth, Sisters and Brothers in Zion:

After many years of underground warfare, years of persecution and suffering, moral and physical suffering, the rebels against the enslaver stand before you, with a blessing of thanks on their lips and a prayer in their heart. The blessing is the one their forefathers used to greet holidays with. It was with this blessing that they tasted new fruit. And it is truly a holiday in our dwellings and a new fruit is visible before our very eyes. The Hebrew revolt of 1944–48 has been crowned with success, the first Hebrew revolt since the Hasmonean insurrection, that has ended in victory. The rule of enslavement of Britain in our country has been beaten, uprooted, has crumbled and been dispersed. The State of Israel has arisen out of a bloody battle, a battle of conquest. The road for the mass return to Zion has been paved. The basis has been laid—but only the basis—for actual

Hebrew independence. One phase of the battle for freedom whose aim it was to return the entire People of Israel to its homeland and return the entire Land of Israel to its nation—its owner, has ended. But only one phase. And if we keep in mind that this great event has happened after seventy generations of dispersion, of disarmament, of enslavement, of neverending wanderings and persecution; if we remember that this thing has happened in the midst of the total campaign of extermination of the Jew wherever he be; if we remember that once again the few overcame the many who would destroy Israel—then, despite the fact that the cup of suffering of our mothers and children has not yet been emptied, it is our right and our duty to give thanks, most humbly, to the Rock and Saviour of Israel for the miracles he has shown our people this day, even as in days of yore. Therefore we shall say today—the first day of our liberation from the yoke of the British enslaver—Blessed be He who kept us alive and brought us hence.

The State of Israel has arisen. And it has arisen "Only Thus": Through blood, fire, a strong hand and a mighty arm, with sufferings and sacrifices. It could not be otherwise. And yet, even before our State has managed to create the normal State institutions, it is forced to fight—or to continue to fight—the satanic enemy and his blood-thirsty mercenaries on land, from the air and from the sea. Under such conditions, the warning that the Philosopher-President Thomas Masaryk sounded in the ears of the Czechoslovak nation when it emerged free after three hundred years of enslavement, has a double meaning for us. In 1918, when Masaryk stepped out onto the Wilson railway station in Prague, he greeted his cheering country-men with the words: "It is difficult to erect a State; but it is even more difficult to keep one going." And in truth, Brothers in Zion, it was difficult for us to erect our state. Tens of generations of wandering from one land of massacre to another were needed; it was necessary that there be exiles, stakes and torture cells; there were needed horrible awakenings out of illusions; there were needed warnings—unheeded warnings—of prophets and seers; there was needed the labour of generations of pioneers and builders; and there was need of an uprising of rebels, to crush the enemy; there was need of gallows and exiles beyond seas and deserts—all this was necessary in order that we might reach the stage where there are seven hundred thousand [blank] homeland, to the state where the direct rule of oppression has been driven out and independence declared in part of the country, the whole of which is ours.

It was difficult to create our state. But it will be still more difficult to keep it going. We are surrounded by enemies who desire our extermination. And that same enslaver, who is both the teacher of Hitler and his pupil; this same dastardly enslaver who has been beaten by us directly, is trying indirectly to make us surrender with the aid of his mercenaries from the south, the north and the east. Our one-day-old state is therefore in the midst of the flames of battle. And the first basis for our state must therefore be victory, total victory, in the war which is raging all over our country. And for this victory, without which we shall have neither freedom nor life, we need arms: weapons of all sorts, in order to strike the enemy, in order to disperse the invader, in order to free the entire length and breadth of the country from its would-be destroyers. But in addition to these arms each and every one of us has need of another spiritual weapon, the weapon of standing without flinching against attacks from the air; standing resolutely in the face of heavy casualties; standing unflinching in the face of local disasters and temporary defeats; standing without retreat before threats and cajolery. One is bound up with the other. If, within the coming days and weeks we shall be armed with this spiritual armour of an undying nation in resurrection—we shall in the meantime receive the blessed arms with which to strike the enemy and bring freedom and peace to our nation and country.

But, even after emerging victorious from this campaign—and victorious we shall be—we shall still need superhuman efforts in order to remain independent, in order to free our country. First of all it will be necessary to increase and strengthen the fighting arm of Israel, without which there will be no freedom and no survival for our homeland. The Hebrew Army can and must be among the best of the armies of the world. In modern warfare it is not numbers that matter. What is decisive is the spirit, and the brain. And what is the spirit of our fighters? This has been demonstrated by the whole of the Hebrew youth, the youth of Haganah, the youth of the F.F.I. and the youth of the Irgun Zvai Leumi, this wonderful Hebrew youth, the like of which has been given to no other people, the like of which no generation of Israel, from Bar-Kochba to the first pioneers of modern times, has been privileged to possess. And as for our brains, the brains of Israel represent the composite essence of thought of 120 generations—of 120 generations of thinkers, of searchers after the Almighty and of his discoverers. This, the greatest of our "natural" resources, is unlimited. And the military science, which will be based on such brains, will be among the most developed in the world. Yes, we shall have power, for we have brains, thinking brains, inventive brains.

We shall need a wise foreign policy in order to free our country and keep up our state. We must make a fact of our declared independence. And we must know this: so long as even one British soldier—or any other foreign soldier—tramples the earth of our homeland, our sovereign independence is nothing but an aspiration, an aspiration for whose fulfilment we must be ready to fight not only on the battlefront but also in the international arena. Secondly, we must also establish and maintain the principle of reciprocity in our relations with the nations of the world. There must be no self-denigration. There must be no surrender, and no favouritism. There must be reciprocity. Enmity for enmity. Aid for aid. Friendship must be repaid with friendship.

We must foster and maintain friendship and understanding with the great American nation. True, the present American government—the Forrestal government—has forgotten what was preached by Jefferson, Washington, Lee and Tom Paine. But there are among the American nation other forces too. They remember. And they will also remember the British Cornwallis and the French Lafayette. We must foster and maintain friendship and understanding with the peoples of the Soviet Union. We must not hide the truth. In the past there was ill-feeling between the land of the revolution and the Hebrew independence movement. For these relations we paid a heavy price in blood and tears. But now, in the wake of the heroic battle of the Hebrew underground, a revolutionary change has taken place in these relations. The Soviet Union has recognized our right to independence in our country. And we shall never forget that the victorious Russian Army saved hundreds of thousands of Jews from the Nazi beasts of prey. We shall never forget that while our nation was standing before the cross-roads of history, the Soviet Union stretched out a helping hand and helped us onto the road of independence. We must foster and maintain friendship and understanding with the nations of Europe who have behind them a long history of struggles for freedom and whence will come within the coming months and years the masses of those returning to Zion. We must foster and maintain friendship and understanding with the great French nation, the bearer of the banner of freedom and light since the days of the Bastille. We must foster friendship and understanding between us and every nation, great or small, strong or weak, near or far, which recognizes our independence, which aids our nation and which is interested, even as we are, in international justice and peace among nations.

Of no less importance is our internal policy. And the primary part of this policy is the Return to Zion. Ships, for heavens sake, bring ships. Let us not be plagued with inertia. Let us not talk empty words about absorptive capacity. Let us not make restrictions for the sake of so-called order. Quickly. Quickly. Our nation has no time. Bring in hundreds of thousands. Immediately. And if there be not enough houses for us all, we shall find tents. And if there be no sufficient tents—it does not matter—there are skies above us, the blue skies of our country. People do not perish because of bad living conditions. We who saw the way the Russian people lived during their fight for freedom and independence know that there is no limit, just that: no limit to the sacrifices a nation is willing to make for its homeland, and its future. We are now in the midst of a war for survival; and our tomorrow and theirs depend on the quickest concentration of our nation's exiles.

And within our homeland—justice must be the supreme ruler, the ruler over the rulers. There must be no tyranny. The officials must be the servants of the nation and not their rulers. There must be no exploitation. There must be no man within our country—citizen or foreigner—who will be hungry, lacking a roof over his head, or lacking the most elementary knowledge. "Remember thou wert a foreigner in Egypt"—this rule must light our way in our relations with the neighbours within our gates. "Thou shalt pursue righteousness" should be our guiding light in our relations amongst ourselves.

And let us remember: It is the state of Israel that we have created. Let us protect the state; let us protect Israel. From this point of view our whole social and state outlook may be summarized in one sentence from Ahad Haam: "It was the Sabbath that kept guard over Israel, rather than Israel over the Sabbath."

For these principles, and within the limits of Hebrew law and Hebrew democracy, the Freedom Movement will fight, the Freedom Movement which will arise out of the depths of the Hebrew underground and which will be created by our great fighting family composed of all classes of people, people from all over the world, people of all classes and tendencies who rallied to the banner of the Irgun Zvai Leumi. The Irgun Zvai Leumi is leaving the underground within the boundaries of the Hebrew independent state. We went underground, we *rose* up in the underground, under a rule of oppression in order to strike at it and liquidate it. And we have struck well. We have driven it away, for ever and ever. Now, for the time being, we have Hebrew rule in part of our homeland. And in this part of the homeland, in this liberated section where there will be Hebrew law—and that is the only legal law in this country—there is no need for a Hebrew underground. In the State of Israel we shall be soldiers and builders. We shall obey its laws—for they are our laws. And we shall respect its government, for it is our government. Only let the Hebrew Government beware, let the Provisional Government and any other government that will come in its place beware that it does not, by appeasement and tyranny create a new underground. Let the Hebrew Government safeguard the independence bought with the blood of heroes and martyrs. Let it not give it up, in surrender, to tyrants and terrorists. And let the government safeguard the rights of man and citizen without discrimination. Let it safeguard the principles of justice and freedom and let our mansion be lighted with the light of brotherly love.

The State of Israel has arisen, but let us remember that our homeland is not yet liberated. The battle continues and you see now that the words of your fighters were not vain words: it is Hebrew arms which will decide the boundaries of the Hebrew State. So it is now in this battle; and so it will be in the future. The homeland is an entity. The attempt to dissect it is not only a crime, but an abortion. Whoever does not recognise our natural right to our entire homeland, does not recognise our right to any part of it. And we shall not foregoe this natural right of ours. We shall continue to bear the vision of full independence. And we shall bring it about. For it is an iron rule of life: That which comes between the people's state and the people's homeland must disappear. The state will cover the homeland. The homeland will be the state. And let us not use foreign words. Let us not talk of irridenta. It is not just the *city* which was stolen from us. We have in mind five–sixths of the territory of our homeland which we can and must fructify for our sakes and for the sake of those who come after us, for our security and the security of our brothers and sons; and for the sake of peace. We shall therefore proudly bear the vision of full salvation, the dream of the liberation under the Hebrew flag, the flag of freedom, the flag of peace and progress. The soldiers of Israel will yet hoist our banner on the Tower of David and our ploughs will yet plough the fields of Gilead.

Citizens of the Hebrew State, soldiers of Israel:

We are in the midst of battle. There are difficult days ahead of us. Much and precious blood will yet be spilled. Strengthen your will, brothers, armour your hearts. For the road is paved with suffering and sacrifices—there is no other. We cannot buy peace from our enemies with appeasement. There is only one kind of "peace" that is purchaseable—the peace of the graveyard, the peace of Treblinka. Be brave of heart and be prepared for grave tests. We shall withstand them. The Lord of Hosts will help us and the bravery of the Hebrew youth, the bravery of the Hebrew mothers who, like Hannah, offer their sons on the altar of God—this bravery will save us from our enemies and deliver us from slavery to freedom, from the danger of extermination to the shore of safety.

And you, brothers of our fighting family, do you remember how we started? With what we started? And now you see that they who plough with blood reap with freedom. We were alone and persecuted. But you fought out of a deep faith and did not retreat, you were tortured but did not surrender, you were thrown into gaol but did not give in, you were exiled from your homeland but were not broken, you were sent to the gallows but went with a song in your hearts. Thus you wrote a glorious page in history. And you shall yet continue to write—not with ink, but with blood and sweat. Not with the pen, but with a sword and plough. You will not remember grudges and will ask for no prize. The only prize we seek is to see our nation truly liberated and fighting, united, for freedom. Our true prize will be Hebrew children playing games without fear; and the aeroplane circling over their heads will be a Hebrew plane, and the soldier coming towards them will be a Hebrew soldier, and the train coming in the distance will be a Hebrew train. Is there a greater joy than this?

But for the time being let us think of the battle, for only the battle will decide our fate and future. And we shall be sent on our way into battle inspired by the spirit of our ancient heroes, from the conquerors of Canaan to the Rebels of Judah. We shall be accompanied into battle by the spirits of the revivers of our nation, Zeev Banjamin Herzl, Max Nordau, Joseph Trumpeldor and the father of the resurrected Hebrew heroism Zeev Jabotinsky. We shall be accompanied by the spirit of David Raziel, the greatest of the Hebrew commanders of our day; and by Dov Gruner, the greatest among the Hebrew soldiers. We shall be accompanied into battle by the spirits of our heroes of the gallows, the conquerors of death. And we shall be accompanied by the spirits of millions of our martyrs, our murdered fathers and butchered mothers, our murdered brothers and strangled children. And in this battle we shall break the enemy and bring salvation to our nation, tried in persecution, thirsting for freedom.

Lord of Israel, safeguard your soldiers and bless their sword which is once again forging the covenent which you made with your people and your chosen country.

Lion of Judah, for our nation, for our country, forward to battle, forward to victory.

[Communiques]

MAY 27, 1948

With the establishment of the Jewish Army, the combat battalions of the Irgun Zvai Leumi will be ready for transfer into the ranks of the unified forces, our battalions led by their battle-expirienced officers will be at the command of the High Command in the execution of their tasks in the people's war.

MAY 24, 1948

The political correspondent of "ha'Aretz" took the liberty of expressing his opinion concerning the part played by the soldiers of the Irgun Zvai Leumi of the Jerusalem front. The political correspondent of "ha' Aretz" has misled the public. For reasons which are well understood by everyone, we have refrained from making public the facts concerning the Battle of Jerusalem. In the long run it is not the pen-prattlers who decide the future of the nation, but its soldiers and fighters. But a day will come—and it is not far off—when we shall be in a position to reveal just what part the soldiers of the Irgun Zvai Leumi have played in the Battle of Jerusalem, both in the Old City and in the New. Then too, the world will come to know under what conditions our soldiers fought and what acts of heroism they committed on the most dangerous sections of the front.

Communique

May 30, 1948

At 5:30 a.m. our combat-units stormed Resh Ra'Ayin (Ras-el-Ain) which had been occupied by strong forces of the Iraqi Army.

Our soldiers advanced on the enemy camp in two columns: from the west and south. In a fierce attack, which developed into a face-to-face battle, the first detachment captured the historic Anti-patrus fortress. This opened the way to the capture of the water-supply station. Our soldiers stormed the station and despite advance preparations, the enemy did not succeed in blowing it up. The water-station, which is the source of water supply for Jerusalem, is in our hands, undamaged.

At the same time the second column advanced from the south, stormed and captured the huge British air-force camp. A second military camp, as well as the railway station, were also captured.

The entire area has been cleared of the enemy who suffered heavy losses.

Our casualties: Six killed and six wounded.

Declaration

The provisional government of the State of Israel have accepted the conditions of Count Bernadotte and agreed to the truce. Provided that Brigadier Clayton will order his hirelings, the invading Arab states, to agree to the armistice, the truce will become a political fact.

The provisional government consisting of the notorious men of the 29th of June committed one of the most deadly blunders. And let us pray that this blunder should not prove to be a fatal one; one to deprive us, by the stroke of a pen, of the advantages gained through the blood sacrifices of our best sons.

Analysis of the letter written by Shertok to Count Bernadotte reveals the following:—

1). The provisional government received under para (iii) of the letter a cease fire *without any stipulation whatsoever.* That is the basic fact of this acceptance. All the other addenda of Mr. Shertok are nothing but pure "belle lettres." Should Count Bernadotte have no literary tastes he will not read them; if he is, however, a lover of literature— he will read them and will be amused.

2). Within our frontiers are invading armies of the aggressors—the hirelings of Britain. No demand was placed on record by the provisional government to remove these armies from our Motherland. *Thus our own provisional government lend[s] a cloak of legality to the invasion of Arab armies.*

3). The provisional government knows well that during the next four weeks—or any other similar period of cease fire—the forces of the invaders will grow without any check whatsoever. There will be no control imposed on supplies to the invading armies, whose presence in the country the provisional government officially recognised. Egypt, for instance, will claim that it is entitled to maintain its army and this claim will be approved. An endless stream of equipment of all kinds will pour through to the enemy. Should, in spite of all, some measure of control be imposed for the sake of appearance, it cannot be effective; the British will see to that, moreover the type of country and the vastness of the area controlled by the Arab states will help them.

4). There will be, however, a most meticulous control over our shores. Shertok handed over to Bernadotte and his British advisers an unlimited authority to check our shipping and you can rely on the British pirates—who perfected this technique over years—that no "unwanted" ship will come to Eretz Israel and should it arrive it will be requisitioned (?) in the name of peace.

5). Immigration will be limited by decision of the most noble Count. The right to limit the homecoming of our Brothers has been conceded to the emissary of Britain by our own government. In para (iv) of his letter Shertok tries, in a flood of verbiage, to say that it is not just to limit the return of the dispersed of our nation. But at the end of the same paragraph our clever Foreign Secretary says clearly that it is up to the "discretion" of the Count. That means that from tomorrow we are under the regime of a new "White Paper" of Bernadotte. And all this by the *agreement* of a Hebrew Government.

6). The spirit of the Jewish Agency—the spirit of political and spiritual cringing subjugation—is very much in evidence in every word of the letter by the man who claims to be the representative of a sovereign state and to speak in the name of an independent government. To the sons of our homecoming nation the Foreign Secretary of the State of Israel assigns the description "Immigrants." The word repatriates is not apparently known to the Agency people who have donned the paraphenalia of Ministers.

7). Whatsoever repercussion the concessions made by the provisional government have is brought out by para (x) of the official letter. The provisional government emphasised that should the other side (Brigadier Clayton) not agree to this Jewish virtual surrender terms, the provisional government will reconsider the situation and will withdraw its agreement to the terms of Count Bernadotte. But the provisional government is again in the wrong. *From such concessions* there is no return. He who has bartered his sovereign rights will not be rescued by any verbal reservations.

8). In the wake of the Shertok letter our political situation deteriorated rapidly. The provisional government made opening to renewed intrigues by Nazi-Britain. Britain has regained the initiative and can at will end the cease fire within days. But should she be satisfied with the observers of Bernadotte and see that we are totally isolated she will prolong the cease fire for weeks and months. Not only Jerusalem will be beleaguered—*we will all be beleaguered*. And, of course, no state will be in a particular hurry to recognise us when our very sovereignty is doubted because of the shameful concessions of the provisional government.

9). Our military position deteriorated enormously. We shall only have a few more weeks of training but our forces will not grow, while those of the enemy expand continually. He will organize without interference his long lines of communications. He will advance his bases; he will replenish his stores—and in a few weeks time we shall be faced by a force much greater than that which is facing us to-day.

The overall conclusion from these facts is obvious:

The provisional government was faced by the alternatives: WAR or SHAME. They chose SHAME but that will not save them from war.

And the people will pay in blood and tears—streams of blood and tears—because of the blunder of the men of the 29th of June.

Declaration of the Irgun Zvai Leumi

A. The Irgun Zvai Leumi, which rose up against the regime of British subjugation, smote it, brought about its disintegration, forced its armies of occupation to evacuate the country and thus made possible the sovereignty and independence of the People of Israel in their homeland—hereby announces its decision to come out from the underground within the territory of the State of Israel and to transfer the thousands of its officers and men, in the framework of distinct military units—battalions—into the Hebrew Army.

B. Having accomplished their task as an armed underground and as an independent military entity, within the present boundaries of the State of Israel, the officers and men of the Irgun Zvai Leumi vow not to rest and not to relax until the final aim to which they gave their oath, is fulfilled—until the entire country is liberated from the yoke of foreign rule and returned to the People of Israel.

C. The Hebrew War of Liberation, the spiritual offspring of the prophet and leader of Hebrew revolt and renaissance in our generation, Zeev Jabotinsky, goes on. In Jerusalem as long as it is not integrated into the boundaries of the Hebrew State, the Irgun will continue as an armed and fighting organisation and will continue to hold high the banner of freedom and complete redemption. In all other areas, outside of the boundaries of Hebrew sovereignty, the Irgun Zvai Leumi will continue to fight as a military and armed organization against the enemies of our nation, for the dignity of the nation and for its complete liberation. But, within the present boundaries of the State of Israel the Irgun Zvai Leumi hereby announces the creation of the Hebrew Freedom Movement which will keep faith with the glorious tradition of the war for liberation, and will fight, within the framework of the Hebrew State law and for the same principles for which the soldiers of the Irgun fought and still continue to fight; fell and still continue to fall.

D. The Hebrew Freedom Movement, founded by the Irgun Zvai Leumi, hereby proclaims its basic principles, the acceptance of which, and the readiness to achieve their realisation, by personal sacrifice and devotion, will be all that will be demanded from whoever wishes to join its ranks.

THE PRINCIPLES OF THE HEBREW FREEDOM MOVEMENT

a. The Hebrew homeland whose area stretches east and west of the river Jordan, is a historic and geographic entity.

b. The dismemberment of the homeland is an illegal act. The agreement to such a partition is illegal and in no way commits the People of Israel.

c. It is the task of our generation to bring back under Hebrew sovereignty all those areas of our homeland which have been torn away from us and given over to foreign rule.

d. The return of the People of Israel to their homeland is not only an acute necessity but also the prerequisite for the very survival of the entire nation. There is no future for the People of Israel in the diaspora. It is the task of our generation to return the majority of the nation to its liberated homeland.

e. The right to repatriation of every Jew who so desires is inalienable and is not susceptible of any qualification. Any attempt to tamper with this right—and it does not matter from what quarter such an attempt may come—is unlawful and it is a primary duty to do away with it—both legally and practically.

f. Within the Hebrew State and liberated homeland a new society has to be established which will be based on the following principles:

1. True democracy which will ensure the people full freedom in deciding both the problems of their national existence as well as the election of their leaders—leaders who must be the *servants* of the people and not its masters.

2. Strict adherence to the basic principles of the human rights of all citizens.

3. Equal rights for every citizen regardless of origin, religion or sex.

4. Social progress: Continuous raising of the standard of living of the working man.

5. Social justice: to assure to every citizen the minimum essentials of life and to aspire to eliminate all economic distinctions between the various classes of the people.

6. Constant development of culture and science.

7. Work and respect for work in all its forms and variations.

8. Respect for the holy traditions and institutions of the Jewish people.

BASIC OUTLINE OF THE PROGRAM OF THE
HEBREW FREEDOM MOVEMENT
(Founded by the Irgun Zvai Leumi)

FOREIGN POLICY:—

1. The prime task of Hebrew foreign policy will be to bring about the unification of all parts of our partitioned homeland under sovereign Hebrew rule.

2. The foreign policy of our state will be a policy of peace.

3. The Hebrew State would see in a new world war a catastrophe for all nations, but first and foremost for the People of Israel, whose very existence will be in jeopardy should such a war break out. The Hebrew State will therefore spare no effort, in cooperation with other freedom-loving nations, to prevent a clash between the world powers and thus will seek to ensu[r]e peace among nation.

4. The Freedom Movement will strive to foster understanding

and friendly relations between the Hebrew State and the Union of Soviet Socialist Republics who consistently helped in achieving the first phase of our independence in our homeland.

5. We shall foster understanding and friendly relations with the great American nation in whose midst there live millions of Jews, devoted supporters of the Hebrew State, many among them potential citizens of Eretz Israel.

6. The Freedom Movement will foster friendship and understanding between our nation and the great French Republic, traditional champion of the ideals of freedom and equality.

7. We shall foster friendship and understanding with the countries of Europe, proud heirs of a long history of wars for liberation and from whose midst there will come the majority of our future citizens—the returners to Zion.

8. There will exist ties of friendship and understanding between our nation and all other nations, big and small, strong and weak, near and far, between us and all who look towards peace and understanding with our nation and country.

9. The Hebrew State will strive for good neighbourliness and a system of mutual help and close cooperation with all the nations of the Middle East, and particularly with those nations in that area which are still oppressed. The fostering of such friendly relations and the building of eventual partnership cannot however be achieved at the price of any of our rights on any part of our homeland. On the contrary, we must make it clear to all concerned, in a manner which cannot be misunderstood, that true friendship between us and our neighbours near and far is possible only on the basis of their recognizing our people's right to our undivided homeland.

10. The guiding principle of Hebrew foreign policy must be: reciprocity; friendship for friendship; help for help; and enmity for enmity.

INTERNAL POLICY:—

a. *National and Religious Minorities*

1. National and Religious minorities will enjoy complete equality of rights in all aspects of civic life and in all activities of the state.

2. Adequate representation in the State and in its institutions must be granted to all religious and national minorities, on the basic condition, however, of their unequivocal allegiance to the State.

3. The State and its institutions must ensure to the minorities full opportunity to educate their children in their own language, in the spirit of their specific culture, religion and tradition.

b. *Social and Economic Policies*

1. The State must guarantee every citizen not only the right to work, but also the opportunity to work.

2. It is the undeniable right of all working men to unite in trade-unions which will strive—alongside the state—for the continuous betterment of the workingman's standard of living.

3. The State institutions must make certain that within the Hebrew State no man will go hungry, or without a roof, or be deprived of the right to at least elementary education.

4. The Freedom Movement will fight against all trusts and monopolies—regardless in whose hands they may be—for such trusts and monopolies lead inevitably to the exploitation of the working man and the "little people."

5. Special attention will be paid to the welfare of mothers and children. After the mass extermination of millions of our people, it is the duty of Israel to assure such conditions as will encourage the maximum natural increase of a healthy Hebrew population.

6. State and Social institutions will provide and care for ex-servicemen and former underground fighters who risked their lives and shed their blood for the liberation of the homeland.

7. Every citizen who works either with hand or brain must be assured of security in old age, in sickness or in case of disability—security both for himself and for his family as well, if he is the breadwinner. And in case of his death his family must be cared for.

8. The State will care for the development of industry, agriculture, commerce and all other resources of national wealth and will strive thereby constantly to increase the capacity of the motherland to absorb new repatriates while maintaining adequate living conditions for the entire population.

9. All public utility works and basic industries must be nationalized and run for the benefit of the people.

10. The State Institutions must strenuously encourage scientific research into natural resources of the State and their exploitation for the good of the nation.

c. *Education*

1. Education within the Hebrew State must be a *unified* system and not along party lines. All spiritual trends of thought and ideas will be included in the general education system.

2. Elementary education will be obligatory for every citizen. The State institutions must create the necessary conditions in order to provide elementary education for every child.

3. The elementary education will be borne entirely by the State. Tuition fees will not be charged in any *government* secondary schools.

4. The State must provide all teachers with decent living conditions and with opportunities for further self-education.

5. Teaching of Hebrew as a subject in schools for Arab children, and of Arabic to Hebrew children will be obligatory.

6. The education which will be given the children of Israel will be based on the following principles: the territorial unity of the homeland; love of the homeland and its people; physical and military training; recognition of the equality of man; good manners; love of freedom and loyalty to democratic principles; pioneering in the upbuilding of the country.

7. The teaching of our Holy Books, tradition and history of the nation will be included among the basic elements of the education which will be given the children of Israel.

d. *Religion*

1. Freedom of religion will be assured to all citizens of the State.

2. Respect for *all* religions will be instilled among the population by the educational, state and civic institutions.

3. The Sabbath is one of the most exalted social ideas which the People of Israel have contributed to world-civilization. Sabbath observance therefore will be the privilege not only of all the *Hebrew* citizens of the state, but will also be enforced in all government and civic institutions; only those services whose continuance is a strict necessity will be excepted. The same rule must apply with regard to the Holy Days and Feasts of Israel. The observance of the Jewish Sabbath will not be obligatory amongst the minorities.

e. *Land Reform*

1. The Government institutions must undertake a Land Reform which will assure every farmer on communal settlement— of any sort—a sufficient acreage of land for the maintenance of a self supporting agricultural economy.

2. Private ownership of land must be limited by the institution of a maximum farm unit.

3. Land which is government property, estates which are not cultivated by their owners or those excessive areas which will be nationalized—after payment of compensation—will create a land resserve from which allocations for farmers, individual and communal, will be made.

4. State institutions must be compelled to encourage pioneering settlement, whether private, communal or cooperative.

5. Special attention will be paid to the task of exploring water resources and to their full exploitation.

f. *Repatriation and Absorption*

1. So long as the process of repatriation has not been completed, the repatriation of all the Returners to Zion and their absorption—both spiritual and economic—must of necessity be the main and primary concern of the Hebrew State and its institutions.

2. Any discrimination on the grounds of party politics in repatriation and settlement must be forbidden.

3. The static "absorptive capacity" of the state cannot serve as a criterion for repatriation. Experience has proved that even under the regime of foreign subjugation, absorptive capacity was a dynamic factor. It is the need of our people to return to Zion which must serve as the criterion for our people's repatriation.

4. It will be the State institutions' concern to provide temporary but adequate housing for the repatriates, until permanent arrangements can be made for them.

5. If the temporary housing arrangements do not suffice to meet the needs of the new repatriates, the government will have to resort to the system of allocating for all citizens of the state a maximum living unit for a transitory period, or to tax the owners of large dwellings and thus obtain the necessary emergency possibilities to provide housing for the new repatriants.

g. *Taxes*

1. The tax system must be progressive. "He who earns more must pay more for the upkeep of the State and Society." This must be the rule of the State.

2. Indirect taxation of essential products, a system which weighs most heavily on the poor, must be reduced to a minimum.

h. *Judiciary*

1. The Courts—of all degrees—must be completely independent of the Executive and all other State institutions in their *work* procedure and acts of judgment.

2. Judges will be appointed by the President of the State. Their transfer from their regular seat of jurisdiction elsewhere, or their release from their duties will be the decision of a special committee which will be chosen by the judges themselves.

3. Only the laws of the State and his own conscience will guide the judge in the discharge of his duties. Any outside interference, political or otherwise, in the process of any trial, or any kind of favoritism, political or otherwise, will be considered a crime against the State and society.

4. In all major trials there will be appointed, in addition to the judges, a sworn jury.

5. Punishment of law-breakers must be of such a nature as to return the citizen to a law-abiding way of life; any degradation or physical mishandling of an accused citizen, will be strictly forbidden. Any state representative who fails to observe this rule will be punished severely.

6. We must strive for the abolition of capital punishment.

i. *Army and Police*

1. We must create a military force based on discipline resulting from free will constantly trained in military science, and equipped with modern weapons.

2. *All* the citizens of the state will serve as a reservoir for the armed forces and will receive military training. Each citizen will be a potential soldier.

3. The Hebrew Army, as well as the internal security forces, must be inculcated with the spirit of democracy in their actions and their dealings with the citizens of the State. The citizens will respect the soldier and policeman; the soldier and policeman will respect the citizen.

j. *State Institutions*

The Freedom Movement proposes the creation of Governmental Institutions along the following lines:

1. The President of the State will be elected in a General Election for a period of four years.

2. The Legislative Branch of the State will be composed of a House of Representatives, an Upper Chamber and a Supreme Supervisory Board.

3. The State Constitution will be adopted by a combined session of both Houses.

4. The remaining State-laws will be promulgated by the House and approved by the Upper Chamber.

5. The Supreme Supervisory Board which will be elected by the Legislative Assembly will be composed of personalities who are outside all legislative and executive institutions of the government. The Supreme Supervisory Board will be enpowered to investigate all monetary and economic acts and transactions of the State Institutions and will be entitled to call their members before them to answer for their stewardship.

6. Every citizen, male or female, from the age of 18 will be entitled to vote. Every citizen from the age of 25 will be eligible for membership of Parliament; for the Upper Chamber the required age should be over 30.

7. The Government will be responsible to both Houses of Parliament.

8. The Principles which will govern the State institutions and our whole public life will be:
   a. Government of the People, by the People and for the People.
   b. "Justice, Justice thou shalt pursue."
   c. "One law there shall be to him that is homeborn and to the stranger in thy land."

The Hebrew Freedom Movement, founded by the Irgun Zvai Leumi, has come into being in order to continue to battle for freedom and in order to instill in the life of our State the principles which form the basis of the war for complete independence. The Hebrew Freedom Movement will resist any attempt to enforce on our State and country any regime of oppression. The Hebrew Freedom Movement will resist any attempt at one-party rule. The Hebrew Freedom Movement extends the hand of friendship to all fighting, patriotic and progressive elements and groups in the State of Israel and calls upon them to create together that great force of public opinion which will lead our nation through the war of liberation to ultimate victory.

APPENDIX

Proclamation of Revolt of the
Irgun Zvai Leumi[1]

TO THE JEWISH NATION IN ZION:

We are now entering into the final stages of this World War. At present each and every people is engaged in evaluating its national position. Which are its victories and which are its defeats? What course shall it embark upon in order to achieve its objective and fulfill its destiny? Who are its friends and who are its enemies? Who is a genuine ally and who is a traitor? And, who will participate in the decisive battle?

Similarly, the people of Israel is obliged to examine its course, to survey the past and arrive at conclusions concerning its future. For, the last few years have been the most horrible in our history; the coming ones—the most crucial in our history.

Let us look at the facts:

1. In 1939 all the political movements in Israel proclaimed that our nation would stand alongside England, France, and Poland in their Holy War against the Hitlerite German aggression.

2. Germany proclaimed this World War a "Jewish War" and that the people of Israel was its Enemy Number One. Nevertheless, the British Government has continuously and stubbornly rejected all proposals to establish a Jewish fighting Force to engage the German armies in direct combat.

3. A truce has been declared between the government and the Jews in the Land of Israel. The Jewish community has offered its unqualified assistance to the Allied Nations in their war against the Hitlerite tyranny.

4. Over 25,000 young men and women volunteers have joined the British Army in the hope that England would establish a National Jewish Army.

5. In 1941 the Arabs of Iraq exploited Britain's desperate position and with German assistance, attacked her armies; the Arabs

---

[1]This document was originally published in Hebrew.

of Syria supported Hitler's agents; the Egyptian fifth column exercised tremendous influence there; the Arabs of the Land of Israel awaited the coming of Rommel, the redeemer while their leader, the Mufti, dispatched orders from Berlin.

6. Jewry stood the test, remaining loyal during the crucial period of 1940–41. The expertise and industrial knowhow of the Jews in the Land of Israel has served the entire Middle East arena. Sons of Israel risked and sacrificed their lives in Syria, Egypt and Iraq.

7. Germany began to exterminate European Jewry. Poland was transformed into a slaughter house; German, Austrian, Dutch and Belgian Jewries have been destroyed; Lithuanian, Latvian and Estonian Jewries lie in their own blood; the remnant of Polish Jewry is battling for its existence in the ghettoes; Roumanian Jewry is in danger of liquidation; Bulgarian Jews are on the verge of deportation. Hungarian Jewry is fearful of its fate. Sword and famine, epidemic and poison are annihilating our European brethren. Throughout all the communities of the diaspora—blood!

8. Our brethren enjoy no refuge. All countries have barred their doors to them. Even those who escaped from Poland, Roumania, and the Baltic countries to Russian Asia are dying of starvation, cold and epidemics. Yet no one will help them—because they are Jews!

9. In response to the horrible slaughter in Europe, the Allied Nations have merely issued a verbal declaration, worth no more than the paper on which it was written.

10. The British government has announced that rescue activities are not possible since they "would interfere with the achievement of victory." Yet, not satisfied with this malicious, satanic declaration alone, she personally authored the bloody chapters in the saga of Jewish immigration to the Land of Israel: Patria, Mauritius, Struma.

11. The government responsible for the White Paper has now attacked the Jewish population in the Land of Israel. Its agents have carried out lawless murders in the cities and villages. Its judges have invented lies and have sought to defame our people and sully its honor throughout the world.

12. The White Paper remains in force, implemented despite Jewish loyalty and Arab treachery; despite the mass mobilization of Jews into the British Army; despite the armistice and the calm prevailing in the Land of Israel; despite the mass slaughter of Jews in Europe. And despite the fact that even now, following the rout of Hitlerism, Jews have no future among the hate-ridden, anti-Semitic nations of Europe.

The facts are both simple and horrible. During the four war years, we have lost millions of the best of our people; other millions face annihilation. Yet the Land of Israel remains sealed because it is ruled by a British regime which enforces the White Paper and aims at destroying our people's last hope.

Sons of Israel. Jewish Youth!

We are now entering the final stage of the war. Our people's destiny shall be determined at this historic juncture. The British regime has violated the armistice agreement which was declared at the outset of the war. The rulers of The Land have disregarded loyalty, concessions and sacrifice. Instead they continue to work toward their goal—the eradication of Zionist efforts to achieve statehood.

Four years have passed. The hopes we had harbored since 1939 have been dashed. We have not been accorded international status; a Jewish Army has not been established; the gates of the Land of Israel have not been opened. The British regime has continued its shameful betrayal of the Jewish Nation and there [is] no moral basis for its continued presence in the Land of Israel.

Let us fearlessly draw the proper conclusions. There can no longer be an armistice between the Jewish Nation and its youth and a British administration in the Land of Israel which has been delivering our brethren to Hitler. Our nation is at war with this regime and it is a fight to the finish. This war will exact many and heavy sacrifices but we shall enter into it in the conviction that we have remained loyal to our slaughtered brethren, that we fight in their name, and remain true to their final testament.

This, then, is our demand!
IMMEDIATE TRANSFER OF POWER IN THE LAND OF ISRAEL TO A PROVISIONAL JEWISH GOVERNMENT.

Immediately after its establishment, the Jewish government of the land of Israel, the only legal representative of the Jewish Nation, shall undertake the following:

a. Establish a National Jewish Army.

b. Negotiate with all authorized bodies to organize the mass evacuation of European Jewry to the Land of Israel.

c. Negotiate with the Russian government for the evacuation of Jewish refugees from Poland and other countries.

d. Create conditions for the absorption of our sons returning to their homeland

e. Effect an alliance with the Allied governments aimed at intensifying the war effort against Germany.

f. Propose—in behalf of the sovereign state of the Land of Israel, on the basis of the Atlantic Charter, and in recognition of the community of interests—a mutual assistance pact with Great Britain, the United States of America, the new French government and any other free nation who recognizes the sovereignty and international rights of the Jewish State. An honorable peace and good neighborliness shall be offered to all the neighbors of the independent Jewish State.

g. Implant the sanctity of the Torah into the life of an emancipated nation in its homeland.

h. Guarantee all citizens of the State employment and social justice.

i. Proclaim the extra-territorial status of all places sacred to Christians and Moslems.

j. Grant full equality to the Arab population.

Jews!

The only way to save our nation, insure our survival and preserve our honor is to establish a Jewish government and implement this program. We shall follow this course for there is none other.

We shall fight. Every Jew in the homeland will fight.

The God of Israel, Lord of Hosts, shall be at our side. There is no retreat. Freedom—or death! Erect an iron wall around your fighting youth! Do not abandon them, for the traitor shall be cursed and the coward held in contempt!

And you too shall be called to raise the banner of this citizen's war. You will be called upon:

a. to refuse to pay taxes to the oppressive regime.

b. to demonstrate in the city streets day and night, demanding the establishment of a Jewish government in The Land.

c. to refuse to obey any order issued by the foreign ruler; you shall violate these orders declaring, "I shall only obey a Jewish government."

d. Workers shall be called upon to proclaim a general strike in all public and private enterprises. Be prepared for hunger and tribulation but under no circumstances break this strike, for it is a holy endeavor.

e. Student youth shall be called upon to boycott the schools and devote all their time and energy to this war.

Jews!

This fighting youth will not be deterred by the prospect of sacrifices and suffering, blood and pain. It will not surrender, nor will it rest until it has succeeded in renewing our days as of yore until it guarantees our people a homeland, freedom, honor, sustenance, and true justice. And if, indeed, you lend them every assistance, very soon, in our own time, you shall behold the return of people to Zion and the restoration of Israel.

May God grant that this comes to pass.

SELECT BIBLIOGRAPHY

Allon, Yigal. *Shield of David: The Story of Israel's Armed Forces.* New York: Bloch Publishing Co., 1970. 376 pp. This a profile of the people and events that molded the first resistance movement in Israel some eighty years ago into the army of the Jewish state.

Andrews, Fannie Fern. *Holy Land Under Mandate.* New York: Houghton, 1931. This book describes the history of Palestine from 1919 to 1931 and is a survey of the Zionist Movement, including the Balfour Declaration and the development of Zionism. It explains the Arab claim to Palestine and traces their policies and actions. It discusses Arab life and organization and the government of Palestine.

Anglo-American Committee of Inquiry on Jewish Problems in Palestine and Europe. *Report to the United States Government and His Majesty's Government in the United Kingdom.* Lausanne, Switzerland. April 20, 1946. Washington: Government Printing Office, 1946. 92 pp. This official report of the committee is invaluable to the study of modern Israel.

Avner (pseud.). *Memoirs of an Assassin.* New York: Yoseloff, 1959. 199 pp. A member of the Stern gang describes some of the assassinations in which he participated.

Begin, Menachem. *The Revolt.* New York: Schuman, 1951. 385 pp. This story of the Jewish underground in Palestine is told by the former leader of the Irgun.

Bell, Bowyer J. *Terror out of Zion: Irgun Zvai Leumi, LEHI, and the Palestine Underground, 1929–1949.* New York: St. Martin's Press, 1977. 374 pp. This is an authentic account based primarily on interviews with surviving participants.

Bilby, Kenneth W. *New Star in the Near East.* New York: Doubleday, 1951. This is a report of events during the struggle between Jews and Arabs for control of Palestine. The author covers the last days of the British mandate to the emergence of Israel as an independent state. He evaluates the leaders and policies of both sides and points to reasons for Jewish success and Arab failure. Bilby discusses the Arab Higher Committee for Palestine, the Arab-Jewish Municipal Council, the Arab League,

David Ben Gurion, British policy in Israel, the refugee problem, and the United Nations' concern over Israel.

Buber, Martin. *Israel and Palestine*. New York: Farrar, Straus and Young, 1952. 165 pp. The history of an idea is explained by a foremost Jewish thinker.

Dekel [Krassner], Ephraim. *Shai: Historical Exploits of Hagannah Intelligence*. New York: Yoseloff, 1959. 369 pp. The commander of the Palestine Jewish defense organization from 1929 to 1946 tells the story of his organization's underground work.

ESCO Foundation for Palestine. *Palestine: A Study of Jewish, Arab and British Policies*. New Haven: Yale University Press, 1947. 2 vols. 1380 pp. This is the most comprehensive treatment of the problem of Palestine from the middle of the nineteenth century through the period of the British mandate.

Frank, Jerold. *The Dead*. New York: Simon and Schuster, 1963. 317 pp. As an account of the assassination of Lord Moyne, the book gives a deep insight into the workings of the Irgun and the Stern gang.

Freulich, Roman. *Soldiers in Judea*. New York: Herzl, 1965. 216 pp. This book relates the story of the Jewish Legion and its role in the conquest of Palestine by the British in World War I.

Garcia-Granados, Jorge. *The Birth of Israel, The Dream As I Saw It*. New York: Alfred A. Knopf, 1948. 291 pp. Dr. Garcia-Granados was the Guatemalan member of the United Nations Special Committee on Palestine, which proposed partition.

Gilner, Elias. *War and Hope*. New York: Herzl Press, 1969. 466 pp. This is the story of the Jewish Legion in World War I by a former Legionnaire and participant in the events described.

Halpern, Ben. *The Idea of the Jewish State*. Cambridge, MA: Harvard University Press, 1961. 492 pp. Avoiding specialized terminology, Dr. Halpern provides a general understanding of Israel. He explores the history of Zionist thought, negotiations over Palestine, and the Arab-Israeli situation.

Hurewitz, Jacob C. *The Struggle for Palestine*. New York: Norton, 1950. 404 pp. The author provides a study of the Arab nationalist-Zionist struggle over the establishment of an independent state in Palestine.

Jabotinksy, Vladimir. *The Story of the Jewish Legion*. New York: Ackerman, 1945. 191 pp. Although created during World War I, the Jewish Legion played an important role as a nucleus for the later Israeli military.

Katz, Samuel. *Days of Fire*. Garden City: Doubleday, 1968. 317 pp. These are the personal memoirs of days in the Irgun Zvai Leumi fighting against the Arabs, British, and the Jewish "establishment."

Koestler, Arthur. *Promise and Fulfillment: Palestine 1917–1949*. New York: Macmillan, 1949. 345 pp. Koestler provides a very factual account, including the underground struggle during the last years of the mandate. He also includes the main military and political forces and events that led to the establishment of Israel.

Mardor, Munya. *Hagannah*. New York: New American Library, 1966. 295 pp. This is the story of the volunteer Jewish defense organization in Palestine.

Memorandum Submitted to the Anglo-American Committee of Inquiry by The Jewish Agency for Palestine. Jerusalem: Jewish Agency for Palestine, 1946. 52 pp. The memorandum contains the Zionist plan for the solution of the Palestine problem.

Meridor, Yaacov. *Long is the Road to Freedom*. New York: United Zionists Revisionists, 1961. 298 pp. This is a personal account of a commander of the Irgun and his capture and imprisonment by the British.

Official Documents, Pledges and Resolutions on Palestine. New York: Palestine Arab Refugee Office, 1959. 161 pp. A compilation beginning with the Hussein-McMahon correspondence in 1916, this includes pertinent material from the Arab viewpoint.

Rifkin, Shepard. *What Ship? Where Bound?* New York: Alfred A. Knopf, 1961. 254 pp. The story of a volunteer crew of seamen on the first Irgun ship to run the British blockade of Palestine in 1946.

Sykes, Christopher. *Crossroads to Israel*. Cleveland: World, 1965, This book discusses in detail the Arab delegation to London, the Arab Higher Committee, the Arab League, the Legion Liberation Army, the National Committee, the Palestine police, and the various events in Palestine.

Unsung Heroes. Brooklyn: Hakibbutz Hameuchad, 1948. 112 pp. This is an account of the Hagannah.